RV Camping in
State Parks

Published by:

Roundabout Publications
P.O. Box 19235
Lenexa, KS 66285

800-455-2207

www.TravelBooksUSA.com

Published by:

Roundabout Publications
P.O. Box 19235
Lenexa, KS 66285

Phone: 800-455-2207
Internet: www.TravelBooksUSA.com

Library of Congress Control Number: 2014943154

ISBN-10: 1-885464-57-6
ISBN-13: 978-1-885464-57-6

Contents

Introduction

About this Book

Millions of Americans enjoy camping in state parks every year. *RV Camping in State Parks* is designed to make finding RV-friendly state parks easier. In it, you'll find information on more than 1,700 state parks, forests, and recreation areas in 49 states (Hawaii is not included) that offer accommodations for RVers. We prepared this book with two assumptions: You are traveling with a state map or atlas and have access to a telephone.

A summary for each state tells you how many state parks have RV campgrounds and the amenities generally available. You'll also find contact information including phone number and web site for each state so you can make reservations, obtain state park brochures and request more information.

Following the summary is a **Park Locator Chart**, which lists all the state parks alphabetically. The number that follows each park corresponds to the map coordinate. This chart is helpful if you already know the name of a state park you'd like to visit.

State maps are provided to aid you in finding state parks with RV facilities. Locations on the map are approximate and are intended to give you the general idea of where parks are located. If you need specific information or directions, it is best to call the state park you plan to visit. GPS coordinates are listed for each park.

Details for each state park include location, general directions, each park's phone number (or a park or office answering for that park) and amenities, such as swimming, fishing, boat ramps, marinas, golf courses, etc. Parks with fishing facilities require a valid state fishing license. You'll also learn how many RV sites are available, the number of sites that have water and electric hookups, and sites with full hookups. Also provided is each park's season of operation and availability of showers and dump stations. (*Note that the addresses for the parks are mailing addresses, which sometimes are not the physical address of that park.*) Parks with equestrian facilities or areas are also identified, as well as parks offering Wireless Internet service.

Camping Fees

We have included a Rate Group guide for each state, which indicates general camping fees charged throughout the state. These rates do not include any entrance fees, if they are charged by a park. Rates were accurate at press time but are subject to change. We advise you call the park you plan to visit to confirm campsite availability and camping fees. Rates are categorized as follows:

Category	Fee Range
A	$12 to $19 per night
B	$20 to $26 per night
C	$27 and up per night

Park Name Abbreviations

F&WA	Fish & Wildlife Area
MSP	Memorial State Park
RA	Recreation Area
SB	State Beach
SF	State Forest
SHP	State Historic Park
SP	State Park
SR	State Reservation
SRA	State Recreation Area
SRP	State Resort Park
SRS	State Recreation Site

About the Author

D.J. Davin is a retired sales and marketing executive. He and his wife, Kay, of 58 years have been enjoying the RV lifestyle since 2000. They have made several cross-country junkets and travelled extensively in the West. They have stayed in many of the parks listed in this book. They also have been volunteer campground hosts with Oregon State Parks. The Davins are the parents of four adult children, have ten grandchildren and three cats, which are RV veterans. When not in their RV, D.J. and his wife reside outside Tucson, Arizona, where he attempts to play golf and Kay does pastel portraits of children and pets.

ALABAMA

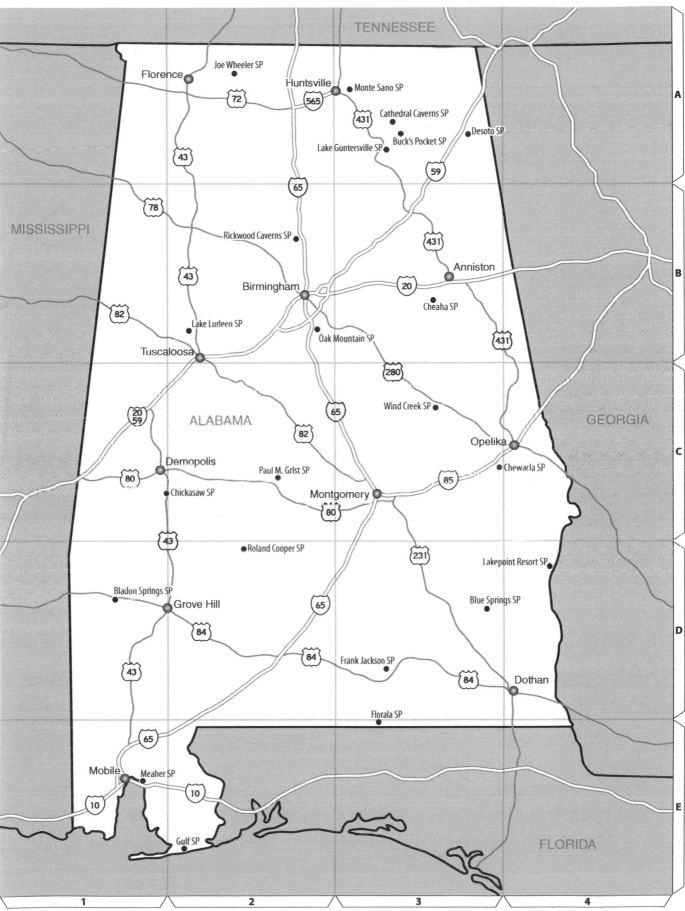

TENNESSEE

Florence ● Joe Wheeler SP

Huntsville ● Monte Sano SP

Cathedral Caverns SP

Buck's Pocket SP ● Desoto SP

Lake Guntersville SP ●

MISSISSIPPI

Rickwood Caverns SP ●

Anniston

Birmingham

Cheaha SP ●

Lake Lurleen SP ●

Oak Mountain SP ●

Tuscaloosa

ALABAMA

Wind Creek SP ●

GEORGIA

Opelika

Demopolis

Paul M. Grist SP ●

Chewacla SP ●

Chickasaw SP ●

Montgomery

Roland Cooper SP ●

Lakepoint Resort SP ●

Bladon Springs SP ●

Grove Hill

Blue Springs SP ●

Frank Jackson SP ●

Dothan

Florala SP ●

Mobile ● Meaher SP

Gulf SP ●

FLORIDA

Alabama

Alabama offers 22 state parks for RVers. Most parks have sites with electric and water hookups and all have showers. Alabama parks accept MasterCard, Visa and American Express credit cards. Seniors, 62 years and older, or disabled persons are eligible for a 15% discount, with proof of age or disability (holidays excluded). All parks are open year-round, weather permitting. If in doubt, call the particular park. Unless noted otherwise, all parks have a sanitary dump station. Rate groups: A, B and C.

Division of State Parks
Alabama Dept. of Conservation & Natural Resources
64 N Union St, Ste 538
Montgomery, AL 36130

Information & Reservations: (800) 252-7275
Internet: www.alapark.com

Alabama Park Locator

Alabama Parks

Bladon Springs State Park

3921 Bladon Rd, Bladon Springs, AL 36919. Phone: (251) 754 9207. Located 12 miles W of Coffeeville via US 84 and CR 31. Centered on four mineral springs. 10 full hook-up sites. Lake in park. Fish; swim GPS: N 31-43.9 W 88-11.8

Blue Springs State Park

2595 State Hwy 10, Clio, AL 36017. Phone: (334) 397-4875. Located 6 miles E of Clio on AL 10 about 15 miles W of US 431. 50 sites with water, electric; 7 w/sewer; showers. Lake in park. Pedal boat rentals. Fish; swim. Wi-Fi. GPS: N 31-39.9 W 85-30.6

Buck's Pocket State Park

393 County Rd 174, Grove Oak, AL 35975. Phone: (256) 659-2000. Located on Lake Guntersville, 2 miles N of Grove Oak. Northbound travelers use exit 205 off I-59 to CR 20 to AL 227. Southbound travelers use exit 218 off I-59 to AL 35 to Rainsville, south on AL 75 to AL 227, follow signs to park. 36 sites with water and electric; laundry; showers. Wi-Fi. GPS: N 34-28.0 W 86-02.9

Cathedral Caverns State Park

837 Cave Rd, Woodville, AL 35776 Phone: (256)728-8193. Primitive sites only. Cave tours. GPS: N 34-34.4; W 86-13.2

Cheaha State Park (Resort)

19644 Hwy 281, Delta, AL 36258. Office: (256) 488-5111. Resort: (800) 610-5801. Located in Talladega National Forest, 12 miles S of I-20 off AL 281 near Anniston. 73 sites with water and electric, (50-amp) sewers; showers. Lake Cheaha in park. Pedal boat rentals. Store in park. Fish, swim. GPS: N 33-28.5 W 85-48.4

Chewacla State Park

124 Shell Toomer Pkwy, Auburn, AL 36830. Phone: (334) 887-5621. Located on Chewacla Lake, 4 miles S of Auburn off I-85 at exit 51. 36 sites with water, electric, sewer; showers. Dump station. Swimming, fishing; boat rentals. GPS: N 32-33.3 W 85-28.9

Chickasaw State Park

26955 US Hwy 43, Gallion, AL 36742. Phone: (334) 295-8230. Located on US 43 about 4 miles N of Linden. 3 sites with water and electric; some primitive sites. GPS: N 32-21.7 W 87-46.8

DeSoto State Park (Resort)

7104 DeSoto Pkwy NE, Fort Payne, AL 35967. Office: (256) 845-5075. Resort: (800) 568-8840. Located 8 miles NE of Fort Payne near I-59 & US 11. 94 full hook-up sites; back-ins; 20 with water, electric, sewer (10 pull-thrus). Swimming pool, tennis courts. Store. GPS: N 34-29.7 W 85-37.1

Florala State Park

439 Victoria Ln, Florala, AL 36442. Phone: (334) 858-6425. Located in the city of Florala on US 331 north of AL/FL state line on Lake Jackson. 28 sites with water, electric, sewer; showers. Boat ramp, rentals. Fish, swim GPS: N 30-59.9 W 86-19.8

Frank Jackson State Park

100 Jerry Adams Dr, Opp, AL 36467. Phone: (334) 493-6988. Located on Lake Jackson, in the town of Opp on US 331. 32 sites (on the

water) with water, electric, sewer. showers. Fishing, swimming. Cable TV, Wi-Fi. GPS: N 31-19.5 W 86-15.8

Gulf State Park (Resort)

20115 State Hwy 135, Gulf Shores, AL 36542. Campground reservations: (251) 948-7275. Resort: (800) 544-4853. Located in the city of Gulf Shores on the Gulf of Mexico. 496 sites with water, electric (50-amp), sewer. Swimming pool, tennis, fishing. Wi-Fi. GPS: N 30-16.2 W 87-34.9

Joe Wheeler State Park (Resort)

201 McLean Dr, Rogersville, AL 35652. Phone: (256) 247-1184. Located on Wheeler Lake, 1.5 miles W of Rogersville on US 72. 116 sites, 110 with water, electric, sewer. Fishing, swimming, golf. Boat rentals, marina. GPS: N 34-47.5 W 87-22.8

Lake Guntersville State Park (Resort)

24 State Campground Rd, Guntersville, AL 35976. Office: (256) 571-5455. Resort: (800) 760-4108. Located 6 miles NE of Guntersville off Hwy 227. 321 sites (five sections) with water, electric, some sewers; showers. Boat rentals. GPS: N 34-22.0 W 86-13.4

Lake Lurleen State Park

13226 Lake Lurleen Rd, Coker, AL 35452. Phone: (205) 339-1558. Located on Lake Lurleen, 12 miles NW of Tuscaloosa via US 82 and CR 21. 318 sites with water and electric; 35 w/sewer; showers. Fishing, swimming. Boat ramp, rentals. Golf. GPS: N 33 17.8 W 87-40.6

Lakepoint Resort State Park

104 Lakepoint Dr, Eufaula, AL 36027. Office: (334) 687-8011. Resort: (800) 544-5253. On Lake Eufaula. Located 7 miles N of Eufaula on US 431 near Georgia state line. 192 sites with water and electric (some 50 amp), some with sewer, some pull-through; (some on the lake) showers; laundry. Fishing, swimming; marina, boat rentals. Golf. GPS: N 31-59.4 W 85-06.9

Meaher State Park

5200 Battleship Pkwy E, Spanish Fort, AL 36577. Phone: (251) 626-5529. Located on US 90 (Old Spanish Trail) north of I-10 exit 30. 56 full hook-up sites. Showers. Fishing. GPS: N 30-40.2 W 87-56.0

Monte Sano State Park

5105 Nolen Ave, Huntsville, AL 35801. Phone: (256) 534-3757. Located in the city of Huntsville, 8 miles SE of city center off US 431. 89 sites with water and electric (some with sewer), some pull-thrus; showers. GPS: N 34-44.7 W 86-30.7

Oak Mountain State Park

200 Terrace Dr, Pelham, AL 35124. Phone: (205) 620-2527. Reservations: (205) 625-2520. Located E of I-65 exit 246 along AL 119 (15 miles S of Birmingham). 85 sites with water, electric, sewer; showers. Largest park in system. Two lakes in park. Boat ramp, rentals, (no gas motors); Golf course. Fishing, swimming. Equestrian area, trails, rentals. Wi-Fi. GPS: N 33-19.3 W 86-46.6

Paul M. Grist State Park

1546 Grist Rd, Selma, AL 36701. Phone: (334) 872-5846. Located 15 miles N of Selma via CR 37. 11 full hook-up sites; showers. Lake in park. Fishing, swimming. Boat/canoe rentals. GPS: N 32-35.7 W 86-59.8

Rickwood Caverns State Park

370 Rickwood Park Rd, Warrior, AL 35180. Phone: (205) 647-9692. Located 4 miles W of I-65 at exit 284 (Warrior). 13 sites with water, electric, sewer; showers; swimming pool. Caverns in park. GPS: N 33-52.6 W 86-52.0

Roland Cooper State Park

285 Deer Run Dr, Camden, AL 35726. Phone: (334) 682-4838. Located on Dannelly Reservoir, 6 miles NE of Camden on AL 41 (about 37 miles SW of Selma). 47 sites with water, electric, sewers; showers; laundry; store. Fishing; Boat rentals. Golf. GPS: N 33-02.9 W 87-14.7

Wind Creek State Park

4325 State Hwy 128, Alexander City, AL 35010. Phone: (256) 329-0845. Located on Lake Martin, 7 miles SE of Alexander City off AL 63 and AL 128. 626 sites (many waterfront) with water and electric (30 amp); showers; 16 equestrian sites; store. Fishing, swimming; Marina, boat rentals. Wi-Fi. GPS: N 32-51.4 W 85-56.8

ALASKA

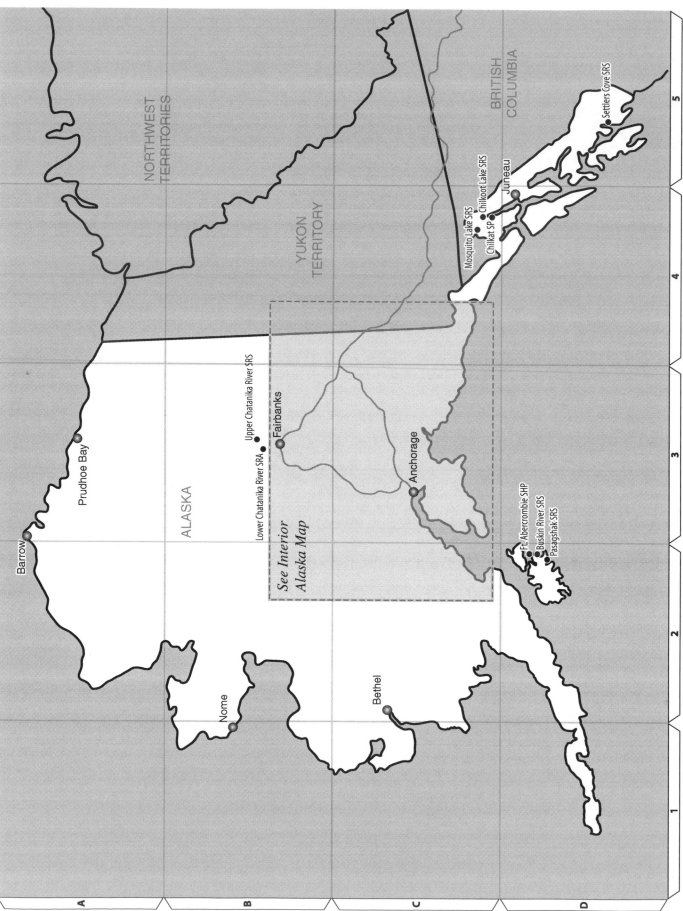

ALASKA INTERIOR

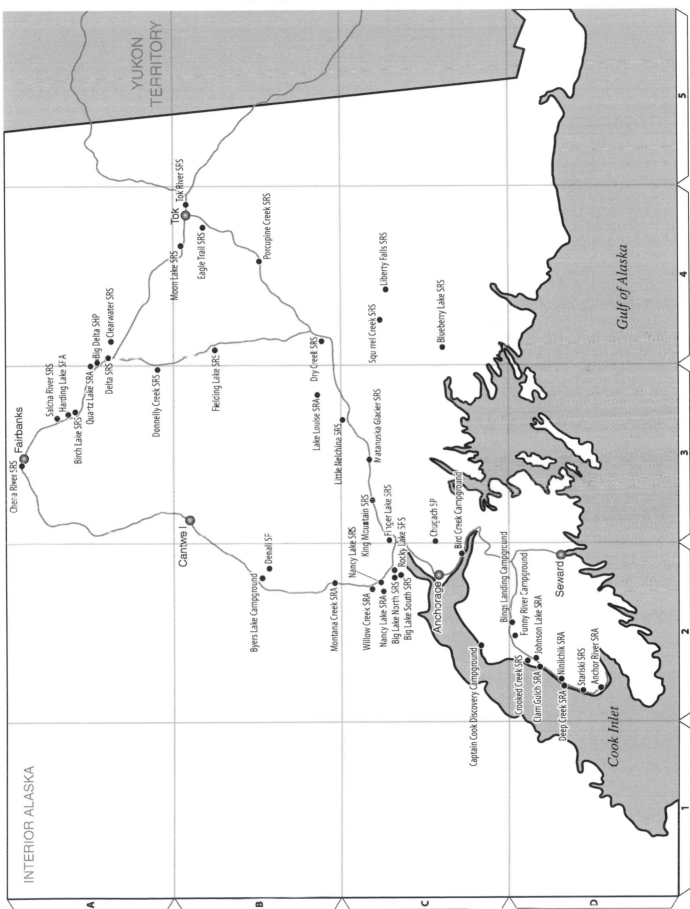

YUKON TERRITORY

INTERIOR ALASKA

Gulf of Alaska

Cook Inlet

Chena River SRS

Fairbanks

Salcha River SRS
Harding Lake SRA
Birch Lake SRS
Quartz Lake SRA
Big Delta SHP
Clearwater SRS
Delta SRS

Donnelly Creek SRS

Fielding Lake SRS

Moon Lake SRS
Eagle Trail SRS

Tok
Tok River SFS

Porcupine Creek SRS

Liberty Falls SRS

Squirrel Creek SRS

Blueberry Lake SRS

Dry Creek SRS

Lake Louise SRA

Little Nelchina SRS

Matanuska Glacier SRS

Cantwell

Denali SF

Byers Lake Campground

Montana Creek SRA

Nancy Lake SRS
King Mountain SRS
Willow Creek SRA
Nancy Lake SRA
Big Lake North SRS
Big Lake South SRS

Finger Lake SRS
Rocky Lake SFS

Chugach SP

Bird Creek Campground

Anchorage

Bings Landing Campground

Funny River Campground

Johnson Lake SRA

Seward

Captain Cook Discovery Campground

Crooked Creek SRS
Clam Gulch SRA
Deep Creek SRA
Ninilchik SRA
Stariski SRS
Anchor River SRA

A   B   C   D

1   2   3   4   5

Alaska

America's largest state also has the most acreage devoted to state parks, but has only 53 locations suitable for RVs. The largest number of these parks is in the Interior of the state. These locations include state parks, recreation sites and recreation areas. Few park sites have facilities. Most locations are on water and fishing is permitted (with Alaska license). The listed addresses are highway mile markers. RVs are limited to 35 feet at some locations because the access roads are difficult to navigate with larger rigs. (You should call to check size restrictions.) Most of these facilities do not have telephones in the locations so all information about a particular park otherwise must come from one of the offices listed below. Several parks have multiple campgrounds within and are listed as a single location. Pets are permitted on leashes. All locations have central drinking water facilities. Reservations are not accepted and usually not required. Rate Groups: A (or less) depending on park facilities. Dump station usage requires an additional fee.

Alaska Dept. of Natural Resources
Public Information Centers

DNR PIC - Anchorage
550 W 7th Ave, Suite 1260, Anchorage, AK 99501

Information: (907) 269-8411
Internet: www.dnr.state.ak.us

DNR PIC - Fairbanks
3700 Airport Way, Fairbanks, AK 99709
Information: (907) 451-2705

Alaska State Parks

Division of Parks & Outdoor Recreation
550 W 7th Ave, Ste 1380, Anchorage, AK 99501

Information: (907) 269-8700
Internet: www.alaskastateparks.org

Alaska Park Locator

Alaska Parks

Anchor River State Recreation Area
Homer, AK 99603. Located on Kenai Peninsula, outside Homer, 157 on AK 1 (Sterling Hwy). 46 sites. GPS: N 59-46.7 W 151-50.0

Big Delta State Historic Park
Delta Junction, AK 99737. Located at mile marker 274.5 on Richardson Hwy, 8 miles N of Delta Junction on AK 2 (Richardson Hwy). 25 sites. GPS: N 64-9.3 W 145-50.1

Big Lake North State Recreation Site
Big Lake, AK 99652. Phone: (907) 317-9094. Located 13 miles W of Wasilla, off AK 3 (Parks Hwy) 5.25 on North Big Lake Rd. 60 sites; no size limit. No alcohol. Fishing, swimming. GPS: N 61-32.1 W 149-48.9

Big Lake South State Recreation Site
Big Lake, AK 99652. Phone: (907) 269-8400. Located 26 miles W of Wasilla, off AK 3 (Parks Hwy) on South Big Lake Rd. 20 sites. Fishing; boat ramp. GPS: N 61-32.0 W 149-48.5

Bings Landing Campground
80 Sterling Hwy, Sterling, AK 99672. Phone: (907) 262-5581. 36 sites; boat ramp. GPS: N60.4 W151.4

Birch Lake State Recreation Site
Fairbanks, AK. Located near Salcha, SE of Fairbanks, 305.5 on AK 2 (Richardson Hwy). 19 sites. GPS: N 64-02.7 W 145-41.9

Bird Creek Campground
Chugach, AK 99540 (Anchorage area). Located at 101.2 Seward Hwy. 28 sites; 35-foot limit. GPS: N39.5 W114.7

Blueberry Lake State Recreation Site
Valdez, AK 99686. Located on Prince William Sound outside Valdez, 23 on AK 4 (Richardson Hwy). 25 sites. GPS: N 61-07.6 W 146-21.2

Buskin River State Recreation Site
4.5 W Rezanof Dr. 15 sites. One of three parks located outside Kodiak. Remote locations. 40 total sites. Also see Ft. Abercrombie SHP and Pasagshak SRS. GPS: N 57-46.4 W 152-24.6

Byers Lake Campground
147 Parks Hwy, Trapper Creek, AK 99683. (907) 269-8400 (Denali area). 147 miles N of Anchorage. 73 sites. 35-foot limit. GPS: N67.7 W150.1

Captain Cook Discovery Campground
39 Kenai Spur Hwy, Nikiski, AK 99635. Located north of Kenai, on N Kenai Rd. 52 sites. GPS: N 60-33.4 W 151-14.9

Chena River State Recreation Site
221 University Ave, Fairbanks, AK. Located in Fairbanks. 61 sites, 11 with water and electric; dump station. GPS: N 64-50.2 W 147-48.8

Chilkat State Park
7 Mud Bay Rd, Haines, AK 99827. Located 7 miles S of Haines on AK 7. 35 sites. 35-foot limit; boat ramp. GPS: N 59-10.9 W 135-22.4

Chilkoot Lake State Recreation Site
10 Lutak Rd, Haines, AK 99827. Located 10 miles N of Haines on Lutak Rd, off AK 7 on Chilkoot Lake. 32 sites. 35-foot limit. GPS: N 59-19.2 W 135-33.3

Chugach State Park
Eagle River, AK 99577. Located NE of Anchorage off AK 1 (Glenn Hwy) near Eagle River. 3 campgrounds: Eklutna Campground - 45 sites; water. Eagle River Campground - 57 sites; water; dump station. Bird Creek Campground - 28 sites; water (plus 20 overflow sites). GPS: N 61-18.6 W 149-34.7

Clam Gulch State Recreation Area
Soldotna, AK 99669. Located SW of Soldotna near Clam Gulch on Sterling Hwy mile marker 117.5. 120 sites. 35-foot limit. GPS: N 60-13.8 W 151-23.8

Clearwater State Recreation Site
Delta Junction, AK 99737. Located outside Delta Junction at 268 AK 2 (Richardson Hwy). 17 sites. GPS: N 64-02.2 W 145-44.1

Crooked Creek State Recreation Site
Soldotna, AK 99669. Located on Cook Inlet, outside Soldotna, off Sterling Hwy, on Coho Loop Rd. 80 sites. 35-foot limit. GPS: N 60-22.3 W 151-19.3

Deep Creek State Recreation Area
Homer, AK 99603. Located NE of Homer on Cook Inlet, on Sterling Hwy mile marker 137.3. 100 sites. 35-foot limit. GPS: N 59-43.3 W 151-53.2

Delta State Recreation Site
Delta Junction, AK 99737. Located outside Delta Junction at 267 AK 4 (Richardson Hwy). 25 sites with water; showers. GPS: N 64-01.5 W 145-43.5

Denali State Park
Trapper Creek, AK 99683. Phone: (907) 269-8400. Located about 163 miles N of Anchorage on AK 3 (George Parks Hwy), mile 135 to mile 164, next to Denali National Park. 3 campgrounds: Denali View Campground - 29 sites. Byers Lake Campground - 79 sites. Lower Troublesome Creek Campground - 10 sites. Boat ramp (Byers Lake). GPS: N 62-33.0 W 150-14.6

Donnelly Creek State Recreation Site
Delta Junction, AK 99737. Located 32 miles S of Delta Junction at 238 AK 4. 12 sites. GPS: N 64-01.1 W 145-43.6

Dry Creek State Recreation Site
Glennallen, AK 99588. Phone: (907)259-4123. Located 4 miles N of Glennallen, at 117.5 Richardson Hwy. 50 sites. GPS: N 62-06.5 W 145-33.2

Eagle Trail State Recreation Site
Tok, AK 99780. Located 16 miles S of Tok at 109.5 Tok Cutoff. 35 sites. GPS: N 63-16.2 W 143-01.8

Fielding Lake State Recreation Site
Delta Junction, AK 99737. Located south of Delta Junction at 200.5 on AK 4 (Richardson Hwy). 17 sites. GPS: N 64-01.1 W 145-43.6

Finger Lake State Recreation Site
Palmer, AK 99645. Phone: (907)745-4801. Located on Bogard Rd near Wasilla, NE of Anchorage, off AK 1 (Glenn Hwy). 36 sites. Boat ramp. GPS: N 61-33.1 W 149-10.9

Ft. Abercrombie State Historic Park

1400 Abercrombe Dr. 13 sites. One of three parks located outside Kodiak. Remote locations. 40 total sites. Also see Buskin River SRS and Pasagshak SRS. GPS: N 57-46.4 W 152-24.6

Funny River Campground

85 Sterling Hwy, Sterling, AK 99672 (Kenai River area). 10 sites; 40-foot limit. GPS: N44.1 W102.5

Harding Lake State Recreation Area

Fairbanks, AK 99714. Located between Fairbanks and Delta Junction at 321.4 AK 2 (Richardson Hwy). 81 sites; dump station. GPS: N 64-25.1 W 146-54.3

Johnson Lake State Recreation Area

Soldotna, AK 99669. Located south of Soldotna, 110 on Sterling Hwy. 51 sites. GPS: N 60-17.3 W 151-16.0

King Mountain State Recreation Site

Palmer, AK 99645. Phone: (907) 746-4644. Located at mile marker 76.1, outside Palmer on AK 1 (Glenn Hwy). 22 sites. GPS: N 61-35.5 W 149-07.3

Lake Louise State Recreation Area

Glennallen, AK 99588. Phone: (907) 441-7575. Located N of Anchorage at mile marker 159.8 on AK 1 (Glenn Hwy) near Glennallen, on Lake Louise. 58 sites. Boat ramp. GPS: N 62-17.2 W 146-33.7

Liberty Falls State Recreation Site

Chitina, AK 99566. Phone: (907) 823-2223. Located outside Chitina, 23.5 on AK 10 (Edgerton Hwy), next to Wrangell-Saint Elias National Park. 10 sites. GPS: N 61-31.6 W 144-26.7

Little Nelchina State Recreation Site

Glennallen, AK 99588. Located at mile marker 137.6 on AK 1 (Glenn Hwy) between Chickaloon and Glennallen. 11 sites. GPS: N 61-47.7 W 148-25.9

Lower Chatanika River State Recreation Area

Fairbanks, AK 99712. Located north of Fairbanks at mile marker 11 on Elliott Hwy. 12 sites. Area passively maintained. GPS: N 64-57.6 W 147-37.0

Matanuska Glacier State Recreation Site

Palmer, AK 99645. Phone: (907) 745-5151. Located NE of Palmer, 101 on AK 1 (Glenn Hwy). 12 sites. GPS: N 61-36.1 W 149-07.1

Montana Creek State Recreation Area

96.6 Parks Hwy, Trapper Creek, AK 99688. Phone: (907) 733-5267. 36 sites. GPS: N44.8 W111.4

Moon Lake State Recreation Site

Tok, AK 99780. Located 15 miles NW of Tok at 1332 AK 2 (Alaska Hwy). 15 sites. Boat ramp. GPS: N 63-22.3 W 143-32.8

Mosquito Lake State Recreation Site

Haines, AK 99827. Located 27 miles NW of Haines at 2.5 AK 7. 5 sites. SMALL RIGS ONLY. Boat ramp. GPS: N 59-24.8 W 135-55.4

Nancy Lake State Recreation Area

Willow, AK 99688. Located outside Willow, off AK 3 (George Parks Hwy), 67 miles N of Anchorage. 2 campgrounds: South Rolly Lake Campgrounds - 98 sites. Canoe rentals. GPS: N 61-42.3 W 150-01.1

Nancy Lake State Recreation Site

Willow, AK 99688. Phone: (907) 495-6273. Located outside Willow, 66.5 on AK 3 (George Parks Hwy). 30 sites. GPS: N 61-44.6 W 149-58.7

Ninilchik State Recreation Area

Homer, AK 99603. Located 40 miles S of Soldotna, 134.5 to 135 on Sterling Hwy. Three areas 57 sites; 35-foot limit. Dump station. GPS: N 60-02.6 W 151-40.0

Pasagshak State Recreation Site

20 Pasagshak Dr. 12 sites. One of three parks located outside Kodiak. Remote locations. 40 total sites. Also see Buskin River SRS and Ft. Abercrombie. GPS: N 57-46.4 W 152-24.6

Porcupine Creek State Recreation Site

Tok, AK 99780. Located about 62 miles S of Tok, 64 on AK 1. 12 sites. GPS: N 62-46.8 W 143-47.3

Quartz Lake State Recreation Area

Delta Junction, AK 99737. Located NW of Delta Junction at 277.8 on AK 2 (Richardson Hwy). 103 sites. Boat ramp. GPS: N 64-09.1 W 145-46.8

Rocky Lake State Recreation Site

Big Lake, AK 99652. Located at 3.5 on Big Lake Rd, off AK 3, SW of Wasilla. 10 sites. GPS: N 61-34.2 W 149-43.5

Salcha River State Recreation Site

Fairbanks, AK 99703. Located outside Salcha at 323.3 on AK 2 (Richardson Hwy). 6 sites. GPS: N 64-48.6 W 147-34.6

Settlers Cove State Recreation Site

18 N Tongass Rd, Ketchikan, AK 99903. Located in southeastern Alaska outside Ketchikan off AK 7. 14 sites. 35-foot limit. Note: Ketchikan is accessible only by ferry. GPS: N 55-19.4 W 131-36.6

Squirrel Creek State Recreation Site

Copper Center, AK 99573. Located about 35 miles S of Glennallen at 79.5 AK 4. 25 sites. GPS: N 61-40.0 W 145-10.6

Stariski State Recreation Site

Homer, AK 99603. Located north of Homer, 152 on AK 1 (Sterling Hwy). 13 sites. GPS: N 59-39.5 W 151-39.1

Tok River State Recreation Site

Tok, AK 99780. Located 4.5 miles E of Tok at 130.9 AK 2 (Richardson Hwy). 43 sites. GPS: N 63-20.1 W 142-59.7

Upper Chatanika River State Recreation Site

Fairbanks, AK 99712. Located NW of Fairbanks at 39 on Steese Hwy, off AK 2. 24 sites. GPS: N 65-06.6 W 147-28.7

Willow Creek State Recreation Area

Willow, AK 99688. Located north of Willow at 70.8 AK 3 (George Parks Hwy), on Willow Creek Pkwy. 140 sites. GPS: N 61-45.4 W 150-04.1

ARIZONA

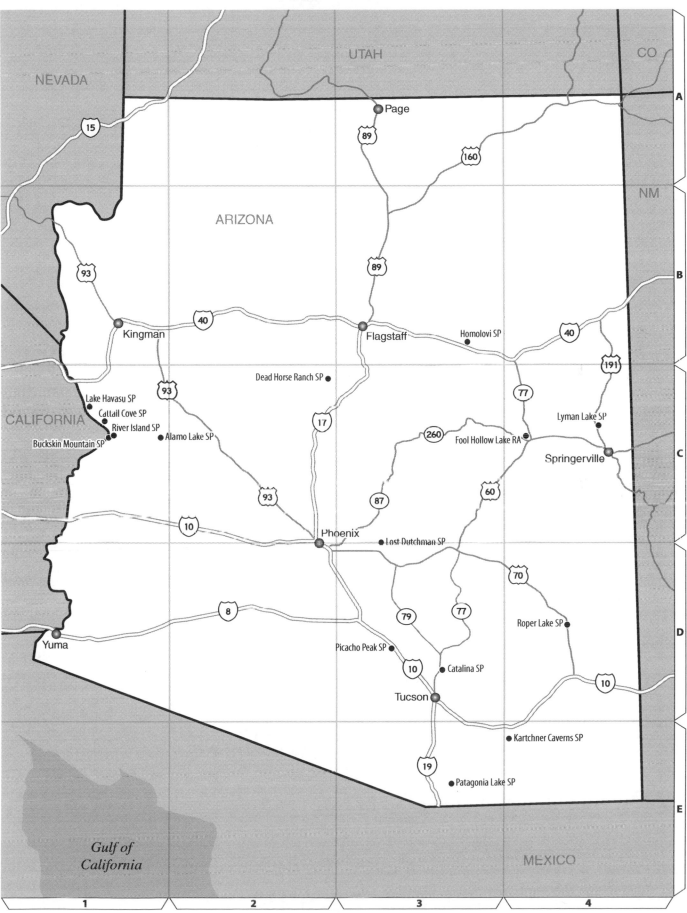

Arizona

Arizona offers the RVer 15 state parks or recreation areas. Most of the facilities have electric hook-ups and in-park showers. Some locations accept reservations but you must check with the park or Central Reservations. Some parks offer extended stays (up to 84 nights). You must check with Central Reservations for details. Pets are allowed and credit cards are accepted. Entrance fees are extra at all parks; the entrance fee at Kartchner Caverns State Park is waived with proof of reservation for cave tour. Rate groups: A and C, depending on facilities and park.

Arizona State Parks
1300 West Washington St.
Phoenix, AZ 85007

Information & Reservations: (602) 586-2283.
Reservation fees required.
Internet: www.azstateparks.com

Arizona Park Locator

Arizona Parks

Alamo Lake State Park

Wenden, AZ 85357. Phone: (928) 669-2088. Remote location in western AZ on Alamo Dam, 34 miles N of US 60 from Wenden on county roads, follow signs. 99 sites, some with electric and water; dump station; boat ramp. Fishing. Note: Located in mountains; recommend you call park ranger for directions and site availability. GPS: N 34-14.0 W 113-33.1

Buckskin Mountain State Park

5476 N US 95, Parker, AZ 85344. Phone: (928) 667-3231. Located in western AZ, 12 miles NE of Parker on AZ 95, on Colorado River. 68 sites with electric, water; 15 full hook up; showers; dump station. Fishing, swimming, boat ramp. GPS: N 34-15.3 W 114-08.1

Catalina State Park

11570 N Oracle Rd, Tucson, AZ 85740. Phone: (520) 628-5798. Located in south-central AZ, 9 miles N of Tucson on AZ 77 at mile marker 81. 120 sites, 95 with electric, water; showers; dump station. Equestrian area, trails. GPS: N 32-25.0 W 110-56.2

Cattail Cove State Park

Lake Havasu City, AZ 86405. Phone: (928) 855-1223. Located in western AZ 15 miles S of Lake Havasu City on AZ 95, on Colorado River (north of Buckskin Mountain SP). 61 sites with electric, (some 50 amp), water; showers; dump station. Fishing, swimming, boat ramp. Reservations recommended, especially in winter months. GPS: N 34-17.3 W 114-06.5

Dead Horse Ranch State Park

675 Dead Horse Ranch Rd, Cottonwood, AZ 86326. Phone: (928) 634-5283. Located in northern AZ, 39 miles W of Sedona on AZ 89A. 106 sites with electric (30/50 amp); showers; dump station. Equestrian area with corrals; fishing, boat ramp (no motors). GPS: N 34-44.9 W 112-01.4

Fool Hollow Lake Recreation Area

1500 N Fools Hollow Lake Rd, Show Low, AZ 85901. Phone: (989) 537-3680. Located in northeastern AZ, 2 miles N of US 60, off AZ 260 near Show Low. 123 sites (31 non-hook-up); 30/50 amps; showers; dump station. Fishing, swimming, boat ramp. GPS: N 34-15.7 W 110-04.2

Homolovi State Park

Winslow, AZ 86047. Phone: (928) 289-4106. Located in north-central AZ, 12 miles NE of I-40 exit 257 on AZ 87. 53 sites with electric (30/50 amps), some pull-throughs, showers; dump station. Horse trails. GPS: N 35-04.4 W 110-37.8

Kartchner Caverns State Park

Benson, AZ 85602. Phone: (520) 586-4100. Cave tour reservations: (520) 586-2283. Located in southeastern AZ, 9 miles S of I-10 exit 302 (Benson) on AZ 90. 62 sites with electric, water; showers; dump station. Big tourist attraction park; reservations strongly recommended for cave tours (limited walk-up tickets available daily); No reservations for campground. Campground gate hours: 7am to 6pm. GPS: N 31-50.4 W 110-20.6

Lake Havasu State Park

699 London Bridge Rd, Lake Havasu City, AZ 86403. Phone: (928) 855-2784. Located in western AZ, 6 miles S of Lake Havasu City on AZ 95. 47 sites; showers; dump station. Location of original London Bridge. Reservations recommended, especially in winter months. GPS: N 34-24.2 W 114-14.3

Lost Dutchman State Park

6109 N Apache Trail, Apache Junction, AZ 85219. Phone: (480) 982-4485. Located 5 miles N of Apache Junction on AZ 88, off US 60 (Superstition Hwy). 70 sites, some 50 amps; 35 non-hook-ups; showers; dump station. GPS: N 33-27.9 W 111-28.9

Lyman Lake State Park

St. Johns, AZ 85936. Phone: (928) 337-4441. Located in eastern AZ near NM state line, 11 miles S of St. Johns (I-40 exit 339) on US 191, on Lyman Lake. 61 sites, 13 with electric; showers; dump station. Fishing, swimming, horse trails; boat ramp. Open June-Sept.15. GPS: N 34-21.8 W 109-22.5

Patagonia Lake State Park

400 Patagonia Lake Rd, Patagonia, AZ 85624. Phone: (520) 287-6965. Remote location in southern AZ near Nogales off AZ 82, 35 miles S of I-10 exit 281. 105 sites, 68 with electric and water (some pull thrus); showers; dump station. 35-foot limit. No reservations. Horse trails, fishing, swimming, boat ramp. GPS: N 31-29.5 W 110-51.5

Picacho Peak State Park

Eloy, AZ 85131. Phone: (520) 466-3183. Located northwest of Tucson at I-10 exit 219. 85 sites with water, electric (some 50 amps); some pull-throughs; showers; dump station. No reservations. GPS: N 32-38.8 W 111-23.9

River Island State Park

5200 N Hwy 95; Parker, AZ 85344. Phone (928) 667-3386. Located SE of Lake Havasu City, 12 miles NW of Parker, off AZ 95, on Colorado River. 37 sites, some on the river (24' limit), water, electric. Showers, dump station. Fishing, swimming. Boat rentals nearby. GPS: N 34-15.1 W 114-08.3

Roper Lake State Park

101 E Roper Lake Rd, Safford, AZ 85546. Phone: (928) 428-6760. Located in southeastern AZ, 28 miles N of I-10 exits 352 or 355 on US 191; south of Safford about 6 miles. 45 sites with electric (some 50 amp), water; showers; dump station. Hot springs tub. Reservations - call park. GPS: N 32-45.5 W 109-42.5

ARKANSAS

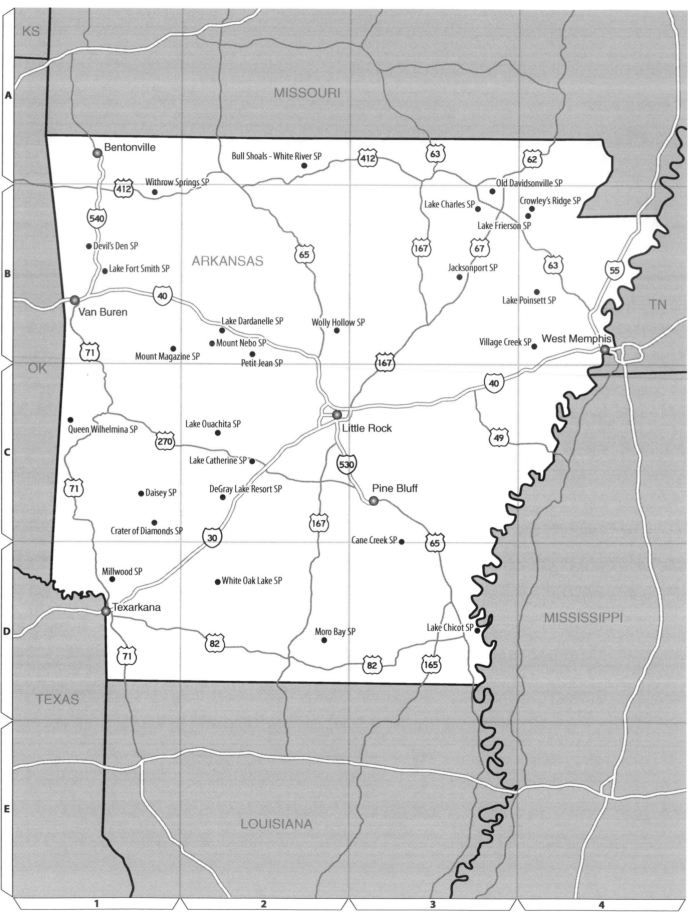

KS

MISSOURI

A

Bentonville

Bull Shoals - White River SP

412

63

62

Withrow Springs SP

Old Davidsonville SP

412

Lake Charles SP

Crowley's Ridge SP

540

Lake Frierson SP

Devil's Den SP

ARKANSAS

65

167

67

Jacksonport SP

B

Lake Fort Smith SP

40

63

55

Van Buren

Lake Dardanelle SP

Wolly Hollow SP

Lake Poinsett SP

TN

71

Mount Nebo SP

Village Creek SP

West Memphis

Mount Magazine SP

Petit Jean SP

167

OK

167

40

Queen Wilhelmina SP

Lake Ouachita SP

Little Rock

C

270

49

Lake Catherine SP

530

71

Daisey SP

DeGray Lake Resort SP

Pine Bluff

Crater of Diamonds SP

30

167

Cane Creek SP

65

Millwood SP

White Oak Lake SP

Texarkana

Lake Chicot SP

MISSISSIPPI

D

82

Moro Bay SP

71

82

165

TEXAS

E

LOUISIANA

1   2   3   4

Arkansas

Of the 52 Arkansas state parks, half are RV friendly. The sites in these parks range from Premium Class A (water, electric, sewer) to Class A (water and electric) to Class B (no hook-ups). Most of the RV parks offer a sanitary dump station and showers. All the listed parks are open year-round but some facilities might be limited because of seasonal adjustments. All parks on reservoir lakes have fishing facilities and boat ramps. All of the state parks accept Visa, MasterCard and Discover credit cards; Resort Parks accept American Express cards as well. Seniors (62 and older) are eligible for rate discount but you must ask. Premium (AAA) parks have full hook up sites. Parks with Class A sites offer 50 amp electric service as an option for a small up-charge. Class B sites have no hook-ups. All parks accept reservations (up to 12 months in advance) and reservations are to be made directly with the individual park. Rate groups: A and B (Resorts are more expensive and rates vary.)

Division of State Parks
Arkansas Dept. of Parks & Tourism
One Capitol Mall
Little Rock, AR 72201

Information: (888) 287-2757
Internet: www.ArkansasStateParks.com

Arkansas Park Locator

Arkansas Parks

Bull Shoals-White River State Park

153 Dam Overlook Ln, Bull Shoals, AR 72619. Phone: (870) 445-3629. 82 sites (along the river) with water, electric; showers; dump station; store. Located about 9 miles S of AR/MO state line in north-central Arkansas on the White River. From Mountain Home, travel 6 miles N on AR 5 and then 8 miles W on AR 178. Boat ramp, rentals. GPS: N 36-22.1 W 93-33.5

Cane Creek State Park

50 State Park Rd, Star City, AR 71667. Phone: (870) 628-4714. 29 Class A/Preferred sites; showers; dump station; store. Located 5 miles E of Star City on AR 293. Star City is located on US 425 about 24 miles SE of Pine Bluff. Boat ramp, rentals. GPS: N 33-56.0 W 91-48.1

Crater of Diamonds State Park

209 State Park Rd, Murfreesboro, AR 71958. Phone: (870) 285-3113. 47 Class AAA sites, some 50 amp; showers; dump station; store. Located on AR 301 about 2 miles SE of Murfreesboro. Diamond search area. GPS: N 34-02.3 W 93-40.1

Crowley's Ridge State Park

2092 Hwy 168 N, Paragould, AR 72450. Phone: (870) 573-6751. 18 Class A sites, electric; showers; dump station; store. Located in northeastern Arkansas 17 miles N of Jonesboro on AR 141 or 9 miles W of Paragould on US 412, then 2 miles S on AR 168. Marina, boat ramp, rentals. GPS: N 36-02.7 W 90-40.0

Daisy State Park

103 East Park, Kirby, AR 71950. Phone: (870) 398-4487. 26 Class A Premium sites, 56 Class B, dump station; store; showers nearby. Located 1/4 mile south of Daisy off US 70 near AR 27 on Lake Greeson. Boat ramp, ATV trails. GPS: N 34-14.2 W 93-44.2

DeGray Lake Resort State Park

2027 State Park Entrance Rd, Bismarck, AR 71929. Phone: (501) 865-5810. 113 Premium/Preferred/Class A sites; showers; dump station; store. Located on DeGray Lake, about 14 miles NW of Arkadelphia on AR 7. Exit 78 off I-30 at Caddo Valley/Arkadelphia, then 7 miles N on AR 7, or 21 miles S of Hot Springs on AR 7. Golf course; boat ramp, rentals, equestrian area. Marina. GPS: N 34-13.0 W 93-05.1

Devils Den State Park

11333 W Arkansas Hwy 74, West Fork, AR 72774. Phone: (479) 761-3325. 58 Class A/Preferred; 143 sites, most with with water and electric, some sewers; showers; dump station. Located about 25 miles S of Fayetteville. Directions: I-540 S from Fayetteville 8 miles to exit 53 then 17 miles SW on AR 170. From south, on I-540 exit at Winslow, exit 45 then 7 miles W on AR 74. Note: Trailers longer than 26 feet and larger RVs with towed vehicles should use exit 53. Equestrian area; swimming pool. GPS: N 35-47.0 W 94-15.5

Jacksonport State Park

205 Avenue St, Newport, AR 72112. Phone: (870) 523-2143. Located on White River in Jacksonport on AR 69, 3 miles N of Newport. 20 Class A sites, all 50 amp; showers; dump station; store; swimming, boat ramp. GPS: N 35-38.3 W 91-18.7

Lake Catherine State Park

1200 Catherine Park Rd, Hot Springs, AR 71913. Phone: (501) 844-4176. 68 Class A sites; showers; dump station; store. Located on Lake Catherine, southeast of Hot Springs on AR 171 near Malvern. Directions: I-30 exit 97, 12 miles N on AR 171. Swimming, equestrian area. GPS: N 34-25.8 W 92-56.8

Lake Charles State Park

3705 Hwy 25, Powhatan, AR 72458. Phone: (870) 878-6595. 60 Class AA & B sites. Showers and dump station are seasonal; store. Located on Lake Charles in northeastern Arkansas near Hoxie. From Hoxie, 8 miles northwest on US 63 then 6 miles S on AR 25. Swimming, boat ramp. GPS: N 36-03.9 W 91-09.3

Lake Chicot State Park

2542 Hwy 257, Lake Village, AR 71653. Phone: (870) 265-5480. 122 sites, including Premium with sewer; Class A and Class B. Located on Lake Chicot on AR 144, 8 miles NE of Lake Village. Exit US 65 at AR 144, east 9 miles to park. Boat ramp, rentals. GPS: N 33-22.4 W 91-11.7

Lake Dardanelle State Park

100 State Park Dr, Russellville, AR 72802. Phone: (479) 967-5516. This park has 2 areas, 74 sites total. Russellville area has Premium sites with sewers, and Class A. Dardanelle area has Class A only; showers, dump station and store. Located on Lake Dardanelle near Russellville in north-central AR. Russellville area: I-40 exit 81 (AR 7) south to AR 326, west 5 miles to park. Dardanelle area: 4 miles W of Dardanelle on AR 22. Swimming; boat ramp, rentals, bicycle rentals. Marina. GPS: N 35-17.5 W 93-12.1

Lake Fort Smith State Park

Mountainburg, AR 72946. Phone: (479)369-2469. Located on Lake Fort Smith, on Shepherd Springs Road, eight miles N of Mountainburg. 30 sites, water, electric. Swimming, marina, boat rentals. GPS: N 35-42.4 W 94-06.3

Lake Frierson State Park

7904 Hwy 141, Jonesboro, AR 72401. Phone: (870) 932-2615. 7 sites, 4 with water, electric; showers and dump station nearby, not in the park. Located on Lake Frierson, 10 miles N of Jonesboro on AR 141. Boat ramp, rentals. GPS: N 35-59.3 W 90-43.1

Lake Ouachita State Park

5451 Mountain Pine Rd, Mountain Pine, AR 71956. Phone: (501) 767-9366. 117 Class A and Class B sites; showers; dump station; store. Located on Lake Ouachita NW of Hot Springs. Directions: 3 miles W on US 270 then 12 miles N on AR 227. Swimming, boat ramp, rentals. Marina. GPS: N 34-36.7 W 93-09.9

Lake Poinsett State Park

5752 State Park Ln, Harrisburg, AR 72432. Phone: (870) 578-2064. 29 Class A and Class B sites; showers; dump station; store. Located on Lake Poinset near Harrisburg in northeastern Arkansas between US 63 and US 49. Directions: From Harrisburg 1 mile E on AR 14 to AR 163, south 3 miles to park. Boat ramp, rentals. GPS: N 35-32.1 W 90-41.3

Millwood State Park

1564 Hwy 32 E, Ashdown, AR 71822. Phone: (870) 898-2800. 115 Class AA & A sites; showers; dump station; store. Located north of Texarkana off US 71. Directions: From Texarkana, north on US 71 to Ashdown (16 miles), E on AR 32 for 9 miles. Boat ramp, rentals. Marina. GPS: N 33-41.1 W 93-59.8

Moro Bay State Park

6071 Hwy 600, Jersey, AR 71651. Phone: (870) 463-8555. 20 sites (5 Class A, 15 Class B); showers and dump station operate seasonally; store. Located on Ouachita River in southeastern Arkansas between El Dorado and Warren on US 63 (23 miles NE from El Dorado; 29 miles SW from Warren). Swimming. Boat ramp, rentals. GPS: N 33-18.0 W 92-21.0

Mount Magazine State Park

16878 Hwy 309 S, Paris, AR 72855. Phone: (479) 963-8502. 18 Premium sites with sewer; showers; dump station; store. Located on AR 309, 17 miles S of Paris; (exit 37 off I-40, about 35 miles S on AR 309). New 60-room lodge, 13 cabins. Equestrian area, ATV trails. GPS: N 35-09.6 W 93-35.9

Mount Nebo State Park

16728 W State Hwy 155, Dardanelle, AR 72834. Phone: (479) 229-3655. Located seven miles W of Dardanelle. 24 Class B sites; showers and dump station; operates seasonally. Note: AR 155 is a zig-zag road and trailers longer than 24 feet are not recommended. Swimming pool. GPS: N 35-13.5 W 93-13.8

Old Davidsonville State Park

7953 Hwy 166 S, Pocahontas, AR 72455. Phone: (870) 892-4708. 24 Class A sites; showers seasonal; dump station; store. Located on Black River in northeastern Arkansas near Pocahontas and Black Rock. Directions: From Pocahontas, go 2 miles W on US 62 then 9 miles S on AR 166. From Black Rock, take US 63 to AR 361, north to AR 166. Boat ramp, rentals (trolling motors only). GPS: N 36-09.5 W 91-03.4

Petit Jean State Park

1285 Petit Jean Mountain Rd, Morrilton, AR 72110. Phone: (501) 727-5441. Four camping areas; 125 Premium/Preferred/Class A sites (some pull-throughs); showers; dump station; store. Located near Morrilton in north-central AR. Directions: From I-40 exit 108 at Morrilton, south 9 miles on AR 9, then 12 miles W on AR 154. From Dardanelle, 7 miles S on AR 7, then 16 miles E on AR 154. Boat rentals, swimming pools. GPS: N 35-09.5 W 92-44.4

Queen Wilhelmina State Park

3877 Hwy 88 W, Mena, AR 71953. Phone: (479) 394-2863 or 394-2864. 35 Class B sites; showers; dump station; store. Located on

Talimena Scenic Drive, 13 miles W of Mena on AR 88. Alt. Route: From Mena go 6 miles N on US 71 then 9 miles W on US 270 to AR 272, then 2 miles south to park. GPS: N 34-41.2 W 94-23.3

Village Creek State Park

201 County Rd 754, Wynne, AR 72396. Phone: (870) 238-9406. Located in NE Arkansas, E of Wynne. I-40 exit 242 (Forrest City) then 13 miles N on AR 284. 96 Class AAA & A sites on Lake Dunn; showers seasonal; dump station; store. Swimming; Golf course; Boat ramp, rentals. Marina. GPS: N 35-12.0 W 90-43.5

White Oak Lake State Park

563 Hwy 387, Bluff City, AR 71722. Phone: (870) 685-2748. 41 Class A & B sites (some on the lake); showers; dump station. Located in a state forest southeast of Prescott. From Prescott on I-30 east 20 miles on AR 24 to AR 299, south 100 yards to AR 387, south 2 miles to park. GPS: N 33-41.3 W 93-07.0

Withrow Springs State Park

33424 Spur 23, Huntsville, AR 72740. Phone: (479) 559-2593. 30 Class AAA sites; showers; dump station. Located in Ozark Mountains on AR 23, 5 miles N of Huntsville. Swimming pool; boat ramp, rentals. GPS: N 36-10.4 W 93-42.9

Woolly Hollow State Park

82 Woolly Hollow Rd, Greenbrier, AR 72058. Phone: (501) 679-2098. 20 Class A, 10 Class B sites; showers; dump station. Located north of Conway. I-40 exit 125 (Conway), 12 miles N on US 65, 6 miles E on AR 285. Swimming; Boat ramp, rentals on Lake Bennett. GPS: N 35-16.9 W 92-17.2

CALIFORNIA

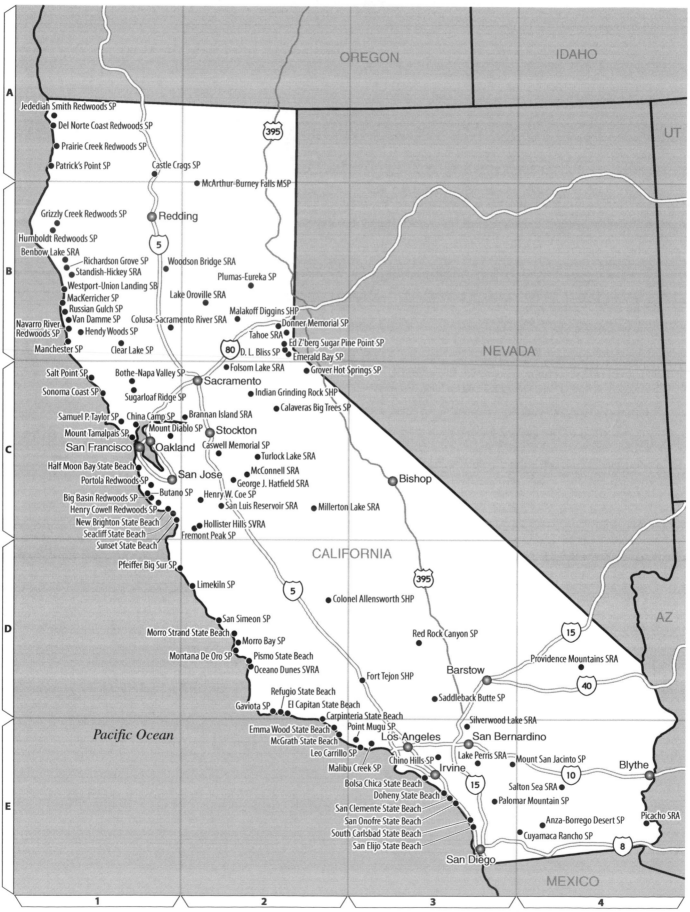

OREGON

IDAHO

UT

Jedediah Smith Redwoods SP

Del Norte Coast Redwoods SP

Prairie Creek Redwoods SP

Patrick's Point SP

Castle Crags SP

McArthur-Burney Falls MSP

Grizzly Creek Redwoods SP

Redding

Humboldt Redwoods SP

Benbow Lake SRA

Richardson Grove SP

Standish-Hickey SRA

Woodson Bridge SRA

Plumas-Eureka SP

Westport-Union Landing SB

MacKerricher SP

Lake Oroville SRA

Russian Gulch SP

Malakoff Diggins SHP

Van Damme SP

Colusa-Sacramento River SRA

Donner Memorial SP

Navarro River Redwoods SP

Hendy Woods SP

Tahoe SRA

Ed Z'berg Sugar Pine Point SP

Manchester SP

Clear Lake SP

D. L. Bliss SP

Emerald Bay SP

NEVADA

Salt Point SP

Bothe-Napa Valley SP

Folsom Lake SRA

Grover Hot Springs SP

Sonoma Coast SP

Sacramento

Sugarloaf Ridge SP

Indian Grinding Rock SHP

Samuel P. Taylor SP

China Camp SP

Brannan Island SRA

Calaveras Big Trees SP

Mount Tamalpais SP

Mount Diablo SP

Stockton

San Francisco

Oakland

Caswell Memorial SP

Half Moon Bay State Beach

Turlock Lake SRA

Portola Redwoods SP

San Jose

McConnell SRA

Big Basin Redwoods SP

Butano SP

George J. Hatfield SRA

Henry W. Coe SP

Bishop

Henry Cowell Redwoods SP

San Luis Reservoir SRA

Millerton Lake SRA

New Brighton State Beach

Hollister Hills SVRA

Seacliff State Beach

Fremont Peak SP

Sunset State Beach

CALIFORNIA

Pfeiffer Big Sur SP

Limekiln SP

395

Colonel Allensworth SHP

5

San Simeon SP

Morro Strand State Beach

Morro Bay SP

Red Rock Canyon SP

Providence Mountains SRA

Montana De Oro SP

Pismo State Beach

15

Oceano Dunes SVRA

Fort Tejon SHP

Barstow

Refugio State Beach

Saddleback Butte SP

40

Gaviota SP

El Capitan State Beach

Carpinteria State Beach

Silverwood Lake SRA

Pacific Ocean

Emma Wood State Beach

Point Mugu SP

San Bernardino

McGrath State Beach

Los Angeles

Leo Carrillo SP

Lake Perris SRA

Mount San Jacinto SP

Blythe

Malibu Creek SP

Chino Hills SP

Irvine

15

10

Bolsa Chica State Beach

Salton Sea SRA

Doheny State Beach

Palomar Mountain SP

Picacho SRA

San Clemente State Beach

San Onofre State Beach

Anza-Borrego Desert SP

South Carlsbad State Beach

Cuyamaca Rancho SP

8

San Elijo State Beach

San Diego

AZ

MEXICO

1   2   3   4

California

RV travelers in The Golden Gate State have their choice of 96 state parks or recreation areas with facilities for recreational vehicles. While services in these locations vary from primitive sites to full hookups, a number of parks offer the RVer an "enroute campsite." These sites are usually in the Day Use parking area and available when the regular camping area is full. Users of these "*enroute*" facilities must be fully self-contained and agree they will vacate the area no later than 9am the following day. Parks with this type facility are designated in the listings by **ER**.

Because of California's administrative assignment of parks to Districts, many parks are not reachable directly by U.S. Mail. Rather, these parks receive mail via the district office. Therefore, in some cases the park's listed address is the city of the district office; in other instances it is the city or town of the park's locale. The park's actual location or nearest city or town is indicated in the "located" section. Many parks have length limits that differ for motor homes and trailers. These differences are indicated in the listings (if different) by *M* for Motorhome and *T* for Trailer. A number of parks have added wireless Internet service. This service is indicated in the particular park's listing. (Parks are continuing to add this service.) Also, some parks are especially attractive to bears and these locations are noted.

Most parks hold several sites out of the reservation system for drive-in campers. You should always check the desired location for space availability and direction particulars, if in doubt. Some parks or areas are not included in the State's reservation network. Those that are not have a strict "first-come, first-served" policy and cannot hold spaces for drive-in visitors. Also, senior citizens (age 62 or older) are entitled to a camping discount. This discount must be requested at check-in and proof of age is necessary. Rate groups: B and C depending on site utilities. (As much as $38/night for Premium Developed sites; check park for clarification, fees.) We recommend making reservations for most parks, especially those locations on the coast.

Note: Some of the listed telephone numbers are answered by a central state park office. You must ask for the desired information by park name. Also, some of these numbers are answered by an automated device. To obtain information, follow the prompts. We recommend you call any park prior to arrival.

State of California
Dept. of Parks and Recreation
PO Box 942896
Sacramento, CA 94296

Information: (916) 653-6995
Reservations: (800) 444-7275 (Reserve America)
Internet: www.parks.ca.gov

California Park Locator

Anza-Borrego Desert State Park.....................E4
Benbow Lake State Recreation Area B1
Big Basin Redwoods State Park.......................C1
Bolsa Chica State Beach E3
Bothe-Napa Valley State Park.........................C1
Brannan Island State Recreation Area...........C2
Butano State Park...C1
Calaveras Big Trees State Park.........................C2
Carpinteria State Beach...................................D2
Castle Crags State Park....................................A1
Caswell Memorial State Park...........................C2
China Camp State Park.....................................C1
Chino Hills State Park.......................................E3
Clear Lake State Park.......................................B1
Colonel Allensworth State Historic Park D2
Colusa-Sacramento River State Recreation Area B1
Cuyamaca Rancho State Park..........................E4
D. L. Bliss State Park B2
Del Norte Coast Redwoods State Park............A1
Doheny State Beach E3
Donner Memorial State Park...........................C2
Ed Z'berg Sugar Pine Point State Park B2
El Capitan State Beach......................................D2
Emerald Bay State Park....................................B2
Emma Wood State Beach E2
Folsom Lake State Recreation Area.................C2
Fort Tejon State Historic Park D3
Fremont Peak State Park..................................C2
Gaviota State Park..D2
George J. Hatfield State Recreation Area........C2
Grizzly Creek Redwoods State Park B1

Carlifornia Parks

Anza-Borrego Desert State Park
200 Palm Canyon Dr, Borrego Springs, CA 92004. Phone: (760) 767-5311. Largest state park in California. Remote location in southern CA east of San Diego, north of I-8, via CA 78 or 79. 158 sites, 52 with electric, water; dump station. 35-foot limit. Wi-Fi. Horse trails. GPS: N 33-15.4 W 116-2.9

Benbow Lake State Recreation Area
1600 Hwy 101, Garberville, CA 95542. Phone: (707) 923-3238 or (707) 247-3318 (winter). Located in northern CA, S of Eureka off US 101, 2 miles S of Garberville. 77 sites with electric, water; showers; dump station. 30-foot limit-M; 24-foot limit-T. Swimming, fishing; boat rentals. ER. Note: Check ahead for operating hours, site availabilty. GPS: N 40-03.9 W 123-47.2

Big Basin Redwoods State Park
Boulder Creek, CA 95006. Phone: (831) 338-8860. Located in central CA, 25 miles N of Santa Cruz on CA 236. (CA 1 is less curvy.) 150 sites; showers; dump station. 27-foot limit-M; 24-foot limit-T. Swimming; horse trails. GPS: N 37-10.0 W 122-12.3

Bolsa Chica State Beach
San Clemente, CA 92672. Phone: (714) 846-3460. Located in southern CA in Huntington Beach. 50 sites with electric, water; dump station. 40-foot limit. ER. Wi-Fi. Swimming, fishing. GPS: N 33-39.2 W 117-59.8

Bothe-Napa Valley State Park
Sonoma, CA 95476. Phone: (707) 942-4575. Located in northern CA, in wine country, 5 miles N of St. Helena on CA 128. 40 sites; dump station. 31-foot limit-M; 24-foot limit-T. Reservations recommended. Swimming; horse trails. GPS: N 38-33.2 W 122-31.5

Brannan Island State Recreation Area
Folsom, CA 95630. Phone: (916) 777-6671. Located in central CA, NW of Stockton, 3 miles SE of Rio Vista on CA 160. 140 sites; showers; dump station. 36-foot limit. Swimming, fishing; boat ramp. Note: Call ahead for site availability. GPS: N 38-04.6 W 121-44.0

Butano State Park

Felton, CA 95018. Phone: (650) 879-2040. Located in central CA, SW of San Jose, 4.5 miles S of Pescadero and east of CA 1. 21 sites. 24-foot limit. GPS: N 37-11.5 W 122-20.5

Calaveras Big Trees State Park

Stockton, CA 95310. Phone: (209) 795-2334. Located in east-central CA, in foothills of Sierra Nevada Mountains, 4 miles NE of Arnold on CA 4. 129 sites, 47 with electric, water; showers; dump station. 30-foot limit. Winter access/facilities limited. GPS: N 38-16.7 W 120-18.6

Carpinteria State Beach

Ventura, CA 93001. Phone: (805) 968-1033. Located on southern CA coast, 12 miles S of Santa Barbara on US 101. 246 sites, 120 with electric, water; dump station. 35-foot limit. Swimming. ER. GPS: N 34-23.6 W 119-31.3

Castle Crags State Park

Oroville, CA 95966. Phone: (530) 235-2684. Located in northern CA off I-5, 6 miles SW of Dunsmuir. 76 sites. 27-foot limit-M; 21-foot limit-T. Swimming, fishing; horse trails. ER. GPS: N 41-09.9 W 122-19.0

Caswell Memorial State Park

Columbia, CA 95310. Phone: (209) 599-3810. Located in central CA, on Stanislaus River, NW of Modesto, 6 miles SW of Ripon on Austin Rd. 60 sites. 24-foot limit-M; 21-foot limit-T. Swimming, fishing. GPS: N 37-42.1 W 121-10.9

China Camp State Park

Duncan Mills, CA 95430. Phone: (415) 456-0766. Located 4 miles E of San Rafael on San Pablo Bay. From US 101, go east on N San Pedro Rd to park. Showers. No size limit. ER only. Swimming, fishing; horse trails. GPS: N 38-00.2 W 122-28.0

Chino Hills State Park

4721 Sapphire Rd, Chino Hills, CA 91709. Phone: (951)780-6222. Located 10 miles northwest of Corona off CA 71, via CA 91. 10 sites. 28-foot limit. Primitive park. Horse trails. GPS: N 33-57.3 W 117-42.1

Clear Lake State Park

Oroville, CA 95966. Phone: (707) 279-2267. Located on Clear Lake in northern CA, SE of Ukiah on CA 281. 147 sites; showers; dump station. 35-foot limit. Wi-Fi. Swimming, fishing; boat ramp. GPS: N 39-00.6 W 122-48.3

Colonel Allensworth State Historic Park

Earlimart, CA 93219. Phone: (661) 849-3433. Located in south-central CA, NW of Bakersfield and SW of Earlimart on CA 43. 15 sites; showers. 35-foot limit-M; 27-foot limit-T. Note: Limited operating hours. GPS:N 35-51.9 W 119-23.1

Colusa-Sacramento River State Recreation Area

Oroville, CA 95966. Phone: (530) 458-4927. Located on Sacramento River in north-central CA, NW of Sacramento in Colusa, 9 miles E of I-5. 12 sites; dump station. 27-foot limit-M; 24-foot limit-T. ER. Wi-Fi. Fishing; boat ramp. GPS: N 39-13.6 W 122-01.0

Cuyamaca Rancho State Park

Descanso, CA 91916. Phone: (760) 765-3020. Located in southern CA on CA 79, NE of San Diego, 5 miles N of I-8 at Descanso. 166 sites, 85 with electric, water; showers; two dump stations. 30-foot limit. Wi-Fi. Fishing; horse trails. GPS: N 32-55.9 W 116-33.8

D. L. Bliss State Park

Tahoma, CA 96142. Phone: (530) 525-7277. Located in east-central CA, 17 miles S of Tahoe City on CA 89. 165 sites. 18-foot limit-M; 15-foot limit-T. Closed in winter. GPS: N 38-58.3 W 120-05.9

Del Norte Coast Redwoods State Park

Crescent City, CA 95531. Phone: (707) 465-7335 ext 5120. Located in northern coast area on US 101, 7 miles S of Crescent City. 142 sites; dump station. 31-foot limit-M; 27-foot limit-T. (Campgrounds open May 1 to Sep 30.) GPS: N 41-42.8 W 124-07.8

Doheny State Beach

Dana Point, CA 92629. Phone: (949) 496-6172. Located in southern CA outside Dana Point, near junction of CA 1 and I-5. 120 sites; showers; dump station. 35-foot limit. Reservations recommended. Fishing. Wi-Fi. GPS: N 32-59.2 W 117-16.4

Donner Memorial State Park

Tahoma, CA 96142. Phone: (530) 582-7892. Located in east-central CA near Donner Pass, 2 miles W of Truckee, off I-80 at Truckee exit. 154 sites; showers. 28-foot limit-M; 24-foot limit-T. Fishing, swimming; boat ramp nearby on Donner Lake. GPS: N 39-19.4 W 120-13.7

Ed Z'berg Sugar Pine Point State Park

Tahoma, CA 96142. Phone: (530)525-7982. Located on Lake Tahoe. 250 sites (limited sites in winter.) Dump station. Fishing, boat ramp. 32-foot limit M; 26-foot T. Wi-Fi. GPS: N39-24.0 W120-2.9

El Capitan State Beach

Ventura, CA 93001. Phone: (805) 968-1033. Located in southern CA, 17 miles W of Santa Barbara on US 101. 132 sites. 42-foot limit. ER. GPS: N 34-27.8 W 120-01.3

Emerald Bay State Park

Tahoma, CA 96142. Phone: (530) 541-3030. Located in east-central CA in Lake Tahoe area, 22 miles S of Tahoe City on CA 89. 120 sites. 21-foot limit-M; 18-foot limit-T. Reservations recommended. GPS: N 38-57.4 W 120-06.5

Emma Wood State Beach

Ventura, CA 93001. Phone: (805) 968-1033. Located in southern CA on US 101, 2 miles W of Ventura. 90 sites (primitive). Two areas: North Beach; Ventura River. 45-foot limit. GPS: N 34-16.9 W 119-18.6

Folsom Lake State Recreation Area

Folsom, CA 95630. Phone: (916) 988-0295. Located in central CA, 25 miles NE of Sacramento, outside Folsom off US 50. 150 sites in two campgrounds; showers; dump station. 31-foot limit. Fishing, boat ramp, horse trails. Marina. Wi-Fi. GPS: N 38-43.2 W 121-10.5

Fort Tejon State Historic Park

Columbia, CA 95310. Phone: (661) 248-6692. Located in southern CA, 70 miles NW of Los Angeles, I-5 Fort Tejon exit (near the "Grapevine"). Open site camping. 36-foot limit-M; 30-foot limit-T. GPS: N 34-52.5 W 118-53.7

Fremont Peak State Park

Monterey, CA 93940. Phone: (831) 623-4255. Located in central CA, NE of Salinas off CA 156. Astronomical observatory. Narrow, steep road, not easy access. 25 sites. 25-foot limit. GPS: N 36-45.6 W 121-30.2

Gaviota State Park

Ventura, CA 93001. Phone: (805) 968-1033. Located 33 miles N of Santa Barbara on US 101. 39 sites; showers. No water for fill-up. 28-foot limit-M; 25-foot limit-T. Fishing, swimming. GPS: N 34-29.4 W 120-13.6

George J. Hatfield State Recreation Area

4394 N Kelly Rd, Hilmar, CA 95310. Phone: (209) 632-1852. Located on Merced River in central CA, on CA 140 between Merced and I-5 Newman exit, east on CR J18. 18 sites. 30-foot limit. No reservations. GPS: N 37-27.0 W 120-57.8

Grizzly Creek Redwoods State Park

16949 Hwy 36, Carlotta, CA 95528. Phone: (707) 777-3683. Located in northern CA on Van Duzen River, 20 miles SE of Eureka on CA 36 off US 101. 30 sites. 30-foot limit-M; 24-foot limit-T. Fishing, swimming. GPS: N 40-29.2 W 123-54.4

Grover Hot Springs State Park

Tahoma, CA 96142. Phone: (530) 694-2248. Located in east-central CA, SE of South Lake Tahoe on CA 4, 4 miles W of Markleeville. Features hot springs pool. 76 sites; showers. 27-foot limit-M; 24-foot limit-T. GPS: N 38-41.7 W 119-50.2

Half Moon Bay State Beach

Felton, CA 95019. Phone: (650) 726-8819. Located in central CA on CA 1, S of San Francisco in Half Moon Bay. 52 sites; showers; dump station. 40-foot limit. ER. Fishing, horse trails. GPS: N 37-27.9 W 122-26.6

Hendy Woods State Park

Mendocino, CA 95460. Phone: (707) 895-3141. Located in northern CA on CA 128, SW of Ukiah, 8 miles NW of Boonville. 82 sites; showers; dump station. 35-foot limit. Swimming. GPS: N39-05.3 W123-28.9

Henry Cowell Redwoods State Park

Felton, CA 95108. Phone: (831)335-4598. Located in central CA, 5 miles N of Santa Cruz on CA 9. 109 sites. 35-foot limit-M; 31-foot limit-T. Fishing. Wi-Fi. GPS: N 37-02.6 W 122-04.3

Henry W. Coe State Park

Morgan Hill, CA 95038. Phone: (408) 779-2728. Remote location in central CA, E of San Jose, 13 miles NE of Morgan Hill on county roads. 20 sites. 22-foot limit-M; 20-foot limit-T. Horse trails. GPS: N 37-05.1 W 121-28.0

Hollister Hills State Vehicular Recreation Area

Hollister, CA 95023. Phone: (831) 637-3874. Off-road vehicle park. Located in central CA, NE of Salinas, 6 miles S of Hollister on CA 25. Open camp sites; showers. 26-foot limit-M; 18-foot limit-T. GPS: N 36-46.8 W 121-24.3

Humboldt Redwoods State Park

Weott, CA 95571. Phone: (707) 946-2409. Located in northern CA, 45 miles S of Eureka off US 101 and CA 254. 260 sites in three campgrounds. 33-foot limit-M; 24-foot limit-T. Horse trails. GPS: N 40-26.6 W 124-01.4

Indian Grinding Rock State Historic Park

14881 Pine Grove-Volcano Rd, Pine Grove, CA 95665. Phone: (209) 296-7488. Located in central CA, E of Sacramento, 11 miles NE of Jackson on CA 88. 22 sites with water. 27-foot limit. GPS: N 38-27.3 W 120-38.6

Jedediah Smith Redwoods State Park

Eureka, CA 95503. Phone: (707)465-7335 ext. 5112. Located on Smith River in northern CA, 9 miles E of Crescent City on US 199. 105 sites; dump station. 36-foot limit-M; 31-foot limit-T. Swimming; horse trails; boat ramp. GPS: N 41-47.9 W 124-05.0

Lake Oroville State Recreation Area

Oroville, CA 95966. Phone: (530) 538-2200. Located in north-central CA, 7 miles E of Oroville (CA 99). 278 sites in two campgrounds, 74 full hook-up; dump station. 40-foot limit-M; 35-foot limit-T. ER. Wi-Fi. Swimming, boat ramp; horse trails. GPS: N 39-31.7 W 121-29.1

Lake Perris State Recreation Area

Perris, CA 92571. Phone: (951) 940-5600. Located in southern CA east of Los Angeles, 11 miles SE of Riverside via CA 60 or I-215, follow signs. 431 sites, 265 with electric, some 50 amp. Water; showers; dump station. 31-foot limit. Wi-Fi. Swimming; horse trails; boat ramp. GPS: N 33-51.6 W 117-8.4

Leo Carrillo State Park

Malibu, CA 90265. Phone: (805) 488-1827 or (818) 880-0363. Located in southern CA, 28 miles NW of Santa Monica on CA 1. 136 sites; showers; dump station. 31-foot limit. Swimming, fishing. Wi-Fi. GPS: N 34-02.7 W 118-56.1

Limekiln State Park

Big Sur, CA 93920. Phone: (831) 667-2403. Located in southern CA on Pacific Coast, 56 miles S of Carmel on CA 1. 29 sites; showers. 24-foot limit-M; 15-foot limit-T. GPS: N 36-00.8 W 121-31.6

MacKerricher State Park

Mendocino, CA 95460. Phone: (707) 964-9112. Located in northern CA on coast, 3 miles N of Fort Bragg on CA 1. 120 sites; showers; dump station. 35-foot limit. Wi-Fi. Swimming; horse trails. GPS: N 39-29.3 W 123-47.2

Malakoff Diggins State Historic Park

Tahoma, CA 96142. Phone: (530) 265-2740. Located in east-central CA about 17 miles NE of Nevada City on steep, unpaved road, off CA 49. 33 sites. 24-foot limit-M; 18-foot limit-T. Swimming; horse trails. GPS: N 39-22.0 W 120-55.5

Malibu Creek State Park

Calabasas, CA 91302. Phone: (818) 880-0367. Located in southern CA, 4 miles S of US 101 near Agoura Hills on Malibu Canyon Rd. 63 sites; showers; dump station. 30-foot limit. Fishing; horse trails. GPS N 34-06.4 W 118-44.2

Manchester State Park

44500 Kinney Ln, Mendocino, CA 95460. Phone: (707) 882-2463. Located in northern CA on Pacific Coast, 7 miles N of Point Arena on CA 1, outside Manchester. 65 sites; dump station. 30-foot limit-M; 22-foot limit-T. GPS: N 38-59.84 W 123-41.4

McArthur-Burney Falls Memorial State Park

Oroville, CA 95966. Phone: (530) 335-2777. Located in north-central CA, NE of Redding, on CA 89 near Burney. 128 sites; showers; dump station. 32-foot limit. ER. Wi-Fi. Swimming, boat ramp; horse trails. GPS: N 41-00.6 W 121-38.9

McConnell State Recreation Area

Columbia, CA 95310. Phone: (209) 394-7755. Located in central CA on Merced River, on CA 99, SE of Modesto, outside Livingston. 20 sites; showers. 30-foot limit-M; 24-foot limit-T. GPS: N 37-24.9 W 120-42.7

McGrath State Beach

Ventura, CA 93001. Phone: (805) 968-1033. Located in southern CA, W of Oxnard five miles S of Ventura, off US 101. 168 sites; dump station. 34-foot limit-M; 30-foot limit-T. Fishing, swimming. GPS: N 34-13.6 W 119-15.4

Millerton Lake State Recreation Area

Columbia, CA 95310. Phone: (559) 822-2332. Located in central CA, 20 miles NE of Fresno via CA 141 and 145, on Millerton Lake. 133 sites, 28 full hook-up; showers; dump station. 36-foot limit. Swimming; boat ramp; horse trails. GPS: N 36-59.2 W 119-41.2

Montana De Oro State Park

San Simeon, CA 93452. Phone: (805) 528-0513. Located in southern CA on Pacific Coast, 7 miles S of Los Osos off CA 1. 52 sites. 27-foot limit. ER. Equestrian area, trails. GPS: N 35-18.0 W 120-51.8

Morro Bay State Park

San Simeon, CA 93452. Phone: (805) 772-2560. Located in southern CA on Pacific Coast, outside Morro Bay on CA 1. 136 sites with electric, water; showers; dump station. 35-foot limit. Surfing. Wi-Fi. GPS: N 35-21.2 W 120-50.6

Morro Strand State Beach

San Simeon, CA 93452. Phone: (805) 772-2560. Located in southern CA 2 miles S of Cayucos, on CA 1. 76 sites; 24-foot limit. Fishing, wind-surfing. GPS: N 36-26.1 W 120-53.3

Mount Diablo State Park

Sonoma, CA 95476. Phone: (925) 837-2525. Located in central CA, NE of Danville, 5 miles E of I-680, east of Oakland. 58 sites; showers. 20-foot limit. Horse trails. GPS: N 37-50.7 W 121-57.0

Mount San Jacinto State Park

Idyllwild, CA 92549. Phone: (951) 659 -2607. Located in south-central CA, SW of Palm Springs, outside Idyllwild via I-10 and CA 243. 76 sites; showers. 24-foot limit. Aerial tramway. Wi-Fi. GPS: N 33-46.9 W 116-44.9

Mount Tamalpais State Park

Duncan Mills, CA 95430. Phone: (415) 388-2070. Located in central CA, NE of Sausalito on Marin Peninsula, off US 101 on CA 1; follow signs. 17 sites; no size limits. ER. Wi-Fi. Horse trails. GPS: N 37-54.3 W 122-36.2

Navarro River Redwoods State Park

Mendocino, CA 95460. Phone: (707) 937-5804. Located in northern CA off CA 1, near Elk, on CA 128; on Navarro River. 28 sites; no water. 30-foot limit-M; 24-foot limit-T. Swimming, fishing. GPS: N 39-09.9 W 123-39.5

New Brighton State Beach

Capitola, CA 95018. Phone: (831) 464-6330. Located in southern CA, 4 miles S of Santa Cruz on CA 1. 10 sites with electric, water; dump station. 36-foot limit. ER. Swimming, fishing. GPS: N 36-59.0 W 121-56.2

Oceano Dunes State Vehicular Recreation Area

Arroyo Grande, CA 93420. Phone: (805) 473-7220. Located in southern CA, 3 miles S of Pismo Beach on CA 1. 1,000 sites; open camping; 40-foot limit. Off-road vehicle park. Sites are on soft sand. Swimming; horse trails. GPS: N 35-01.6 W 120-36.8

Palomar Mountain State Park

Borrego Springs, CA 92004. Phone: (760) 742-3462. Located in southern CA, NE of Oceanside, off CA 76 (off I-15). 31 sites. Showers. 27-foot limit-M; 24-foot limit-T. GPS: N 33-19.5 W 116-53.6

Patrick's Point State Park

Trinidad, CA 95570. Phone: (707) 677-3570. Located in northern CA, 25 miles N of Eureka on US 101. 12 sites; showers. 31-foot limit. GPS: N 41-08.2 W 124-09.0

Pfeiffer Big Sur State Park

Big Sur, CA 93920. Phone: (831) 667-2315. Located in central CA, 26 miles S of Carmel, in Big Sur, off CA 1. 10 sites; showers; dump station. 32-foot limit-M; 27-foot limit-T. ER. Wi-Fi. Swimming. GPS: N 36-15.1 W 121-47.2

Picacho State Recreation Area

Borrego Springs, CA 92004. Phone: (760) 996-2963. Remote location in southeast corner of CA, on Colorado River, near Yuma, AZ, N of Winterhaven on unpaved road. 54 sites; showers; dump station. 35-foot limit-M; 30-foot limit-T. Swimming; boat ramp. No reservations. GPS: N 33-01.3 W 114-36.9

Pismo State Beach

Oceano, CA 93445. Phone: (805) 489-1869. Located in southern CA, 2 miles W of Pismo Beach (City) on CA 1. 173 sites, 42 with electric, water; showers. 36-foot limit-M; 31-foot limit-T. Swimming, fishing. Horse trails. Wi-Fi. GPS: N 35-08.4 W 120-38.6

Plumas-Eureka State Park

Blairsden, CA 96103. Phone: (530) 836-2380. Located in central CA, 5 miles W of Blairsden, off CA 89 on CR A-14. 67 sites; showers;

dump station. 30-foot limit-M; 24-foot limit-T. Fishing. GPS: N 39-45.5 W 120-41.7

Point Mugu State Park

Malibu, CA 90265. Phone: (805) 488-1827. Located in southern CA, 15 miles S of Oxnard on CA 1. 126 sites; dump station. 31-foot limit. Swimming; horse trails; surf fishing. Wi-Fi. GPS: N 34-04.2 W 119-00.7

Portola Redwoods State Park

Felton, CA 95018. Phone: (650) 948-9098. Located in central CA, W of Saratoga, 6.5 miles W of CA 35, via steep and winding road. 53 sites; showers. 24-foot limit-M; 21-foot limit-T. (Campground closed Dec.to May 1.) GPS: N 37-16.0 W 122-12.4

Prairie Creek Redwoods State Park

Eureka, CA 95503. Phone: (707) 465-7335. Located in northern CA, 50 miles N of Eureka on US 101, in Redwoods National Park. 63 sites; dump station. 27-foot limit-M; 24-foot limit-T. GPS: N 41-27.2 W 124-02.6

Providence Mountains State Recreation Area

Perris, CA 92571. Phone: (760) 928-2586. Located in southeastern CA in Mojave Desert, 56 miles W of Needles, 15 miles NW of I-40 at Essex exit. 6 sites. 32-foot limit-M; 31-foot limit-T. (Caverns with tours for extra fee.) Reservations not accepted. GPS: N 34-57.0 W 115-27.5

Red Rock Canyon State Park

Perris, CA 92571. Phone: (661) 946-6092 (info only). Located in south-central CA, 25 miles N of Mojave on CA 14. 50 primative sites; dump station; water available. 30-foot limit. ER. Horse trails. No reservations. GPS: N 35-19.5 W 117-59.9

Refugio State Beach

10 Refugio Beach Rd, Goleta, CA 93117. Phone: (805) 968-1033. Located in southern CA, 20 miles W of Santa Barbara on US 101. 80 sites. 30-foot limit-M; 27-foot limit-T. Swimming, fishing. GPS: N 34-27.7 W 120-03.8

Richardson Grove State Park

Garberville, CA 95440. Phone: (707) 247-3318 (recorded message). Located in northern CA, 7 miles S of Garberville on US 101. 175 sites; showers. 30-foot limit-M; 24-foot limit-T. ER. Wi-Fi. Swimming. Bear country. GPS: N 40-01.6 W 123-47.6

Russian Gulch State Park

Mendocino, CA 95460. Phone: (707) 937-5804. Located in northern CA, 2 miles N of Mendocino on CA 1. 28 sites; showers. 24-foot limit. Swimming, fishing. GPS: N 39-19.9 W 123-48.3

Saddleback Butte State Park

Perris, CA 92571. Phone: (661) 946-6092 or (661) 942-0662. Remote location in southern CA, 17 miles E of Lancaster (CA 14). 50 sites; water available; dump station. 30-foot limit. Horse trails. GPS: N 34-41.4 W 117-49.5

Salt Point State Park

Duncan Mills, CA 95430. Phone: (707) 847-3221. Located in northern CA, 12 miles W of Healdsburg on CA 1. 109 sites. 31-foot limit-M; 27-foot limit-T. ER. Water available. Fishing; horse trails. GPS: N 38-34.9 W 123-19.9

Salton Sea State Recreation Area

North Shore, CA 92254. Phone: (760) 393-3052 or 393-3059 (ranger). Located in southern CA, 30 miles SE of Indio (I-10) on CA 111. Five campgrounds; 1,600 sites; many full hook-up. 28-foot limit-M; 24-foot limit-T. Reservations accepted. Swimming, fishing; boat ramp. Wi-Fi. GPS: N 33-30.5 W 115-55.2

Samuel P. Taylor State Park

8889 Sir Francis Drake Blvd, Lagunitas, CA 94938. Phone: (415) 488-9897. Located in central CA, 15 miles W of San Rafael, off CA 1. 84 sites; showers; dump station. 31-foot limit-M; 27-foot limit-T. No reservations. Swimming. Wi-Fi. GPS: N 38-00.3 W 122-42.5

San Clemente State Beach

San Clemente, CA 92672. Phone: (949) 492-3156. Located in southern CA, south end of San Clemente just off I-5. 72 sites with electric, water; showers; dump station. 30-foot limit. Wi-Fi. Swimming, fishing. GPS: N 33-24.4 W 117-36.2

San Elijo State Beach

San Diego, CA 92108. Phone: (760) 753-5091. Located in southern CA, N of San Diego, on Old 101, off I-5 Rancho Santa Fe exit. 171 sites; dump station. 35-foot limit. Surfing. Wi-Fi. GPS: N 32-59.2 W 117-16.4

San Luis Reservoir State Recreation Area

31426 Gonzaga Rd, Gustine, CA 95322. Phone: (209) 826-1197. Located in central CA, SE of San Jose, 12 miles W of Los Banos on CA 152. 132 sites, 70 with electric, water; showers; dump station. 30-foot limit. Swimming, fishing; horse trails; boat ramp. Note: Lake level and wind affect accessibility. Call ahead. GPS: N 37-05.0 W 121-06.0

San Onofre State Beach

San Clemente, CA 92672. Phone: (949) 492-4872. Located in southern CA, off I-5, 3 miles S of San Clemente. 334 sites (includes San Mateo campground), 67 with electric, water; showers; dump station. 36-foot limit. Fishing, surfing. No alcohol. GPS: N 33-23.0 W 117-34.8

San Simeon State Park

Cambria, CA 93428. Phone: (805) 927-2020. Located in southern CA, 5 miles S of San Simeon on CA 1. 115 sites; showers; water fill-up; dump station. 35-foot limit. Reservations recommended March through September. GPS: N 35-36.0 W 121-11.4

Seacliff State Beach

Felton, CA 95018. Phone: (831) 685-6442. Located in central CA, 5.5 miles S of Santa Cruz on CA 1. 26 sites with electric, water; showers. 40-foot limit-M; 36-foot limit-T. Swimming, fishing. GPS: N 36-58.4 W 121-54.8

Silverwood Lake State Recreation Area

Perris, CA 92571. Phone: (760) 389-2281. Located in southern CA, N of San Bernardino, 11 miles E of I-15 on CA 138. 258 sites; showers; dump station. 34-foot limit-M; 31-foot limit-T. Fishing; Boat ramp. Wi-Fi. GPS: N 34-16.7 W 117-20.6

Sonoma Coast State Park

Duncan Mills, CA 95430. Phone: (707) 875-3483. Located in northern CA on Pacific Coast, SW of Santa Rosa, north of Bodega Bay on CA 1. 156 sites in four campgrounds; no hook-ups; showers in one campground; dump station. RV limits vary by campground; maximum 31 feet. Call for details, site assignments. Reservations recommended. ER. Horse trails; boat ramp. GPS: N 38-26.5 W 123-07.4

South Carlsbad State Beach

7201 Carlsbad Blvd, Carlsbad, CA 92008. Phone: (760) 438-3143. Located in southern CA, 3 miles S of Carlsbad off I-5. 222 sites; showers; dump station. 35-foot limit. Reservations recommended. Swimming, fishing. Wi-Fi. GPS: N 33-08.8 W 117-20.7

Standish-Hickey State Recreation Area

Leggett, CA 95455. Phone: (707) 925-6482. Located in northern CA, 2 miles N of Leggett on US 101 near junction of CA 1. 161 sites; showers. 27-foot limit-M; 24-foot limit-T. GPS: N 39-52.7 W 123-43.1

Sugarloaf Ridge State Park

2605 Adobe Canyon Rd, Kenwood, CA 95452. Phone: (707) 833-5712. Located in central CA, 7 miles E of Santa Rosa off CA 12 on Adobe Canyon Rd. 47 sites. 27-foot limit-M; 24-foot limit-T. Horse trails. Ferguson observatory in park. GPS: N 38-26.2 W 122-30.5

Sunset State Beach

Felton, CA 95018. Phone: (831) 763-7062. Located in central CA just south of Watsonville off CA 1. 90 sites. 31-foot limit. Wi-Fi. Swimming, fishing; horse trails. GPS: N 36-53.9 W 121-50.1

Tahoe State Recreation Area

Tahoma, CA 96142. Phone: (530) 583-3074. Located in east-central CA on Lake Tahoe, 1/4 mile E of Tahoe City on CA 28. 28 sites. 21-foot limit-M; 15-foot limit-T. No camping from September 16 to Memorial Day. Bear country. GPS: N 39-11.0 W 120-07.3

Turlock Lake State Recreation Area

LaGrange, CA 95329. Phone: (209) 874-2056. Located in central CA, 25 miles E of Modesto off CA 132. 66 sites. 27-foot limit-M; 24-foot limit-T. Swimming, fishing; boat ramp. GPS: N 37-37.7 W 120-35.1

Van Damme State Park

Mendocino, CA 95460. Phone: (707) 937-5804. Located in northern CA on Pacific Coast, 3 miles S of Mendocino on CA 1. 84 sites; showers; dump station. 35-foot limit. ER. Swimming, fishing. Wi-Fi. GPS: N 39-16.4 W 123-47.4

Westport-Union Landing State Beach

Mendocino, CA 95460. Phone: (707) 937-5804. Located in northern CA on Pacific Coast, 1.5 miles N of Westport on CA 1. Open camping; no size limits. Reservations recommended in summer. GPS: N 39-39.5 W 123-47.1

Woodson Bridge State Recreation Area

Oroville, CA 95966. Phone: (530) 839-2112. Located in central CA, 6 miles E of I-5 Corning exit. 37 sites; showers. 31-foot limit. Fishing. Boat ramp nearby. GPS: N 39-54.6 W 122-05.4

COLORADO

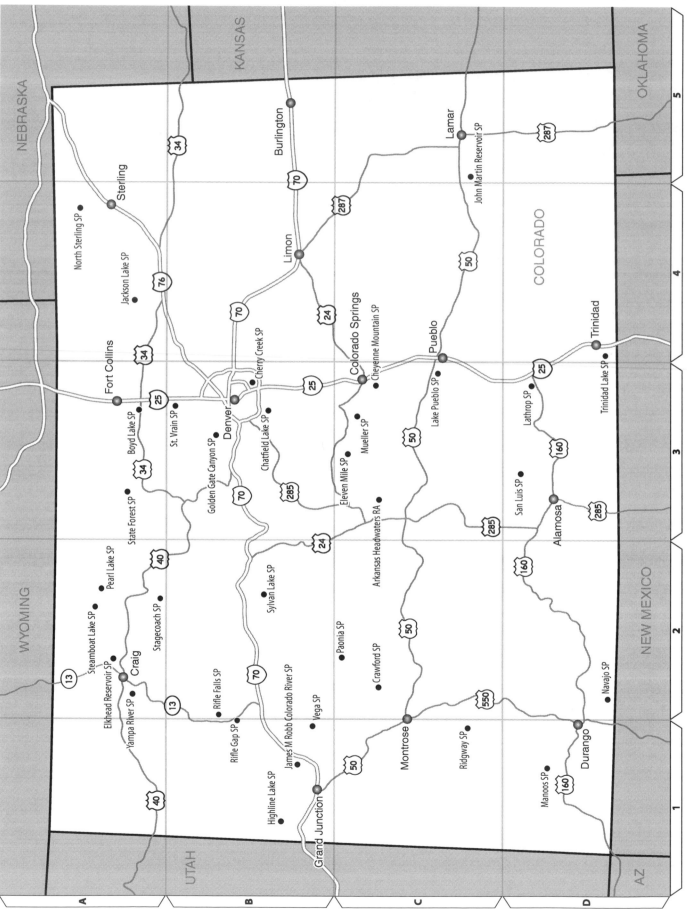

Colorado

Twenty-six of Colorado's 33 RV-friendly state parks are located west of I-25. Many locations are near or on major roadways. While these are open year-round, some of the facilities are curtailed in winter months. Reservations are available through the state-wide system but sites are also available on a drive-in basis. It is important to check with the particular park for site availability. Pets are permitted but must be on leashes. There are some "primitive" (no facilities) sites available, but most sites are developed and offer upgraded amenities. Rate groups: A and B, depending on hook-ups. Vehicle fee extra.

Colorado State Parks
1313 Sherman St., Room 618
Denver, CO 80203

Information: (303) 866-3437
Reservations: (800) 678-2267
Internet: www.parks.state.co.us

Colorado Park Locator

Arkansas Headwaters Recreation Area....C3
Boyd Lake State Park....A3
Chatfield Lake State Park....B3
Cherry Creek State Park....B3
Cheyenne Mountain State Park....C3
Crawford State Park....C2
Eleven Mile State Park....C3
Elkhead Reservoir State Park....A2
Golden Gate Canyon State Park....B3
Highline Lake State Park....B1
Jackson Lake State Park....A4
James M. Robb Colorado River State Park....B1
John Martin Reservoir State Park....C5
Lake Pueblo State Park....C3
Lathrop State Park....D3
Mancos State Park....D1
Mueller State Park....C3
Navajo State Park....D3
North Sterling State Park....A4
Paonia State Park....C2
Pearl Lake State Park....A2
Ridgway State Park....C1
Rifle Falls State Park....B2
Rifle Gap State Park....B1
San Luis State Park....D3
St. Vrain State Park....B3
Stagecoach State Park....A2
State Forest State Park....A3
Steamboat Lake State Park....A2
Sylvan Lake State Park....B2
Trinidad Lake State Park....D4
Vega State Park....B1
Yampa River State Park....A2

Colorado Parks

Arkansas Headwaters Recreation Area

307 W Sackett Ave, Salida, CO 81201. Phone: (719) 539-7289. Located NW of Salida near junction of CO 291 and US 24 along Arkansas River. Six campgrounds, 86 sites; no hook-ups or drinking water. Fishing. White water boating. GPS: N 38-36.2 W 106-02.9

Boyd Lake State Park

3720 N CR 11-C, Loveland, CO 80538. Phone: (970) 669-1739. Located 1 mile E of Loveland off US 34 (I-25 exit 257B). 148 pull-thru sites with electric; showers; dump station; fishing, boat ramp. GPS: N 40-26.0 W 105-02.7

Chatfield Lake State Park

11500 N Roxborough Park Rd, Littleton, CO 80125. Phone: (303) 791-7275. Located south of Denver off CO 470 along CO 121. 197 sites, all with electric, some full hook-up; showers; dump station. Horse trails; boat ramp. GPS: N 39-31.8 W 105-03.3

Cherry Creek State Park

4201 S Parker Rd, Aurora, CO 80014. Phone: (303) 690-1166. Located in Aurora south of I-225 exit 4. 125 full hook-up sites; showers; dump station; swimming, boat ramp. GPS: N 39-37.9 W 104-52.6

Cheyenne Mountain State Park

410 JL Ranch Heights, Colorado Springs, CO 80926. Phone: (719) 576-2016. Located 4 miles SW of I-25 Exit 135. 51 full hook-up sites; showers; laundry; hiking trails. GPS: N 38-44.1 W 104-49.1

Crawford State Park

40468 Hwy 92, Crawford, CO 81415. Phone: (970) 921-5721. Located on CO 92 about 25 miles E of Delta (US 550 & 50). 66 sites, 45 with electric, water; showers. Fishing, swimming; Boat ramp (restricted boating.) GPS: N 38-42.5 W 107-37.1

Eleven Mile State Park

4229 CR 92, Lake George, CO 80827. Phone: (719) 748-3401. Remote location about 38 miles W of Colorado Springs via US 24 and CR 92. Nine campgrounds, 349 sites, 75 with electric; showers; dump station. GPS: N 38-56.9 W 105-31.6

Elkhead Reservoir State Park

6185 US 4; Hayden, CO 81639. Phone: (970) 276-2061. Located 9 miles NE of Craig, W of Steamboat Springs on the reservoir. 16 basic sites. Boat ramp; fishing, swimming. Closed Nov. 30 to April 15.GPS: N 40-36.4 W 107- 24.5

Golden Gate Canyon State Park

92 Crawford Gulch Rd, Golden, CO 80403. Phone: (303) 582-3707. Located NW of Golden via CR 70 and CO 46. 97 sites, 59 with electric; showers; dump station; fishing, horse trails. GPS: N 39-50.2 W 105-26.0

Highline Lake State Park

1800 11.8 Rd, Loma, CO 81524. Phone: (970) 858-7208. Located north of Loma (I-70 exit 15) off CO 139 and Q Road. 31 sites; showers; laundry; dump station; swimming, fishing; boat ramp. GPS: N 39-16.2 W 108-50.1

Jackson Lake State Park

26363 CR 3, Orchard, CO 80649. Phone: (970) 645-2551. Located about 11 miles from US 34/I-76 interchange via CO 39 through Goodrich. 260 sites, 54 with electric; showers; dump station; swimming, fishing; boat ramp, marina. GPS: N 40-24.5 W 104-04.2

James M. Robb Colorado River State Park

Clifton, CO 81520. Phone: (970) 434-3388. Two areas:

a. Island Acres: Located off I-70 exit 47, 5 miles E of Palisades on Colorado River. 80 sites with electric, sewers; showers; laundry; dump station. GPS N 39-10.0 W 108-18.1

b. Fruita: Located off I-70 exit 19, south on CO 340. 63 sites with electric, sewers; showers; laundry; dump station. Swimming, fishing, non-gas motors. GPS: N 39-08.5 W 108-44.2

John Martin Reservoir State Park

30703 CR 24, Hasty, CO 81044. Phone: (719) 829-1801. Located in eastern CO, 93 miles E of Pueblo, off US 50, 4 miles S of Hasty. 213 sites (2 areas); 109 sites with electric; water available; showers; dump station; laundry. Swimming, fishing; boat ramp; horse trails. GPS: N 38-03.8 W 102-55.6

Lake Pueblo State Park

640 Pueblo Reservoir Rd, Pueblo, CO 81005. Phone: (719) 561-9320. Located west of Pueblo (I-25 exit 102) via US 50; follow signs. Three areas, 400 sites, some with electric; showers; dump station; fishing, swimming, boat ramp. GPS: N 38-15.5 W 104-42.3

Lathrop State Park

70 CR 502, Walsenburg, CO 81089. Phone: (719) 738-2376. Located off US 160, 3 miles W of Walsenburg (I-25 exit 49). Two areas, 103 sites, 82 with electric; showers; dump station. Golf course; fishing, swimming, boat ramp. GPS: N 37-36.2 W 104-50.0

Mancos State Park

42545 CR N, Mancos, CO 81328. Phone: (970) 533-7065. Located NW of Durango in southwestern Colorado; N of Mancos off US 160 and CO 184; follow signs. 32 sites; dump station; horse trails; fishing, boat ramp, rentals. GPS: N 37-24.0 W 108-16.0

Mueller State Park

21045 Hwy 675, Divide, CO 80814. Phone: (719) 687-2366. Located 3.5 miles S of Divide, 25 miles W of Colorado Springs, via US 24 and CO 67. 132 sites, most with electric; showers; dump station.Horse trails (No pets on trails.) GPS: N 38-53.1 W 105-09.5

Navajo State Park

1526 CR 982, Arboles, CO 81121. Phone: (970) 883-2208. Located near New Mexico state line SW of Pagosa Springs (US 160) off CO 151 south. 118 sites, 80 with electric, some with sewer; showers; laundry; dump station. Fishing, swimming. Marina, boat ramp, rentals. GPS: N 37-04.3 W 107-24.3

North Sterling State Park

24005 CR 330, Sterling, CO 80751. Phone: (970) 522-3657. Located in northeastern Colorado, 12 miles N of Sterling (I-76 exit 125) via CR 39 and CR 37. 141 sites, 97 with electric; showers; dump station; swimming, marina. GPS: N 40-44.4 W 103-16.0

Paonia State Park

Crawford, CO 81415. Phone: (970) 921-5721. Located on CO 133, 16 miles N of Paonia. 13 sites, no water or electric. Boat ramp, fishing. GPS: N 39-00.0 W 107-18.4

Pearl Lake State Park

Clark, CO 80428 Phone: (970) 879-3922. Located in northern CO, near Steamboat Springs, SE of Columbine, 23 miles N of US 40. 36 sites (size limits); showers. Fishing; boat ramp (no wake lake). GPS: N 40-47.7 W 106-54.2

Ridgway State Park

28555 Hwy 550, Ridgway, CO 81432. Phone: (970) 626-5822. Located on Uncompahgre River, 22 miles S of Montrose on US 550. 258 sites, some with electric, water; showers; dump station. Golf nearby; fishing, swimming; boat ramp. GPS: N 38-12.5 W 107-43.8

Rifle Falls State Park

5775 Hwy 325, Rifle, CO 81650. Phone: (970) 625-1607. Located north of Rifle (I-70 exit 90) on CO 325, off CO 13. 13 sites with electric. Fishing, swimming; boat ramp. GPS: N 39-41.7 W 107-42.0

Rifle Gap State Park

5275 CO 325, Rifle, CO 81650. Phone: (970) 625-1607. Located in western CO, off CO 325, 9 miles N of I-70 at Rifle exit. 89 sites (5 areas); some full hook-up, some electric, water; showers; dump station. Swimming, fishing; boat ramp. GPS: N 39-37.6 W 107-45.7

San Luis State Park

Mosca, CO 81146. Phone: (719) 378-2020. Located on San Luis Lake about 17 miles NE of Alamosa (US 160 and 285) between CO 17 and CO 150 on Six Mile Lane. 51 sites; electric; showers; dump station. Fishing, boat ramp. GPS: N 37-39.8 W 105-43.5

St. Vrain State Park

3785 Weld CR 24 1/2, Freestone, CO 80504. Phone: (303) 678-9402. Located near Longmont just west of I-25 exit 240. 87 sites, 42 with electric, 45 full hook-up; dump station; fishing, boat ramp (no gas motors.) GPS: N 40-10.1 W 104-59.2

Stagecoach State Park

25500 R CR 14, Oak Creek, CO 80467. Phone: (970) 736-2436. Remote location off CO 131 about 43 miles N of I-70 exit 157. 92 sites with electric, water; showers; dump station; fishing. Marina. GPS: N 40-16.9 W 106-52.1

State Forest State Park

56750 Hwy 14, Walden, CO 80480. Phone: (970) 723-8366. Remote location in northern Colorado, 75 miles W of Fort Collins off CO 14. Four campgrounds; 158 sites. Equestrian area (32 sites). Fishing; wakeless boats. GPS: N 40-32.5 W 106-02.1

Steamboat Lake State Park

61105 R CR 129, Clark, CO 80428. Phone: (970) 879-3922. Remote location about 28 miles NW of Steamboat Springs off CR 129, (off US 40). 188 sites, 83 with electric; showers; dump station; fishing, horse trails. Marina. GPS: N 40-48.3 W 106-56.6

Sylvan Lake State Park

10200 Brush Creek Rd, Eagle, CO 81631. Phone: (970) 328-2021. Located 18 miles S of I-70 exit 147 (Eagle) off Brush Creek Rd. 46 sites; showers; dump station. Horse trails, fishing, boat rentals (electric motors only). GPS: N 39-28.9 W 107-48.6

Trinidad Lake State Park

32610 Hwy 12, Trinidad, CO 81082. Phone: (719) 846-6951. Located 3 miles W of Trinidad (I-25 exit 13) on CO 12. 62 sites with electric; showers; dump station; fishing, boat ramp. GPS: N 37-09.0 W 104-32.8

Vega State Park

15247 N 6/10 Rd, Collbran, CO 81624. Phone: (970) 487-3407. Located 29 miles E of I-70 exit 49 via CO 65 and CO 330. 99 sites, 33 with electric, water; showers; dump station. Fishing, boat ramp. GPS: N 39-13.6 W 107 48.6

Yampa River State Park

Headquarters, Hayden, CO 81639. Phone: (970) 276-2061. Located S of Craig on CO 13, off US 40. 35 sites with electric; showers; dump station. Note: Some RV sites are also available at the Yampa River location and at Yampa/Elkhead. Both areas are accessible off US 40. Check with park rangers. Boat ramp. GPS: N 40-29.4 W 107-34.6

CONNECTICUT

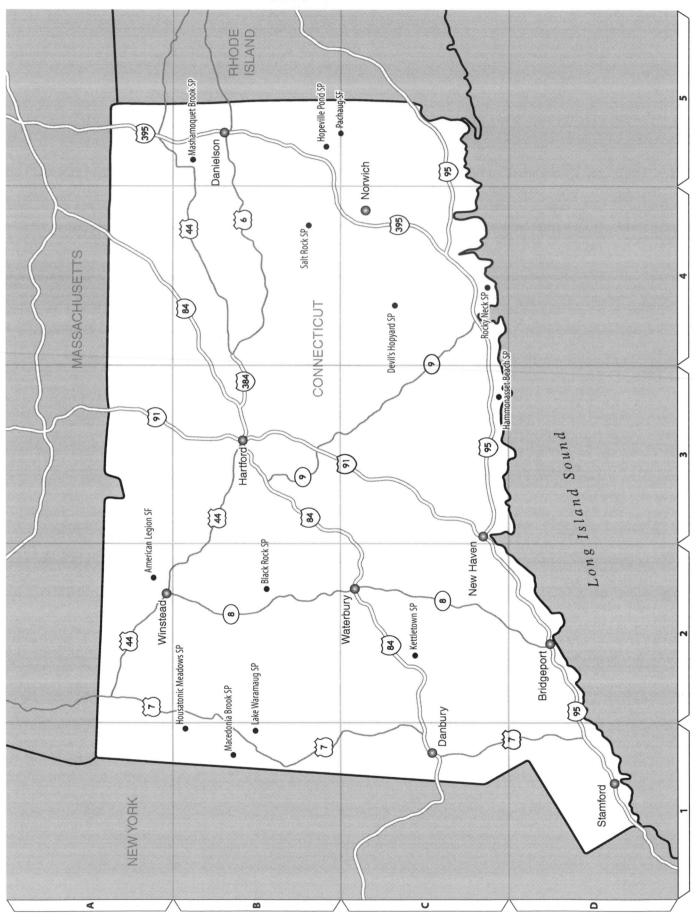

Connecticut

Connecticut has 13 state parks or forests with RV campgrounds. Only one park, Salt Rock, has utilities at the sites. The other locations have facilities within the campground but individual sites are "dry camp" sites. Some of the parks are alcohol-free; check listings below. Only Salt Rock State Park and the two state forest areas allow pets. Most of the locations are open mid-April through September. Some are open through October and one, Housatonic State Park, is open mid-April until December 31. In some cases the listed address is for mail only. RVs cannot exceed 35-feet in any state campground; some parks have shorter limits. Check by telephone. Reservation service is available but requires 48 hours advance request. Rate groups: A (Salt Rock State Park: C); plus processing fee for reservations.

State Parks Division
Bureau of Outdoor Recreation
Dept. of Environmental Protection
79 Elm St., Hartford, CT 06106

Information: (860) 424-3200
Reservations: (877) 668-2267
Internet: www.dep.state.ct.us/stateparks
Reservations: www.reserveamerica.com

Connecticut Park Locator

Connecticut Parks

American Legion (People's) State Forest

West River Rd, Pleasant Valley, CT 06063. Phone: (860) 379-0922. Located in northwestern Connecticut near the junction of US 44 and CT 318. 30 sites; showers; dump station. Fishing. GPS: N 41-56.6 W 73-00.5

Black Rock State Park

Route 6, Thomaston, CT 06787. Phone: (860) 283-8088. Located on US 6 off CT 8 exit 38, SW of Thomaston. 96 sites; showers; dump station. Swimming. No alcohol or pets in campground. GPS: N 41-39.1 W 73-05.8

Devil's Hopyard State Park

366 Hopyard Rd, East Haddam, CT 06423. Phone: (860) 526-2336. Located NE of East Haddam off CT 11 exit 5; remote location. 21 sites. Fishing. No pets. GPS: N 41-28.7 W 72-20.5

Hammonasset Beach State Park

1288 Boston Post Rd, Madison, CT 06443. Phone: (203) 245-1817. Located on Long Island Sound on US 1, off I-95 exit 62, between New Haven and New London. 552 sites; showers; dump station. Swimming, fishing. GPS: N 41-16.4 W 72-33.7

Hopeville Pond State Park

193 Roode Rd, Jewett City, CT 06351. Phone: (860) 376-2920 or (860) 376-0313. Located west of Pachaug State Forest off CT 201 (I-395 exit 86). 80 sites; showers; dump station. Swimming, fishing; boat ramp; horse trails. GPS: N 41-36.4 W 71-55.3

Housatonic Meadows State Park

Route 7, Cornwall Bridge, CT 06754. Phone: (860) 672-6772. Located on US 7 in northwestern CT between Cornwall Bridge and West Cornwall. 95 sites; showers; dump station. Fishing. No alcohol. No pets. GPS: N 41-50.4 W 73-22.8

Kettletown State Park

1400 Georges Hill Rd, Southbury, CT 06488. Phone: (203) 264-5678 or 938-2285. Located on the Housatonic River SE of I-84 exit 14 on CT 172. 68 sites; showers; dump station. 26-foot limit. Swimming, fishing. GPS: N 41-25.7 W 73-12.0

Lake Waramaug State Park

30 Lake Waramaug Rd, New Preston, CT 06777. Phone: (860) 868-0220. Located off CT 478 NW of New Preston (US 202). 77 sites; showers; dump station. Seasonal. GPS: N 41-42.4 W 73-23.0

Macedonia Brook State Park

159 Macedonia Brook Rd, Kent, CT 06757. Phone: (860) 927-3238. Located in northwestern Connecticut off CT 41, W of US 7. 51 sites. Fishing. No alcohol. No pets. GPS: N 41-45.7 W 73-29.6

Mashamoquet Brook State Park

147 Wolf Den Dr, Pomfret Center, CT 06259. Phone: (860) 928-6121. Located on US 44, SW of Putnam. 55 sites (two campgrounds); showers (Wolf Den Campground only); dump stations. Swimming, fishing. GPS: N 41-51.6 W 71-59.2

Pachaug State Forest

Route 49, Voluntown, CT 06384. Phone: (860) 376-4075. Largest forest in state system. Green Falls Campground located on CT 138, 3 miles E of Voluntown. 18 sites. Mt. Misery Campground located 1 mile N of Voluntown on CT49. 22 sites. Equestrian area. No reservations. GPS: N 41-35.3 W 71-52.3

Rocky Neck State Park

244 W Main St, Niantic, CT 06357. Phone: (860) 739-5471. Located on CT 156 off I-95 exits 71 or 72. 160 sites; showers; dump station. Swimming, fishing. GPS: N 41-19.0 W 72-14.4

Salt Rock State Park

173 Scotland Rd, Baltic, CT 06330. Phone: (860) 822-0884. Located 2 miles N of Baltic on CT 97. 71 sites, some with full hook-ups; showers; dump station. GPS: N 41-38.0 W 72-05.3

DELAWARE

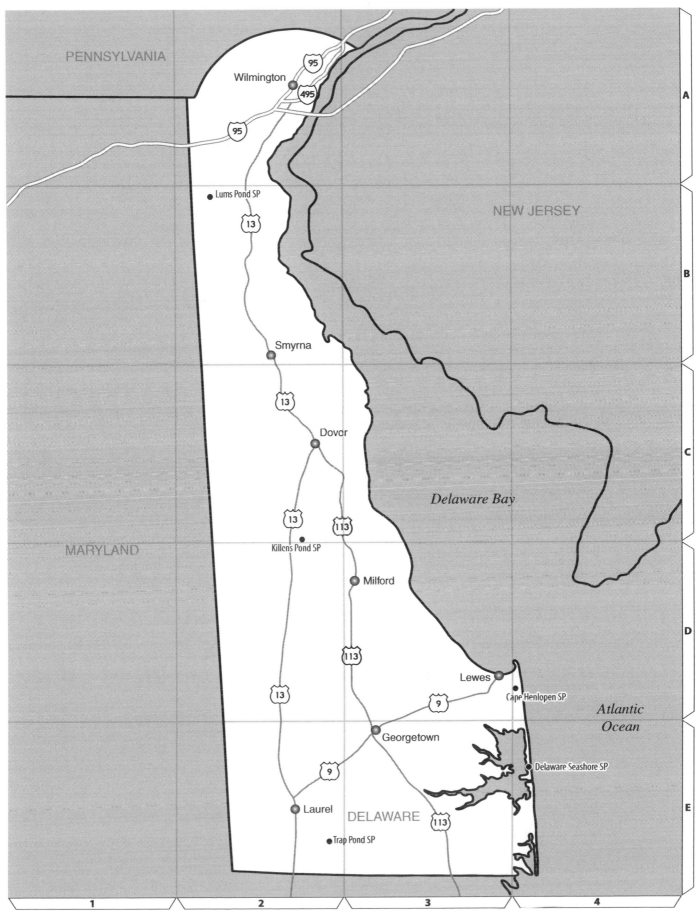

Delaware

Although Delaware has only five state parks with RV facilities, there are more than 800 sites available, most of which have at least electric hook-ups. All the parks have dump stations and drinking water in the park, if not at the particular site. All the parks accept reservations, which can be executed in as little as 24 hours. Pet policies can vary by park, so it is wise to call ahead for particulars. All the parks are on water; two on the Atlantic Ocean. Some campgrounds are seasonal with limited winter services. There are resident and non-resident and summer and winter rates. Rate Group: C.

Delaware Division of Parks & Recreation
89 Kings Highway
Dover, DE 19901

Information: (302) 739-9220 or (302) 739-9200
Reservations: (877) 987-2757
Internet: www.destateparks.com

Delaware Park Locator

Delaware Parks

Cape Henlopen State Park
15099 Cape Henlopen Dr, Lewes, DE 19958. Phone: (302) 645-8983. Located in Lewes and east end of US 9 on the Atlantic Ocean. 150 sites with water; 17 no hook-ups; showers; dump station. Seasonal: March through November. Horse trails. GPS: N 38-46.9 W 75-06.2

Delaware Seashore State Park
39415 Inlet Rd, Rehoboth Beach, DE 19971. Phone: (302) 227-2800. Located along DE 1 south of Dewey Beach on the Atlantic Ocean. 151 full hook-up sites; and 156 "overflow" sites (self-contained units only); showers; dump station. Fishing, swimming; marina; boat ramp. Open all year; limited services. GPS: N 38-38.0 W 75-04.3

Killens Pond State Park
5025 Killens Pond Rd, Felton, DE 19943. Phone: (302) 284-4526. Located south of Felton one mile E of US 13. 59 sites with water and electric; showers; dump station. Boat ramp, rentals. Open all year. GPS: N 38-58.5 W 75-32.2

Lums Pond State Park
1068 Howell School Rd, Bear, DE 19701. Phone: (302) 368-6989. Located on DE 71 south of Newark, off DE 896. 68 sites, 6 with electric; showers; dump station. Four horse sites. Boat ramp, rentals. GPS: N 39-34.2 W 75-44.0

Trap Pond State Park
33587 Baldcypress Ln, Laurel, DE 19956. Phone: (302) 875-5153. Located on DE 24 about 4 miles E of Laurel. 130 sites, water, electric; showers; dump station. Boat ramp, rentals. GPS: N 38-31.4 W 75-28.0

FLORIDA

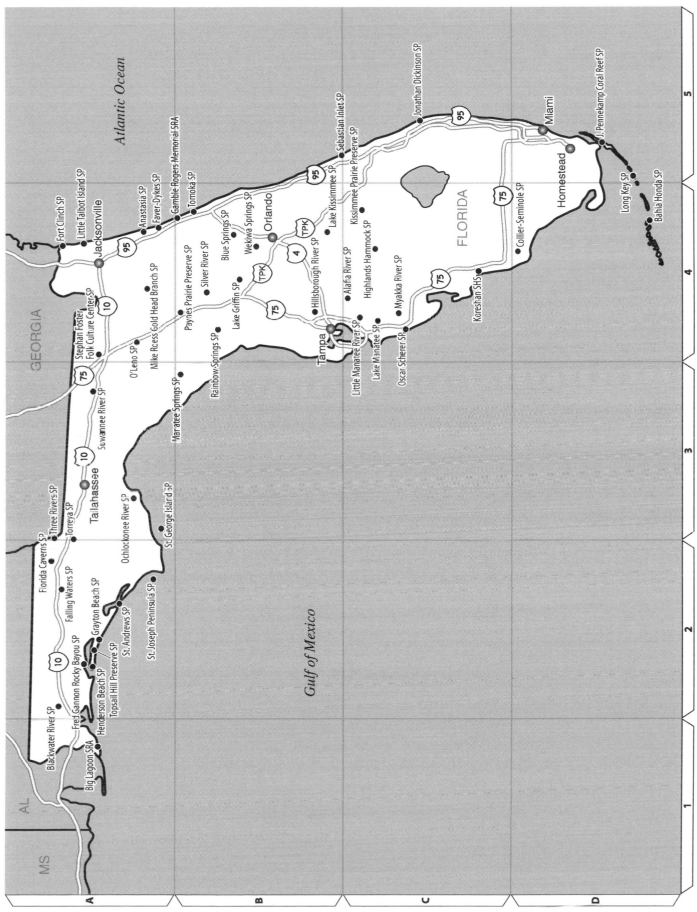

Atlantic Ocean

GEORGIA

Fort Clinch SP
Little Talbot Island SP
Jacksonville
Anastasia SP
Faver-Dykes SP
Gamble Rogers Memorial SRA
Tomoka SP

Stephan Foster
Folk Culture Center SP
O'Leno SP
Mike Roess Gold Head Branch SP
Paynes Prairie Preserve SP
Silver River SP
Blue Springs SP
Wekiwa Springs SP
Orlando
Lake Griffin SP
Rainbow Springs SP
Manatee Springs SP
Suwannee River SP

Sebastian Inlet SP
Kissimmee Prairie Preserve SP
Lake Kissimmee SP
Jonathan Dickinson SP

Hillsborough River SP
Alafia River SP
Highlands Hammock SP
Myakka River SP
Tampa
Little Manatee River SP
Lake Manatee SP
Oscar Scherer SP
Koreshan SHS

FLORIDA

Miami
Homestead
Collier-Seminole SP

J. Pennekamp Coral Reef SP
Long Key SP
Bahia Honda SP

AL
MS
Blackwater River SP
Fred Gannon Rocky Bayou SP
Big Lagoon SRA
Henderson Beach SP
Topsail Hill Preserve SP
Grayton Beach SP
St. Andrews SP
St. Joseph Peninsula SP
Falling Waters SP
Florida Caverns SP
Three Rivers SP
Torreya SP
Tallahassee
Ochlocktonee River SP
St. George Island SP

Gulf of Mexico

TPK

10
75
95
4

Florida

There are 47 state parks or recreation areas in Florida with RV accommodations. These parks are some of the most RV-friendly locations in the country. Most sites in these parks include water and electric hookups and at least one dump station in the park. Some parks do not allow pets, as noted by park. All pets must have current vaccinations and some parks charge a pet fee. All parks have showers. Reservations require a minimum of 24 hours advance notice and, depending upon the park, could require 48 hours. It is imperative you call the particular park to verify space, especially in the Spring and Summer months. All parks are open year-round. Senior discounts are available for Florida residents. Rate groups: A, B and C depending upon the season.

Florida Division of Recreation & Parks
3900 Commonwealth Blvd.
Tallahassee, FL 32399

Information: (850) 488-9872 or (850) 245-2157
Reservations: (800) 326-3521 (Reserve America)
Internet: www.FloridaStateParks.org

Florida Park Locator

Florida Parks

Alafia River State Park

14326 S CR 39, Lithia, FL 33547. Phone: (813) 672-5320. Located 10 miles SE of Tampa. 30 sites; showers; dump station; 12 equestrian sites. Fishing, canoeing. GPS: N 27-47.05 W 82-8.25

Anastasia State Park

1340-A A1A South, St. Augustine, FL 32080. Phone: (904) 461-2033. Located near Saint Augustine on FL A1A, 1.5 miles N of FL 312. 139 sites; laundromat. Swimming, fishing; canoe/kayak rentals. 40-foot limit. GPS: N 29-52.5 W 81-17.1

Bahia Honda State Park

36850 Overseas Hwy, Big Pine Key, FL 33043. Phone: (305) 872-2353. Located 12 miles S of Marathon in Florida Keys, on US 1. 78 sites; some length and height limits within the three campgrounds. Canoe and kayak rentals. Swimming, fishing; marina, boat ramp. GPS: N 24-39.6 W 81-16.5

Big Lagoon State Recreation Area

12301 Gulf Beach Hwy, Pensacola, FL 32507. Phone: (850) 492-1595. Located on CR 292A, 10 miles SW of Pensacola. 68 sites; dump station. Swimming, fishing; boat ramp. 30-foot limit. GPS: N 30-19.3 W 87-24.1

Blackwater River State Park

7720 Deaton Bridge Rd, Holt, FL 32564. Phone: (850) 983-5363.

Located 15 miles NE of Milton, off US 90. 30 sites. Swimming, fishing; boat ramp. 45-foot limit. GPS: N 30-42.3 W 86-52.5

Blue Springs State Park

2100 W French Ave, Orange City, FL 32763. Phone: (386) 775-3663. Located in Orange City (US 17), 2 miles W on West French Ave. 52 sites; dump station. Canoe rentals;fishing, swimming. 30-foot limit. GPS: N 28-54.4 W 81-18.5

Collier-Seminole State Park

20200 E Tamiami Trail, Naples, FL 34114. Phone: (239) 394-3397. Located on US 41, 17 miles S of Naples on Tamiami Trail. 108 sites. Fishing; boat ramp. 40-foot limit. GPS: N 25-59.6 W 81-35.5

Falling Waters State Park

1130 State Park Rd, Chipley, FL 32428. Phone: (850) 638-6130. Located 3 miles S of Chipley, off FL 77A. 19 sites; showers; dump station. Swimming, fishing; horse trails. 40-foot limit. GPS: N 30-44.1 W 85-33.2

Faver-Dykes State Park

1000 Faver-Dykes Rd, St. Augustine, FL 32086. Phone: (904) 794-0997. Located 15 miles S of St. Augustine near intersection of I-95 and US 1 exit 298. 27 sites. Fishing, canoe rentals; boat ramp. 30-foot limit. GPS: N 29-40.1 W 81-16.1

Florida Caverns State Park

3345 Caverns Rd, Marianna, FL 32446. Phone: (850) 482-9598. Located 3 miles N of Marianna on FL 166. 35 sites. Canoe/kayak rentals, fishing; boat ramp. 40-foot limit. Cave tours available. GPS: N 30-48.4 W 85-12.8

Fort Clinch State Park

2601 Atlantic Ave, Fernandina Beach, FL 32034. Phone: (904) 277-7274. Located about 16 miles E of Fernandina Beach off FL A1A (I-95 exit 373). 58 sites (all back ins). Swimming, fishing. 40-foot limit. GPS: N 30-40.1 W 81-26.1

Fred Gannon Rocky Bayou State Park

4281 SR 20, Niceville, FL 32578. Phone: (805) 833-9144. Located on FL 20, 5 miles E of Hwy 85. 38 sites; showers. Fishing, boat ramp. 40-foot limit.Boat ramp, canoe, kayak rentals. GPS: N 30-30.0 W 86-25.8

Gamble Rogers Memorial State Recreation Area

3100 S A1A, Flagler Beach, FL 32136. Phone: (386) 517-2086. Located in Flagler Beach along FL A1A. 30 sites. 40-foot limit. Fishing, swimming; canoe, kayak rentals; boat ramp. GPS: N 29-26.1 W 81-06.6

Grayton Beach State Park

357 Main Park Rd, Santa Rosa, FL 32459. Phone: (805) 231-4210. Located on FL 30A near Grayton Beach, S of US 98, between Panama City and Destin on Gulf of Mexico. 34 sites; showers. Fishing, swimming, boat ramp. 40-foot limit. GPS: N 30-18.2 W 86-04.6

Henderson Beach State Park

17000 Emerald Coast Pkwy, Destin, FL 32541. Phone: (850) 837-7550. Located on US 98, E of Destin. 60 sites (some pull-thru) with electric (some 50-amp); water; 45-foot limit. Showers. Fishing, swimming. GPS: N 30-23.2 W 86-26.8

Highlands Hammock State Park

5931 Hammock Rd, Sebring, FL 33872. Phone: (863) 386-6094. Located on CR 634, 4 miles W of Sebring, off US 27. 138 sites plus 19 sites for vans & pop-ups. Equestrian area/trails. 50-foot limit. GPS: N 27-28.6 W 81-33.4

Hillsborough River State Park

15402 US 301 N, Thonotosassa, FL 33592. Phone: (813) 987-6771. Located 12 miles N of Tampa and 6 miles S of Zephyrhills, on US 301. 112 sites. Fishing, swimming; canoe and kayak rentals. 50-foot limit. GPS: N 28-09.1 W 82-13.2

John Pennekamp Coral Reef State Park

US 1, Mile 102.5, Key Largo, FL 33037. Phone: (305) 451-1202. Located on US 1 at mile marker 102.5, N of Key Largo. 47 sites with sewer. Swimming, fishing; boat ramp. 45-foot limit. GPS: N 25-07.7 W 80-24.6

Jonathan Dickinson State Park

16450 SE Federal Hwy, Hobe Sound, FL 33455. Phone: (772) 546-2771. Located 12 miles S of Stuart on US 1. 90 sites. Canoe, kayak rentals. Swimming, fishing; boat ramp. 40-foot limit. Equestrian area/trails. GPS: N 27-00.2 W 80-06.0

Kissimmee Prairie Preserve State Park

33104 NW 192nd Ave, Okeechobee, FL 34972. Phone: (863) 462-5360. Located 25 miles NW of Okeechobee via US 441 and CR 724. 35 regular and equestrian sites. GPS: N 27-29.7 W 80-50.5

Koreshan State Historic Site

3800 Corkscrew Rd, Estero, FL 33928. Phone: (239) 992-0311. Located in Estero on US 41 at Corkscrew Rd (I-75 exit 123). 60 sites. Canoe rentals; boat ramp. 40 foot limit. GPS: N 26-25.9 W 81-48.7

Lake Griffin State Park

3089 US 441/27, Fruitland Park, FL 34731. Phone: (352) 360-6760. Located 3 miles N of Leesburg and 30 miles SE of Ocala on US 27/441. 40 sites. Canoe rentals; boat ramp, fishing. 40-foot limit. GPS: N 28-51.4 W 81-54.2

Lake Kissimmee State Park

14248 Camp Mack Rd, Lake Wales, FL 33853. Phone: (863) 696-1112. Located off FL 60, 15 miles E of Lake Wales (US 27 and FL 60). 60 sites. Horse trails. Fishing. GPS: N 27-58.3 W 81-22.8

Lake Manatee State Park

20007 Hwy 64 E, Bradenton, FL 34202. Phone: (941) 741-3028. Located 15 miles E of Bradenton on FL 64. 60 sites. Swimming, fishing; boat ramp. 65-foot limit. GPS: N 27-28.5 W 82-20.2

Little Manatee River State Park

215 Lightfoot Rd, Wimauma, FL 33598. Phone: (813) 671-5005. Located 5 miles S of Sun City, off US 301 on Lightfoot Rd. 34 full hook-up sites. 4 equestrian sites, trails. Fishing. 68-foot limit. GPS: N 27-39.4 W 82-22.4

Little Talbot Island State Park

12157 Heckscher Dr, Jacksonville, FL 32226. Phone: (904) 251-2320. Located 17 miles NE of Jacksonville on FL A1A. 40 sites. Fishing, swimming; canoe, kayak rentals. 30-foot limit. GPS: N 30-27.6 W 81-25.3

Long Key State Park

67400 Overseas Hwy, Long Key, FL 33001. Phone: (305) 664-4815. Located on US 1 at mile marker 67.5 in Florida Keys, between Key Largo and Marathon. 60 sites. Canoe rentals. Swimming, fishing. 45-foot limit. GPS: N 24-49.3 W 80-49.2

Manatee Springs State Park

11650 NW 115th St, Chiefland, FL 32626. Phone: (352) 493-6072. Located at the end of FL 320, off US 98, 6 miles W of Chiefland. 78 sites. Canoe, kayak rentals. Swimming, fishing. 40-foot limit. GPS: N 29-29.8 W 82-57.5

Mike Roess Gold Head Branch State Park

6239 State Rte 21, Keystone Heights, FL 32656. Phone: (352) 473-4701. Located 6 miles NE of Keystone Heights on FL 21, between US 301 & 17. 74 sites in 3 campgrounds. Canoe rentals; horse trails; swimming, fishing. 45-foot limit. GPS: N 29-50.9 W 81-57.7

Myakka River State Park

13208 FL 72, Sarasota, FL 34241. Phone: (941) 361-6511. Located 9 miles E of Sarasota on FL 72. 90 sites; some 50 amp; some pull-thrus. Canoe and kayak rentals. Fishing; boat ramp. Horse trails. 35-foot limit. GPS: N 27-14.6 W 82-19.9

O'Leno State Park

410 SE O'Leno Park Rd, High Springs, FL 32643. Phone: (386) 454-1853. Located 6 miles N of High Springs on US 41/441, off I-75 exits 414 or 404, on Santa Fe River. 61 sites. 50-foot limit. Equestrian area, trails. GPS: N 29-54.9 W 82-36.6

Ochlockonee River State Park

429 State Park Rd, Sopchoppy, FL 32358. Phone: (850) 962-2771. Located 4 miles S of Sopchoppy on US 319. 30 sites; showers. Swimming, fishing; boat ramp, rentals. 40-foot limit. GPS: N 29-60.0 W 84-24.9

Oscar Scherer State Park

1843 S Tamiami Trail, Osprey, FL 34229. Phone: (941) 483-5956. Located on US 41, 2 miles S of Osprey. 104 sites. Canoe rentals. Fishing; canoe ramp. GPS: N 27-10.1 W 82-28.6

Paynes Prairie Preserve State Park

100 Savannah Blvd, Micanopy, FL 32667. Phone: (352) 466-3397. Located 10 miles S of Gainesville on US 441 between I-75 exits 374 and 382. 50 sites. Fishing, (electric motors only); horse trails. 50-foot limit. GPS: N 29-31.1 W 82-17.9

Rainbow Springs State Park

19158 SW 81st Place Rd, Dunnellon, FL 34432. Phone: (352) 465-8555. Located 3 miles N of Dunnellon on US 41. Camping Entrance: 2 miles N of CR 484 off SW 180th Ave. 105 sites with sewers. Fishing, swimming; canoe, kayak rentals. 40-foot limit. GPS: N 29-04.8 W 82-26.3

Sebastian Inlet State Park

9700 S A1A, Melbourne Beach, FL 32951. Phone: (321) 984-4852. Located on FL A1A, 15 miles S of Melbourne Beach. 51 sites. Canoe, kayak rentals; swimming, fishing; boat ramp. 40-foot limit. GPS: N 27-52.1 W 80-27.2

Silver River State Park

1425 NE 58th Ave, Ocala, FL 34470. Phone: (352) 236-7148. Located NE of Ocala, 1 mile S of FL 40 on FL 35. 59 sites with water, electric, (Two campgrounds.) Canoe/kayak rentals; equestrian area. GPS: N 29-13.1 W 82-00.9

St. Andrews State Park

4607 State Park Ln, Panama City, FL 32408. Phone: (850) 233-5140. Located 3 miles E of Panama City Beach off FL 392 (Thomas Drive). 176 sites; showers. Swimming, fishing. 40-foot limit. No pets. GPS: N 30-08.2 W 85-44.9

St. George Island State Park

1900 E Gulf Beach Dr, St. George Island, FL 32328. Phone: (850) 927-2111. Located on St. George Island (via bridge) 10 miles SE of Eastpoint, off US 98. 60 sites; showers. Swimming, fishing; boat ramp. 43-foot limit. GPS:N 29-40.9 W 84-48.1

St. Joseph Peninsula State Park

8899 Cape San Blas Rd, Port St. Joe, FL 32456. Phone: (850) 227-1327. Located between Port St. Joe and Apalachicola on Cape San Blas Rd, off CR 30. 119 sites; showers. Swimming, fishing; boat ramp. 38-foot limit. No pets. GPS: N 29-44.7 W 85-23.7

Stephan Foster Folk Culture Center State Park

11016 Lillian Saunders Dr, White Springs, FL 32096. Phone: (386) 397-2733. Located on Suwannee River in White Springs off US 41 north. 45 sites. Horse trails; fishing. 100-foot limit. GPS: N 30-19.8 W 82-45.6

Suwannee River State Park

3631 201st Path, Live Oak, FL 32060. Phone: (386) 362-2746. Located 13 miles W of Live Oak, off US 90. 30 sites. Canoe rentals, boat ramp; fishing. GPS: N 30-23.4 W 83-09.5

Three Rivers State Park

7908 Three Rivers Park Rd, Sneads, FL 32460. Phone: (850) 482-9006. Located on FL 271, 2 miles N of Sneads. 30 sites. Canoe rentals; boat ramp, fishing. 40-foot limit. GPS: N 30-52.2 W 84-57.5

Tomoka State Park

2099 N Beach St, Ormond Beach, FL 32174. Phone: (386) 676-4050. Located on Tomoka River, 3 miles N of Ormond Beach on North Beach St. 100 sites. Canoe, kayak rentals; fishing; boat ramp. 34-foot limit (11-foot height limit). GPS: N 28-42.6 W 81-05.2

Topsail Hill Preserve State Park

7525 W Scenic Hwy 30A, Santa Rosa Beach, FL 32459. Phone: (850) 267-8330. Located in Santa Rosa Beach on US 98. 156 sites with electric (30 and 50 amp); showers. Swimming, fishing; boat rentals. 45-foot limit. GPS: N 30-22.5 W 86-17.7

Torreya State Park

2575 NW Torreya Park Rd, Bristol, FL 32321. Phone: (850) 643-2674. Located 12 miles N of Bristol, off FL 12 on CR 271. 30 sites. 30-foot limit. GPS: N 30-33.4 W 84-57.0

Wekiwa Springs State Park

1800 Weklwa Cir, Apopka, FL 32712. Phone: (407) 884-2008. Located NE of Orlando, off FL 434 or FL 436, W of I-4 exit 94. 60 sites. Canoe and kayak rentals; swimming, fishing; Equestrian area/trails. 50-foot limit. GPS: N 28-42.6 W 81-27.8

GEORGIA

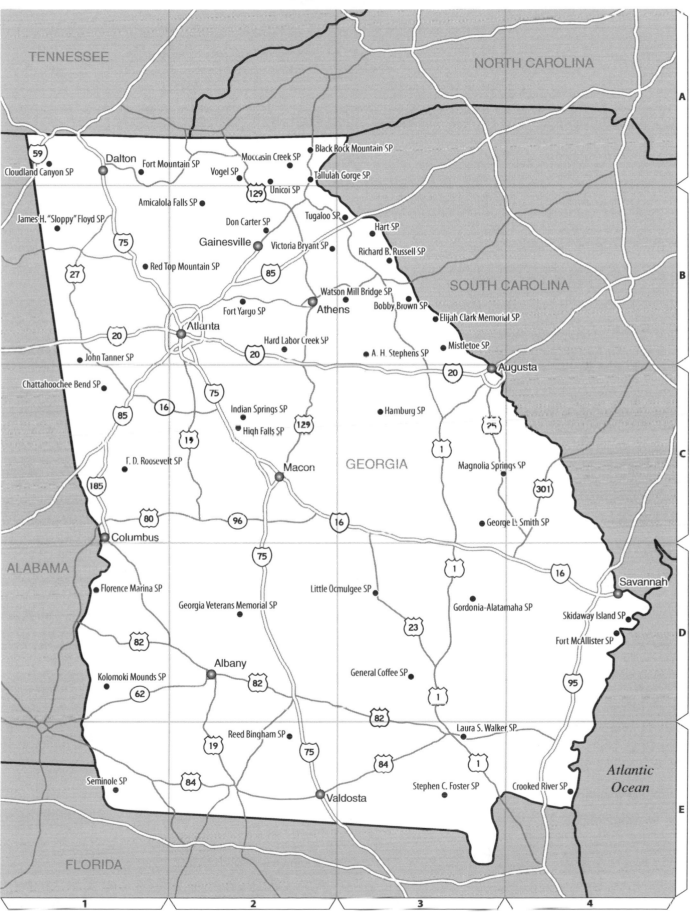

TENNESSEE

NORTH CAROLINA

59

Cloudland Canyon SP

Dalton

Fort Mountain SP

Moccasin Creek SP

Black Rock Mountain SP

Vogel SP

Tallulah Gorge SP

129

Unicoi SP

Amicalola Falls SP

James H. "Sloppy" Floyd SP

Don Carter SP

Tugaloo SP

Hart SP

75

Gainesville

Victoria Bryant SP

Richard B. Russell SP

27

Red Top Mountain SP

85

SOUTH CAROLINA

B

Watson Mill Bridge SP

Fort Yargo SP

Athens

Bobby Brown SP

Atlanta

Elijah Clark Memorial SP

20

Hard Labor Creek SP

Mistletoe SP

John Tanner SP

20

A. H. Stephens SP

Augusta

20

Chattahoochee Bend SP

75

25

85

16

Indian Springs SP

Hamburg SP

1

19

129

High Falls SP

F. D. Roosevelt SP

Macon

GEORGIA

Magnolia Springs SP

C

185

301

80

96

16

George L. Smith SP

Columbus

75

1

ALABAMA

16

Savannah

Florence Marina SP

Little Ocmulgee SP

Georgia Veterans Memorial SP

Gordonia-Alatamaha SP

Skidaway Island SP

82

23

Fort McAllister SP

D

Albany

Kolomoki Mounds SP

82

General Coffee SP

1

95

62

82

Laura S. Walker SP

Reed Bingham SP

19

75

84

1

Seminole SP

84

Stephen C. Foster SP

Crooked River SP

Atlantic
Ocean

Valdosta

E

FLORIDA

1   2   3   4

Georgia

Georgia is unique in that all its state parks with RV sites (43) have water and electric hookups at each developed site. All parks with camping sites also have shower facilities and dump stations. Several parks offer cable TV hookups. Georgia has a state-wide reservation network (48-hour lead time) and requires a two-night minimum stay on weekends only. All parks offer drive-in space, depending upon availability. You should call to verify space. Many parks have pull-through sites and most have laundry facilities. Unless noted, there are no length limitations. All parks are open year-round and offer discounts to seniors (62 and older: 20 percent off published fees) and senior disabled veterans receive an extra discount. Pets are allowed in campgrounds. Rate groups: A and B.

Georgia State Parks & Historic Sites
2 MLK Jr Dr SE, Suite 1352
Atlanta, GA 30334

Information & Reservations: (800) 864-7275
Internet: www.gastateparks.org

Georgia Park Locator

Georgia Parks

A.H. Stephens State Park
456 Alexander St N, Crawfordville, GA 30631. Phone: (706) 456-2602. Located 3 miles N of I-20 exit 148 via GA 22 or US 278. 22 sites. Equestrian area (18 sites), trails. Swimming; boat rentals. GPS N 33-33.4 W 82-53.8

Amicalola Falls State Park
418 Amicalola Falls State Park Rd, Dawsonville, GA 30534. Phone: (706) 265-4703. Located 15 miles NW of Dawsonville on GA 52. 24 sites. Fishing. GPS: N 34-33.3 W 84-15.8

Black Rock Mountain State Park
3085 Black Rock Mtn Pkwy, Mountain City, GA 30562. Phone: (706) 746-2141. Located 3 miles N of Clayton off US 23/441. Follow signs from Mountain City. 49 sites, 38 with electric. Fishing. GPS: N 34-54.1 W 83-24.9

Bobby Brown State Park
2509 Bobby Brown State Park Rd, Elberton, GA 30635. Phone: (706) 213-2046. Located 21 miles SE of Elberton off GA 72. On Clark's Hill Lake. 61 sites. Boat ramp, rentals. GPS: N 33-59.2 W 82-38.2

Chattahoochee Bend State Park
425 Bobwhite Way; Newnan, GA 30263. Phone: (770)254-7271. One of Georgia's largest state parks. Located NW of Newnan. 33 RV sites; showers. 40-foot limit. Fishing; boat ramp. GPS: N33-25.2 W84-59.0

Cloudland Canyon State Park
122 Cloudland Canyon Park Rd, Rising Fawn, GA 30738. Phone: (706) 657-4050. Located 8 miles E of Trenton and I-59 exit 11 on GA 136. 72 sites; showers. Fishing, disc golf. GPS: N 34-29.8 W 85-17.5

Crooked River State Park

6222 Charlie Smith Sr. Hwy, St. Mary's GA 31558. Phone: (912) 882-5256. Located 7 miles N of St. Mary's on GA Spur 40; 8 miles E of I-95 exit 3. On Georgia coast. 52 sites; showers. Miniature golf course; boat ramp, rentals; fishing. GPS: N 30-50.5 W 81-33.0

Don Carter State Park

500 North Browning Bridge Rd, Gainesville, GA 30506. (State's newest park.) Phone: (678)450-7726. Located N of Gainesville on Lake Lanier, off Clarks Bridge Road. 41 sites; showers. Boat ramp, fishing, swimming. Store. GPS: N34-23.4 W83-45.2

Elijah Clark Memorial State Park

2959 McCormick Hwy, Lincolnton, GA 30817. Phone: (706) 359-3458. Located 7 miles NE of Lincolnton on US 378. 175 sites. Miniature golf; swimming, fishing; boat ramp. GPS: N 33-50.9 W 82-24.0

Florence Marina State Park

Omaha, GA 31821. Phone: (229) 838-6870. Located 16 miles W of Lumpkin at end of GA 39C. 43 sites. Fishing; boat ramp, rentals; miniature golf. GPS: N 32-07.2 W 85-03.6

Fort McAllister State Park

3894 Fort McAllister Rd, Richmond Hill, GA 31324. Phone: (912) 727-2339. Located 10 miles E of I-95 exit 90 to GA Spur 144. 65 sites. Fishing; boating, rentals. GPS: N 31-53.4 W 81-11.9

Fort Mountain State Park

181 Fort Mountain Park Rd, Chatsworth, GA 30705. Phone: (706) 422-1932. Located 8 miles E of Chatsworth via GA 52 (I-75 exit 333) to GA 411. 70 sites. Fishing, swimming; boat rentals; miniature golf; horse trails. GPS: N 34-45.8 W 84-41.4

Fort Yargo State Park

210 S Broad St, Winder, GA 30680. Phone: (770) 867-3489. Located 1 mile S of Winder on GA 81. 48 sites. Fishing, swimming; boat ramp, rentals; miniature and disc golf. GPS: N 33-58.3 W 83-44.6

Franklin D. Roosevelt State Park

2970 GA 190, Pine Mountain, GA 31822. Phone: (706) 663-4858. (Largest GA park.) Located on GA 190 off I-185 exits 34 or 42, W of Warm Springs. 105 sites. Swimming, fishing; boat rentals; horse trails. GPS: N 32-50.3 W 84-48.8

General Coffee State Park

46 John Coffee Rd, Nicholls, GA 31554. Phone: (912) 384-7082. Located 6 miles E of Douglas on GA 32. 50 sites; 10 equestrian sites. Fishing; canoe rentals. (Electric motors.) GPS: N 31-30.7 W 82-44.7

George L. Smith State Park

371 George L Smith State Park Rd, Twin City, GA 30471. Phone: (478) 763-2759. Located between Metter and Twin City off GA 23 (I-16 exit 104). 25 sites. Fishing; canoe, boat rentals; boat ramp, (10 h.p. limit.) GPS: N 32-34.2 W 82-06.2

Georgia Veterans Memorial State Park

2459 US Hwy 280 W, Cordele, GA 31015. Phone: (229) 276-2371. Located 9 miles W of I-75 exit 101 on US 280. On Lake Blackshear. 73 sites. Golf course. War museum. Fishing, swimming; boat ramp, rentals. GPS: N 31-57.5 W 83-54.2

Gordonia-Alatamaha State Park

322 Park Ln, Hwy 280 W, Reidsville, GA 30453. Phone: (912) 557-7744. Located in Reidsville off US 280, south of I-16 exit 98. 29 sites. Golf course; fishing; boat rentals. GPS: N 32-05.0 W 82-07.2

Hamburg State Park

6071 Hamburg State Park Rd, Mitchell, GA 30820. Phone: (478) 552-2393. Located 20 miles N of Sandersville via GA 15 and GA 102. 30 sites. Fishing; boat rentals; (electric motors). GPS: N 33-12.5 W 82-46.5

Hard Labor Creek State Park

Knox Chapel Rd, Rutledge, GA 30663. Phone: (706) 557-3001. Located 2 miles N of Rutledge (I-20 exit 105) on Fairplay Rd. 47 sites(11 horse). Golf course. Fishing, swimming; boatramp, rentals; horse trails. GPS: N 33-39.3 W 83-35.7

Hart State Park

330 Hart State Park Rd, Hartwell, GA 30643. Phone: (706) 376-8756 or 213-2045. Located just north of Hartwell off US 29 via Ridge Rd. 78 sites. Fishing, swimming; boat ramp, rentals. GPS: N 34-22.6 W 82-54.6

High Falls State Park

76 High Falls Park Dr, Jackson, GA 30233. Phone: (478) 993-3053. Located 1.8 miles E of I-75 exit 198. 99 sites. Swimming, fishing; boat rentals, ramp; miniature golf. GPS: N 33-10.7 W 84-0.9

Indian Springs State Park

678 Lake Clark Rd, Flovilla, GA 30216. Phone: (770) 504-2277. Located off GA 42 about 15 miles from I-75 exits 188 or 205. 54 sites. Swimming, fishing; boat ramp, rentals; miniature golf. GPS: N 33-14.6 W 83-55.8

James H. "Sloppy" Floyd State Park

2800 "Sloppy" Floyd Lake Rd, Summerville, GA 30747. Phone: (706) 857-0826. Located 3 miles S of Summerville to park road via US 27. On Sloppy Floyd Lake. 25 sites. Fishing; boat ramp, rentals. GPS: N 34-26.4 W 85-20.9

John Tanner State Park

354 Tanner's Beach Rd, Carrollton, GA 30117. Phone: (770) 830-2222. Located 6 miles W of Carrollton off GA 16. 31 sites. Swimming; boat rentals. (Electric motors.) GPS: N 33-36.6 W 85-09.9

Kolomoki Mounds State Park

205 Indian Mounds Rd, Blakely, GA 39823. Phone: (229) 724-2150. Located 6 miles N of Blakely off US 27; on two lakes. 24 sites. Fishing, swimming; boat rentals; miniature golf. GPS: N 31-28.0 W 84-57.1

Laura S. Walker State Park

5653 Laura Walker Rd, Waycross, GA 31503. Phone: (912) 287-4900. Located 9 miles SE of Waycross on GA 177. 44 sites. Golf course. Fishing, swimming. Boat ramp; canoe rentals. GPS: N 31-08.5 W 82-12.9

Little Ocmulgee State Park

80 Live Oak Trail, Helena, GA, 31037. Phone: (229) 868-7474. Located 2 miles N of McRae off US 319/441. 54 sites. Golf course. Fishing; boat rentals; bike rentals. GPS: N 32-05.8 W 82-53.1

Magnolia Springs State Park

1053 Magnolia Springs Dr, Millen, GA 30442. Phone: (478) 982-1660. Located 5 miles N of Millen on US 25. 26 sites. Swimming, fishing; boat rentals. GPS: N 32-52-5 W 81-57.8

Mistletoe State Park

3723 Mistletoe Rd, Appling, GA 30802. Phone: (706) 541-0321. Located 8 miles N of I-20 exit 175 via GA 150 and Mistletoe Rd; on Clark's Hill Lake. 96 sites. Swimming, fishing. Boat ramp. GPS: N 33-38.2 W 82-23.6

Moccasin Creek State Park

3655 State Hwy 197, Clarkesville, GA 30523. Phone: (706) 947-3194. Located 20 miles N of Clarkesville on GA 197; on Lake Burton. 55 sites. Fishing; boat rentals. GPS: N 34-40.0 W 83-32.1

Red Top Mountain State Park

50 Lodge Rd SE, Cartersville, GA 30121. Phone: (770) 975-0055. Located near Cartersville, 1.5 miles E of I-75 exit 285; on Lake Allatoona. 36 sites. Swimming, fishing; boat ramp; miniature golf. Marina. GPS: N 34-08.8 W 84-42.4

Reed Bingham State Park

542 Reed Bingham Rd, Adel, GA 31620. Phone: (229) 896-3551. Located 6 miles W of Adel (I-75 exit 39) and 14 miles E of Moultrie on GA 37. 46 sites. Fishing, swimming; boat, canoe rentals; miniature golf. GPS: N 31-09.3 W 83-31.4

Richard B. Russell State Park

2650 Russell State Park Rd, Elberton, GA 30635. Phone: (706) 213-2045. Located 8 miles NE of Elberton via GA 77 and GA 368; follow signs. 28 sites. Golf course. Swimming, fishing; boat rentals. Disc golf. GPS: N 34-13.7 W 83-45.8

Seminole State Park

7870 State Park Rd, Donalsonville, GA 39845. Phone: (229) 861-3137. Located in southwest corner of Georgia, 16 miles S of Donalsonville via GA 39; on Lake Seminole. 50 sites. Swimming, fishing; boat ramp, rentals; miniature golf. GPS: N 30-48.3 W 84-52.5

Skidaway Island State Park

52 Diamond Causeway, Savannah, GA 31411. Phone: (912) 598-2300. Located 15 miles SE of Savannah. Use I-16 exit 164A to DeRenne Ave, Waters Ave to Causeway; follow signs. On Intercoastal Waterway. 87 sites. Swimming; bike rentals. GPS: N 31-56.4 W 81-03.4

Stephen C. Foster State Park

17515 Hwy 177, Fargo, GA 31631. Phone: (912) 637-5274. Located in Okefenokee Swamp; remote location. 18 miles NE of Fargo via GA 177 to end. 64 sites. Fishing; boat ramp, rentals, (10 h.p. limit.) GPS: N 30-49.5 W 82-21.7

Tallulah Gorge State Park

338 Jane Hurt Dr, Tallulah Falls, GA 30573. Phone: (706) 754-7981. Located in Tallulah Falls, on US 441 in NE corner of state. 50 sites. Swimming, fishing. GPS: N 34-44.2 W 83-23.5

Tugaloo State Park

1763 Tugaloo State Park Rd, Lavonia, GA 30553. Phone: (706) 356-4362. Located off GA 328 via I-85 exit 173, GA 17. Follow signs. On Lake Hartwell. 113 sites. Fishing; boat ramp; canoe rentals; miniature golf. GPS: N 34-30.3 W 83-05.2

Unicoi State Park

1788 Hwy 356, Helen, GA 30545. Phone: (706)878-4726 Located 2 miles NE of Helen via GA 356. 82 sites. Fishing, swimming; boat rentals. GPS: N 34-42.5 W 83-43.0

Victoria Bryant State Park

1105 Bryant Park Rd, Royston, GA 30662. Phone: (706) 245-6270. Located 2 miles N of Franklin Springs on GA 327; I-85 exit 160, follow signs. 35 sites. Golf course. Swimming, fishing. GPS: N 34-17.9 W 83-09.5

Vogel State Park

405 Vogel State Park Rd, Blairsville, GA 30512. Phone: (706) 745-2628. Located 11 miles S of Blairsville off US 19/129. 103 sites. Swimming, fishing; boat rentals; miniature golf. GPS: N 34-46.0 W 83-55.3

Watson Mill Bridge State Park

650 Watson Mill Rd, Comer, GA 30629. Phone: (706) 783-5349. Located 3 miles S of Comer off GA 22; on South Fork River. 20 sites; 11 horse sites. Fishing; boat, canoe rentals; horse trails. GPS: N 34-01.6 W 83-04.4

IDAHO

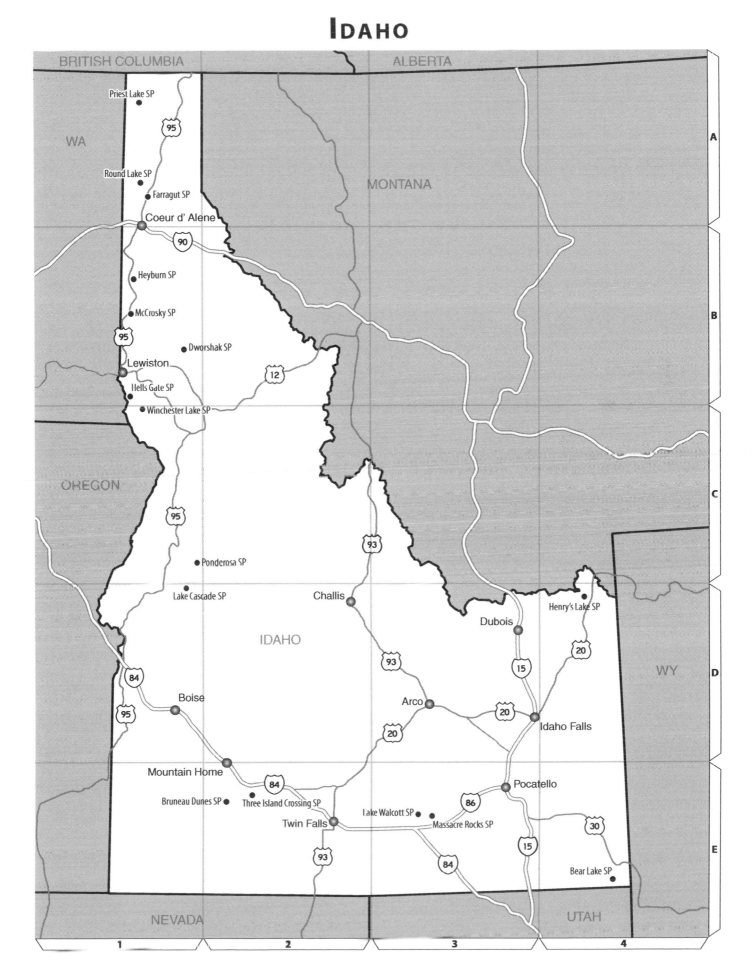

BRITISH COLUMBIA

ALBERTA

MONTANA

WA

Priest Lake SP

95

Round Lake SP

Farragut SP

Coeur d' Alene

90

Heyburn SP

McCrosky SP

95

Dworshak SP

Lewiston

12

Hells Gate SP

Winchester Lake SP

OREGON

95

Ponderosa SP

93

Lake Cascade SP

Challis

Henry's Lake SP

IDAHO

Dubois

20

93

15

WY

84

Boise

Arco

20

Idaho Falls

95

20

Mountain Home

84

Pocatello

Bruneau Dunes SP

Three Island Crossing SP

86

Lake Walcott SP

Twin Falls

Massacre Rocks SP

30

93

15

Bear Lake SP

84

NEVADA

UTAH

A

B

C

D

E

1 2 3 4

Idaho

There are 16 state parks in The Gem State with RV camping spaces but few have site facilities. Most parks do offer centralized drinking water. Lake Cascade State Park, located north of Boise on the Cascade Reservoir, has 11 different camping locations around the lake but only two locations have any desired facilities (see listing under Lake Cascade). Despite Idaho's mountainous terrain, most of the parks are open year-round; you should check with the particular park before proceeding to it. One park, Dworshak State Park near Orofino, has a 10 percent downgrade approach road and is not recommended for larger RVs. Reservations are accepted at some parks by contacting the park but all locations operate on a "first-come" basis. Numerous locations offer Internet (Wi-Fi) access. Credit cards are accepted and pets are OK but must be leashed. Rate groups: A or B, depending on facilities. Motorized Vehicle Entrance fee extra. *Note*: A number of these parks offer a 50% discount on camping fees Mondays through Thursdays to persons 62 years or older. You must ask the attendant at check-in or when phoning for space availability if that park offers this discount.

Idaho Dept. of Parks & Recreation
5657 Warm Springs Ave
Boise, ID 83716

Information: (208) 334-4199
Reservations: (866) 634-3246
Internet: www.idahoparks.org

Idaho Park Locator

Idaho Parks

Bear Lake State Park

3rd N 10th E, St. Charles, ID 83272. Phone: (208)945-2325. Located 11 miles S of Montpieler, off ID 89 & 30, (southeastern corner of Idaho) on Bear Lake. Seasonal. 47 sites with electric; some pull-thrus. Dump station. 60-foot limit. Swimming, fishing; boat ramp. Wi-Fi. GPS: N 42-11.5 W 111-24.1

Bruneau Dunes State Park

27608 Sand Dunes Rd, Mountain Home, ID 83647. Phone: (208) 366-7919. Located 18 miles S of I-84 exit 95 via ID 51. 113 sites; 82 with water, electric; showers; dump station. 65-foot limit. Equestrian sites. Fishing, swimming, boat ramp (electric motors). Wi-Fi. GPS: N 42-54.6 W 115-42.6

Dworshak State Park

9934 Freeman Creek, Orofino, ID 83544. Phone: (208) 476-5994. Remote location on Snake River about 24 miles NW of Orofino (US 12) on county roads. Note: 10 percent downgrade on entrance road. 103 sites; electric; showers; 50-foot limit. Swimming, fishing; boat ramp. Wi-Fi. GPS: N 46-34.0 W 116-18.0

Farragut State Park

13550 E Hwy 54, Athol, ID 83801. Phone: (208) 683-2425. Located in northern Idaho along ID 54 on Lake Pendoreille, 4 miles E of Athol and US 95. 217 sites; some with water, electric; showers; dump station; pull-thrus. 60-foot limit. Swimming, fishing; boat ramp; horse sites, trails; disc golf. GPS: N 47-57.2 W 116-36.1

Hells Gate State Park

5100 Hells Gate Rd, Lewiston, ID 83501. Phone: (208) 799-5015. Located 4 miles S of Lewiston on Snake River Ave. 80 sites with water, electric; some pull-thrus; showers; dump station. 60-foot limit. Swimming, fishing; boat ramp; horse trails. GPS: N 46-22.8 W 117-02.7

Henrys Lake State Park

3917 E 5100 N, Island Park, ID 83429. Phone: (208) 558-7532; (208)558-7368 (winter) Located near Yellowstone National Park on US 20 mile post 401, 45 miles N of Ashton. 43 sites; electric; dump station. 40-foot limit. Fishing, boat ramp. Wi-Fi. GPS: N 44-36.5 W 111-20.2

Heyburn State Park

57 Chatcolet Rd, Plummer, ID 83851. Phone: (208) 686-1308. Located between Plummer and St. Maries, southeast of Coeur d'Alene, along ID 5. (Three lakes in park.) 129 sites with electric, sewer; showers; dump station. 55-foot limit. Fishing; boat ramp. Wi-Fi. GPS: N 47-21.2 W 116-44.8

Lake Cascade State Park

Cascade, ID 83611. Phone: (208) 382-6544 (telephone number for all Cascade Park units). All units located along Cascade Reservoir, starting at main park about 75 miles N of Boise on ID 55. (Office is in Cascade, near intersection of Dam Road and Lakeshore Drive.) All units have central water and 55-foot limit and most are seasonal; dump station(s). Fishing, swimming, boat ramps (all). GPS: N 44-31.0 W 116-02.4

a) Big Sage - Open area (undefined sites)
b) Blue Heron - Open area
c) Buttercup - 28 sites
d) Crown Point - 31 sites; some pull-thrus
e) Huckleberry - 28 sites; some pull-thrus
f) Poison Creek - 18 primitive sites; (open year round) Wi-Fi
g) Sugarloaf - 45 sites
h) Van Wyck Central - 40 primitive sites
i) Van Wyck Main - Open area; dump station
j) West Mountain - 26 primitive sites; dump station
k) Curlew - Open area

Lake Walcott State Park

959 E Minidoka Dam, Rupert, ID 83350. Phone: (208) 436-1258. Located on Lake Walcott in southern ID, 11 miles NE of Rupert on ID 24, I-84 exit 211. 40 sites; water, electric; dump station. 60-foot limit. Fishing, swimming; boat ramp. Wi-Fi. GPS: N 42-40.7 W 113-35.3

Massacre Rocks State Park

3592 N Park Ln, American Falls, ID 83211. Phone: (208) 548-2672. Located 10 miles W of American Falls just off I-86 exit 28; on Snake River. 42 sites; water, electric; dump station; pull-thrus. 55-foot limit. Fishing; boat ramp; disc golf. Wi-Fi. GPS: N 42-40.6 W 112-59.2

McCrosky State Park

2750 Kathleen Ave, Coeur d'Alene, ID 83851. Phone: (208) 686-1308. Located south of Coeur d'Alene. 35 primitive sites. Not good for large RVs (over 26-feet). Horse trails. GPS: N 47-5.1 W 116-55.6

Ponderosa State Park

1920 N Davis Ave, McCall, ID 83638. Phone: (208) 634-2164. Located 2 miles NE of McCall off ID 55, 110 miles N of Boise on Payette Lake. 185 sites, 163 with electric, water; some sewers, pull-thrus; showers; dump station. 35-foot limit. Seasonal. Swimming, fishing; boat ramp. Wi-Fi. GPS: N 44-55.3 W 116-05.4

Priest Lake State Park

314 Indian Creek Park Rd, Coolin, ID 83821. Phone: (208) 443-2200. Located 33 miles N of city of Priest Lake. Three units; remote location in northern Idaho on Priest Lake. 151 sites with electric; showers; dump station. 50-foot limit. Wi-Fi. GPS: N 48-28.0 W 116.50.9

a) Dickensheet - located 4 miles south of Coolin
b) Indian Creek - 11 miles north of Coolin
c) Lionhead - 23 miles north of Coolin. Swimming, fishing; boat ramp.

Round Lake State Park

1880 Dufort Rd, Sagle, ID 83860. Phone: (208) 263-3489. Located on US 95, 10 miles S of Sandpoint in Idaho Panhandle. 51 sites; showers; dump station. 35-foot limit motorhomes; 24-foot limit trailers. Swimming, fishing; canoe rentals; (electric motors). GPS: N 48-10.0 W 116-38.1

Three Island Crossing State Park

1083 S Three Island Fork Dr, Glenns Ferry, ID 83623. Phone: (208) 366-2394. Located in Glenns Ferry on Madison Street about 4 miles from I-84 exit 121. 82 sites with electric, water; showers; dump station. 60-foot limit. Fishing. Wi-Fi. GPS: N 42-56.7 W 115-18.9

Winchester Lake State Park

1786 Forest Rd, Winchester, ID 83555. Phone: (208) 924-7563. Located 35 miles SE of Lewiston on US 95, W of Winchester on Winchester Lake. 68 sites, 46 with electric, water; showers; dump station. 70-foot limit. Fishing, boat ramp, rentals. Wi-Fi. GPS: N 46-13.9 W 116-38.1

ILLINOIS

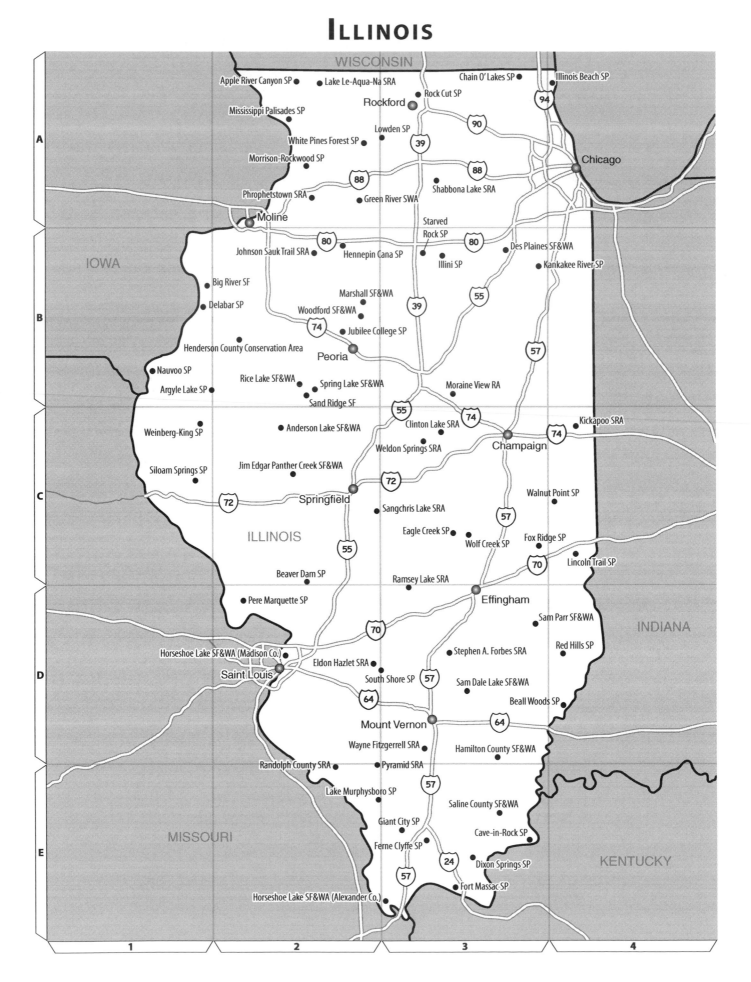

WISCONSIN

Apple River Canyon SP ●   ● Lake Le-Aqua-Na SRA   Chain O' Lakes SP ●   ● Illinois Beach SP

Rock Cut SP ●

Rockford ◉

Mississippi Palisades SP ●

Lowden SP ●   39   90

White Pines Forest SP ●   Chicago ◉

Morrison-Rockwood SP ●

88   88

Phrophetstown SRA ●   88   Shabbona Lake SRA ●

● Green River SWA

Moline ◉

Starved Rock SP ●

IOWA   80   80   Des Plaines SF&WA ●

Johnson Sauk Trail SRA ●   Hennepin Cana SP ●   Illini SP ●   ● Kankakee River SP

Big River SF ●

Marshall SF&WA ●

Delabar SP ●   55

Woodford SF&WA ●   39

74   ● Jubilee College SP

Henderson County Conservation Area ●

Peoria ◉   57

Nauvoo SP ●

Rice Lake SF&WA ●   Spring Lake SF&WA ●

Argyle Lake SP ●   Moraine View RA ●

Sand Ridge SF ●

55   74   Kickapoo SRA ●

Weinberg-King SP ●   ● Anderson Lake SF&WA   Clinton Lake SRA ●

Weldon Springs SRA ●   Champaign ◉   74

Siloam Springs SP ●   Jim Edgar Panther Creek SF&WA ●

72   Walnut Point SP ●

72   Springfield ◉   57

ILLINOIS   Sangchris Lake SRA ●

Eagle Creek SP ●   Fox Ridge SP ●

Wolf Creek SP ●   70

55   Lincoln Trail SP ●

Beaver Dam SP ●   Ramsey Lake SRA ●

● Pere Marquette SP   Effingham ◉

70   Sam Parr SF&WA ●   INDIANA

Horseshoe Lake SF&WA (Madison Co.) ●   Stephen A. Forbes SRA ●   Red Hills SP ●

Saint Louis ◉   Eldon Hazlet SRA ●

South Shore SP ●   57   Sam Dale Lake SF&WA ●

64   Beall Woods SP ●

Mount Vernon ◉   64

Wayne Fitzgerrell SRA ●   Hamilton County SF&WA ●

Randolph County SRA ●   ● Pyramid SRA

57

Lake Murphysboro SP ●   Saline County SF&WA ●

Giant City SP ●   Cave-in-Rock SP ●

Ferne Clyffe SP ●

24   Dixon Springs SP ●   KENTUCKY

MISSOURI   57   Fort Massac SP ●

Horseshoe Lake SF&WA (Alexander Co.) ●

1   2   3   4

A   B   C   D   E

Illinois

Sixty-four state parks or recreation areas in Illinois have RV sites. The state classifies these areas as AA, A, B/E, B/S and C (see list below) and the charges for these sites vary as to facilities available. All patrons of these campgrounds must pay a basic entrance fee plus a fee for site use. Many of the parks are self-register and it is imperative that all users check in at the park office to obtain a camping permit. Some parks or facilities in a park are seasonal so it is wise to call ahead. Some parks accept or require reservations, which are handled at the particular park. (Some parks require a reservation fee.) Most parks, however, are on a first-come, first-served basis and most do not allow alcohol. Discounts are available to Illinois senior residents, all disabled veterans and ex-POWs. Rate groups: A, B and C, depending on facilities.

Site classifications:

Class AA: electric, water, sewer; showers.
Class A: electric; showers in campground.
Class B/E: electric.
Class B/S: showers in campground.
Class C: vehicle access; showers nearby.

Illinois Dept. of Natural Resources
Office of Land Management and Education
One Natural Resources Way
Springfield, IL 62702

Information/reservations: (800) 226-6632 (Reserve America)
Internet: www.dnr.state.il.us

Illinois Park Locator

Illinois Parks

Anderson Lake State Fish & Wildlife Area

647 N Hwy 100, Astoria, IL 61501. Phone: (309)759-4484. On Anderson Lake, 11 miles N of Browning on Route 100. 30 C sites; dump station. Fishing, boat ramp. GPS: N40-12.o W90-12.0

Apple River Canyon State Park

8763 E Canyon Rd, Apple River, IL 61001. Phone: (815) 745-3302. Located in the northwestern corner of state near Apple River between US 20 and IL 78. 49 C sites. Dump station. No reservations. Fishing. GPS: N 42-26.6 W 90-03.2

Argyle Lake State Park

640 Argyle Park Rd, Colchester, IL 62326. Phone: (309) 776-3422. Located off US 136 2 miles N of Colchester. 86 A, 24 B, 18 C sites. Dump station. Fishing; equestrian area; boat ramp. GPS: N 40-26.8 W 90-48.0

Beall Woods State Park

9285 Beall Woods Ave, Mt. Carmel, IL 62863. Phone: (618) 298-2442. Located 6 miles S of Mount Carmel on IL 1, on Wabash River. 16 C sites. Dump station. Fishing; boat ramp (electric motors only). GPS: N 38-21.1 W 87-50.2

Beaver Dam State Park

14548 Beaver Dam Ln, Plainview, IL 62685. Phone: (217) 854-8020. Located 7 miles SW of Carlinville off IL 111. 64 A sites; dump station. Fishing; boat ramp (no gas motors). GPS: N 39-12.9 W 89-57.6

Big River State Forest

Keithsburg, IL 61442. Phone: (309) 374-2496. Located on Mississippi River S of Keithsburg off IL 94. 65 C sites. Dump station. Horse rentals, trails. Fishing; boat ramp. GPS: N 41-05.0 W 90-56.3

Cave-in-Rock State Park

#1 New State Park Rd, Cave-in-Rock, IL 62919. Phone: (618) 289-4325. Located on the Ohio River on IL 1 near junction of IL 146. 34 A sites. Dump station. Fishing; marina, boat ramp. Golf one mile away. GPS: N 37-28.1 W 88-10.0

Chain O'Lakes State Park

8916 Wilmot Rd, Spring Grove, IL 60081. Phone: (847) 587-5512. Located 60 miles N of Chicago, near Wisconsin state line off US 12. (Bordering three lakes.) 151 A, 87 B sites. Dump station. Equestrian area. Fishing, boat ramp, rentals. No alcohol. GPS: N 42-27.6 W 88-12.7

Clinton Lake State Recreation Area

7251 Ranger Rd, DeWitt, IL 61735. Phone: (217) 935-8722. Located about 3 miles NE of Clinton (US 51 & IL 54) on IL 54. 17 AA, 286 A and 5 B sites; showers; dump station. Swimming, fishing, boat ramp. GPS: N 40-09.8 W 88-47.3

Delabar State Park

Oquawka, IL 61469. Phone: (309) 374-2496. Located on Mississippi River about 1.5 miles N of Oquawka off IL 164; follow signs. 54 B/E sites. Dump station. Fishing; boat ramp. GPS: N 40-57.4 W 90-55.9

Des Plaines State Fish & Wildlife Area

24621 North River Rd, Wilmington, IL 60481. Phone: (815) 423-5326. Located just west of I-55 exit 241 near Wilmington, on Illinois River. 20 C sites. Dump station. Horse trails; fishing, boat ramp. No camping Nov/Dec. GPS: N 41-18.7 W 88-11.7

Dixon Springs State Park

Route 146, Golconda, IL 62938. Phone: (618) 949-3394. Located 10 miles W of Golconda on IL 146 in southern Illinois. 38 B/E sites. Dump station. Swimming. GPS: N 37-22.9 W 88-40.2

Eagle Creek State Park

Findlay, IL 62534. Phone: (217) 756-8260. Located on Lake Shelbyville off IL 128 between Effingham and Decatur. 56 A, 24 B/E sites; showers. Pool, fishing, boat ramp. GPS: N 39-31.3 W 88-42.7

Eldon Hazlet State Recreation Area

20100 Hazlet Park Rd, Carlyle, IL 62231. Phone: (618) 594-3015. Located on Carlyle Lake 3 miles N of Carlyle (US 50), off IL 127. 328 A sites with 30 & 50 amp service (most sites on the lake); store; dump station. Swimming, fishing; boat ramp. GPS: N 38-41.4 W 89-20.3

Ferne Clyffe State Park

Goresville, IL 62939. Phone: (618) 995-2411. Located 1 mile S of Goresville on IL 37; (I-57 use exit 40; I-24 use exit 7.) 30 A and 25 equestrian sites. Dump station. Fishing. GPS: N37-09.2 W88-58.2

Fort Massac State Park

1308 E Fifth St, Metropolis, IL 62960. Phone: (618) 524-4712. Located on the Ohio River at junction of US 45 & IL 145. 50 A sites. Dump station. Fishing; boat ramp. GPS: N 37-09.7 W 88-41.6

Fox Ridge State Park

18175 State Park Rd, Charleston, IL 61920. Phone: (217) 345-6416. Located on IL 130 about 8 miles S of Charleston. 43 A sites. Dump station. Horse trails; fishing. GPS: N 39-24.4 W 88-08.1

Giant City State Park

460 Giant City Lodge Rd, Makanda, IL 62958. Phone: (618) 457-4836. Located S of Carbondale off US 51; follow signs. 85 A sites. Dump station. Equestrian area. GPS: N 37-36.7 W 89-10.9

Green River State Wildlife Area

375 Game Rd, Harmon, IL 61042. Phone: (815) 379-2324. Located 6 miles NW of Ohio (IL) off IL 26. Open camping (dry). Dump station. Horse trails. GPS: N 41-38.7 W 89-28.3

Hamilton County State Fish & Wildlife Area - (Dolan Lake)

McLeansboro, IL 62859. Phone: (618) 773-4340. Located off IL 14 near US 45, 8 miles SE of McLeansboro. 81 A sites. Dump station. GPS: N 38-04.3 W 88-23.1

Henderson County Conservation Area

Keithsburg, IL 61442. Phone: (309) 374-2496. Located 20 miles S of Monmouth. 20 C sites. Fishing; boat ramp. GPS: N40-08.0 W90-09.1

Hennepin Canal State Park

16006 875 E St, Sheffield, IL 61361. Phone: (815) 454-2328. Located

1 mile S of I-80, exit 45, W of US 40. 24 C sites. Fishing, boat ramp. Equestrian area. GPS: N41-04.8 W89-03.6

Horseshoe Lake State Fish & Wildlife Area (Alexander Co.)

Miller City, IL 62962. Phone: (618) 776-5689. Located on IL 3, 7 miles NW of Cairo. 38 A, 40 B/E, 10 C sites. Dump station. GPS: N 37-07.8 W 89-19.2

Horseshoe Lake State Fish & Wildlife Area (Madison Co.)

3321 Hwy 111, Granite City, IL 60240. Phone: (618) 931-0270. Located on IL 111 east of St. Louis, MO. 48 C sites; showers; dump station. Fishing, boat ramp. No reservations. GPS: N 38-41.1 W 90-08.9

Illini State Park

2660 E 2350th Rd, Marseilles, IL 61341. Phone: (815) 795-2448. Located on Illinois River near Marseilles on US 6. 50 A, 50 B/S sites. Dump station. Fishing; boat ramp. GPS: N 41-19.1 W 88-42.7

Illinois Beach State Park Lake Front

Zion, IL 60099. Phone: (847) 662-4811. Located on Lake Michigan, just N of Waukegan. 241 A sites. Dump station. Note: this park is especially busy in summer months. It would be wise to telephone first. Reservations are recommended, if possible (must be made by mail). Weekends are especially crowded. Fishing, swimming. (Some alcohol restrictions.) GPS: N 42-25.8 W 87-49.5

Jim Edgar Panther Creek State Fish & Wildlife Area

10149 Hwy 11, Chandlerville, IL 62627. Phone: (217) 452-7741. Located on IL 78, NE of Virginia (IL). 18 AA and 64 A sites. Dump station. Canoe rentals; fishing, boat ramp. No reservations. GPS: N 39-55.8 W 90 02.4

Johnson-Sauk Trail State Recreation Area

28616 Sauk Trail Road Ave, Kewanee, IL 61443. Phone: (309) 853-5589. Located 5 miles N of Kewanee off IL 78. 70 A sites. Dump station. Lake in park. Fishing; boat ramp, rentals. (Electric motors). GPS: N 41-19.7 W 89-52.2

Jubilee College State Park

13921 W Rt 150, Brimfield, IL 61517. Phone: (309) 446-3758. Located 15 miles NW of Peoria near Kickapoo off US 150. 107 A, 40 C sites. Dump station. Fishing; equestrian area, trails. GPS: N 40-50.6 W 89-49.6

Kankakee River State Park

5314 W Rt 102, Bourbonnais, IL 60914. Phone: (815) 933-1383. Located on IL 102 about 6 miles NW of Kankakee, on Kankakee River. 110 A, 150 B sites. Dump station. (Two campgrounds.) Equestrian area. Fishing. Busy weekend park. Call ahead. No alcohol. GPS: N 41-12.2 W 88-00.6

Kickapoo State Recreation Area

10906 Kickapoo Park Rd, Oakwood, IL 61858. Phone: (217) 442-4915. Located off I-74 exit 206 west of Danville. 184 A sites. Dump station. Swimming, fishing, boat ramp. Lakes in area. No reservations. GPS: N 40-08.7 W 87-43.6

Lake Le-Aqua-Na State Recreation Area

8542 N Lake Rd, Lena, IL 61048. Phone: (815) 369-4282. Located 3 miles N of Lena, 10 miles N of US 20, off IL 73. 112 A sites. Dump station. Equestrian area. Seasonal. Swimming, fishing; boat ramp, rentals. GPS: N 42-25.4 W 89-49.4

Lake Murphysboro State Park

52 Cinder Hill Dr, Murphysboro, IL 62966. Phone: (618) 684-2867. Located 1.5 miles W of Murphysboro off IL 149. 3 A, 54 B/E sites. Fishing; boat ramp, rentals; (10 hp limit). GPS: N 37-46.3 W 89-23.0

Lincoln Trail State Park

16985 E 1350th Rd, Marshall, IL 62441. Phone: (217) 826-2222. Located 2 miles S of Marshall off IL 1. 173 A sites. (Some Class C.) Dump station. Fishing, boat ramp. GPS: N 39-28.8 W 87-41.8

Lowden State Park

1411 N River Rd, Oregon, IL 61061. Phone: (815) 732-6828. Located near Oregon (IL 2 & 64); follow signs. 80 A sites. Dump station. Fishing; boat ramp. GPS: N 42-02.1 W 89-19.5

Marshall State Fish & Wildlife Area

236 SR 26, Lacon, IL 61540. Phone: (309) 246-8351. Located off IL 26 about 27 miles NE of Peoria, on Illinois River. 22 B/E, 6 C sites. Dump station. Fishing; boat ramp. GPS: N 40-57.0 W 89-25.4

Mississippi Palisades State Park

16327A Rt 84, Savanna, IL 61074. Phone: (815) 273-2731. Located about 4 miles N of Savanna on IL 84, near confluence of Mississippi and Apple rivers. 241 A & B sites. Dump station. Fishing; boat ramp. GPS: N 42-07.7 W 90-09.5

Moraine View Recreation Area

27374 Moraine View Park Rd, Le Roy, IL 61752. Phone: (309) 724-8032. Located SE of Bloomington off US 150 via County Rd 36. 137 A sites. Equestrian campground with 30 A sites. Dump station. Lake. Horse trails; swimming, fishing; boat ramp, rentals. No alcohol. GPS: N 40-25.5 W 88-43.8

Morrison-Rockwood State Park

18750 Lake Rd, Morrison, IL 61270. Phone: (815) 772-4708. Located N of Morrison (US 30 & IL 78) on IL 78. 92 A sites. Dump station. Fishing, boat ramp. GPS: N 41-50.4 W 89-59.3

Nauvoo State Park

Nauvoo, IL 62354. Phone: (217) 453-2512. Located on IL 96 about 8 miles N of Hamilton and US 136. 75 A and 75 B/S sites. Dump station. Lake. Fishing; boat ramp (electric motors only). GPS: N 40-32.6 W 91-23.2

Pere Marquette State Park

13112 Visitor Center Ln, Grafton, IL 62037. Phone: (618) 786-3323. Located NW of St. Louis, MO on IL 100 near Grafton. 80 A sites; showers. Dump station. Horse trails; fishing, boat ramp. GPS: N 38-58.3 W 90-27.5

Prophetstown State Recreation Area

Riverside Drive & Park Ave, Prophetstown, IL 61277. Phone: (815) 537-2926. Located on northeast edge of Prophetstown on IL 78, on the Rock River. 44 A, 42 B/E sites. Dump station. Swimming, fishing. GPS: N 41-40.3 W 89-55.2

Pyramid State Recreation Area

1562 Pyramid Park Rd, Pinckneyville, IL 62274. Phone: (618) 357-2574. Located 5 miles S of Pinckneyville off IL 127/13. 28 C sites. Dump station. Equestrian area. Fishing; boat ramp (10 hp limit). GPS: N 38-00.2 W 89-25.3

Ramsey Lake State Recreation Area

Ramsey Lake Rd, Ramsey, IL 62080. Phone: (618) 423-2215. Located 1 mile NW of Ramsey off US 51. 90 A, 45 C sites. Dump station.

Fishing; boat ramp, rentals (electric motors only). GPS: N 39-09.6 W 89-07.6

Randolph County State Recreation Area

4301 S Lake Dr, Chester, IL 62233. Phone: (618) 826-2706. Located 5 miles NE of Chester off IL 150. 51B/E and 95 C sites. Dump station. Fishing; boat ramp, rentals. Equestrian area. GPS: N 37-58.4 W 89-46.1

Red Hills State Park

3571 Ranger Ln, Sumner, IL 62466. Phone: (618) 936-2469. Located on US 50 between Olney and Lawrenceville. 103 A sites (some pull-thru & 50 amp electric). Dump station. Fishing; boat ramp, rentals (electric motors only). Horse trails. GPS: N 38-443.0 W 87-50.6

Rice Lake State Fish & Wildlife Area

19721 N US 24, Canton, IL 61520. Phone: (309) 647-9184. Located 18 miles N of Havana on US 24. 34 B/E sites. Dump station. Two lakes in park. Fishing. GPS: N 40-27.8 W 89-54.3

Rock Cut State Park

7318 Harlem Rd, Loves Park, IL 61111. Phone: (815) 885-3311. Located 1.5 miles N of Riverside Blvd exit from I-90, follow signs. 210 A, 60 B/E sites. Dump station. Two lakes in park. Equestrian area; swimming, fishing; boat rentals. GPS: N 42-20.5 W 88-57.9

Saline County State Fish & Wildlife Area

85 Glen O. Jones Rd, Equality, IL 62934. Phone: (618) 276-4405. Located 5 miles SW of Equality near Shawnee National Forest, off IL 13 & 142. 25 C sites. Dump station. Equestrian area. Fishing; boat ramp, rentals. GPS: N 37-41.6 W 88-24.2

Sam Dale Lake State Fish & Wildlife Area

620 CR 1910 N, Johnsonville, IL 62850. Phone: (618) 835-2292. Located 3 miles NW of Johnsonville on IL 161. 68 B/E sites. Dump station. Fishing; boat ramp, rentals. GPS: N 38-31.6 W 88-34.9

Sam Parr State Fish & Wildlife Area

13225 E State Hwy 23, Newton, IL 63448. Phone: (618) 783-2661. Located 3 miles NE of Newton near junction of IL 30 & 133. 16 B/E, 18 C sites. Dump station. Fishing; horse trails; boat ramp (10 hp limit). GPS: N 39-01.5 W 88-05.4

Sand Ridge State Forest

25799 E CR 2300, Forest City, IL 61532. Phone: (309) 597-2212. Located 25 miles SW of Peoria; access via US 136 from Chatauqua Park, follow signs. 27 C sites. Dump station. Equestrian area, trails. GPS: N 40-24.7 W 89-54.2

Sangchris Lake State Recreation Area

9898 Cascade Rd, Rochester, IL 62563. Phone: (217) 498-9208. Located SE of Springfield via IL 29 and CR 20, on Sangchris River. 80 A, 40 B/S sites. Dump station. Fishing; boat ramp. GPS: N 39-39.0 W 89-28.4

Shabbona Lake State Recreation Area

4201 Shabbona Grove Rd, Shabbona, IL 60550. Phone: (815) 824-2106. Located off US 30, between DeKalb and LaSalle-Peru, just W of Chicago. 150 A sites. Dump station. Fishing; boat ramp. GPS: N 41-43.9 W 88-51.9

Siloam Springs State Park

938 E 3003rd Ln, Clayton, IL 62324. Phone: (217) 894-6205. Located SW of Mt. Sterling off US 24 or N of IL 104; follow signs. 98 A, 84 B/

S sites. Dump station. Fishing; boat ramp, rentals (electric motors only). No reservations. GPS: N 39-54.0 W 90-57.3

South Shore State Park

20100 Hazlet Park Rd, Carlyle, IL 62231. Phone: (618) 594-3015. Located on Carlyle Lake (south shore) 3 miles E of Carlyle, off US 50. 33 C sites. Fishing; boat ramp. GPS: N 38-36.6 W 89-18.9

Spring Lake State Fish & Wildlife Area

7982 S Park Rd, Manito, IL 61546. Phone: (309) 968-7135. Located 25 miles SW of Peoria on the Illinois River. Access via US 136 & IL 29, follow signs. 70 C sites. Dump station. Fishing, boat ramp. GPS: N 40-27.8 W 89-52.7

Starved Rock State Park

Routes 178 and 71, North Utica, IL 61373. Phone: (815) 667-4726. Located 1 mile S of North Utica off US 6, SE of LaSalle, on Illinois River. 129 A sites. Dump station. Equestrian area; fishing, boat ramp. No alcohol. GPS: N 41-21.2 W 88-55.9

Stephen A. Forbes State Recreation Area

6924 Omega Rd, Kinmundy, IL 62854. Phone: (618) 547-3381. Located off IL 37, 15 miles NE of Salem (US 50 & I-57). 115 A sites. Dump station. Equestrian area. Swimming, fishing; boat ramp. GPS: N 38-42.8 W 88-44.6

Walnut Point State Park

2331 E CR 370 N, Oakland, IL 61943. Phone: (217) 346-3336. Located 20 miles NE of Charleston off IL 133 and US 57. 34 A sites. Dump station. Fishing. GPS: N 39-42.3 W 88-01.6

Wayne Fitzgerrell State Recreation Area

11094 Ranger Rd, Whittington, IL 62897. Phone: (618) 629-2320. Located on Rend Lake 3 miles W of I-57 exit 77 and 6 miles N of Benton, on IL 154. 243 A sites. Dump station. Horse trails. Fishing; boat ramp. No reservations. GPS: N 38-05.4 W 88-56.2

Weinberg-King State Park

Augusta, IL 62311. Phone: (217) 392-2345. Located 3 miles E of Augusta, off IL 101. 60 C and 19 B/E equestrian sites; trails. Dump station. Fishing. GPS: N 40-13.6 W 90-54.0

Weldon Springs State Recreation Area

4734 Weldon Springs Rd, Clinton, IL 61727. Phone: (217) 935-2644. Located 3 miles SE of Clinton off US 51. 75 A (5 pull-thru) sites. Dump station. Fishing; boat ramp. GPS: N 40-07.5 W 88-56.1

White Pines Forest State Park

6712 West Pines Rd, Mt. Morris, IL 61054. Phone: (815) 946-3717. Located about 9 miles SW of Mt. Morris (IL 64). 103 B/S sites. Dump station. No alcohol. GPS: N 41-59.3 W 89-27.9

Wolf Creek State Park

Windsor, IL 61957. Phone: (217) 459-2831. Located on Lake Shelbyville, 8 miles NW of Windsor, off IL 16. 304 A, 140 B/E sites. Equestrian area. Swimming, fishing; boat ramp. GPS: N 39-31.2 W 88-41.3

Woodford State Fish & Wildlife Area

Low Point, IL 61545. Phone: (309) 822-8861. Located NE of Peoria on the Illinois River, off IL 26. 40 C sites. Dump station. Fishing, boat ramp. (Call ahead.) GPS: N 40-54.6 W 89-28.0

INDIANA

MICHIGAN

Indiana Dunes SP

Gary

South Bend

Pokagon SP

Potato Creek SP

Chain O'Lakes SP

Fort Wayne

ILLINOIS

Tippecanoe River SP

J. Edward Roush Lake

Salamonie Lake

OHIO

Ouabache SP

Mississinewa Lake

INDIANA

Prophetstown SP

Mounds SP

Summit Lake SP

Turkey Run SP

Shades SP

Richmond

Cecil M. Harden Lake

Indianapolis

Whitewater Memorial SP

Terre Haute

Brookville Lake

Cagles Mill Lake

McCormick's Creek SP

Shakamak SP

Brown County SP

Columbus

Versailles SP

Monroe Lake

Hardy Lake

Clifty Falls SP

Spring Mill SP

Glendale F&WA

Charlestown SP

Patoka Lake

O'Bannon Woods SP

Harmonie SP

Lincoln SP

Evansville

KENTUCKY

Indiana

Indiana offers 21 state parks and 11 reservoir/recreation areas that are RV friendly. All the locations have basic amenities; three offer full hook-ups. RV sites are classified AA for full hook-ups to Class C for primitive. Camping fees for each reflect these classifications. Some parks offer seasonal "specials" and you have to ask about these offers when calling. Indiana residents are eligible for senior discounts. However, there are senior discounts (60 years or older) available to all, Sunday through Wednesday in April and May and again in September and October when the parks are less busy. It is always wise to call ahead because some parks do not accept reservations. Rate groups: A, B and C depending on site and facilities. (Weekends and holidays carry premiums.)

Indiana Dept. of Natural Resources
402 West Washington St., Room W298
Indianapolis, IN 46204

Information: (574) 656-8186
Reservations: (866) 622-6746
Internet: www.in.gov/dnr/parklake
Reservations: www.indiana.reserveworld.com

Indiana Park Locator

Indiana Parks

Brookville Lake

Brookville, IN 47012. Phone: (765) 647-2657. Located 5 miles N of Brookville, off IN 101. 404 sites, (two areas); 388 with electric, 62 full hook-up sites. Dump station. Swimming, fishing; boat ramp. GPS: N 39-25.8 W 85-00.8

Brown County State Park

1405 Hwy 46 W, Nashville, IN 47448. Phone: (812) 988-6406. Located on IN 46 between Bloomington and Columbus. 401 sites with electric; 28 non-electric. Dump station. Equestrian sites, trails; fishing, swimming. GPS: N 39-11.8 W 86-12.9

Cagles Mill Lake (Lieber State Recreation Area)

1317 W Lieber Rd, Cloverdale, IN 46120. Phone: (765) 795-4576. Located S of I-70, SW of Cloverdale, off US 231. 150 sites with electric; 96 primitive. Dump station. Swimming, fishing; boat ramp, rentals. GPS: N 39-29.2 W 86-52.5

Cecil M. Harden Lake (Raccoon State Recreation Area)

1588 S Raccoon Pkwy, Rockville, IN 47872. Phone: (765) 344-1412. Located 9 miles E of Rockville at Hollandsburg, off US 36. 245 sites with electric, 56 primitive. Dump station. Swimming, fishing; boat ramp, rentals. GPS: N 39-45.5 W 87-04.2

Chain O'Lakes State Park

2355 E 75 South, Albion, IN 46701. Phone: (260) 636-2654. Located SW of Kendallville on IN 9. 331 sites with electric; 49 non-electric; 33 primitive. Dump station. (Nine lakes in the park.) Swimming; fishing, boat ramp, rentals (electric motors only). GPS: N 41-20.2 W 85-25.4

Charlestown State Park

12500 Hwy 62, Charlestown, IN 47111. Phone: (812) 256-5600. Located in Charlestown in southern Indiana near KY state line at junction of IN 62 & 160; on Ohio River. 61 sites with full hook-ups; 131 sites with electric; showers. Dump station. Fishing. GPS: N 38-26.3 W 85-38.8

Clifty Falls State Park

2221 N Clifty Dr, Madison, IN 47250. Phone: (812) 273-8885. Located in southeastern Indiana near junction of IN 256 & 7. Entrance off IN 62 and 56. 106 sites with electric; showers; 63 primitive sites. Dump station. Store. Swimming pool; tennis courts. GPS: N 38-46.3 W 85-26.2

Glendale Fish & Wildlife Area

6001 E 600 S; Montgomery, IN 47558. Phone: (812) 644-7711. Located NE of Hudsonville on Dogwood Lake. 121 sites, 67 with electric. Fishing; boat ramp, (some restrictions), rentals. GPS: N38-33.0 W87-02.4

Hardy Lake

5620 N. Hardy Lake Rd, Scottsburg, IN 47170. Phone: (812) 794-3800. Located in SE IN, 7.5 miles N of Scottsburg, off US 31. 167 sites, 149 with electric. Dump station. Swimming, fishing; boat ramp, rentals. GPS: N 38-44.2 W 85-41.3

Harmonie State Park

3451 Harmonie State Park Rd, New Harmony, IN 47631. Phone: (812) 682-4821. Located on Wabash River, 25 miles NW of Evansville, off IN 69. 200 sites with electric; showers. Dump station. Store. Fishing, swimming; horse trails; boat ramp. GPS: N 38-05.4 W 87-56.4

Indiana Dunes State Park

1600 N 25 E, Chesterton, IN 46304. Phone: (219) 926-1952. Located N of Chesterton, off US 12, on Lake Michigan. 140 sites with electric (50 amp); 3 water fill stations; showers. Dump station. Swimming, fishing. GPS: N 41 39.2 W 87-03.7

J. Edward Roush Lake (Huntington Lake)

517 N Warren Rd, Huntington, IN 46750. Phone: (260) 468-2165. Located 3.4 miles SE of Huntington, off US 224, on Wabash River. 67 primitive, 25 electric sites. Fishing; boat ramp. GPS: N 40-50.3 W 85-27.9

Lincoln State Park

Hwy 162, Lincoln City, IN 47552. Phone: (812) 937-4710. Located in southern Indiana on US 231 near junction with IN 162; I-64 exit 57; on Lake Lincoln. 150 sites with electric; showers; 120 primitive sites. Dump station. Store. Boat ramp, rentals (electric motors only). GPS: N 38-07.1 W 86-58.8

McCormick's Creek State Park

250 McCormick's Creek Park Rd, Spencer, IN 47460. Phone: (812) 829-2235. Located on White River outside Spencer near junction of US 231 & IN 46 and 43. 189 sites with electric; 32 primitive; showers. Dump station. Store. Horse rentals. Swimming; tennis courts. GPS: N 39-17.0 W 86-43.6

Mississinewa Lake

4673 S 625 E, Peru, IN 46970. Phone: (765) 473-6528. Located 4 miles NW of Mt. Vernon, off IN 13. 374 sites: 335 with electric, 39 full hook-up. Dump station. Swimming, fishing; boat ramp. GPS: N 40-41.1 W 85-54.0

Monroe Lake

4850 South SR 446, Bloomington, IN 47401. Phone: (812) 837-9546. Located 9.3 miles SE of Bloomington, off of IN 37. Resort. Marina. 320 sites, 226 with electric; dump station. Swimming, fishing; boat ramp, rentals. GPS: N 39-04.2 W 86-25.0

Mounds State Park

4306 Mounds Rd, Anderson, IN 46017. Phone: (765) 642-6627. Located E of Anderson, I-69 & IN 32. 75 sites with electric; showers. Dump station. Store. Swimming, fishing. GPS: N 40-05.7 W 85-37.1

O'Bannon Woods State Park

7234 Old Forest Rd SW, Corydon, IN 47112. Phone: (812) 738-8232. Located on Ohio River in southern Indiana, SW of New Albany, S of I-64 off IN 62. 281 sites with electric; 25 primitive sites. Dump station. Equestrian area (47 sites); fishing. GPS: N 38-11.6 W 86-17.6

Ouabache State Park

4930 E State Rd 201, Bluffton, IN 46714. Phone: (260) 824-0926. Located on the Wabash River, outside Bluffton on IN 201. 77 sites with electric; showers; 47 non-electric. Dump station. Swimming, fishing; tennis courts. GPS: N 40-43.7 W 85-06.6

Patoka Lake

3084 N Dillard Rd, Birdseye, IN 47513. Phone: (812) 685-2464. Located in southern Indiana, 11.4 miles NE of Jasper (US 231). 455 sites with electric. Dump station. Swimming, fishing; boat ramp. Disc golf. GPS: N 38-25.3 W 86 43.4

Pokagon State Park

450 Lane 100 Lake James, Angola, IN 46703. Phone: (260) 833-2012. Located on Lake James near Angola, I 69 exit 154 & IN 727. 200 sites with electric; showers; 73 non-electric. Dump station. Store. Fishing; boat rentals. GPS: N 41-42.5 W 85-01.3

Potato Creek State Park

25601 State Rd 4, North Liberty, IN 46554. Phone: (574) 656-8186. Located 12 miles SW of South Bend on IN 4, off US 31. 287 sites with electric; showers; 70 equestrian sites with electric. Store. Dump station. Fishing, swimming; boat ramp, rentals (electric motors only). GPS: N 41-32.1 W 86 20.4

Prophetstown State Park

5545 Swisher Rd, West Lafayette, IN 479067. Phone: (765) 567-4919. Located in north central Indiana, NE of West Lafayette and Battle Ground, I-65 exit 178, on Wabash and Tippecanoe rivers. 55 full hook-up; 55 sites with electric. Dump station. GPS: N 40-30.3 W 86-49.3

Salamonie Lake

9214 West Lost Lake Bridge W, Andrews, IN 46702. Phone: (260) 468-2125. Located 6.3 miles SE of Largo, off US 24. 246 sites with electric; 50 equestrian sites. Dump station. Marina. Swimming, fishing. GPS: N 40-47.0 W 85-38.9

Shades State Park

7751 S 890W, Waveland, IN 47989. Phone: (765) 435-2810. Seasonal. Located 17 miles SW of Crawfordsville off IN 47. 105 sites, non-electric; showers. Dump station. Fishing. GPS: N 39-56.5 W 87-03.5

Shakamak State Park

6265 W State Rd 48, Jasonville, IN 47438. Phone: (812) 665-2158.

Located about 10 miles E of US 41/150 from Shelburn on IN 159. 122 sites with electric; 94 primitive sites; showers. Dump station. Three lakes in park. Swimming pool. Store. Fishing; boat ramp, rentals (electric motors only); tennis courts. GPS: N 39-10.8 W 87-13.9

Spring Mill State Park

3333 State Rd 600 E, Mitchell, IN 47446. Phone: (812) 849-4129. Located in south central Indiana, E of Mitchell, off IN 37 on IN 60. 187 sites with electric; 36 primitive sites; showers. Dump station. Store. Primitive caves; swimming, fishing. GPS: N 38-43.4 W 86-26.4

Summit Lake State Park

5993 N Messick Rd, New Castle, IN 47362. Phone: (765) 766-5873. Located on US 36, NE of New Castle. 125 sites with electric; showers. Dump station. Store. Fishing, swimming; boat ramp, rentals. GPS: N 40-00.8 W 85-15.6

Tippecanoe River State Park

4200 N US 35, Winamac, IN 46996. Phone: (574) 946-3213. Located on US 35, 6 miles N of Winamac on Tippecanoe River. 112 sites with electric; showers. 56 primitive equestrian sites. Dump station. Fishing; boat ramp. GPS: N 41-07.0 W 86-36.2

Turkey Run State Park

8121 E Park Rd, Marshall, IN 47859. Phone: (765) 597-2635. Located SW of Crawfordsville on IN 47, E of US 41. 213 sites with electric; showers. Dump station. Store. Swimming; fishing; horse rentals; tennis courts. GPS: N 39-52.9 W 87-12.2

Versailles State Park

1004 Hwy 50, Versailles, IN 47042. Phone: (812) 689-6424. Located in SE Indiana, near Versailles on US 50 near junction of US 421. 226 sites with electric; showers. Dump station. Store; swimming, fishing; boat ramp, rentals (electric motors only). GPS: N 39-04.5 W 85-17.0

Whitewater Memorial State Park

1418 S State Rd 101, Liberty, IN 47353. Phone: (765) 458-5565. Located in SE Indiana, E of Connorsville, near junction of IN 101 & 44. Whitewater Lake in park. 236 sites with electric; showers; 45 non-electric. Dump station. Store. Equestrian area; swimming, fishing; boat ramp, rentals. GPS: N 39-36.5 W 84-56.7

IOWA

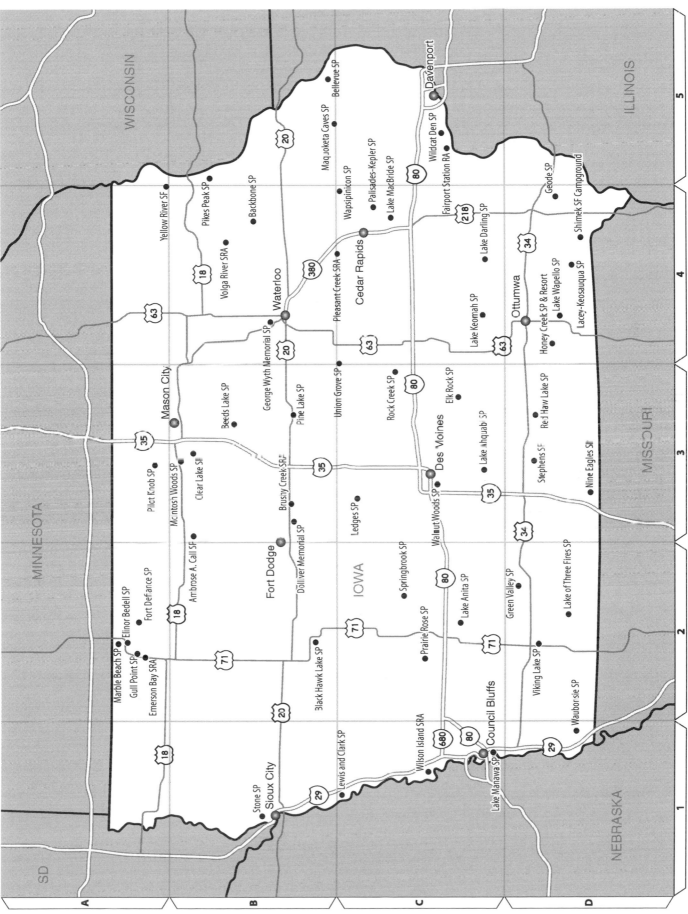

Iowa

Of Iowa's state park and recreation areas, 54 locations have RV facilities. These locations have two categories of sites: Modern (M) - showers in the park and Non-Modern (NM) - no facilities nearby. Most locations have electric at the site; some have sewer hookups. Most locations also have dump stations. Iowa has a reservation system but all parks hold some sites for a first-come, first-served basis. Unless noted, there are no rig size limitations. All the parks have direction signs from major highways and Interstates. Rate group: B (less in off season). No entrance fees are charged.

State Parks Bureau
Iowa Department of Natural Resources
Wallace State Office Bldg.
502 E 9th Street
Des Moines, IA 50319

Information: (515) 281-8368
Reservations: (877) 427-2757
Internet: www.exploreiowaparks.com
Reservations: www.reserveiaparks.com

Iowa Park Locator

Iowa Parks

Ambrose A. Call State Park

Route 1, Algona, IA 50511. Phone: (641) 581-4835. Located in north-central IA, 1.5 miles SW of Algona, off US 169. 16 sites, 13 with electric; NM. Swimming. GPS: N 43-04.1 W 94-13.6

Backbone State Park

1347 129th St, Dundee. IA 52038. Phone: (536) 924-2000. Located in northeastern IA, 4 miles SW of Strawberry Point on IA 410, near IA 3. Two campgrounds; 125 sites, 49 with electric; showers; dump station. M & NM. Swimming, fishing; boat ramp, rentals. GPS: N 42-36.9 W 91-33.7

Beeds Lake State Park

1422 165th St, Hampton, IA 50441. Phone: (641) 456-2047. Located in north-central IA on Beeds Lake, 3 miles NW of Hampton (US 65 & IA 3) on CR 134. 144 sites, 99 with electric; showers; dump station. M. Swimming, fishing; boat ramp, rentals. GPS: N 42-46.0 W 93-14 4

Bellevue State Park

24668 Hwy 52 Bellevue, IA 52031. Phone: (563) 872-4019. Located in eastern IA, 21 miles S of Bellevue on US 52; near Mississippi River. 46 sites, 31 with electric; showers; dump station. M. GPS: N 42-14.9 W 90-25.1

Black Hawk Lake State Park

228 S Blossom, Lake View, IA 51450. Phone: (712) 657-8712. Located in west-central IA in Lake View on Black Hawk Lake, near US 71 & IA 175. 128 sites, 89 with electric; showers; dump station. M. Swimming, fishing; boat ramp. GPS: N 42-17.5 W 95-00.8

Brushy Creek State Recreation Area

3175 290th St, Lehigh, IA 50557. Phone: (515) 543-8298. Located in central IA, 4 miles S of Duncombe on CR P-73, off US 20. 47 sites, 39 with electric, 8 full hook-up; showers; dump station. M. Equestrian area with 125 sites, 50 with electric. Swimming, fishing; boat ramp. GPS: N 42-22.1 W 93-58.3

Clear Lake State Park

6490 South Shore Dr, Clear Lake, IA 50428. Phone: (641) 357-4212. Located in north-central IA west of Mason City, 2 miles S of Clear Lake on IA 107, near US 18 and I-35. 200 sites, 95 with electric; showers; dump station. M. Swimming, fishing; boat ramp. GPS: N 43-06.5 W 93-23.8

Dolliver Memorial State Park

2757 Dolliver Park Ave, Lehigh, IA 50557. Phone: (515) 359-2539. Located on Des Moines River in central IA south of Fort Dodge, 3 miles NW of Lehigh on IA 50, off US 169. 33 sites with electric; showers; dump station. M. Fishing; boat ramp. GPS: N 42-22.6 W 94-05.2

Elinor Bedell State Park

1619 260th Ave, Spirit Lake, IA 51360. Phone: (712) 337-3211. Located in northwestern IA on East Lake Okoboji, near MN state line, 2 miles W of Spirit Lake on 250th Ave, off US 71. 8 full hook-up sites; showers. M. Swimming, fishing; boat ramp. GPS: N 43-29.5 W 95-07.5

Elk Rock (Red Rock) State Park

811 146th Ave, Knoxville, IA 50138. Phone: (641) 842-6008. Located in south-central IA, SE of Des Moines, 7 miles N of Knoxville on IA 14; on Red Rock Lake. 30 sites, 21 with electric; showers; dump station. M. Equestrian area with 60 sites, 24 with electric. Swimming, fishing; boat ramp. GPS: N 41-24.0 W 93-03.8

Emerson Bay State Recreation Area

3100 Emerson St, Okoboji, IA 51351. Phone: (712) 337-3211. Located in northwestern IA near MN state line, 2.5 miles N of Milford on IA 86, off US 71. 117 sites, 57 with electric; showers; dump station. M. Fishing; boat ramp. GPS: N 43-21.7 W 95-11.0

Fairport Station Recreation Area

3280 Hwy 22 E, Muscatine, IA 52761. Phone: (563) 263-4337. Located on Mississippi River in southeastern IA, 5 miles E of Muscatine on IA 22. 42 sites with electric; showers; dump station. M. Fishing; boat ramp. GPS: N 41-26.5 W 90-53.7

Fort Defiance State Park

3642 174th St, Estherville, IA 51334. Phone: (712) 337-3211. Located in northwestern IA near MN state line, 1 mile W of Estherville (IA 9 & 4) on IA 9. 16 sites. NM. GPS: N 43-23.7 W 94-51.3

Geode State Park

3249 Racine Ave, Danville, IA 52623. Phone: (319) 392-4601. Located in southeastern IA on Lake Geode, 4 miles SW of Danville (NW of Burlington), off IA 79. 168 sites, 87 with electric; showers; dump station. M. Fishing, swimming. GPS: N 40-49.0 W 91-22.8

George Wyth Memorial State Park

3659 Wyth Rd, Waterloo, IA 50703. Phone: (319) 232-5505. Located in east-central IA, NW of Waterloo, E of Cedar Falls on Cedar River. 69 sites with electric; showers; dump station. M. Three lakes in park. Fishing; boat ramp (motor restrictions). GPS: N 42-32.0 W 92-23.9

Green Valley State Park

1480 130th St, Creston, IA 50801. Phone: (641) 782-5131. Located in southwestern IA, on Green Valley Lake, NW of Creston, on IA 186, off US 34. 100 sites, 83 with electric; 18 full hook-up; showers; dump station. M. Fishing; boat ramp (no inboard boats). GPS: N 41-06.9 W 94-22.6

Gull Point State Park

1500 Harper St, Milford, IA 51351. Phone: (712) 337-3211. Located in northwestern IA, near MN state line, 3.5 miles N of Milford via US 71 and IA 86, in Iowa Lakes area. 112 sites, 60 with electric; showers; dump station. M. Fishing; boat ramp. GPS: N 43-22.2 W 95-11.0

Honey Creek State Park & Resort

12194 Honey Creek Rd, Moravia, IA 52571. Phone: (641) 724-3739. Located on Rathbun Lake in south-central IA, 12 miles W of Moravia on IA 142. 149 sites, 75 with electric, 28 full hook-up; showers; dump station. M. Fishing; boat ramp. GPS: N 40-53.5 W 92-59.0

Lacey-Keosauqua State Park

22895 Lacey Trail, Keosauqua, IA 52565. Phone: (319) 293-3502. Located in southeastern IA on Des Moines River, near MO state line, 5 miles S of Keosauqua on IA 1. 113 sites, 45 with electric; showers; dump station. M. Swimming, fishing; boat ramp (electric motors only). GPS: N 40-43.7 W 91-57.6

Lake Ahquabi State Park

1650 118th Ave, Indianola, IA 50125. Phone: (515) 961-7101. Located about 22 miles S of Des Moines via US 69 and IA 349. 141 sites, 85 with electric; showers; dump station. M. Lake in park. Swimming, fishing; boat ramp. GPS N 41-17.2 W 93-34.9

Lake Anita State Park

55111 750th St, Anita, IA 50020. Phone: (712) 762-3564. Located in southwestern IA, 5 miles S of Anita on IA 83, off I-80 exit 70. 161 sites, 52 with electric, 40 full hook-up; showers; dump station. Lake in park. M. Swimming, fishing; boat ramp. Golf near-by. GPS: N 41-26.0 W 94-45.7

Lake Darling State Park

111 Lake Darling Rd, Brighton, IA 52540. Phone: (319) 694-2323. Located in southeastern IA, 3 miles W of Brighton (SW of Washington), off IA 78 on Lake Darling. 118 sites, 81 with electric;

showers; dump station. M. Swimming, fishing; boat ramp. GPS: N 41-10.6 W 91-53.1

Lake Keomah State Park

2720 Keomah Ln, Oskaloosa, IA 52577. Phone: (641) 673-6975. Located in southeastern IA, 6 miles E of Oskaloosa via IA 92. 65 sites, 41 with electric; showers; dump station. M. Swimming, fishing; boat ramp (electric motors only). GPS: N 41-17.1 W 92-32.3

Lake MacBride State Park

3225 Hwy 382 NE Solon, IA 52333. Phone: (319) 624-2200. Located in eastern IA, on Lake MacBride, 4 miles NW of Solon (SE of Cedar Rapids), on IA 382. 111 sites, 37 with electric; showers; dump station. M. Swimming, fishing; boat ramp, rentals; (10 h.p. limit). GPS: N 41-48.2 W 91-34.3

Lake Manawa State Park

1100 South Shore Dr, Council Bluffs, IA 51501. Phone: (712) 366-0220. Located in southwestern IA, 2.5 miles S of I-80 exit 3, 2.5 miles W of I-29 exit 47, S of Council Bluffs, on Lake Manawa. 72 sites, 37 with electric; showers; dump station. M. Swimming, fishing; boat ramp, rentals. GPS: N 41-12.9 W 95-51.5

Lake of Three Fires State Park

2303 Lake Rd, Bedford, IA 50833. Phone: (712) 523-2700. Located in southwestern IA, on the lake, 3 miles N of Bedford on IA 49. 140 sites, 30 with electric; showers; dump station. M. Swimming, fishing; boat ramp, rentals. GPS: N 40-42.4 W 94-41.1

Lake Wapello State Park

15248 Campground Rd, Drakesville, IA. 52552. Phone: (641) 722-3371. Located in southeastern IA, 6 miles W of Drakesville on IA 273, off US 63, on Lake Wapello. 80 sites, 42 with electric; showers; dump station. M. Fishing, swimming; boat ramp. GPS: N 40-49.5 W 92-34.1

Ledges State Park

1515 P Ave, Madrid, IA 50156. Phone: (515) 432-1852. Located in central IA west of Ames, on Des Moines River, 6 miles S of Boone, off US 30 on IA 164. 95 sites, 40 with electric; showers; dump station. M. Fishing; boat ramp. GPS: N 41-59.9 W 93-53.6

Lewis and Clark State Park

21914 Park Loop, Onawa, IA 51040. Phone: (712) 423-2829. Located in western IA near NE state line, 5 miles W of Onawa, off IA 175 & I-29 exit 112; follow signs. 112 sites, 100 with electric, 12 full hook-up; showers; dump station. M. Lake in park. Swimming, fishing; boat ramp. GPS: N 42-02.5 W 96-09.8

Maquoketa Caves State Park

10970 98th St, Maquoketa, IA 52060. Phone: (563) 652-5833. Located in eastern IA, 7 miles NW of Maquoketa (US 61 & IA 64). 29 sites, 17 with electric; showers; dump station. M. GPS: N 42-07.2 W 90-46.7

Marble Beach State Park

12320 240th Ave, Spirit Lake, IA 51360. Phone: (712) 337-3211. Located in northwestern IA near MN state line, 2 miles NW of Orleans, off US 71 & IA 276. 224 sites, 100 with electric; showers; dump station. M. Fishing, swimming; boat ramp. GPS: N 43-27.1 W 95-07.8

McIntosh Woods State Park

1200 E Lake St, Ventura, IA 50482. Phone: (641) 829-3847. Located in north-central IA about 8 miles W of Clear Lake (city), on Clear Lake, on US 18. 49 sites, 45 with electric; showers; dump station. M. Swimming, fishing; boat ramp. GPS: N 43-08.0 W 93-27.5

Nine Eagles State Park

Davis City, IA 50065. Phone: (641) 442-2855. Located in southern IA near MO state line, 6 miles SE of Davis City (I-35 exit 4) on county road. 68 sites, 28 with electric; showers; dump station. M. Fishing, swimming; boat ramp. GPS: N 40-35.5 W 94-45.9

Palisades-Kepler State Park

700 Kepler Dr, Mt. Vernon, IA 52314. Phone: (319) 895-6039. Located in eastern IA, on Cedar River, SE of Cedar Rapids, 3.5 miles W of Mt. Vernon on US 30. 44 sites, 26 with electric; showers; dump station. M. Fishing; boat ramp. GPS: N 41-55.0 W 91-29.8

Pikes Peak State Park

32264 Oikes Peak Rd, McGregor, IA 52157. Phone: (563) 873-2341. Located in northeastern IA, 3 miles SE of McGregor (US 18/52, IA 340), on Mississippi River. 77 sites, 60 with electric; showers; dump station. M. GPS: N 43-00.0 W 91-10.8

Pilot Knob State Park

2148 340th St, Forest City, IA 50436. Phone: (641) 581-4835. Located in north-central IA, NW of Mason City, 4 miles E of Forest City on IA 9. 60 sites, 48 with electric; showers; dump station. M. Lake in park. Fishing; boating (electric motors). GPS: N 43-15.6 W 93-33.4

Pine Lake State Park

22620 County Hwy S56, Eldora, IA 50627. Phone: (641) 858-5832. Located in central IA, on Iowa River, next to Eldora, off IA 14/175 on CR 556. 124 sites with electric; showers; dump station. M. Lake in park. Fishing, swimming; boat ramp. GPS: N 42-21.8 W 93-04.8

Pleasant Creek State Recreation Area

4530 McClintock Rd, Palo, IA 52324. Phone: (319) 436-7716. Located in east-central IA, 15 miles NW of Cedar Rapids, off I-380 exit 35. 69 sites, 43 with electric; showers; dump station. M. Lake in park. Fishing, swimming; boat ramp. GPS: N 42-07.1 W 91-48.3

Prairie Rose State Park

680 Road M47, Harlan, IA 51537. Phone: (712) 773-2701. Located in southwest Iowa on Prairie Lake, 3 miles SE of Harlan via IA 44 and Road M47. 97 sites, 61 with electric; showers; dump station. M. Fishing, swimming; boat ramp. GPS: N 41-36.1 W 95-12.7

Red Haw Lake State Park

24550 US Hwy 34, Chariton, IA 50049. Phone: (641) 774-5632. Located in south-central IA, on Red Haw Lake, 1 mile S of Chariton, off US 34. 80 sites, 60 with electric; showers; dump station. M. Fishing, swimming; boat ramp. GPS: N 41-00.2 W 93-16.8

Rock Creek State Park

5627 Rock Creek E, Kellogg, IA 50135. Phone: (641) 236-3722. Located in central IA between Newton and Grinnell, 6 miles NE of Kellogg via county roads. 200 sites, 101 with electric; showers; dump station. M. Fishing; boat ramp. GPS: N 41-45.6 W 92-50.1

Shimek State Forest Campground

33653 Rt J56, Farmington, IA 52626. Phone: (319) 878-3811. Located in southeastern IA, 1 mile E of Farmington on IA 2. 56 sites. NM. Equestrian area. Fishing, swimming, boating. GPS: N 40-37.5 W 91-43.1

Springbrook State Park

2437 160th Rd, Guthrie Center, IA 50115. Phone: (641) 747-3591. Located in west-central IA, 8 miles NE of Guthrie Center on IA 384, off IA 25. 120 sites, 81 with electric; showers; dump station. M. Lake in park. Fishing, swimming; boat ramp. GPS: N 41-46.5 W 94-28.4

Stephens State Forest

1111 N 8th St, Chariton, IA 50049. Phone: (641) 774-5632. Located in south-central IA, 2.5 miles S of Lucas on US 65. 85 sites. NM. Equestrian park. GPS: N 41-01.0 W 93-28.5

Stone State Park

5001 Talbot Rd, Sioux City, IA 51103. Phone: (712) 255-4698. Located in western IA, 8 miles NW of Sioux City on IA 12. 30 sites, 10 with electric. NM. Fishing, boating. GPS: N 42-33.4 W 96-28.6

Union Grove State Park

1215 220th St, Gladbrook, IA 50635. Phone: (641) 473-2556. Located in central IA, NE of Marshalltown, 4 miles S of Gladbrook via CR T47. 26 sites, 7 with electric. NM. Fishing, swimming, boating. GPS: N 42-07.4 W 92-43.5

Viking Lake State Park

2780 Viking Lake Rd, Stanton, IA 51573. Phone: (712) 829-2235. Located in southwestern IA, on Viking Lake, SE of Red Oak off US 34 on CR 115. 120 sites, 94 with electric 12 full hook-up; showers; dump station. M. Fishing, swimming; boat ramp. GPS: N 40-58.4 W 95-02.9

Volga River State Recreation Area

10225 Ivy Rd, Fayette, IA 52142. Phone: (563) 425-4161. Located in northeastern IA, on Volga River, 4 miles NE of Fayette on IA 150. 49 sites. NM. Lake in park. Equestrian area. Fishing, boat ramp. GPS: N 42-53.9 W 91-48.6

Walnut Woods State Park

3155 Walnut Woods Dr, West Des Moines, IA 50265. Phone: (515) 285-4502. Located in south-central IA on Raccoon River, 4 miles SW of Des Moines on IA 5, near I-35. 22 sites, 13 with electric, 8 full hook-up. NM. Fishing; boat ramp. GPS: N 41-32.2 W 93-44.8

Wapsipinicon State Park

21301 CR E34, Anamosa, IA 52205. Phone: (319) 462-2761. Located on Wapsipinicon River, about 15 miles NE of Cedar Rapids via US 51. 26 sites, 14 with electric; showers; dump station. M. Fishing, boat ramp. GPS: N 42-05.7 W 91-17.9

Waubonsie State Park

2585 Waubonsie Park Rd, Hamburg, IA 51640. Phone: (712) 382-2786. Located in southwest corner of IA, S of Sidney, off I-29 exits 1 or 10, on IA 239 at IA 2. 40 sites, 24 with electric; showers; dump station. M. Equestrian campground. Fishing; boat ramp, (electric motors). GPS: N 40-40.5 W 95-41.2

Wildcat Den State Park

1884 Wildcat Dr, Muscatine, IA 52761. Phone: (563) 263-4337. Located in southeastern IA, 10 miles E of Muscatine on IA 22. 28 sites. NM. GPS: N 41-28.0 W 90-52.5

Wilson Island State Recreation Area

32801 Campground Ln, Missouri Valley, IA 51555. Phone: (712) 642-2069. Located in southwestern IA on Missouri River, 5 miles W of Loveland, off I-29 exit 72 on IA 362. 135 sites, 63 with electric; showers; dump station. M. GPS: N 41-29.5 W 96-00.6

Yellow River State Forest

729 State Forest Rd, Harpers Ferry, IA 52146. Phone: (563) 586-2196 . Located in northeastern IA on Missouri River, 14 miles SE of Waukon, off IA 76, near junction IA 360. 162 sites. NM. Equestrian area. Fishing; boat ramp. GPS: N 43-11.5 W 91-13.4

KANSAS

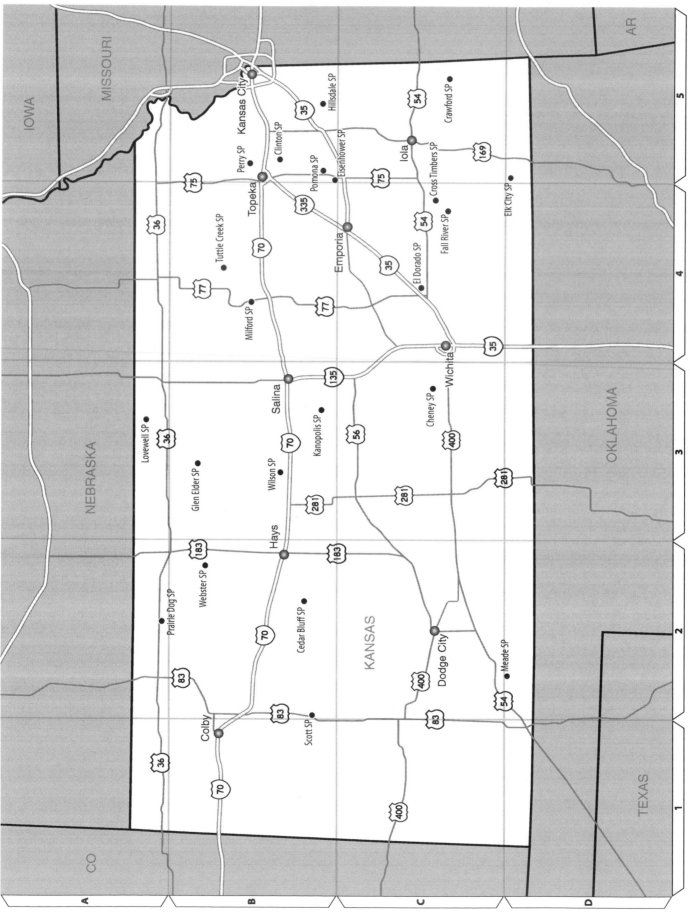

Kansas

There are 22 state parks with RV facilities in Kansas. They range from full hookups to electric-only sites. In most cases the electric service is 50 amps at all campgrounds. All parks require a daily ($6.50 per vehicle) or annual usage fee plus an additional fee for utility sites. Senior and disabled discounts available. Reservations are accepted at some parks, as listed, and some parks charge a reservation fee. Some telephone numbers are for that park's area office. Visa and MasterCard accepted. Rate group: B (Rate includes vehicle fee.)

Kansas Dept. of Wildlife & Parks
512 SE 25th Ave
Pratt, KS 67124

Information: (620) 672-5911
Internet: www.kdwp.state.ks.us

Kansas Park Locator

Kansas Parks

Cedar Bluff State Park
32001 147 Hwy, Ellis, KS 67637. Phone: (785) 726-3212. Located on Cedar Bluff Reservoir on KS 147, S of I-70 exit 135. 11 full hook-up, 85 water & electric; showers, dump station(s). All 50 amp electric. Reservable sites available. Fishing; boat ramp. GPS: N 38-46.2 W 99-46.8

Cheney State Park
16000 NE 50th St, Cheney, KS 67025. Phone: (316) 542-3664. Located on Cheney Reservoir about 20 miles W of Wichita off US 54. 223 water & electric, 100 premium sites; showers, dump station(s). All 50 amp electric. Fishing; marina, boat ramps. GPS: N 37-44.0 W 97-50.7

Clinton State Park
798 N 1415 Rd, Lawrence, KS 66049. Phone: (785) 842-8562. Located off Kansas Turnpike exit 197 & US 40, on Clinton Lake, 4 miles W of Lawrence. 496 sites, 240 premium sites; showers; dump station(s). Reservable sites available. Swimming, fishing. Marina, boat ramps. GPS: N 38-56.8 W 95-20.2

Crawford State Park
1 Lake Rd, Farlington, KS 66734. Phone: (620) 362-3671. Located off KS 7, 9 miles N of Girard, W of US 69. Seven campgrounds. 500 sites; 74 water & electric; showers, dump station. Fishing, swimming; boat ramp, marina. GPS: N 37-38.1 W 94-48.9

Cross Timbers State Park
144 Hwy 105, Toronto, KS 66777. Phone: (620) 637-2213. Located in SE Kansas on Toronto Lake, about 12 miles W of Yates Center (US 75 & 54) on KS 105. 15 full hook-up sites, 37 water & electric, 10 electric, 180 non-utility sites; showers, dump station. Reservable sites available. Fishing, boat ramp. GPS: N 37-48.1 W 95-57.0

Eisenhower State Park
29810 S Fairlawn Rd, Osage City, KS 66523. Phone: (785) 528-4102. Located SW of Lyndon off KS 278, on Melvern Lake. Use I-35 exit 155 and then north on US 75 to KS 278. 186 utility sites (water, electric, some sewers); showers, dump station(s). Reservable sites available. Laundry. Equestrian area (18 sites). Swimming, fishing; kayak rentals. GPS: N 38-32.0 W 95-44.6

El Dorado State Park
618 NE Bluestem Rd, El Dorado, KS 67042. Phone: (316) 321-7180. Located on El Dorado Lake NE of Wichita at Kansas Turnpike exit 76. 1056 sites: 128 full hook-up, 352 water & electric, 566 non-utility sites; showers, dump station(s). Reservable sites available. Swimming, fishing; boat ramps. GPS: N 37-50.0 W 96-47.1

Elk City State Park
4825 Squaw Creek Rd, Independence, KS 67301. Phone: (620) 331-6295. Located on Elk City Lake, 5 miles NW of Independence off US 75. 95 sites with water & electric, (some 50 amp); showers, dump station(s). Boat ramp. GPS: N 37-15.1 W 95-46.5

Fall River State Park
144 Hwy 105, Toronto, KS 66777. Phone: (620) 637-2213. Located on Fall River Lake about 14 miles NW of Fredonia via US 400. 45

water & electric, 100+ non-utility sites; showers, dump station. Swimming, fishing; boat ramp. GPS: N 37-38.8 W 96-02.5

Glen Elder State Park

2131 180 Rd, Glen Elder, KS 67446. Phone: (785) 545-3345. Located in north-central KS on Waconda Lake, along US 24 about 26 miles E of Osborne. 120 water & electric, 300 non-utility sites; showers, dump station(s). Reservable sites available. Swimming, fishing; boat ramp; marina. GPS: N 39-29.9 W 98-18.5

Hillsdale State Park

26001 W 255th St, Paola, KS 66071. Phone: (913) 783-4507. Located about 16 miles E of Ottawa (I-35 exit 187) on KS 68. 200 sites: 99 water & electric, 101 non-utility sites; showers, dump station. Swimming, fishing; boat ramp. Equestrian area. GPS: N 38-39.1 W 94-53.5

Kanopolis State Park

200 Horsethief Rd, Marquette, KS 67464. Phone: (785) 546-2565. Located on Kanopolis Reservoir about 18 miles W of Lindsborg (I-135 exit 72 or 78) via KS 4 and KS 141. 119 water & electric (some full hook-up); 200 non-utility; showers, dump station(s). Reservable sites available. Marina. Horse trails. Swimming, fishing; boat ramp, marina. GPS: N 38-38.3 W 97-58.8

Lovewell State Park

2446 250 Rd, Webber, KS 66970. Phone: (785) 753-4971. Located in north-central KS on Lovewell Reservoir about 9 miles NE of Mankato via US 36 and KS 14. 118 sites with utilities (some full hook-up); 300 non-utility; showers, dump station(s). Marina. Swimming, fishing; boat ramp. GPS: N 39-51.4 W 98-03.1

Meade State Park

13051 V Rd, Meade, KS 67864. Phone: (620) 873-2572. Located in southwestern Kansas on Meade Lake, on KS 14, off US 54 near Meade. Five areas: 42 water & electric, 150 non-utility sites; showers, dump station. Swimming, fishing; boat ramp. Marina. GPS: N 37-09.8 W 100-26.5

Milford State Park

3612 State Park Rd, Milford, KS 66514. Phone: (785) 238-3014. Located on Milford Lake near Junction City; I-70 exit 295 N on US 77 to KS 57. 120 sites with electric & water; some with sewers; 108 non-utility; showers, dump station(s). Equestrian area. Fishing, swimming; boat ramp. GPS: N 39-06.2 W 96-53.3

Perry State Park

5441 W Lake Rd, Ozawkie, KS 66070. Phone: (785) 246-3449. Located NE of Topeka on Perry Lake; US 24 east to KS 237, north to park. 124 water & electric sites, 200+ non-utility sites; showers, dump station(s). Equestrian area. Swimming, fishing; boat ramp. GPS: N 39-08.6 W 95-29.4

Pomona State Park

22900 S Hwy 368, Vassar, KS 66543. Phone: (785) 828-4933. Located on Pomona Lake, about 30 miles S of Topeka near US 75 and KS 268. 142 water & electric sites, 200+ non-utility sites; showers, dump station(s). Reservable sites available. Marina. Swimming, fishing; boat ramp. Disc golf. GPS: N 38-39.6 W 95-36.1

Prairie Dog State Park

13037 Hwy 261, Norton, KS 67654. Phone: (785) 877-2953. Located on Sebelius Reservoir, 4 miles SW of Norton off US 36 on KS 383. 58 utility, 130 non-utility sites; showers, dump station(s). Reservable sites available. Fishing. GPS N 39-48.7 W 99-57.8

Scott State Park

101 W Scott Lake Dr, Scott City, KS 67871. Phone: (620) 872-2061. Located in western KS, N of Scott City, off US 83 on KS 95. 55 water & electric sites (some 50 amp), 100 non-utility sites; showers, dump station. Swimming, fishing; boat rentals. GPS: N 38-40.0 W 100-55.0

Tuttle Creek (Spillway) State Park

5800 A River Pond Rd, Manhattan, KS 66502. Phone: (785) 539-7941. Located near Manhattan on Tuttle Creek Lake about 16 miles N of I-70 exit 313. 118 water & electric, 500 non-utility sites; showers, dump station(s). Reservable sites available. Equestrian area, (13 sites). Fishing GPS: N39-17.5 W 96-34.6

Webster State Park

1210 Nine Rd, Stockton, KS 67669. Phone: (785) 425-6775. Located 8 miles W of Stockton via US 24. 66 water & electric, 6 electric, 100 non-utility sites; showers, dump station. Reservable sites available. Fishing; boat ramp. GPS: N 39-24.9 W 99-26.2

Wilson State Park

#3 State Park Rd, Sylvan Grove, KS 67481. Phone: (785) 658-2465. Located on Wilson Lake about 5 miles N of I-70 exit 206 via KS 232. 99 water & electric, 36 electric, 100 non-utility sites; showers, dump station(s). Reservable sites available. Swimming, fishing; boat ramp, rentals. Marina. GPS: N 38-54.9 W 98-29.8

KENTUCKY

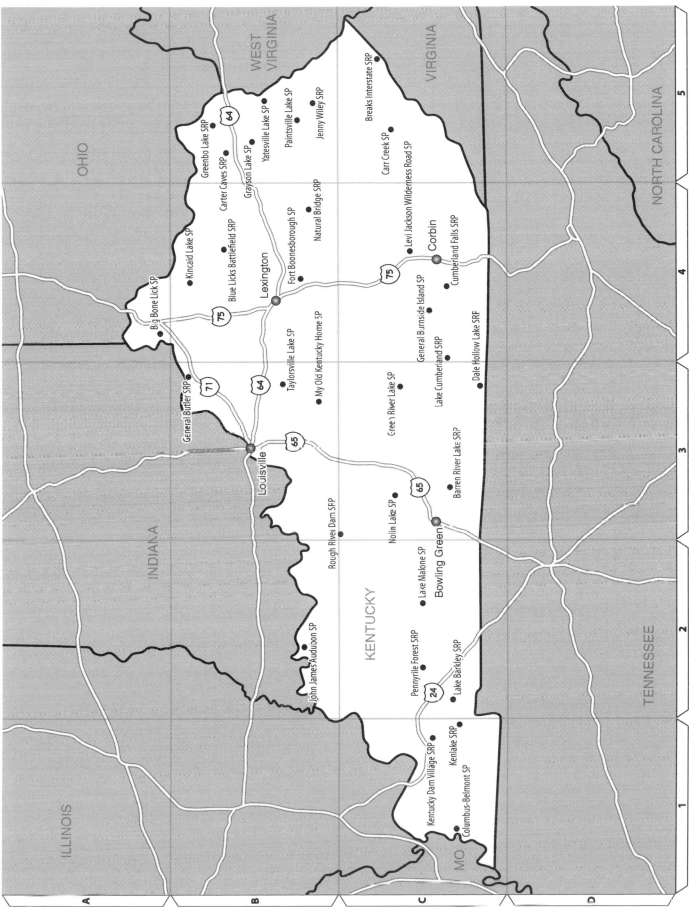

Kentucky

Kentucky is very rich in state parks and resorts with RV facilities. There are 32 state parks or resorts with facilities and all offer water and electricity, although some parks are seasonal, as listed. Fourteen of these locations have golf courses. Seasonal parks are open April 1 through October 31. All parks have a dump station and showers. All are pet friendly. And all parks except Breaks Interstate Park have laundry facilities. Reservations are recommended at the state-run resorts. Resort telephone numbers are listed with each park. Rate groups: B and C. (Holidays have premium fees.)

Kentucky State Parks
500 Mero Street
Frankfort, KY 40601

Information: (800) 255-7275
Reservations: 1-888-459-7275
Internet: www.kystateparks.com

Kentucky Park Locator

Kentucky Parks

Barren River Lake State Resort Park
1149 State Park Rd, Lucas, KY 42156. Resort: (270) 646-2151. Located about 14 miles SW of Glasgow and Cumberland Pkwy exit 11 via US 31E. 99 sites; seasonal. Golf course. Marina. Swimming, fishing; boat ramp, rentals. GPS: N 36-50.0 W 86-02.4

Big Bone Lick State Park
3380 Beaver Rd, Union, KY 41091. Phone: (859) 384-3522. Located 22 miles S of Covington on KY 338 west of I-75 exit 175. 61 sites; year-round. Swimming, fishing. GPS: N 38-53.3 W 84-44.9

Blue Licks Battlefield State Resort Park
10299 Maysville Rd, Carlile, KY 41064. Phone: (859) 289-5507 Located 48 miles NE of Lexington on US 68, near junction of KY 165. 49 sites; year-round. Swimming. GPS: N 38-26.1 W 83-59.5

Breaks Interstate State Resort Park
627 Commission Circle, Breaks, VA 24607. Phone: (540) 865-4413. Resort: (800) 982-5122. Located on KY/VA border, 7 miles E of Elkhorn City, KY on KY/VA 80. 38 sites, most with utilities. Swimming pool. Horse trails. Fishing; boat rentals. GPS: N 37-18.0 W 82-18.5

Carr Creek State Park
2086 Smithboro Rd, Sassafras, KY 41759. Phone: (606) 642-4050. Located 15 miles SE of Hazard in southeastern Kentucky on KY 15 S. From Daniel Boone Pkwy, exit at Hazard (exit 59) to KY 15 S; about 15 miles to park. 38 sites; seasonal. Marina. Swimming, fishing; boat ramp, rentals. GPS: N 37-14.7 W 83-00.3

Carter Caves State Resort Park
344 Caveland Dr, Olive Hill, KY 41164. Phone: (606) 286-4411. Located 30 miles W of Ashland. From I-64 exit 161, KY 182 north about 5 miles. 90 utility sites; year-round. Equestrian area/sites. Golf course. Cave tours. Fishing, swimming; boat ramp. Wi-Fi. GPS: N 38-22.3 W 83-06.5

Columbus-Belmont State Park
350 Park Rd, Columbus, KY 42032. Phone: (270) 677-2327. Located 36 miles SW of Paducah on KY 80; use KY 123, KY 58 or KY 80. 38 sites. Boat ramp. Wi-Fi. GPS: N 36-45.7 W 89-06.4

Cumberland Falls State Resort Park
7351 Hwy 90, Corbin, KY 40701. Resort: (800) 325-0063. Located in southeastern Kentucky. From I-75 exit 25 (Corbin) US 25 W to KY 90, west to park. 29 sites; seasonal. Horse rentals. Swimming, fishing. GPS: N 36-50.1 W 84-21.3

Dale Hollow Lake State Resort Park

5970 State Park Rd, Burkesville, KY 42717. Resort: (800) 325-2282. Located SE of Bowling Green on KY/TN state line. From Bowling Green, I-65 exit 43 (Cumberland Pkwy), take KY 90 E to KY 449 S to park. 145 sites; seasonal. Golf course. Equestrian area. Marina. Swimming, fishing; boat ramp, rentals. GPS: N 36-39.7 W 85-17.8

Fort Boonesborough State Park

4375 Boonesborough Rd, Richmond, KY 40475. Phone: (859) 527-3131. Located on Kentucky River, about 38 miles SE of Lexington on KY 627. From I-75, use exit 75. From I-64, use Winchester exits 94 or 96. 167 sites; year-round. Swimming pool. Fishing; boat ramp. Store. GPS: N 37-53.9 W 84-16.2

General Burnside Island State Park

8801 S Hwy 27, Burnside, KY 42519. Phone: (606) 561-4104. Located 8 miles S of Somerset on US 27. 93 sites; seasonal. Swimming pool, golf course. Marina. Fishing; boat ramp, rentals. GPS: N 36-54.9 W 84-35.7

General Butler State Resort Park

1608 Hwy 227, Carrollton, KY 41008. Phone: (502) 732-4384. Located 44 miles NE of Louisville, I-71 exit 44, north to Carrollton, follow signs. 109 sites; year-round. Swimming, fishing; rentals (no motors). Wi-Fi. GPS: N 38-40.2 W 85-08.7

Grayson Lake State Park

314 Grayson Lake Park Rd, Olive Hill, KY 41164. Phone: (606) 474-9727. Located 25 miles SW of Ashland. From I-64 exit 172 (KY 7) south about 16 miles to park. 69 sites. Seasonal. Golf course. Marina. Swimming; boat ramp, rentals. GPS: N 38-12.5 W 83-00.9

Green River Lake State Park

179 Park Office Rd, Campbellsville, KY 42718. Phone: (270) 465-8255. Located about 4 miles S of Campbellsville on KY 55. 156 sites; seasonal. Marina. Swimming, fishing; boat ramp, rentals. Wi-Fi. GPS: N 37-17.5 W 85-21.8

Greenbo Lake State Resort Park

965 Lodge Rd, Greenup, KY 41144. Resort: (800) 325-0083. From I-64 exit 172 (Grayson) N 18 miles to park. 92 sites with utilities. Swimming, fishing; boat ramp, rentals. Wi-Fi. GPS: N 38-28.7 W 82-52.1

Jenny Wiley State Resort Park

75 Theater Ct, Prestonsburg, KY 41653. Resort: (606) 889-1790. Located on KY 3 off US 23/460, N of Prestonsburg. 91 sites. Disc golf. Fishing, swimming; boat ramp. GPS: N 37-43.8 W 82-44.2

John James Audubon State Park

3100 US Hwy 41 N, Henderson, KY 42419. Phone: (270) 826-2247. Located on US 41 in Henderson on the Ohio River about 10 miles S of Evansville, Indiana. 87 sites; year-round. Golf course. Fishing. Boat ramp, rentals. Wi-Fi. GPS: N 37-53.4 W 87-33.4

Kenlake State Resort Park

542 Kenlake Rd, Hardin, KY 42048. Resort: (270) 474-2211. Located 40 miles SE of Paducah on Kentucky Lake. From Paducah take I-24 east to Purchase Pkwy (exit 25), south to US 68 (exit 47) to Resort. From I-24 West, exit US 68/KY 80 (exit 65) west to Resort. 87 sites; seasonal. Golf course. Marina. Swimming, fishing; boat ramp, rentals. GPS: N 36-46.3 W 88-08.3

Kentucky Dam Village State Resort Park

113 Administration Dr, Gilbertsville, KY 42044. Resort: (270) 362-4271. Located on Kentucky Lake 21 miles SE of Paducah. Exit 27 off I-24 to US 62 to US 641, east to Resort. 214 sites; year-round. Marina. Swimming, fishing; boat ramp, rentals. GPS: N 36-59.9 W 88-17.3

Kincaid Lake State Park

565 Kincaid Park Rd, Falmouth, KY 41040. Phone: (859) 654-3531. Located 48 miles SE of Covington and 61 miles NE of Lexington. From Covington or Lexington, US 27 to Falmouth then KY 159 to park. 84 sites; seasonal. Golf course. Marina. Swimming, fishing; boat ramp, rentals. Wi-Fi. GPS: N 38-41.6 W 84-17.6

Lake Barkley State Resort Park

3500 State Park Rd, Cadiz, KY 42211. Phone: (270) 924-1131; Located 29 miles W of Hopkinsville. From I-24 exit 65, follow US 68 west to park. 79 sites; seasonal. Golf course. Swimming, fishing; boat ramp, rentals. GPS: N 36-49.9 W 87-55.7

Lake Cumberland State Resort Park

5465 State Park Rd, Jamestown, KY 42629. Resort: (800) 325-1709. Located between Glasgow and Somerset, S of Cumberland Pkwy on Lake Cumberland. From I-65 exit 43, Cumberland Pkwy, E to US 127, S about 8 miles. From I-75 exit 41 (KY 80) west to Somerset & Cumberland Pkwy to US 127, south to Resort. 112 sites; seasonal. Golf course. Marina. Swimming, fishing; boat ramp, rentals. GPS: N 36-55.8 W 85-02.4

Lake Malone State Park

331 State Route Rd 8001, Dunmore, KY 42339. Phone: (270) 657-2111. Located 22 miles S of Central City and Western Kentcuky Pkwy exit 58 via US 431 and KY 973. 25 sites; seasonal. Swimming, fishing; boat ramp. GPS: N 37-04.3 W 87-03.5

Levi Jackson Wilderness Road State Park

998 Levi Jackson Mill Rd, London, KY 40744. Phone: (606) 330-2130. Located about 7 miles SE of London. I-75 exit 38, east on KY 80 to park. 136 sites; year-round. Swimming pool. Store. Wi-Fi. GPS: N 37-05.2 W 84-02.8

My Old Kentucky Home State Park

501 E Stephen Foster Ave, Bardstown, KY 40004. Phone: (502) 348-3502. Located in Bardstown on US 150. 39 sites. Golf course. GPS: N 37-48.4 W 85-27.2

Natural Bridge State Resort Park

2135 Natural Bridge Rd, Slade, KY 40376. Resort: (800) 325-1710. Located 52 miles SE of Lexington off Combs Mountain Pkwy, on KY 11. Exit 33 off Mountain Pkwy (KY 402) at KY 11, south about 3 miles. 82 sites with utilities; seasonal. Swimming pool. Fishing, boat rentals. GPS: N 37-46.5 W 83-40.5

Nolin Lake State Park

2998 Brian Creek Rd, Mammouth Cave, KY 42259. Phone: (270) 286-4240. Located 7 miles N of Mammoth Cave National Park via KY 728 & KY 1827. From I-65 exit 53, follow KY 70 to KY 259 and then north to KY 728. From Western Kentucky Pkwy exit 107, follow

KY 259 south to KY 728. 92 sites (60 primitive). Fishing, swimming; boat ramp. GPS: N 37-18.0 W 86-12.7

Paintsville Lake State Park

1551 KY 2275, Staffordsville, KY 41256. Phone: (606) 297-8486. Located 4 miles W of Paintsville on KY 172, from US 460 and KY 40. 42 sites, 32 with full hookup. Marina; Swimming, fishing; boat ramp, rentals. Wi-Fi. GPS: N 37-52.0 W 82-50.2

Pennyrile Forest State Resort Park

20781 Pennyrile Lodge Rd, Dawson Springs, KY 42408. Resort: (800) 325-1711. Located 20 miles NW of Hopkinsville and 5 miles S of Western Kentucky Pkwy exit 24, on KY 109. 88 sites. Golf course. Swimming, fishing; boat rentals. Equestrian area. GPS: N 37-07.4 W 87-39.0

Rough River Dam State Resort Park

450 Lodge Rd, Falls of Rough, KY 40119. Resort: (800) 325-2311. From Western Kentucky Pkwy exit 94 (Caneyville), follow KY 79 north about 17 miles. 34 sites; seasonal. Golf course. Swimming, fishing; boat ramp, rentals. GPS: N 37-37.1 W 86-30.1

Taylorsville Lake State Park

1320 Park Rd, Taylorsville, KY 40071. Phone: (502) 477-8713. Located 20 miles SE of I-64 exit 32. From I-64 travel S on KY 55 to KY 44 east to KY 248 then south to park. 55 sites. Equestrian area (10 sites). Marina. Fishing; boat ramp, rentals. GPS: N 38-02.0 W 85-15.2

Yatesville Lake State Park

2667 Pleasant Ridge Rd, Louisa, KY 41230. Phone: (606) 673-1490. Located about 30 miles S of Ashland in eastern KY. From US 23, exit at Louisa (KY 3) west 3 miles to park. 47 sites, 27 with utilities. Golf course. Marina. Swimming, fishing; boat ramp. GPS: N 38-07.7 W 82-38.8

LOUISIANA

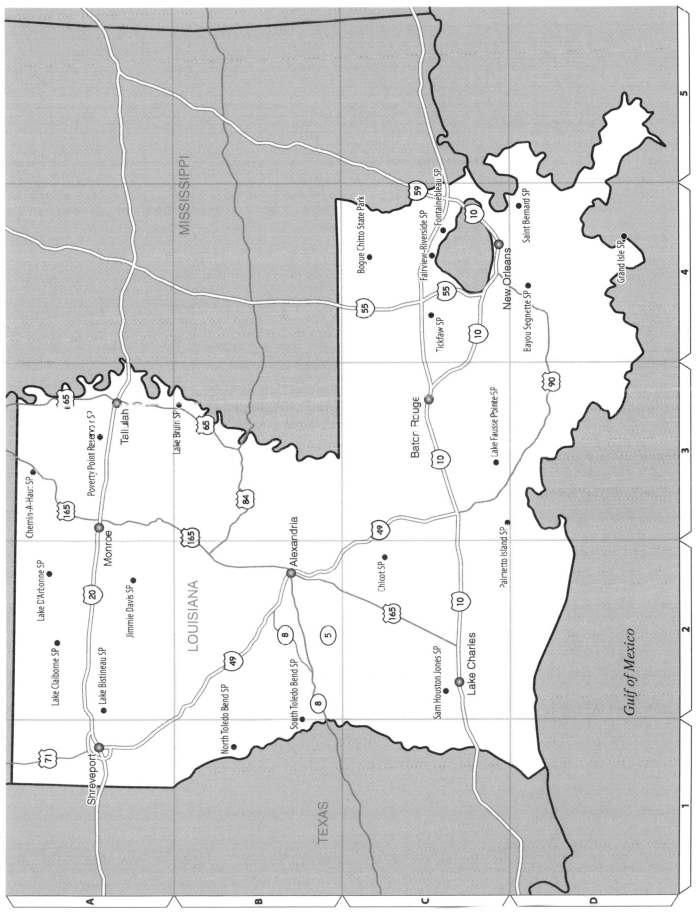

Louisiana

Louisiana maintains 20 state parks with RV facilities. Most of these parks (16) have "improved" campsites, which are a designated site with water and electricity on site and toilet and shower facilities nearby. "Unimproved" sites are not designated spaces and have no utilities but may have toilet and shower facilities in the area. All Louisiana parks are open year-round. (Holders of America the Beautiful or Access Passes are entitled to a discount on camping fees. Entrance fee waived for seniors.) There is a state reservation system (see below) but drive-up users are welcome. Rate groups: A and B, depending on type of site (improved or unimproved).

Louisiana Dept. of Culture, Recreation and Tourism
Office of State Parks
PO Box 44426
Baton Rouge, LA 70804

Information: (888) 677-1400
Reservations: (877) 226-7652
Internet: www.lastateparks.com

Louisiana Park Locator

Louisiana Parks

Bayou Segnette State Park

7777 Westbank Expwy, Westwego, LA 70094. Phone: (504) 736-7140 or (888) 677-2296. Located in Westwego off the Westbank Expwy (Bus. 90 E). I-10 east from New Orleans, across Greater New Orleans Bridge to the Westbank Expwy, west to Westwego. From east I-10 to US 90 south, cross the Huey P. Long Bridge to Westbank Expwy. 98 improved sites; dump station, laundry. Swimming, fishing; boat ramp. GPS: N 29-54.2 W 90-09.2

Bogue Chitto State Park

17049 State Park Blvd, Franklinton, LA 70438. Phone: (985) 839-5707. Located in SE Louisiana, near Mississippi. About 20 miles from US 190 and LA 25. 81 premium sites all pull-through, some with sewers. Equestrian area. Swimming. GPS: N 30-43.4 W 90-14.4

Chemin-A-Haut State Park

14656 State Park Rd, Bastrop, LA 71220. Phone: (318) 283-0812, (888) 677-2436. Located 10 miles N of Bastrop. From I-20 take US 165 north from Monroe to Bastrop then US 425 10 miles N to LA 2229 (Loop Park Rd). 26 improved sites (also primitive area); dump station; laundry. Swimming, fishing, boat rentals, ramp. GPS: N 32-54.8 W 91-50.8

Chicot State Park

3469 Chicot Park Rd, Ville Platte, LA 70586. Phone: (337) 363-2403 or (888) 677-2442. Located 7 miles N of Ville Platte (US 167 & LA 10) on LA 3042. From Ville Platte, 7 miles N on LA 3042. From I-49 exit 46 to LA 106 south 6 miles to LA 3042. 208 improved sites (also primitive area); dump station; laundry. Swimming, fishing; boat rentals, ramp. GPS: N 30-49.8 W 92-16.7

Fairview-Riverside State Park

119 Fairview Dr, Madisonville, LA 70447. Phone: (985) 845-3318 or (888) 677-3247. Located 2 miles E of Madisonville on LA 22; 4 miles from I-12 at LA 21 to LA 22. 81 improved or premium sites; dump station; laundry. Fishing, boat ramp. GPS: N 30-24.5 W 90-08.4

Fontainebleau State Park

67883 Hwy 1089, Mandeville, LA 70448. Phone: (985) 624-4443 or (888) 677-3668. Located on US 190, 4 miles SE of Mandeville. I-12 exit 63A at LA 434 to US 190. 120 improved/premium (some full hook-up) and 237 unimproved sites; dump station; laundry. Swimming. GPS: N 30-21.1 W 90-02.3

Grand Isle State Park

Admiral Craik Dr, Grand Isle, LA 70358. Phone: (985) 787-2559 or (888) 787-2559. Located on the Gulf of Mexico on Grand Island, end of LA 1 (off US 90 at Matthews LA). 49 improved, pull-through sites; dump station. Swimming, fishing; boat rentals. GPS: N 29-15.5 W 89-57.4

Jimmie Davis State Park

1209 State Park Rd, Chatham, LA 71226. Phone: (318) 249-2595 or (888) 677-2263. Located 12 miles E of Jonesboro off LA 4 on Caney Lake. From LA 4 take Lakeshore Drive to LA 1209. 64 improved, 9 premium sites; dump station; laundry. Swimming, fishing; boat ramp. GPS: N 32-17.7 W 92-27.5

Lake Bistineau State Park

103 State Park Rd, Doyline, LA 71023. Phone: (318) 745-3503 or (888) 677-2478. Located 7 miles S of Doyline on LA 163. From I-20, exit at Minden and take US 371 south to Sibley, then LA 164 W to Doyline and LA 163 south to park. 61 improved or premium sites (some pull-through); dump station. Swimming, fishing; boat ramp, rentals. GPS: N 32-27.5 W 93-22.1

Lake Bruin State Park

201 State Park Rd, St. Joseph, LA 71366. Phone: (318) 766-3530 or (888) 677-2784. Located E of US 65, NE of St. Joseph via LA 128, 605 & 604. 48 improved or premium sites; dump station; laundry. Swimming, fishing; boat ramp, rentals. GPS: N 31-57.3 W 91-11.9

Lake Claiborne State Park

225 State Park Rd, Homer, LA 71040. Phone: (318) 927-2976 or (888) 677-2524. Located 7 miles SE of Homer (US 79 & LA 2) on LA 146. 87 improved or premium sites, some pull-through; dump station; laundry. Swimming, fishing; boat ramp, rentals. GPS: N 32-43.0 W 93-56.1

Lake D'Arbonne State Park

3628 Evergreen Rd, Farmerville, LA 71241. Phone: (318) 368-2086 or (888) 677-5200. Located 5 miles W of Farmerville. 65 improved/premium sites; dump station; laundry. Swimming, fishing; boat ramp, rentals. GPS: N 32-46.2 W 92-24.9

Lake Fausse Pointe State Park

5400 Levee Rd, St. Martinville, LA 70582. Phone: (337) 229-4764 or (888) 677-7200. Located about 18 miles SE of St. Martinsville (Use I-10 exit 115, S on LA 352 19 miles). 50 improved or premium sites; dump station; laundry. Swimming, fishing; boat ramp, rentals. GPS: N 30-04.1 W 91-36.9

North Toledo Bend State Park

2907 N Toledo Park Rd, Zwolle, LA 71486. Phone: (318) 645-4715 or (888) 677-6400. Located 9 miles SW of Zwolle, near Texas state line, off LA 3229 and US 171. 63 improved or premium sites; dump station; laundry. Swimming, fishing; boat ramp, rentals. GPS: N 31-32.8 W 93-43.9

Palmetto Island State Park

19501 Pleasant Rd, Abbeville, LA 70510. Phone: (337) 893-3930 or (888) 677-0094. Located S of Abbeville, off Hwy 690. 96 improved sites; dump station. Fishing, boat ramp. GPS: N31-02.0 W82-20.4

Poverty Point Reservoir State Park

1500 Poverty Point Pkwy, Delhi, LA 71232. Phone: (318) 878-3576 or (800) 474-0392. Located 3 miles N of Delhi exit off I-20. 54 improved or premium sites, water; dump station. Laundry. Marina. Swimming, fishing; boat ramp, rentals. GPS: N 32-37.8 W 91-24.3

Saint Bernard State Park

501 Saint Bernard Pkwy, Braithwaite, LA 70040. Phone: (504) 682-2101 or (888) 677-7823. Located on LA 39, 18 miles SE of New Orleans. 51 improved sites; dump station; laundry; swimming pool. GPS: N 29-51.9 W 89-54.2

Sam Houston Jones State Park

107 Sutherland Rd, Lake Charles, LA 70611. Phone: (337) 855-2665 or (888) 677-7264. Located 12 miles N of Lake Charles (I-10 & US 171) on LA 378. 59 improved or premium sites; dump station. Fishing, swimming; boat ramp, rentals. GPS: N 30-18.3 W 93-15.5

South Toledo Bend State Park

120 Bald Eagle Rd, Anacoco, LA 71403. Phone: (337) 286-9075 or (888) 398-4770. Located on Toledo Bend Reservoir, about 15 miles SW of Anacoco (US 171) via LA 111/392 to LA 191. 55 improved/premium sites; dump station. Swimming, fishing; boat ramp; canoe rentals. GPS: N 31-12.7 W 93-34.7

Tickfaw State Park

27225 Patterson Rd, Springfield, LA 70462. Phone: (225) 294-5020 or (888) 981-2020. Located 32 miles E of Baton Rouge (SW of I-12 & I-55 junction) off I-12 exit 32, S on LA 43 to LA 42 to LA 1037 (W) to Patterson Rd, south to park. 30 improved, 20 unimproved (water only) sites; dump station; laundry. Fishing, swimming; boat ramp, canoe rentals. GPS: N 30-22.9 W 90-37.9

MAINE

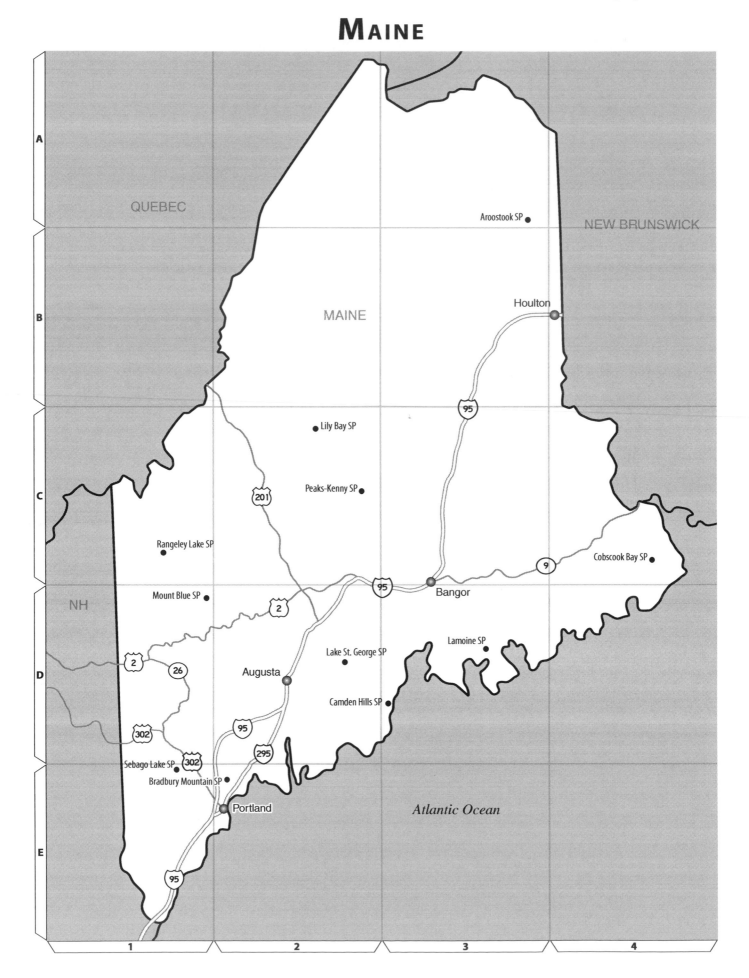

QUEBEC

NEW BRUNSWICK

MAINE

Aroostook SP ●

Houlton ⊙

95

Lily Bay SP ●

Peaks-Kenny SP ●

201

Rangeley Lake SP ●

Cobscook Bay SP ●

9

NH

Mount Blue SP ●

2

95

Bangor ⊙

Lamoine SP ●

2

26

Lake St. George SP ●

Augusta ⊙

302

Camden Hills SP ●

95

Sebago Lake SP ● 302

295

Bradbury Mountain SP ●

Portland ⊙

Atlantic Ocean

95

1   2   3   4

A   B   C   D   E

Maine

Of Maine's 32 state parks, 11 offer RV sites. All campgrounds have potable water but there are no hook-ups at the campsites; neither water or electricity. Only one of the listed parks, Bradbury Mountain, is open all year. The season for the other parks varies from May 1 through October 1, depending upon the park. You should call the particular park to verify opening, space availability and size limitation. Maine does not charge a day-use fee in addition to the site fee. Reservation requests require a 48-hour advance notice. Visa, MasterCard and Discover cards are accepted. There are no rig size limitations. Rate groups: A and B, depending on site facilities. Non-resident fees are higher.

Maine Bureau of Parks & Lands
22 State House Station
Augusta, ME 04333

Information: (207) 287-3821
Reservations: (207) 624-9950 (M-F) out of state; (800)
332-1501 in state
Internet: www.maine.gov/doc/parks
Reservations: www.CampWithMe.com

Maine Park Locator

Maine Parks

Aroostook State Park

87 State Park Rd, Presque Isle, ME 04769. Phone: (207) 768-8341. Located off US 1 near Presque Isle (northeast tip of state). 30 sites; showers. Swimming; boat rentals. No alcohol. GPS: N 46-36.9 W 68-00.4

Bradbury Mountain State Park

528 Hallowell Rd, Pownal, ME 04069. Phone: (207) 688-4712. Located off ME 9, at I-95 (Freeport) exit 35. 31 sites. Horse trails. GPS: N 43-53.9 W 70-10.8

Camden Hills State Park

280 Belfast Rd, Camden, ME 04843. Phone: (207) 236-3109. (Off season: 207-236-5849.) Located 2 miles N of Camden on the Atlantic Coast on US 1. 107 sites; showers; dump station. Horse trails. GPS: N 44-13.9 W 69-02.8

Cobscook Bay State Park

40 S. Edmunds Rd, Edmunds Twp, ME 04628. Phone: (207) 726-4412. Located on US 1, 4 miles S of Dennysville. 106 sites; showers; dump station. Boat rentals, ramp. GPS: N 44-51.3 W 67-10.3

Lake St. George State Park

278 Belfast-Agusta Rd, Liberty, ME 04949. Phone: (207) 589-4255. Located on ME 3 between Augusta (20 miles) and Belfast on Lake St. George. 38 sites; showers; dump station. Fishing, swimming; boat ramp, rentals. GPS: N 44-23.9 W 69-20.8

Lamoine State Park

23 State Park Rd, Lamoine, ME 04605. Phone: (207) 667-4778. (Off season: 207-941-4014.) Located on ME 184, off US 1 between Ellsworth and Bar Harbor on the Atlantic Coast. 61 sites; showers. Fishing; boat ramp. GPS: N 44-27.4 W 68-17.9

Lily Bay State Park

13 Myrle's Way, Greenville, ME 04441. Phone: (207) 695-2700. (Off season: 207-941-4014.) Located on Moosehead Lake off Lily Bay Rd, off ME 6 & 15; 9 miles NE of Greenville. 65 sites; dump station. Fishing, swimming; boat ramp. GPS: N 45-34.7 W 69-31.5

Mount Blue State Park

299 Center Hill Rd, Weld, ME 04285. Phone: (207) 585-2347. (Off season: 207-585-2261.) Located on ME 156, off US 2 at Farmington. 136 sites; showers; dump station. Horse trails. Fishing, swimming; boat ramp; canoe rentals. GPS: N 44-43.6 W 70-25.0

Peaks-Kenny State Park

401 State Park Rd, Dover-Foxcroft, ME 04426. Phone: (207) 564-2003. (Off season: 207-941-4014.) Located on ME 153 at Sebec Lake. 56 sites; showers; dump station. Fishing, swimming; boat ramp, rentals. GPS: N 45-15.4 W 69-15.3

Rangeley Lake State Park

HC 32 Box 5000, Rangeley, ME 04970. Phone: (207) 864-3858. (Off season: 207-624-6080.) Located on Rangeley Lake, 30 miles NW of Rumford (US 2 & ME 17). 50 sites; showers; dump station. Fishing, swimming; boat ramp, rentals. GPS: N 44-55.2 W 70-41.8

Sebago Lake State Park

11 Park Access Rd, Casco, ME 04055. Phone: (207) 693-6613. (Off season: 207-963-6231.) Located on Sebago Lake on US 302, 30 miles NE of Portland. 250 sites; showers; dump station. Fishing, swimming; boat ramp. GPS: N 43-56.0 W 70-34.2

MARYLAND

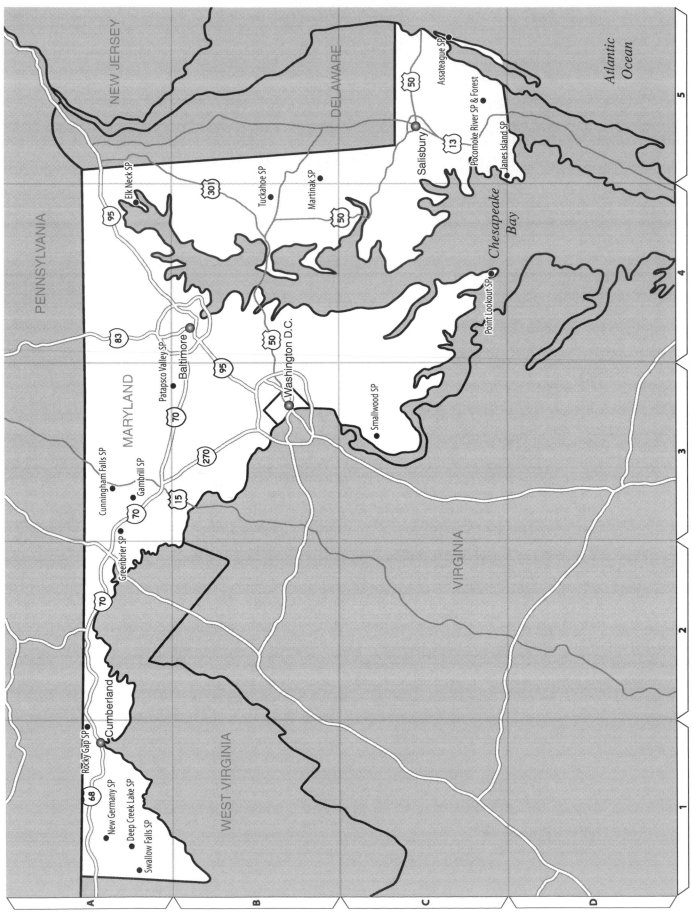

Maryland

Sixteen of Maryland's 58 state parks have RV facilities. Most feature sites with electric hook-ups but few have water at the site. However, all the parks have drinking water available and you can fill holding tanks. All of the parks have reservable sites but several hold some spaces for a "first-come" basis. You can verify availability by calling the particular park. Most of the parks are open for camping seasonally. Some parks offer senior (62+) discounts Sunday through Thursday but you must ask at check-in. Rate Groups: B, C+, depending on site facilities.

Maryland Department of Natural Resources
State Forest & Park Service
580 Taylor Ave., E-3
Annapolis, MD 21401

Information: (877) 620-8367 (in state) or
(410) 260-8367
Reservations: (888) 432-2267
Internet: dnr.state.md.us/publiclands
Internet reservations: reservations.dnr.state.md.us

Maryland Park Locator

Maryland Parks

Assateague State Park

6915 Stephan Decauter Hwy, Berlin, MD, 21811. Phone: (410) 641-2918. Located on Assateague Island on the Atlantic Ocean (only Maryland oceanfront park), about 9 miles S of Ocean City, via US 50 and MD 611. 350 sites some electric; showers; dump station. Store. Swimming, fishing; boat ramp, rentals. GPS: N 38-14.3 W 75-08.4

Cunningham Falls State Park

14038 Catoctin Hollow Rd, Thrumont, MD 21788. Phone: (301) 271-7574. Located 18 miles N of Frederick on US 15. (Two areas.) 140 sites, 33 with with electric; showers; dump station. Store. Swimming, fishing; boat ramp, rentals; horse trails. GPS: N 39-37.5 W 77-27.6

Deep Creek Lake State Park

898 State Park Rd, Swanton, MD 21561. Phone: (301) 387-5563. Located 10 miles NE of Oakland on Deep Creek Lake, off US 219. (Four areas); 112 sites, 26 with electric; showers; dump station. (Narrow roadways, limited sites for units larger than 30'.) Swimming, fishing; boat ramp. GPS: N 39-30.9 W 79-16.6

Elk Neck State Park

4395 Turkey Point Rd, North East, MD 21901. Phone: (410) 287-5333. Located 9 miles SW of North East (US 40) on MD 272. 268 sites, many with full hook-ups; showers; dump station. (Some camping areas prohibit pets.) Store. Swimming, fishing; boat ramp. No alcohol. GPS: N 39-28.8 W 75-59.0

Gambrill State Park

8602 Gambrill Park Rd, Frederick, MD 21702. Phone: (301) 271-7574. Located 6 miles NW of Frederick off I-70 exit 48. 34 sites; showers; dump station. Fishing. Horse trails. GPS: N 39-28.1 W 77-29.7

Greenbrier State Park

21843 National Pike, Boonsboro, MD 21713. Phone: (301) 791-4767. Located 10 miles SE of Hagerstown on US 40. 165 sites, 40 with electric; showers; dump station. Fishing, swimming; boat ramp, rentals. GPS: N 39-32.5 W 77-36.5

Janes Island State Park

26280 Alfred Lakson Dr, Crisfield, MD 21817. Phone: (410) 968-1565. Located on Chesapeake Bay near Crisfield, off MD 413. 104 sites, 49 with electric; showers; dump station. Store. Fishing, swimming; boat ramp, rentals. GPS: N 38-00.4 W 75-50.2

Martinak State Park

137 Deep Shore Rd, Denton, MD 21629. Phone: (410) 820-1668. Located on east shore of Chesapeake Bay, 2 miles E of Denton, off MD 404, on Deep Shore Rd. 63 sites, 30 with electric; showers; dump station. Fishing; boat ramp. GPS: N 38-52-0 W 75-49.4

New Germany State Park

349 Headquarters Ln, Grantsville, MD 21536. Phone: (301) 895-5453. Located 5 miles S of Grantsville off I-68 exit 22. 39 sites; showers; dump station. Swimming, fishing, boat ramp, rentals. (No gas motors). GPS: N 39-38.1 W 79-07.5

Patapsco Valley State Park

8020 Baltimore National Pike, Ellicott City, MD 21043. Phone: (410) 461-5005. Five areas, located W of Baltimore along Patapsco River off I-70 exit 83. 73 sites, some with electric; showers; dump station. Fishing. Some pet restrictions in campgrounds. Call park for campground locations, information. Fishing, swimming; horse trails. GPS: N 39-17.8 W 76-47.1

Pocomoke River State Park and Forest

3461 Worcester Hwy, Snow Hill, MD 21863. Phone: (410) 632-2566. Two areas (Shad Landing and Milburn Landing) located SW of Snow Hill on Pocomoke River, on MD 364, off US 113. 207 sites, (two areas) some with electric; showers; dump station. Store. Fishing, swimming; boat ramp, rentals. Call park for campground locations and site directions. GPS: N 38-07.7 W 75-26.4

Point Lookout State Park

11175 Point Lookout Rd, Scotland, MD 20687. Phone: (301) 872-5688. Located SE of St. Mary's City on MD 5 where the Potomac River meets Chesapeake Bay. 143 sites; 26 with full hook-ups, 33 with electric; showers; dump station. Store. Swimming, fishing; boat ramp, rentals. GPS: N 38-03.9 W 76-20.2

Rocky Gap State Park Lodge & Golf Resort

12900 Lakeshore Dr, Flintstone, MD 21530. Phone: (301) 722-1480. Located 7 miles NE of Cumberland off I-68 exit 50. 278 sites, 30 with electric; showers; dump station. Fishing; boat ramp, rentals. (Electric motors). GPS: N 39-41.9 W 78-39.1

Smallwood State Park

2750 Sweden Point Rd, Marbury, MD 20640. Phone: (301) 743-7613. Located W of St. Charles off MD 224, near Potomac River. 15 sites with electric; showers. Marina. Fishing. GPS: N 38-33.2 W 77-11.0

Swallow Falls State Park

2470 Maple Glade Rd, Oakland, MD 21550. Phone: (301) 387-6938. Located near West Virginia state line, NW of Oakland on Swallow Falls Rd (follow signs from Oakland). 65 sites with electric; showers; dump station. GPS: N 39-30.4 W 79-26.9

Tuckahoe State Park

13070 Crouse Mill Rd, Queen Anne, MD 21657. Phone: (410) 820-1688. Located 6 miles N of Queen Anne (west of Denton) off MD 404 via MD 480. 54 sites, 33 with electric; showers; dump station. Fishing; boat ramp, rentals. (Electric motors.) GPS: N 38-58.0 W 75-56.6

MASSACHUSETTS

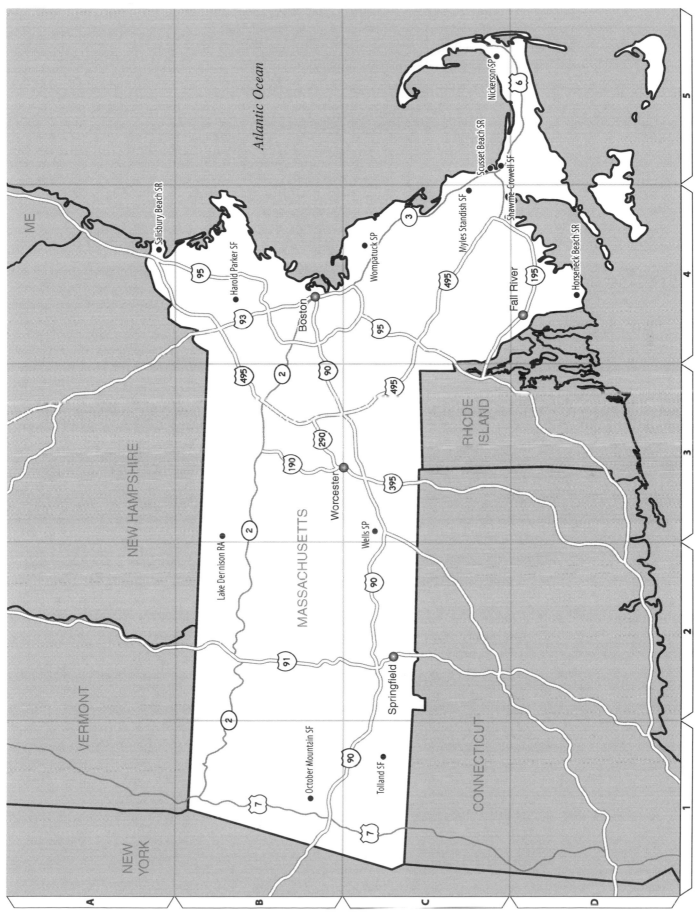

Massachusetts

The Bay State has 13 state parks or recreation areas with RV sites; most do not have in-site facilities. Alcoholic beverages are not permitted on state lands. Pets on leashes are permitted; pets must have current rabies vaccination. Most of the facilities are seasonal and heavily used in summer months. It is advisable to call the particular park to check conditions, facilities and availability. Reservations require a 48-hour lead time. No camping discounts. Rig limits are not a problem. Rate groups: A and B. (Reservation fee extra.)

Department of Conservation & Recreation
Division of State Parks & Recreation
251 Causeway St., Ste 600
Boston, MA 02114

Information: (617) 626-1250
Reservations: (877) 422-6762
Internet: www.massparks.org
Reservations: www.ReserveAmerica.com

Massachusetts Park Locator

Massachusetts Parks

Harold Parker State Forest

133 Jenkins Rd, North Andover, MA. 01810. Phone: (978) 686-3391. Located on MA 114 between I-95 & 495, north of Boston. 89 sites; showers; dump station. Swimming, fishing. (No motor boats.) Horse trails. GPS: N 42-37.2 W 71-04.9

Horseneck Beach State Reservation

5 John Reed Rd, Westport Point, MA 02791. Phone: (508) 636-8816. Located in SE Massachusetts, at south end of MA 88, S of Fall River (I-195) on Rhode Island Sound. 100 sites; showers; dump station. Swimming, fishing; boat ramp. GPS: N 41-30.4 W 71-03.3

Lake Dennison Recreation Area

219 Baldwinville State Rd, Winchendon, MA 01475. Phone: (978)297-1609. Located N of Baldwinville off MA 2 & US 202 near Otter River State Forest. 150 sites; showers; dump station. Swimming, fishing; boat ramp. Horse trails. GPS: N 42-37.3 W 72-01.7

Myles Standish State Forest

194 Cranberry Rd S, Carver, MA 02366. Phone: (508) 866-2526. Located between MA 3 exit 5 & I-495 exit 2, SW of Plymouth off MA 58. 475 sites in five areas on four ponds; showers; dump station. Equestrian camping, trails. Swimming, fishing; boat ramp. GPS: N 41-53.4 W 70-37.9

Nickerson State Park

Route 6A, (Main Street), Brewster, MA 02631. Phone: (508) 896-3491. Located at east end of Cape Cod on MA 6A, E of Brewster. 420 sites; showers; dump station. Fishing and swimming ponds; boat ramp (no motors). GPS: N 41-56.5 W 70-01.9

October Mountain State Forest

317 Woodland Rd, Lee, MA 01238. Phone: (413) 243-1778. Located N of Stockbridge (I-90 exit 2) to US 20 west, follow signs. 36 sites; showers; dump station. 34-foot limit. ATV area. Fishing; boat ramp (no motors). GPS: N 42-20.9 W 73-14.3

Salisbury Beach State Reservation

Beach Rd Rt 1A, Salisbury, MA 01952. Phone: (978) 462-4481. Located in far northeastern MA on the Atlantic Ocean, off I-95 exit 58A to US 1 & MA 110. 484 sites, 324 with electric; showers; dump station. Swimming, fishing; boat ramp. GPS: N 42-49.8 W 70-49.1

Scusset Beach State Reservation

20 Scusset Beach Rd, Sandwich, MA 02562. Phone: (508) 888-0859. Located on the Atlantic Ocean, SE of Plymouth off MA 3 at Sagamore Bridge. 98 sites with electric; showers; dump station. Swimming, fishing. GPS: N 41-47.6 W 70-31.0

Shawme-Crowell State Forest

42 Main St, Sandwich, MA 02563. Phone: (508) 888-0351. Located on Cape Cod, off US 6 exit 2 (MA 130), follow signs. 285 sites; showers; dump station. Swimming. Horse trails. GPS: N 41-46.2 W 70-29.2

Tolland State Forest

410 Tolland Rd, Otis, MA 01253. Phone: (413) 269-6002. Located on Otis Reservoir, S of I-90 between exits 2 & 3, in southwestern MA off MA 23 or MA 8; follow signs. 93 sites; showers; dump station. Swimming, fishing; boat ramp. ATV area. GPS: N 42-07.3 W 73-00.9

Wells State Park

159 Walker Pond Rd, Sturbridge, MA 01379. Phone: (508) 347-9257. Located on MA 49 just N of I-90 exit 9 and Sturbridge Village; follow signs from MA 49 & US 20 junction. 60 sites; showers; dump station. Swimming beach. Fishing; boat ramp. Horse trails. GPS: N 42-08.5 W 72-02.5

Wompatuck State Park

204 Union St, Hingham, MA 02043. Phone: (781) 749-7160. Located SE of Boston off I-93 and MA 228. 262 sites, 140 with electric; showers; dump station. Fishing (car top boats only, no motors). Horse trails. GPS: N 42-13.7 W 70-52.6

MICHIGAN

ONTARIO

Lake Superior

Fort Wilkins Historic SP

McLain SP

Porcupine Mountains Wilderness SP

Twin Lakes SP

Baraga SP

Muskallonge Lake SP

Van Riper SP

Marquette

Tahquamenon Falls SP

Sault Ste. Marie

Lake Gogebic SP

(28)

(2)

Bewabic SP

(41)

(28)

Brimley SP

Indian Lake SP

(2)

Straits SP

Wilderness SP

Cheboygan SP

Fayette Historic SP

Aloha SP

P.H. Hoeft SP

Burt Lake SP

Onaway SP

J.W. Wells SP

Petoskey SP

Fisherman's Island SP

Clear Lake SP

Leelanau SP

Young SP

(75)

WISCONSIN

Otsego Lake SP

Keith J. Charters Traverse City SP

Lake Huron

Harrisville SP

Interlochen SP

Hartwick Pines SP

(31)

North Higgins Lake SP

Orchard Beach SP

South Higgins Lake SP

Rifle River RA

William Mitchell SP

Tawas Point SP

Ludington SP

Wilson SP

(75)

Albert E. Sleeper SP

Port Crescent SP

Charles Mears SP

(10)

Silver Lake SP

(131)

Bay City RA

(31)

Newaygo SP

MICHIGAN

Muskegon SP

(127)

Lakeport SP

P.J. Hoffmaster SP

(75)

Metamora-Hadley RA

Grand Haven SP

Grand Rapids

Sleepy Hollow SP

Flint

(69)

Lake Michigan

Ionia RA

Seven Lakes SP

Holly RA

(94)

Holland SP

Lansing

Pontiac Lake RA

Algonac SP

(96)

Highland RA

Proud Lake RA

Yankee Springs RA

Detroit

(196)

Pinckney RA

Brighton RA

Van Buren SP

Fort Custer RA

Waterloo RA

(94)

(94)

Walter J. Hayes SP

Warren Dunes SP

(131)

(69)

(12)

Sterling SP

Lake Hudson RA

ILLINOIS

INDIANA

OHIO

Michigan

Michigan offers the traveling RVer 69 state parks or recreation areas with facilities. While most of these locations have electric hook-ups, showers and dump stations, three parks (Holland, Hartwick Pines and Sterling state parks) have full hook-up facilities. Michigan has a unique definition method to classify its parks and area sites:

F - Full Hookup Camping: electric, (20, 30 or 50 amp), water, sewer at site
M - Modern Campground: electric; showers and dump station
R - Rustic Campground: primitive sites, no showers, water is by hand pump
Se - Semi-modern Campground: electric; no showers

Pets on leashes are permitted in all locations. Alcoholic beverages are prohibited in some parks, as listed. If in doubt you should call the destination park. Some parks/areas have reservable sites, others accept reservations directly at the park. Nearly all the parks host an annual Harvest Festival sometime in the Autumn months. These events usually fill the respective park so you will need to call ahead to check if you're a Fall traveler. All parks require an admission fee in addition to the camping charges. *Note*: Some park campgrounds are open in the winter but shut off water service; these locations change (rotate) each year. You have to call the particular park. Plowing in these parks is "iffy." Rate groups: A, B and C depending on site facilities and park (see each park listing for rate groups). Advance reservation fees are extra.

Michigan Dept. of Natural Resources
Parks and Recreation
Box 30257
Lansing, MI 48909

Information: (517) 373-9900
Reservations: (800) 447-2757
Internet: www.michigan.gov/dnr

Michigan Park Locator

Michigan Parks

Albert E. Sleeper State Park

6573 State Park Rd, Caseville, MI 48725. Phone: (989) 856-4411. Remote location in eastern MI at the mouth of Saginaw Bay on Lake Huron; 5 miles E of Caseville and 55 miles E of I-75 exit 161 (Bay City). 226 M sites. Group B. Swimming. Wi-Fi. GPS: N 43-58.4 W 83-12.3

Algonac State Park

8732 River Rd, Marine City, MI 48039. Phone: (810) 765-5605. Located NE of Detroit, on St. Clair River, 22 miles from I-94 exit 243; follow signs. 220 M sites (50 amp). Groups A & C. Fishing. GPS: N 42-39.3 W 82-30.9

Aloha State Park

4347 Third St, Cheboygan, MI 49721. Phone: (231) 625-2522. Located in northern MI on Mullett Lake, 5 miles S of Cheboygan on MI 33. 285 M sites. Groups A & C. Swimming, fishing; boat ramp. GPS: N 45-31.5 W 84-27.8

Baraga State Park

1300 US 41 S, Baraga, MI 49908. Phone: (906) 353-6558. Located 1/2 mile S of Baraga on US 41. 116 M and 10 Se sites. Group A. Fishing, swimming. Wi-Fi. GPS: N 46-45.3 W 88-29.9

Bay City Recreation Area

3582 State Park Dr, Bay City, MI 48706. Phone: (989) 684-3020. Located in east-central MI on Lake Huron, outside Bay City, 5 miles E of I-75 exit 168. 193 M sites. Group B. No alcohol. Swimming, fishing. GPS: N 43-40.0 W 83-54.6

Bewabic State Park

720 Idlewild Rd, Crystal Falls, MI 49920. Phone: (906) 875-3324. Located on southern edge of Peninsula, next to WI state line, 4 miles W of Crystal Falls on US 2. 133 M and 4 Se sites. Swimming, fishing; boat ramp. Groups A & B. GPS: N 46-05.7 W 88-25.4

Brighton Recreation Area

6360 Chilson Rd, Howell, MI 48843. Phone: (810) 229-6566. Located in southeastern MI, 4 miles W of Brighton, off I-96 exit 147; follow signs from Brighton. 163 M, 50 R 25 rustic sites. Groups A & C. No alcohol. Equestrian area; 19 sites. Swimming, fishing; boat ramp, canoe/kayak rentals. GPS: N 42-30.5 W 83-51.5

Brimley State Park

9200 W 6 Mile Rd, Brimley, MI 49715. Phone: (906) 248-3422. Located in eastern portion of Peninsula near Canadian border, SW of Sault Ste. Marie on Whitefish Bay; I-75 exit 386 to MI 28, W 7 miles, follow signs. 237 M and some semi-modern sites. Swimming, fishing. Groups A & B. GPS: N 46-24.8 W 84-33.3

Burt Lake State Park

6635 State Park Dr, Indian River, MI 49749. Phone: (231) 238-9392. Located in northern MI just W of I-75 exit 310; on Burt Lake. 306 M sites. Groups A & C. Swimming, fishing; boat ramp. GPS: N 45-24.1 W 84-37.2

Charles Mears State Park

400 W Lowell St, Pentwater, MI 49449. Phone: (231) 869-2051. Located in western MI, 12 miles S of Ludington off US 31, on Lake Michigan. 175 M sites. Group C. Wi-Fi. Swimming, fishing. GPS: N 43-48.4 W 86-25.4

Cheboygan State Park

4490 Beach Rd, Cheboygan, MI 49721. Phone: (231) 627-2811. Located at northern tip of peninsula on Lake Huron, 18 miles NE of I-75 exit 326, via CR 66; follow signs. 76 M sites. Groups A & B. Swimming, fishing; boat ramp. GPS: N 45-38.7 W 84-25.2

Clear Lake State Park

20500 MI 33 N, Atlanta, MI 49709. Phone: (989) 785-4388. Located in northern MI on Clear Lake, 10 miles N of Atlanta, 20 miles E of I-75 exit 290 (Vanderbilt) via county road. 200 M sites. Group B. Swimming, fishing; boat ramp. GPS: N 45-07.6 W 84-10.4

Fayette Historic State Park

4785 11 Rd, Garden, MI 49835. Phone: (906) 644-2603. Located in southern portion of Peninsula on Lake Michigan, 18 miles S of Garden Corners (US 2) on MI 183. 61 Se sites. Swimming, fishing; boat ramp. Group A. GPS: N 45-43.1 W 86-39.9

Fisherman's Island State Park

Bell's Bay Rd, Charlevoix, MI 49720. Phone: (231) 547-6641. Located in northwestern MI at mouth of Grand Traverse Bay on Lake Michigan, on US 31, SW of Petoskey. 81 R sites. Group A. Swimming. GPS: N 45-18.1 W 85-18.3

Fort Custer Recreation Area

5163 Fort Custer Dr, Augusta, MI 49012. Phone: (269) 731-4200. Located in southwestern MI on Eagle Lake, 16 miles E of Kalamazoo, on MI 96, off I-94 exit 92. Three lakes in park. 219 M sites. Group B. No alcohol. Horse trails. Swimming, fishing; boat ramp. Store. GPS: N 42-19.7 W 85-20.9

Fort Wilkins Historic State Park

15223 US 41, Copper Harbor, MI 49918. Phone: (906) 289-4215. Located in far northern tip of Peninsula, at end of US 41, outside Copper Harbor; on Lake Superior. 159 M sites. (Some with 50-amp service.) Groups A, B & C. Swimming, fishing; boat ramp. GPS: N 47-26.6 W 87-45.5

Grand Haven State Park

1001 Harbor Ave, Grand Haven, MI 49417. (616) 847-1309. Located in southwestern MI just S of Grand Haven on US 31, on Lake Michigan. 174 M sites. (Some 50-amp.) Groups A & C. Wi-Fi. No alcohol. Swimming, fishing. GPS: N 43-03.4 W 86-14.8

Harrisville State Park

248 State Park Rd, Harrisville, MI 48740. Phone: (989) 724-5126. Located in northeastern MI in Harrisville on US 23, on Lake Huron. 195 M sites. Group C. Swimming. GPS: N 44-38.9 W 83-17.8

Hartwick Pines State Park

4216 Ranger Rd, Grayling, MI 49738. Phone: (989) 348-7068. Located in north-central MI, north of Grayling off I-75 exit 259. 100 sites, some full hook-up, some M. Groups B & C. Fishing. GPS: N 44-45.0 W 84-41.3

Highland Recreation Area

5200 Highland Rd, White Lake, MI 48383. Phone: (248) 889-3750. Located NW of Detroit, 12 miles E of US 23 on MI 59 (Highland Rd) on Teeple Lake. 25 R sites. Group A. Equestrian area. Swimming, fishing; boat ramp. GPS: N 42-39.3 W 83-34.2

Holland State Park

2215 Ottawa Beach Rd, Holland, MI 49424. Phone: (616) 399-9390. Located in western MI, 7 miles NW of Holland, off US 31; follow signs. 309 sites; some full hook-up, some M. (Two areas on water.) No alcohol. Group C. Wi-Fi. Swimming, fishing; boat ramp. GPS: N 42-46.7 W 86-12.0

Holly Recreation Area

8100 Grange Hall Rd, Holly, MI 48442. Phone: (248) 634-8811. Located in southeastern MI on Heron Lake, 14 miles SE of Flint, near I-75 exit 101; follow signs. 144 M and 15 Se sites. No alcohol. Group B. Swimming, fishing; boat ramp, boat/canoe/kayak rentals. GPS: N 42-50.8 W 83-34.2

Indian Lake State Park

8970 W CR 442, Manistique, MI 49854. Phone: (906) 341-2355. Located in southern portion of Peninsula, W of Manistique via US 2, MI 149 and CR 442. 145 M and 72 Se sites. Groups A & B. Swimming, fishing; boat ramp, rentals. GPS: N 45-57.1 W 86-17.5

Interlochen State Park

4167 MI 37, Interlochen, MI 49643. Phone: (231) 276-9511. Located in northwestern MI, between two lakes, 15 miles SW of Traverse City on MI 137, via US 31. 59 R and 421 M sites. Groups A & B. Swimming, fishing; boat ramp. GPS: N 44-37.7 W 85-45.9

Ionia State Recreation Area

2880 W David Hwy, Ionia, MI 48846. Phone: (616) 527-3750. Located in west-central MI on Sessions Lake 28 miles E of Grand Rapids, N of I-96 exit 67 and MI 66; follow signs. 100 M and 49 R sites. Group B. Equestrian area. Swimming, fishing; boat ramp. GPS: N 42-55.8 W 85-07.9

J.W. Wells State Park

N 7670 MI 35, Cedar River, MI 49887. Phone: (906) 863-9747. Located in southwestern portion of Peninsula, 30 miles SW of Escanaba on MI 35, on Lake Michigan. 150 M sites. Group B. Swimming, fishing. GPS: N 45-25.2 W 87-22.0

Keith J. Charters Traverse City State Park

1132 US 31N, Traverse City, MI 49686. Phone: (231) 922-5270. Located in northwestern MI, 3 miles E of Traverse City, off US 31, at south end of Grand Traverse Bay. 343 M sites. Group C. Wi-Fi. Swimming, fishing; boat rentals. GPS: N 44-44.9 W 85-33.2

Lake Gogebic State Park

N 9995 MI 64, Marenisco, MI 49947. Phone: (906) 842-3341. Located in western portion of Peninsula, S of Merriweather, on MI 64 between US 2 and MI 28. 105 M and 22 Se sites. Groups A & B. Swimming, fishing; boat ramp. GPS: N 46-28.1 W 89-35.9

Lake Hudson Recreation Area

5505 Morey Hwy, Clayton, MI 49235. Phone: (517) 445-2265. Located in southeastern MI, 8 miles E of Hudson, off MI 34 on MI 156. 50 Se sites. Group A. Swimming, fishing; boat ramp. GPS: N 41-59.1 W 84-14.1

Lakeport State Park

7605 Lakeshore Rd, Lakeport, MI 48059. Phone: (810) 327-6224. Located in eastern MI, 13 miles N of Port Huron on MI 25, on Lake Huron. 250 M sites in two areas. Group B. Swimming. GPS: N 43-07.8 W 82-29.8

Leelanau State Park

15310 N Lighthouse Point Rd, Northport, MI 49670. Phone: (231) 386-5422. Located in northwestern MI at end of MI 201 on Lake Michigan, N of Traverse City. 52 R sites. Group A. Swimming. GPS; N 45-12.5 W 85-32.7

Ludington State Park

8800 W. M-116, Ludington, MI 49431. Phone: (231) 843-2423. Located 8 miles N of Ludington (US 10/31) on Hamlin Lake. 344 M sites (in two areas); 10 R sites. Groups A & C. Wi-Fi. Swimming, fishing; boat ramp, canoe/kayak rentals. GPS: N 44-01.0 W 86-28.2

McLain State Park

18350 Hwy M-203, Hancock, MI 49930. Phone: (906) 482-0278. Located on northwestern arm of Peninsula on Lake Superior, N of Houghton, off US 41, 9 miles N on MI 203. 98 M sites. Group A & C. Swimming, fishing. No alcohol. GPS: N 47-14.4 W 88-35.2

Metamora-Hadley Recreation Area

3871 Herd Rd, Metamora, MI 48455. Phone: (810) 797-4439. Located N of Detroit off I-69 exit 155, off MI 24 on Lake Minnewanna; follow signs. 214 M sites (50 amp). No alcohol. Groups A & C. Swimming, fishing; boat ramp, canoe/kayak rentals. GPS: N 43-56.7 W 83-21.5

Muskallonge Lake State Park

30042 CR 407, Newberry, MI 49868. Phone: (906) 658-3338. Located 28 miles N of Newberry via MI 123 and CR 407. 159 M sites. Group

A. Swimming, fishing; boat ramp. GPS: N 46-40.7 W 85-38.0

Muskegon State Park

3560 Memorial Dr, Muskegon, MI 49445. Phone: (231) 744-3480. Located in western MI on Lake Michigan, off US 31, 4 miles N of Muskegon; follow signs. 244 M sites. Group C. No alcohol. Swimming, fishing; boat ramp. GPS: N 43-14.9 W 86-20.5

Newaygo State Park

2793 Beech St, Newaygo, MI 49337. Phone: (231) 856-4452. Located in west-central MI south of Big Rapids, off US 131 exit 125; follow signs. 99 R sites. Group A. Swimming, fishing; boat ramp. GPS: N 43-30.1 W 85-34.9

North Higgins Lake State Park

11747 N Higgins Lake Dr, Roscommon, MI. Phone: (989) 821-6125. Located in north-central MI between US 27 and I-75 exit 244 on Higgins Lake. 174 M sites. Groups B & C. Swimming, fishing; boat ramp. GPS: N 44-30.9 W 84-44.1

Onaway State Park

3622 N MI 211, Onaway, MI 49765. Phone: (989) 733-8279. Remote location in northern MI, 6 miles N of Onaway on MI 211, on Black Lake. 96 M sites. Groups A & B. Swimming, fishing; boat ramp. GPS: N 45-25.8 W 84-13.7

Orchard Beach State Park

2064 N Lakeshore Rd, Manistee, MI 49660. Phone: (231) 723-7422. Located in northwestern MI off US 31 and MI 110, 4 miles N of Manistee, on Lake Michigan. 166 M sites. Groups A & C. Swimming; boat ramp. GPS: N 44-16.7 W 86-18.9

Otsego Lake State Park

7136 Old 27 S, Gaylord, MI 49735. Phone: (989) 732-5485. Located in north-central MI on Old MI 27, off I-75 exit 270, N of Waters. 155 M sites. Groups A & C. Swimming, fishing; boat ramp. GPS: N 44-55.7 W 84-41.3

P.H. Hoeft State Park

5001 US 23 N, Rogers City, MI 49779. Phone: (989) 734-2543. Located in northern MI on Lake Huron, 5 miles NW of Rogers City on US 23. 144 M sites. Group B. Swimming, fishing. GPS: N 45-27.9 W 83-53.2

P.J. Hoffmaster State Park

6585 Lake Harbor Rd, Muskegon, MI 49441. Phone: (231) 798-3711. Located in western MI on Lake Michigan, 10 miles S of Muskegon on US 31; off I-96 exit 4, follow signs. 293 M sites. No alcohol. Group C. Swimming. GPS: N 43-06.9 W 86-15.3

Petoskey State Park

2475 MI 119 Hwy, Petoskey, MI 49712. Phone: (231) 347-2311. Located in northwestern MI on MI 119, off US 31, 1.5 miles N of Petoskey. 178 M sites. Groups A & C. Swimming. GPS: N 45-23.6 W 84-54.4

Pinckney Recreation Area

8555 Silver Hill Rd, Pinckney, MI 48169. Phone: (734) 426-4913. Located in southeastern MI, northwest of Ann Arbor, 11 miles W of US 23 exit 49; follow signs. On three lakes. 186 M and 35 R sites.

No alcohol. Swimming, fishing; boat ramp, canoe/kayak rentals. Equestrian area. GPS: N 42-24.5 W 83-57.8

Pontiac Lake Recreation Area

7800 Gale Rd, Waterford, MI 48327. Phone: (248) 666-1020. Located NW of Greater Detroit, W of Pontiac, off I-75 at MI 59, W 12 miles. 176 M sites. Groups A & B. No alcohol. 24 site equestrian area. Swimming, fishing; boat ramp. GPS: N 42-40.4 W 83-26.4

Porcupine Mountains Wilderness State Park

33303 Headquarters Rd, Ontonagon, MI 49953. Phone: (906) 885-5275. Located 15 miles W of Ontonagon via MI 64 and MI 107. 100 M and 63 R sites. Groups A & C. Swimming, fishing; boat ramp. Canoe/kayak rentals. GPS: N 46-49.5 W 89-43.5

Port Crescent State Park

1775 Port Austin Rd, Port Austin, MI 48467. Phone: (989) 738-8663. Remote location in eastern MI on Lake Huron near Saginaw Bay, 5 miles SW of Port Austin on MI 25. 142 M sites. Group C. Swimming, fishing. GPS: N 44-00.5 W 83-03.1

Proud Lake Recreation Area

3500 Wixom Rd, Commerce Township, MI 48382. Phone: (248) 685-2433. Located in southeastern MI, 7 miles N of I-96 exit 159. 130 M sites. Group B. No alcohol. Fishing; boat ramp, canoe/kayak rentals. Horse trails. GPS: N 42-34.7 W 83-33.6

Rifle River Recreation Area

2550 E Rose City Rd, Lupton, MI 48635. Phone: (989) 473-2258. Located in northeastern MI, 4.5 miles E of Rose City, off MI 33, 20 miles N of I-75 exit 202; on Jewett Lake. 75 M and 83 R sites. Groups A & B. Swimming, fishing; boat ramp. GPS: N 44-25.3 W 84-01.4

Seven Lakes State Park

14390 Fish Lake Rd, Holly, MI 48442. Phone: (248) 634-7271. Located S of Flint in southeastern MI about 5 miles W of I-75 exit 101. 70 M sites. Group B. No alcohol. Swimming, fishing; boat ramp. GPS: N 42-49.0 W 83-38.9

Silver Lake State Park

9679 W State Park Rd, Mears, MI 48436. Phone: (231) 873-3083. Located in western MI on Lake Michigan, off US 31 at Shelby or Hart exits; follow signs. 200 M sites. Groups A & C. No alcohol. Off-road area. Swimming, fishing; boat ramp. GPS: N 43-40.6 W 86-29.8

Sleepy Hollow State Park

7835 E Price Rd, Laingsburg, MI 48848. Phone: (517) 651-6217. Located in south-central MI, 5.5 miles E of US 27, Price Rd exit. 181 M sites. Group B. Swimming, fishing; boat ramp. Horse trails. GPS: N 42-55.5 W 84-24.5

South Higgins Lake State Park

106 State Park Dr, Roscommon, MI 48653. Phone: (989) 821-6374. Located in north-central MI south of Roscommon on CR 100, off I-75 exit 239 and MI 18. 400 M sites. Group C. Swimming, fishing; boat ramp, boat/canoe rentals. GPS: N 44-25.6 W 84-04.3

Sterling State Park

2800 State Park Rd, Monroe, MI 48162. Phone: (734) 289-2715.

Located on Lake Erie in southeastern MI, 3 miles NE of Monroe, off I-75 exit 15. 256 sites; some full hook-up, M sites. Groups B & C. No alcohol. Swimming, fishing; boat ramp. GPS: N 44-55.3 W 83-20.6

Straits State Park

720 Church St, St. Ignace, MI 49781. Phone: (906) 643-8620. Located at southern tip of Peninsula, off I-75 exit 344 (N of Mackinac Bridge) off US 2. 255 M and 15 Se sites. Group A & C. Swimming. GPS: N 45-51.5 W 84-43.2

Tahquamenon Falls State Park

41382 W MI 173, Paradise, MI 49768. Phone: (906) 492-3415. Located in northeast portion of Peninsula between Paradise and Eckerman on MI 123, on Lake Superior Whitefish Bay. 296 M sites in three campgrounds. Groups A & B. Fishing; boat ramp. Canoe/kayak rentals. GPS: N 46-36.6 W 85-11.9

Tawas Point State Park

686 Tawas Beach Rd, East Tawas, MI 48730. Phone: (989) 362-5041. Located in northeastern MI on Tawas Bay, off US 23 in East Tawas. 193 M sites. Group C. Swimming, fishing. GPS: N 44-15.4 W 83-26.8

Twin Lakes State Park

6204 E Poyhonan Rd, Toivola, MI 49965. Phone: (906) 288-3321. Located in northwestern portion of Peninsula, 26 miles SW of Houghton on MI 26. 62 M sites. Group B. Swimming, fishing; boat ramp. ATV area. GPS: N 46-58.0 W 88-45.4

Van Buren State Park

23960 Ruggles Rd, South Haven, MI 49090. Phone: (269) 637-2788. Located in southwestern MI on US 31 between Benton Harbor and South Haven off CR 380; on Lake Michigan. 220 M sites. Groups A & B. No alcohol. Swimming. GPS: N 42-20.0 W 86-18.3

Van Riper State Park

851 CR AKE, Champion, MI 49814. Phone: (906) 339-4461. Located in northwestern portion of Peninsula, 3 miles NW of Champion off US 41. 147 M and 40 R sites. Groups A & B. Swimming, fishing; boat ramp. GPS: N 46-29.3 W 87-58.6

Walter J. Hayes State Park

1220 Wampers Lake Rd, Onsted, MI 49265. Phone: (517) 467-7401. Located in southeastern MI, 9 miles W of Clinton on US 12 and MI 124 on Wampers Round Lake. 185 M sites. Group B. Swimming, fishing; boat ramp. GPS: N 42-04.3 W 84-07.6

Warren Dunes State Park

12032 Red Arrow Hwy, Sawyer, MI 49125. Phone: (269) 426-4013. Located in southwestern MI just north of IN state line, 2 miles S of I-94 exit 16, on Lake Michigan. 218 M & R sites. Groups A & C. No alcohol. Swimming. GPS: N 41-54.1 W 86-35.7

Waterloo Recreation Area

16345 McClure Rd, Chelsea, MI 48118. Phone: (734) 475-8307. Located in southeastern MI, NW of Ann Arbor, near Chelsea. (Includes 2 lakes.) Four Camping areas: I-94 exits 147, 150 and 153. Contact Park office for directions and site assignment. 325 M and R sites. Groups A, B & C. No alcohol. 25 R-site equestrian area. Swimming, fishing; boat ramp. GPS: N 42-19.9 W 84-06.7

Wilderness State Park

903 Wilderness Park Dr, Carp Lake, MI 49718. Phone: (231) 436-5381. Located in northern MI, on Lake Michigan, 11 miles W of Mackinac City, I-75 exit 339. 250 M sites. Groups A & C. Swimming, fishing; boat ramp. GPS: N 45-44.9 W 84-58.5

William Mitchell State Park

6093 E MI 115, Cadillac, MI 49601. Phone: (231) 775-7911. Located in northwestern MI, 3 miles N of Cadillac, on MI 115, off US 131, on Lake Mitchell. 221 M sites. Group C. Swimming, fishing; boat ramp. GPS: N 44-13.8 W 85-26.7

Wilson State Park

910 N First St, Harrison, MI 48625. Phone: (989) 539-3021. Located in north-central MI, on Budd Lake, 3.5 miles E of US 27, Harrison exit. 160 M sites. Group B. Swimming, fishing. GPS: N 44-01.8 W 84-48.4

Yankee Springs Recreation Area

2104 S Briggs Rd, Middleville, MI 49333. Phone: (269) 795-9081. Located in southwestern MI off MI 179 (US 131 exit 61, east 3.5 miles). On two lakes. 200 M and 120 R sites. Groups B & C. No alcohol. 25 R-site equestrian area. Swimming, fishing; boat ramp. GPS: N 42-37.6 W 85-30.8

Young State Park

2280 Boyne City Rd, Boyne City, MI 49712. Phone: (231) 582-7523. Located on Lake Charlevoix in northern MI, 7 miles NW of Boyne City, off US 131 on CR 56. 240 M sites, (three areas). Group C. Swimming, fishing; boat ramp. GPS: N 45-13.9 W 85-02.1

MINNESOTA

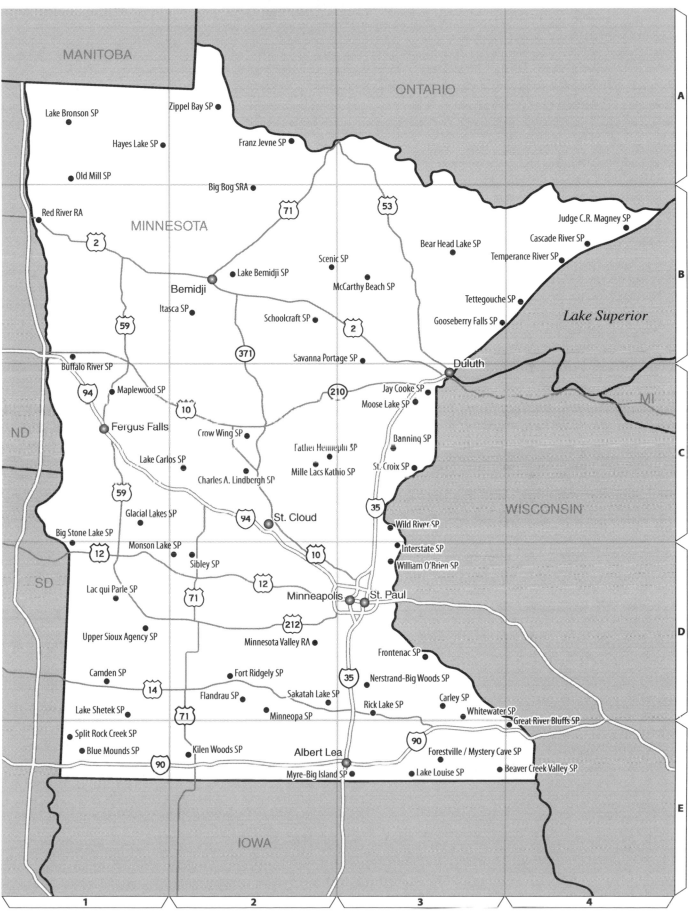

MANITOBA

ONTARIO

Lake Bronson SP
Zippel Bay SP

Hayes Lake SP
Franz Jevne SP

Old Mill SP

Big Bog SRA

Red River RA

MINNESOTA

71

53

Judge C.R. Magney SP

Cascade River SP

Bear Head Lake SP

Temperance River SP

2

Scenic SP

Lake Bemidji SP

Bemidji

McCarthy Beach SP

Tettegouche SP

59

Itasca SP

Schoolcraft SP

2

Gooseberry Falls SP

Lake Superior

371

Savanna Portage SP

Duluth

Buffalo River SP

94

Maplewood SP

210

Jay Cooke SP

Moose Lake SP

MI

10

Fergus Falls

Crow Wing SP

Father Hennepin SP

Banning SP

ND

Lake Carlos SP

Mille Lacs Kathio SP

St. Croix SP

59

Charles A. Lindbergh SP

35

WISCONSIN

Glacial Lakes SP

94

St. Cloud

Wild River SP

Big Stone Lake SP

12

Monson Lake SP

10

Interstate SP

Sibley SP

William O'Brien SP

Lac qui Parle SP

71

12

SD

Minneapolis

St. Paul

212

Upper Sioux Agency SP

Minnesota Valley RA

Frontenac SP

Camden SP

14

Fort Ridgely SP

35

Nerstrand-Big Woods SP

Flandrau SP

Sakatah Lake SP

Carley SP

Lake Shetek SP

71

Minneopa SP

Rick Lake SP

Whitewater SP

Great River Bluffs SP

Split Rock Creek SP

Kilen Woods SP

90

Blue Mounds SP

Albert Lea

Forestville / Mystery Cave SP

Beaver Creek Valley SP

90

Myre-Big Island SP

Lake Louise SP

IOWA

A

B

C

D

E

1   2   3   4

Minnesota

The Gopher State has 59 parks or recreation areas with RV facilities; more than 4,000 sites are available and only two parks, Carley State Park and Franz Jevne, have 30-foot maximum length limits. (Length measurements are from the front of the main vehicle to the rear of the towed vehicle.) The remaining 57 locations will accept big rigs easily. While all the locations are open year-round, some of the facilities (i.e. showers and flush toilets) are shut down after Labor Day. Reservations are not required but are recommended during the summer season. (There is an $8.50 reservation fee.) About 1/3 of the state's sites are on a first-come basis and no reservations are needed from November through April. Pets are permitted in the campgrounds. Rate groups: A and B.

Minnesota Department of Natural Resources
500 Lafayette Road
Saint Paul, MN 55155

Information: (888) 646-6367
Reservations: (866) 857-2757
Internet: www.dnr.state.mn.us
Reservations: www.stayatmnparks.com

Minnesota Park Locator

Minnesota Parks

Banning State Park

61101 Banning Park Rd, Sandstone, MN 55072. Phone: (320) 245-2668. Located on MN 23 off I-35 exit 195, N of Sandstone. 38 sites with electric; showers; dump station. Seasonal. 50-foot limit. Fishing. GPS: N 46-10.8 W 92-51.3

Bear Head Lake State Park

9301 Bear Head Lake State Park Rd, Ely, MN 55731. Phone: (218) 365-7229. Located on Bear Head Lake on CR 128 off US 169, about

11 miles E of Tower. 73 sites, 45 with electric; showers; dump station. 60-foot limit. Fishing, swimming. GPS: N 47-47.6 W 95-05.0

Beaver Creek Valley State Park

15954 CR 1, Caledonia, MN 55921. Phone: (507) 724-2107. Located W of Caledonia on CR 1, 24 miles S of I-90 exit 257 (MN 76). 42 sites, 16 with electric; showers; dump station. 55-foot limit. Fishing. GPS: N 43-38.4 W 91-34.5

Big Bog State Recreation Area

55716 Hwy 72 NE, Waskish, MN 56685. Phone: (218) 647-8592. Located on MN 72 just N of Waskish. 58 sites, 1 pull-through, 26 with electric; showers. 60-foot limit. Swimming, fishing. GPS: N 48-14.0 W 94-30.5

Big Stone Lake State Park

35889 Meadowbrook State Park Rd, Ortonville, MN 56278. Phone: (320) 839-3663. Located 7 miles N of Ortonville on MN/SD line, via MN 7; follow signs. 37 sites, 10 with electric; showers; dump station. 48-foot limit. Swimming, fishing; boat ramp. GPS: N 45-23.4 W 96-30.8

Blue Mounds State Park

1410 161st St, Luverne, MN 56156. Phone: (507) 283-1307. Located 3 miles N of Luvern on Blue Mounds Lake; (I-90, exit 12) off US 75 on CR 20. 73 drive in sites; 40 with electric; showers; dump station. 50-foot limit. Swimming, fishing. (No boat motors.) GPS: N 43-42.9 W 96-11.0

Buffalo River State Park

565 155th St S, Glyndon, MN 56547. Phone: (218) 498-2124. Located 14 miles E of Moorhead off US 10 on Buffalo River. From I-94 exit 22, follow MN 9 about 20 miles N to park. 41 sites, 35 with electric (50, 30, 20 amp); showers; dump station. 60-foot limit. Swimming, fishing. Golf course next to park. GPS: N 46-52.1 W 96-28.3

Camden State Park

1897 Camden Park Rd, Lynd, MN 56157. Phone: (507) 865-4530. Located 10 miles SW of Marshall off MN 23 on Brawner Lake and Redwood River. 80 sites, 7 pull-through; 29 with electric; showers; dump station. 50-foot limit (60-foot for pull-thru sites). Swimming, fishing; boat ramp; canoe rentals. (Electric motors only.) GPS: N 44-21.8 W 95-55.0

Carley State Park

c/o Whitewater State Park, 19041 Hwy 74, Altura, MN 55910. Phone: (507) 932-3007 (Whitewater SP). Located 15 miles NE of Rochester on Wabasha CR 4. 20 primitive sites. 30-foot limit. GPS: N 44-06.7 W 92-10.2

Cascade River State Park

3481 Hwy 61, Lutsen, MN 55612. Phone: (218) 387-3053. Located on Lake Superior between Lutsen and Grand Marais on MN 61 at mile post 101. 40 sites, 4 pull-through; showers; dump station. 35-foot limit. Fishing. GPS: N 47-42.7 W 90-30.3

Charles A. Lindbergh State Park

1615 Lindbergh Dr, South Little Falls, MN 56345. Phone: (320) 616-2525. Located on Mississippi River, 1 mile SW of Little Falls off US 10. 38 sites, 15 with electric; showers; dump station. 50-foot limit. Fishing. GPS: N 45-58.6 W 94-23.3

Crow Wing State Park

3124 State Park Rd, Brainerd, MN 56401. Phone: (218) 825-3075. Located on Mississippi River 9 miles SW of Brainerd off US 371 on CR 27. 59 sites, 12 with electric; showers; dump station. 45-foot limit. Fishing, swimming. GPS: N 46-16.4 W 94-19.0

Father Hennepin State Park

41294 Father Hennepin Park Rd, Isle, MN 56342. Phone: (320) 676-8763. Located 1 mile W of Isle, on Mille Lacs Lake, off MN 27. 103 sites, 51 with electric; showers; dump station. 60-foot limit. Swimming, fishing; boat ramp. GPS: N 46-08.7 W 93-29.1

Flandrau State Park

1300 Summit Ave, New Ulm, MN 56073. Phone: (507) 233-9800. Located in New Ulm (US 14 & MN 15) on Big Cottonwood River; follow signs. 93 sites, 1 pull-through; 34 with electric; showers; dump station. 66-foot limit. Swimming, fishing. GPS: N 44-17.7 W 94-27.6

Forestville / Mystery Cave State Park

21071 CR 118, Preston, MN 55965. Phone: (507) 352-5111. Located E of Wykoff, 4 miles S of MN 16, on CR 5 to CR 118. 73 sites, 23 with electric; showers; dump station. 50-foot limit. 60-site equestrian camp. Mystery Cave tours May through October. Fishing. GPS: N 43-38.4 W 92-12.9

Fort Ridgely State Park

72158 CR 30, Fairfax, MN 55332. Phone: (507) 426-7840. Located SE of Redwood Falls off MN 4, 6 miles S of Fairfax (MN 19). 31 sites, 1 pull-through; 15 with electric; showers; dump station. 60-foot limit. Golf course. 25-site equestrian area (15 with electric). GPS: N 44-27.3 W 94-43.1

Franz Jevne State Park

State Hwy 11, Birchdale, MN 56629. Phone: (218) 783-6252. Located on Rainey River, E of Birchdale on MN 11. 18 sites, 1 with electric. 30-foot limit. Fishing. GPS: N 48-37.6 W 94-04.1

Frontenac State Park

29223 County 28 Blvd, Frontenac, MN 55026. Phone: (651) 345-3401. Located on US 61 10 miles SE of Red Wing, on Mississippi River, on CR 2. 58 sites, 19 with electric; showers; dump station. 53-foot limit. Fishing. GPS: N 44-31.5 W 92-20.3

Glacial Lakes State Park

25022 CR 41, Starbuck, MN 56381. Phone: (320) 239-2860. Located off MN 29 on CR 41, S of Starbuck, on Mountain Lake. 39 sites, 1 pull-through; 14 with electric; showers; dump station. 45-foot limit. Swimming, fishing; boat ramp (electric motors only). GPS: N 45-32.4 W 95-31.8

Gooseberry Falls State Park

3206 Hwy 61 E, Two Harbors, MN 55616. Phone: (218) 834-3855. Located on Lake Superior, 13 miles NE of Two Harbors on MN 61. 69 sites, 3 pull-thru; showers; dump station. 40-foot limit. GPS: N 47-08.7 W 91-27.8

Great River Bluffs State Park

43605 Kipp Dr, Winona, MN 55987. Phone: (507) 643-6849. Located 20 miles SE of Winona via US 14/61 and CR 3. Can also be reached from I-90 exit 266 by following CR 3 north 1 mile to park entrance. 31 sites; showers. 60-foot limit. GPS: N 43-56.3 W 91-25.8

Hayes Lake State Park

48990 CR 4, Roseau, MN 56751. Phone: (218) 425-7504. On Hayes Lake, entrance to the park is 15 miles S of Roseau on MN 89, then 9 miles E on CR 4. 35 sites, 18 with electric; showers; dump station. 40-foot limit. Seasonal. Fishing, swimming; boat ramp. GPS: N 48-38.5 W 95-34.3

Interstate State Park

307 Milltown Rd, Taylors Falls, MN 55084. Phone: (651) 465-5711. Located on St. Croix River, 1 mile S of Taylors Falls, on US 8. 37 sites, 22 with electric; showers; dump station. 45-foot limit. GPS: N 45-23.8 W 92-38.2

Itasca State Park

36750 Main Park Dr, Park Rapids, MN 56470. (Oldest MN state park.) Phone: (218) 669-7251. Located 21 miles N of Park Rapids on Mississippi River, on US 71. 223 sites, 160 with electric; showers; dump station. 60-foot limit. Fishing, swimming. Wi-Fi. GPS: N 47-13.5 W 95-11.3

Jay Cooke State Park

780 Hwy 210, Carlton, MN 55718. Phone: (218) 384-4610. Located 3 miles SE of Carlton (near I-35, southwest of Duluth) on MN 210. 79 sites, 1 pull-through; 21 with electric; showers; dump station. 60-foot limit. GPS: N 46-39.3 W 92-22.4

Judge C.R. Magney State Park

4051 E Hwy 61, Grand Marais, MN 55604. Phone: (218) 387-3039. Located in northeastern tip of Minnesota on Brule River, 14 miles NE of Grand Marais on MN 61. 27 sites; showers. 45-foot limit. GPS: N 47-49.1 W 90-03.1

Kilen Woods State Park

50200 860th St, Lakefeld, MN 56150. Phone: (507) 831-2900, ext. 221. Located off MN 86, N of I-90 exit 64, on CR 24 on Des Moines River. 33 sites, 3 pull-through; 11 with electric; showers; dump station. 50-foot limit. GPS: N 43-43.9 W 95-04.3

Lac qui Parle State Park

14047 20th St NW, Watson, MN 56295. Phone: (320) 734-4450. Located 10 miles NW of Montevideo, off MN 7 on US 59 on Lac qui River. 67 sites; 58 with electric, 8 pull-through, three with full hookup; showers; dump station. 60-foot limit. Swimming, fishing; boat ramp. GPS: N 45-01.4 W 95-53.8

Lake Bemidji State Park

3401 State Park Rd, Bemidji, MN 56601. Phone: (218) 308-2300. On Lake Bemidji NE of town via US 71 and CR 20. 95 sites, 5 pull-through; 43 with electric; showers; dump station. 50-foot limit. Fishing, swimming; boat ramp. Wi-Fi. GPS: N 47-32.2 W 94-49.9

Lake Bronson State Park

CR 28, Lake Bronson, MN 56734. Phone: (218) 754-2200. Located on Lake Bronson, 2 miles E of Lake Bronson on MN 28 in northwestern Minnesota. 152 sites, 67 with electric, 6 pull-through; showers; dump station. 50-foot limit. Swimming, fishing; boat ramp. GPS: N 48-43.9 W 96-37.8

Lake Carlos State Park

2601 CR 38 NE, Carlos, MN 56319. Phone: (320) 852-7200. Located on Lake Carlos on CR 38 off MN 29, N of Alexandria (I-94 exit 103). 121 sites, 81 with electric; showers; dump station. 50-foot limit.

Equestrian area. No reservations. Swimming, fishing; boat ramp. GPS: N 46-00.1 W 95-18.7

Lake Louise State Park

c/o Forestville/Mystery Cave SP, 21071 CR 118, Preston, MN 55965. Phone: (507) 352-5111. Located N of LeRoy in southeastern MN on Little Iowa and Upper Iowa rivers, near Iowa state line off MN 56. 20 sites, 11 with electric; showers; dump station. 45-foot limit. Swimming, fishing; boat ramp. Horse trails. GPS: N 43-32.0 W 92-30.6

Lake Shetek State Park

163 State Park Rd, Currie, MN 56123. Phone: (507) 763-3256. Remote location in southwestern Minnesota, N of Currie on CR 38 on Lake Shetek. 70 sites, 1 pull-through; 64 with electric; showers; dump station. 60-foot limit. Swimming, fishing; boat ramp. GPS: N 44-06.4 W 95-42.0

Maplewood State Park

39721 Park Entrance Rd, Pelican Rapids, MN 56572. Phone: (218) 863-8383. Located 7 miles E of Pelican Rapids off MN 108. 71 sites, 32 with electric; showers; dump station. 50-foot limit. Equestrian area with 25 sites. Swimming, fishing; boat ramp. GPS: N 46-33.0 W 95-57.7

McCarthy Beach State Park

7622 McCarthy Beach Rd, Side Lake, MN 55781. Phone: (218) 254-7979. Located in northern Minnesota off US 69, on CR 5, N of Chisholm on Sturgeon Lake. 86 sites, 21 with electric; showers; dump station. 45-foot limit. Campground has narrow roads, sharp turns. Fishing, swimming; boat ramp. GPS: N 47-40.4 W 93-01.6

Mille Lacs Kathio State Park

15066 Kathio State Park Rd, Onamia, MN 56359. Phone: (320) 532-3523. Located off MN 27, 1/2 mile W of US 169 near Onamia on Mille Lacs Lake. 70 sites, 3 pull-through; 22 with electric; showers; dump station. 60-foot limit. Swimming; boat rentals. GPS: N 46-09.6 W 93-45.5

Minneopa State Park

54497 Gadwall Rd, Mankato, MN 56001. Phone: (507) 389-5464. Located in southern MN, 5 miles W of Mankato on MN 68 and US 169. 61 sites, 6 with electric; showers. 60-foot limit. Fishing. GPS: N 44-09.7 W 94-06.6

Minnesota Valley Recreation Area

19825 Park Blvd, Jordan, MN 55352. Phone: (952) 492-6400. Located 40 miles SW of Minneapolis off US 169; follow signs. 25 sites. 50-foot limit. No reservations. Horse trails. GPS: N 44-39.7 W 93-42.2

Monson Lake State Park

1690 15th St NE, Sunburg, MN 56289. Phone: (320) 366-3797. Located off MN 9, between Sunburg and Benson on Monson Lake. 20 sites; showers. 60-foot limit. No reservations. Fishing. GPS: N 45-19.4 W 95-16.3

Moose Lake State Park

4252 CR 137, Moose Lake, MN 55767. Phone: (218) 485-5420. Located 1/4 mile E of I-35 between exits 214 & 220 on Echo Lake. 33 sites, 20 with electric; showers. 60-foot limit. Swimming, fishing; boat rentals. GPS: N 46-26.2 W 92-44.6

Myre-Big Island State Park

19499 780th Ave, Albert Lea, MN 56007. Phone: (507) 379-3403. Located 3 miles S of Albert Lea on Albert Lea Lake, on CR 38, near intersection of I-90 & I-35; follow signs. 93 sites, 32 with electric; showers; dump station. 60-foot limit. Fishing; boat ramp. GPS: N 43-38.2 W 93-18.5

Nerstrand-Big Woods State Park

9700 170th St E, Nerstrand, MN 55053. Phone: (507) 333-4840. Located in SE Minnesota, E of I-35 between exits 56 & 66, on CR 29. 51 sites, 1 pull-through; 27 with electric; showers; dump station. 60-foot limit. GPS: N 44-20.5 W 93-06.6

Old Mill State Park

33489 240th Ave NW, Argyle, MN 56713. Phone: (218) 437-8174. In northwestern Minnesota, 15 miles E of Argyle via CR 4. 26 sites, 10 with electric; showers. 67-foot limit. Swimming. GPS: N 48-22.2 W 96-34.2

Red River Recreation Area

515 2nd St NW, East Grand Forks, MN 56721. Phone: (218) 773-4950. Located near ND/MN state line on the Red River in East Grand Forks, off US 2. 109 sites, 79 full hook-ups, 24 with electric; 42 pull-through; showers; dump station. 40-foot limit. Swimming, fishing; boat ramp. GPS: N 47-54.1 W 97-00.8

Rice Lake State Park

8485 Rose St, Owatonna, MN 55060. Phone: (507) 455-5871. Located on Rice Lake, 7 miles E of Owatonna (I-35 exit 42) on Rose St. 40 sites, 18 with electric; showers; dump station nearby. 55 foot limit. All back-ins. Lake very shallow. GPS: N 44-04.8 W 93-09.2

Sakatah Lake State Park

50499 Sakatah Lake State Park Rd, Waterville, MN 56096. Phone: (507) 362-4438. Located off MN 60, NE of Mankato, near intersection of MN 60 & 13 at Waterville on Sakatah Lake. 62 sites, 14 with electric; showers; dump station. 55-foot limit. Fishing. GPS: N 44-13.0 W 93-30.6

Savanna Portage State Park

55626 Lake Place, McGregor, MN 55760. Phone: (218) 426-3271. Remote location at end of CR 14, N of McGregor (MN 65). 61 sites, 4 pull-through, 18 with electric; showers; dump station. 55-foot limit. Several lakes in park. Swimming, fishing. GPS: N 46-49.1 W 93-10.6

Scenic State Park

56956 Scenic Hwy 7, Bigfork, MN 56628. Phone: (218) 743-3362. Remote location 7 miles E of Bigfork (MN 38) on CR 7. 93 sites, 21 pull-through, 23 with electric; showers; dump station. 50-foot limit. Two lakes in park. Fishing, swimming. Open in winter. GPS: N 47-42.1 W 93-33.9

Schoolcraft State Park

9042 Schoolcraft Ln NE, Deer River, MN 56636. Phone: (218) 743-3362. (Hill Annex SP.) Located on CR 74, about 17 miles W of Grand Rapids on Misissippi River, off MN 6 via US 2. 28 rustic sites. 35-foot limit. Boat ramp. GPS: N 47-15.1 W 93-48.0

Sibley State Park

800 Sibley Park Rd NE, New London, MN 56273. Phone: (320) 354-2055. Located on Lake Andrew, 16 miles N of Wilmar on US 71.

132 sites, 53 with electric; showers; dump station. 60-foot limit. Equestrian area. Swimming, fishing; boat ramp. GPS: N 45-19.1 W 95-00.7

Split Rock Creek State Park

336 50th Ave, Jasper, MN 56144. Phone: (507) 348-7908. Located in SW Minnesota on Split Rock Lake, near SD state line, on MN 23, SW of Pipestone (US 75). 34 sites, 21 with electric; showers; dump station. 52-foot limit. Swimming, fishing; boat ramp, rentals; equestrian area. GPS: N 43-54.4 W 96-22.1

St. Croix State Park

30065 St. Croix Park Rd, Hinckley, MN 55037. Phone: (320) 384-6591. Located 15 miles E of Hinckley (I-35 exit 183) on MN 48 on St. Croix and Kettle rivers. 211 sites, 81 with electric; showers; dump station. 60-foot limit. Equestrian area. Swimming, fishing. GPS: N 46-00.7 W 92.37.0

Temperance River State Park

(mail c/o Tettegouche SP) 7620 W Hwy 61, Schroeder, MN 55613. Phone: (218) 663-7476. Remote location in northeastern Minnesota on MN 61, just N of Schroeder. 52 sites, 2 pull-through; 18 with electric; showers. 50-foot limit. GPS: N 47-33.5 W 90-52.1

Tettegouche State Park

5702 Hwy 61, Silver Bay, MN 55614. Phone: (218) 226-6365. Located on MN 61 near Silver Bay on Lake Superior. 28 sites, 22 with electric; showers. 60-foot limit. Fishing. GPS: N 47-20.1 W 91-12.2

Upper Sioux Agency State Park

5908 Hwy 67, Granite Falls, MN 56241. Phone: (320) 564-4777. Located on MN 67, 8 miles SE of Granite Falls (US 212 & MN 23). 34 sites, 14 with electric (some 50 amp); showers; dump station nearby. 60-foot limit. Horse trails. GPS: N 44-44.1 W 95-27.4

Whitewater State Park

19041 Hwy 74, Altura, MN 55910. Phone: (507) 932-3007. Located 3 miles S of Elba on MN 74, E of Rochester on Whitewater River. 104 sites, 5 pull-through; 47 with electric (50-amp); showers; dump station. 50-foot limit. Fishing, swimming. GPS: N 44-04.1 W 92-02.4

Wild River State Park

39797 Park Trail, Center City, MN 55012. Phone: (651) 583-2125. Located on CR 12 east of I-35 exit 147 (MN 95) on St. Croix River. 94 sites, 2 pull-through, 17 with electric; showers; dump station. 60-foot limit. Swimming, fishing. Horse trails. GPS: N 45-32.8 W 92-51.4

William O'Brien State Park

16821 O'Brien Trail N, Marine on St. Croix, MN 55047. Phone: (651) 433-0500. Located on St. Croix River along MN 95 about 16 miles E of I-35 exit 129. 120 sites, 77 with electric; showers; dump station. 60-foot limit. Fishing, swimming; boat ramp. (Golf nearby.) GPS: N 45-13.5 W 92-46.0

Zippel Bay State Park

3684 54th Ave NW, Williams, MN 56686. Phone: (218) 783-6252. Located on CR 8, NW of Baudette and E of Roosevelt, in northern Minnesota on Lake of the Woods. 57 sites; showers; dump station. 60-foot limit. Marina. Swimming, fishing; boat ramp. GPS: N 48-50.4 W 94-51.0

MISSISSIPPI

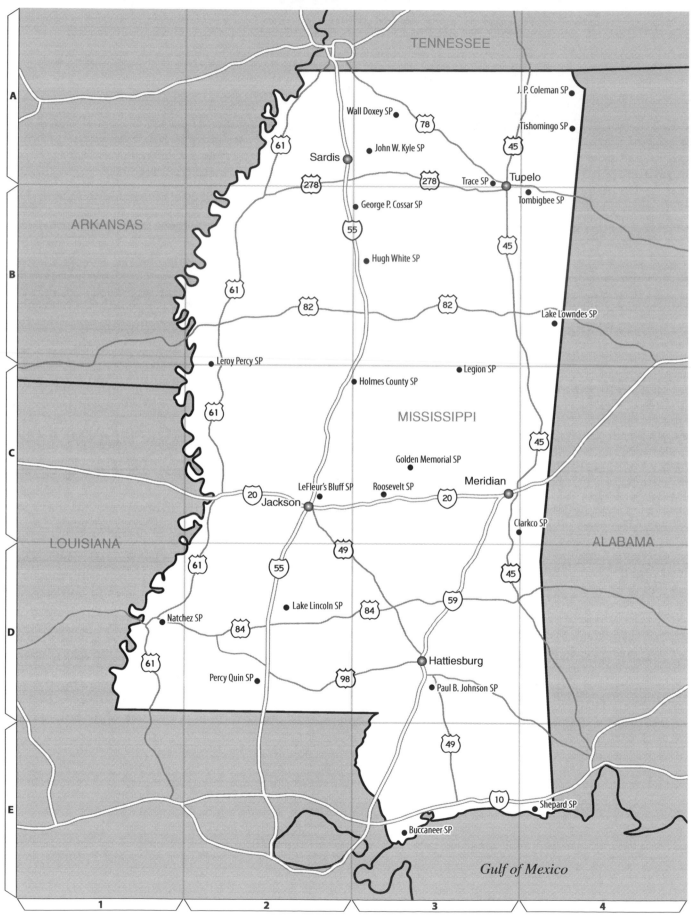

TENNESSEE

J. P. Coleman SP

Wall Doxey SP

78

Tishomingo SP

45

61

John W. Kyle SP

Sardis

278

278

Trace SP

Tupelo

ARKANSAS

George P. Cossar SP

Tombigbee SP

55

45

Hugh White SP

61

82

82

Lake Lowndes SP

Leroy Percy SP

Legion SP

61

Holmes County SP

MISSISSIPPI

Golden Memorial SP

45

20

LeFleur's Bluff SP

Roosevelt SP

Meridian

Jackson

20

Clarkco SP

LOUISIANA

ALABAMA

61

49

55

45

Lake Lincoln SP

84

59

Natchez SP

84

Hattiesburg

61

Percy Quin SP

98

Paul B. Johnson SP

49

10

Shepard SP

Buccaneer SP

Gulf of Mexico

A

B

C

D

E

1   2   3   4

Mississippi

Of the 28 state parks and recreation areas in Mississippi, 22 locations have RV facilities ranging from "primitive" sites (no hookups) to "improved" or "developed" sites with concrete pads, water, and electric connections. All listed parks also have showers and at least one dump station. Reservations are accepted year-round at most locations for a limited number of sites and reservations can be made 24 months in advance. Some parks offer 30-day stays. All other sites are available on a first-come, first-served basis. We recommend calling the particular park to check availability. Offices in all parks are open from 8 AM to 5 PM, 7 days a week. Seniors 65 years and older and the disabled are eligible for a discount, but you must ask and show proof of age. Visa and MasterCard are accepted. Rate groups: A and B depending on site facilities; entrance fee is additional.

Mississippi Dept. of Wildlife, Fisheries and Parks
1505 Eastover Dr.
Jackson, MS 39211

Information/Reservations: (800) 467-2757
Internet: www.mdwfp.com

Mississippi Park Locator

Mississippi Parks

Buccaneer State Park

1150 South Beach Blvd, Waveland, MS 39576. Phone: (228) 467-3822. Located 2 miles off US 90 on Beach Blvd in Waveland. 206 premium sites, 70 with water, electric; laundry. Disc golf. GPS: N 30-15.6 W 89-24.5

Clarkco State Park

386 Clarko Rd, Quitman, MS 39355. Phone: (601) 776-6651. Located 20 miles S of Meridian, off US 45. 43 full hook-up sites; laundry. Swimming, fishing; boat ramp. Disc golf. GPS: N 32-06.5 W 88-41.6

George P. Cossar State Park

165 CR 170, Oakland, MS 38948. Phone: (622) 623-7356. Located on Enid Lake, 5 miles E of I-55 exit 227 (Oakland) on MS 32. 76 developed sites; laundry. Swimming, fishing; boat ramp. GPS: N 34-07.3 W 89-52.9

Golden Memorial State Park

2104 Damascus Rd, Walnut Grove, MS 39180. Phone: (601) 253-2237. Located off Hwy 492, 3.7 miles NE of Walnut Grove. 8 sites with water, electric. Fishing. GPS: N32.6 W89.4

Holmes County State Park

5369 State Park Rd, Durant, MS 39063. Phone: (662) 653-3351. Located on two lakes, on MS 424 just E of I-55 exit 150, 4 miles S of Durant. 28 developed sites; laundry. Fishing; boat ramp. GPS: N 33-01.6 W 89-55.2

Hugh White State Park

3170 State Park Rd, Grenada, MS 38902. Phone: (662) 226-8963. Located on Grenada Lake, 5 miles E of Grenada (I-55 & MS 8) off MS 8. 150 developed sites; laundry. Swimming, fishing; boat ramp. Golf course. GPS: N 33-47.8 W 89-44.6

J. P. Coleman State Park

613 CR 321, Iuka, MS 38852. Phone: (662) 423-6515. Located in northeast MS on Pickwick Lake (Tennessee River), 13 miles N of Iuka off MS 25 on CR 321. 69 developed sites; laundry. Swimming, fishing; boat ramp, rentals. GPS: N 34-56.1 W 88-10.8

John W. Kyle State Park

4235 State Park Rd, Sardis, MS 38666. Phone: (662) 487-1345. Located 9 miles E of Sardis (I-55 exit 252) off MS 315 on Sardis Reservoir. 200 developed sites; laundry. Golf course. Swimming, fishing; boat ramp. GPS: N 34-26.4 W 89-48.6

Lake Lincoln State Park

2573 Sunset Rd NE, Wesson, MS 39191. Phone: (601) 643-9044. Located off US 51, 4.5 miles E of Wesson (I-55 Wesson exit). 71 improved sites, 22 lakeside; showers; laundry. Swimming, fishing; boat ramp. GPS: N 31-40.5 W 90-18.7

Lake Lowndes State Park

3319 Lake Lowndes Rd, Columbus, MS 39702. Phone: (662) 328-2110. Located 8 miles SE of Columbus (US 82 & 45) off MS 69 on Lake Lowndes. 50 lakeside full hook-up sites; showers; laundry. Fishing, swimming; boat ramp. Marina. Horse trails. GPS: N 33-26.4 W 88-18.7

LeFleur's Bluff State Park

2140 Riverside Dr, Jackson, MS 39202. Office: (601) 987-3923. Northeast of downtown Jackson at I-55 exit 98. 28 sites with water, electric; showers; dump station. Golf course. Fishing; boat ramp. Disc golf. GPS: N 32-18.3 W 90-09.2

Legion State Park

635 Legion State Park Rd, Louisville, MS 39339. Phone: (662) 773-8323. Located 2 miles N of Louisville on North Columbus Ave. 15 sites with full hook-ups. Fishing; boat ramp. GPS: N 33-09.1 W 89-02.6

Leroy Percy State Park

1400 Hwy 12 W, Hollandale, MS 38748. Phone: (662) 827-5436. Located 5 miles W of Hollandale (US 61 & MS 12) off MS 12. 16 improved sites; laundry. Fishing; boat ramp. Disc golf. No alcohol. GPS: N 33-09.6 W 90-56.3

Natchez State Park

230-B Wickliff Rd, Natchez, MS 39120. Phone: (601) 442-2658. Located 10 miles NE of Natchez off US 61 at Stanton. 44 developed, 6 full hook-up sites; showers. Fishing; boat ramp. Disc golf. GPS: N 31-35.4 W 91-56.3

Paul B. Johnson State Park

319 Geiger Lake Rd, Hattiesburg, MS 39401. Phone: (601) 582-7721. Located 15 miles S of Hattiesburg off US 49. 125 full hook-up sites showers; laundry. Swimming area & beach. Fishing; boat ramp. GPS: N 31-08.0 W 89-14.0

Percy Quin State Park

2036 Percy Quin Dr, McComb, MS 39648. Phone: (601) 684-3938. Located 6 miles S of McComb off I-55 exit 13. 100 full hook-up sites; showers. Golf course. Swimming, fishing; boat ramp. Marina. GPS: N 31-11.3 W 90-30.6

Roosevelt State Park

2149 Hwy 13 S, Morton, MS 39117. Phone: (601) 732-6316. Located just N of I-20 exit 77 (MS 13). 109 sites, 82 full hook-up, 27 with electric and water; showers; laundry. Swimming, fishing; boat ramp. No alcohol. GPS: N 32-19.2 W 89-40.0

Shepard State Park

1034 Graveline Rd, Gautier, MS 39553. Phone: (228) 497-2244. Operated by City of Gautier. Located 3 miles W of Pascagoula on Gulf of Mexico, off US 90 at Gautier. 28 developed sites; showers. Fishing; boat ramp. Disc golf. GPS: N 30-22.3 W 88-37.7

Tishomingo State Park

105 CR 90, Tishomingo, MS 38873. Phone: (662) 438-6914. Located off the Natchez Trace at mile marker 304. 62 developed sites; showers, laundry. (Reservations strongly recommended.) Swimming, fishing; boat ramp. Disc golf. GPS: N 34-36.6 W 88-11.5

Tombigbee State Park

254 Cabin Dr, Tupelo, MS 38804. Phone: (662) 842-7669. Located 6 miles SE of Tupelo off MS 6. 20 sites, 18 full hook-up; showers; laundry. Fishing; boat ramp. GPS: N 34-13.9 W 88-37.7

Trace State Park

2139 Faulkner Rd, Belden, MS 38826. Phone: (662) 489-2958. Located midway between Pontotoc and Tupelo off MS 6. 52 full-hook-up sites; showers. Swimming, fishing; boat ramp. Golf course adjacent; ATV area; horse trails. Disc golf. GPS: N 34-15.6 W 88-53.2

Wall Doxey State Park

3946 Hwy 7 S, Holly Springs, MS 38635. Phone: (662) 252-4231. Located 7 miles S of Holly Springs (US 78 & MS 7) off MS 7. 64 developed sites; showers; laundry. Fishing; boat ramp (electric motors only); disc golf. GPS: N 34-39.8 W 89-27.6

MISSOURI

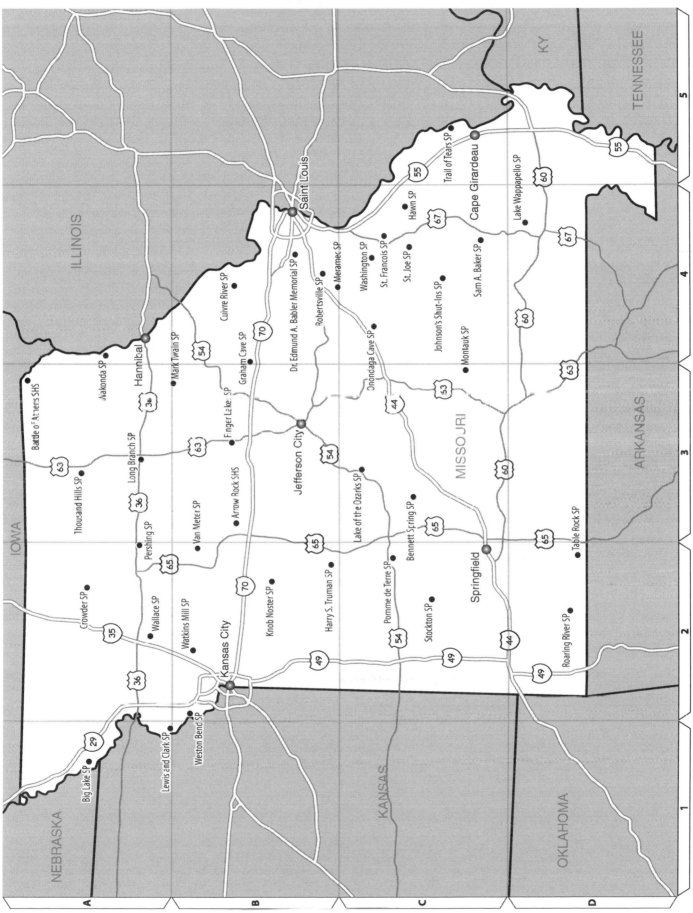

Missouri

Thirty-eight state parks in Missouri have RV camping facilities, ranging from basic (dry-camp) sites to sites with full hook-ups; most offer 50-amp service. All have dump stations and Wi-Fi. Water is available in all parks but not necessarily at each site. State parks are open year-round but water service and showers (in parks so equipped) are available normally from April 1 through October 31. (You should call ahead to determine facilities availability.) Pets are permitted but must be leashed. Seniors (age 65 and older) and persons with disabilities are entitled to a reduced camping fee, with proof of age and/or disability. Missouri has a centralized reservation system. There is an additional fee to use this system. Reservations require a 48-hour lead time and reservations can be made at the individual park. MasterCard, Visa and Discover credit cards are accepted. Rate groups: A and B.

Missouri Dept. of Natural Resources
Division of State Parks
PO Box 176
Jefferson City, MO 65102

Information: (800) 334-6946
Reservations: (877) 422-6766
Internet: www.mostateparks.com

Missouri Park Locator

Missouri Parks

Arrow Rock State Historic Site

39521 Visitor Center Rd, Arrow Rock, MO 65320. Phone: (660) 837-3330. Located on Missouri River, 13 miles N of I-70 exit 98 on MO 41. 47 sites, 34 with electric, one full hook-up; showers. Historic village in park. Fishing. GPS: N 39-04.1 W 92-56.6

Battle of Athens State Historic Site

Revere, MO 63465. Phone: (660) 877-3871. Located on Hwy CC, off MO 81, near Iowa state line, on Des Moines River. 29 sites, 15 with electric; water available. Fishing. GPS: N 40-35.1 W 91-41.8

Bennett Spring State Park

26250 Hwy 64A, Lebanon, MO 65536. Phone: (417) 532-4338. Located on MO 64, 12 miles NW of Lebanon (I-44 exit 129). 191 sites, 128 with electric, water, 48 sites with sewers; showers; laundry. Note: Open year-round but water available April through October only. Wi-Fi. Swimming, fishing; canoe rentals. Reservable. GPS: N 37-43.5 W 92-51.4

Big Lake State Park

204 Lake Shore Dr, Craig, MO 64437. Phone: (660) 442-3770. Located SW of Mound City near Kansas state line on MO 111. 75 sites, 57 with electric; showers; laundry. Wi-Fi. Swimming, fishing; boat ramp. GPS: N 40-05.5 W 95-20.8

Crowder State Park

76 Hwy 128, Trenton, MO 64683. Phone: (660) 359-6473. Located off US 65, on MO 146, 4 miles W of Trenton. 41 sites, 31 with electric; showers. Lake in park. Horse trails; fishing, swimming. GPS: N 40-04.9 W 93-40.1

Cuivre River State Park

678 State Rt 47, Troy, MO 63379. Phone: (636) 528-7247. Located on Cuivre River, 3 miles NE of Troy (US 61 & MO 47) on MO 47. 92 sites, 31 full hook-up; showers. Equestrian area with 8 electric and 5 basic sites. Fishing, swimming. GPS: N 39-03.9 W 90-56.1

Dr. Edmund A. Babler Memorial State Park

800 Guy Park Dr, Wildwood, MO 63005. Phone: (636) 458-3813. Located 20 miles W of St. Louis off MO 109, between US 40 and MO 100. 73 sites, 43 with electric (50 amp); showers; dump station; laundry. Swimming. Horse trails. GPS: N 38-37.1 W 90-41.4

Finger Lakes State Park

1505 E Peabody Rd, Columbia, MO 65202. Phone: (573) 443-5315. Located 10 miles N of Columbia (1-70 exit 123) off US 63. 35 sites, 16 with electric; showers. ATV trails. Swimming, fishing. Reservable. Wi-Fi. GPS: N 39-04.7 W 92-21.6

Graham Cave State Park

217 Hwy TT, Danville, MO 63361. Phone: (573) 564-3476. Located on Loutre River, 2 miles W of Danville (I-70 exit 170) on Hwy TT. 52 sites, 18 with electric; showers. Cave tours. Fishing; boat ramp. GPS: N 38-54.5 W 91-34.6

Harry S. Truman State Park

28761 State Park Rd, Warsaw, MO 65355. Phone: (660) 438-7711. Located off MO 7 on Hwy UU, on Lake of the Ozarks (Truman Lake), W of US 65 at Warsaw. 198 sites, 127 with electric; showers; laundry. Marina. Swimming, fishing; boat ramp, rentals. Reservable. GPS: N 38-16.4 W 93-26.5

Hawn State Park

12096 Park Dr, Sainte Genevieve, MO 63670. Phone: (573) 883-3603. Located 14 miles SW of I-55 exit 150 via MO 32 and MO 144. 45 sites, 26 with electric (some open year-round); showers; laundry. Reservable. GPS: N 37-50.0 W 90-14.5

Johnson's Shut-Ins State Park

148 Taum Sauk Tr, Middlebrook, MO 63656. Phone: (573) 546-2450. Located in remote section of southeast MO near Mark Twain National Forest, on Hwy N, SW of Park Hills and US 67. 55 sites, 21 with electric, 20 full hook-up; showers; laundry; store. Swimming, fishing. Reservable. Horse trails. Wi-Fi. GPS: N 37-32.9 W 90-51.2

Knob Noster State Park

873 SE 10, Knob Noster, MO 65336. Phone: (660) 563-2463. Located on MO 23, outside Knob Noster, off US 50. 68 sites, 27 with electric; showers; laundry. Lakes in park. Equestrian area. Fishing; boat ramp. GPS: N 38-48.2 W 93-34.6

Lake of the Ozarks State Park

403 Hwy 134, Kaiser, MO 65047. Phone: (573) 348-2694. Located on Lake of the Ozarks S of Osage Beach (US 54) via MO 42 and MO 134. 189 sites, 127 with electric (50 amp); showers; laundry. Equestrian area, rentals. Cave tours. Swimming, fishing; boat ramp, rentals; marina. Reservable. GPS: N 38-08.0 W 92-33.9

Lake Wappapello State Park

Hwy 172, Williamsville, MO 63967. Phone: (573) 297-3232. Located 16 miles N of Popular Bluff off US 67. 74 sites, 70 with electric; showers; laundry. Equestrian area. Swimming, fishing; boat ramp. Reservable. GPS: N 36-56.5 W 90-20.7

Lewis and Clark State Park

801 Lake Crest Blvd, Rushville, MO 64484. Phone: (816) 579-5564. Located on MO 138, on the Missouri River, 20 miles SW of St. Joseph. 69 sites, 62 with electric (some 50 amp & pull-through); showers; laundry. Swimming, fishing; boat ramp. GPS: N 39-32.3 W 95-03.1

Long Branch State Park

28615 Visitor Center Rd, Macon, MO 63552. Phone: (660) 773-5229. Located on Long Branch Lake, 2 miles W of the US 63/US 36 junction, outside Macon. 72 sites, 63 with electric (50 amp); showers. Fishing; boat ramp. Marina. GPS: N 39-46.1 W 92-31.6

Mark Twain State Park

37352 Shrine Rd, Florida, MO 65283. Phone: (573) 565-3440. Located on MO 107, NE of Moberly, N of MO 154 on Mark Twain Lake. Three campgrounds. 97 sites, 75 with electric; showers; laundry; dump station. Swimming, fishing. Reservable. Boat ramp. GPS: N 39-29.1 W 91-47.7

Meramec State Park

115 Meramec Park Dr, Sullivan, MO 63080. Phone: (573) 468-6072. Located on Meramec River, 3 miles NE of Sullivan (1-44 exit 225) on MO 185. 209 sites, 124 with electric, (21 full hook-up); showers; laundry. Cave tours. Fishing, swimming; raft/canoe rentals. Store. Reservable. GPS: N 38-12.9 W 91-07.4

Montauk State Park

345 CR 6670, Salem, MO 65560. Phone: (573) 548-2201. Located on Current River, 21 miles SW of Salem on MO 119, off US 63, S of I-44 exit 186. 154 sites, 123 with electric; showers; laundry. Store. Fishing. Reservable. GPS: N 37-27.3 W 91-41.5

Onondaga Cave State Park

7556 Hwy H, Leasburg, MO 65535. Phone: (573) 245-6576. Located 7 miles SE of I-44 exit 214 (Leasburg) on Hwy H. 66 sites, 47 with water, electric; showers; laundry. Cave tours. Open year-round. Fishing, swimming; boat ramp. GPS: N 38-03.8 W 91-13.7

Pershing State Park

29277 Hwy 130, Laclede, MO 64651. Phone: (660) 963-2299. Located 7 miles W of Brookfield or 18 miles E of Chillicothe, off US 36 on MO 130. 38 sites, 26 with electric (50 amp); showers; laundry. Four lakes in park. Swimming, fishing, boat ramp. GPS: N 39-46.6 W 93-12.7

Pomme de Terre State Park

Hwy 64B, Pittsburg, MO 65724. Phone: (417) 852-4291. Located S of Hermitage on Pomme de Terre Lake, via MO 254 and MO 64. (Two separate areas.) 253 total sites, 212 with electric, some sewers; showers; laundry. Store. Marina. Swimming, fishing; boat ramp. Reservable. GPS: N 37-52.5 W 93-19.1

Roaring River State Park

12716 Farm Rd, Cassville, MO 65625. Phone: (417) 847-2539. Located 7 miles S of Cassville on MO 112, near Arkansas state line. 184 sites, 137 with electric, two full hook-up; showers; laundry. Swimming, fishing. Store. Open year-round. Reservable. GPS: N 36-35.4 W 93-50.1

Robertsville State Park

900 State Park Dr, Robertsville, MO 63072. Phone: (636) 257-3788. Located on Meramec River, 5 miles E of I-44 exit 247 on Hwy O at Hwy N. 26 sites, 14 with electric; showers; laundry. Fishing; boat ramp. GPS: N 38-25.8 W 90-49.0

Sam A. Baker State Park

Patterson, MO 63956. Phone: (573) 856-4411. Located on St. Francois River, 4 miles N of Patterson on MO 143, W of US 67. 187 sites, 140 with electric; showers; laundry. Equestrian area. Swimming, fishing; boat ramp, canoe rentals. Store. Open year-round. Reservable. GPS: N 37-15.2 W 90-30.3

St. Francois State Park

8920 US Hwy 67 N, Bonne Terre, MO 63628. Phone: (573) 358-2173. Located on US 67 about 10 miles N of Park Hills (west of I-55 in southeast MO). 110 sites, 63 with electric; showers; laundry. Equestrian area. Swimming, fishing. Reservable. GPS: N 37-58.4 W 90-32.2

St. Joe State Park

2800 Pimville Rd, Park Hills, MO 63601. Phone: (573) 431-1069. Located SW of Park Hills on MO 32, off US 67. 75 sites, 40 with electric (50 amp); showers; laundry. Off road vehicle and equestrian areas. Swimming, fishing; boat ramp (electric motors only). Open year-round. Reservations recommended. GPS: N 37-49.5 W 90-32.2

Stockton State Park

19100 Hwy 215, Dadeville, MO 65635. Phone: (417) 276-4259. Located on Stockton Lake about 9 miles S of Stockton via MO 39 and MO 215. 74 sites, 60 with electric; showers; laundry. Swimming, fishing; boat ramp; marina; store. Reservable. GPS: N 37-37.4 W 93-45.6

Table Rock State Park

5272 Hwy 165, Branson, MO 65616. Phone: (417) 334-4704. Located on Table Rock Lake on MO 165, 5.4 miles W of US 65, SW of Branson. 162 sites, 78 with electric, 41 with sewers; showers. Swimming, fishing; boat ramp, rentals. Open year-round. Marina; store; dive shop. GPS: N 36-35.0 W 93-18.5

Thousand Hills State Park

29431 MO Hwy 157, Kirksville, MO 63501. Phone: (660) 665-6995. Located on Forest Lake, 2.5 miles SW of Kirksville (US 63) via MO 6 and MO 157. 57 sites, 42 with electric (50 amp); showers. Marina; store. Swimming, fishing; boat ramp. Open year-round. GPS: N 40-09.6 W 92-36.6

Trail of Tears State Park

429 Moccasin Springs, Jackson, MO 63755. Phone: (573) 290-5268. Located on Mississippi River, 10 miles E of Fruitland (I-55 exit 105) via US 61 and MO 177. 52 sites, 18 with electric, some with sewers, water; showers; laundry. Lake Boutin in park. Equestrian area. Swimming, fishing; boat ramp. Reservable. GPS: N 37-27.2 W 89-29.5

Van Meter State Park

32146 122 N, Miami, MO 65344. Phone: (660) 886-7537. Located on Missouri River, 12 miles NW of Marshall via MO 41 and MO 122. 21 sites, 12 with electric; showers. (Minimum Fri-Sat stay in season.) Fishing. Boat ramp. GPS: N 39-15.8 W 93-16.0

Wakonda State Park

32836 State Park Rd, LaGrange, MO 63448. Phone: (573) 655-2280. Located on Mississippi River, 3 miles S of LaGrange on US 61/24. 81 sites (some pull-thru), 65 with water, electric, some sewers; showers; laundry. Swimming, fishing; boat ramp, rentals. GPS: N 40-00.3 W 91-31.5

Wallace State Park

10621 NE Hwy 121, Cameron, MO 64429. Phone: (816) 632-3745. Located 6 miles S of Cameron, off I-35 exit 42. 77 sites, 42 with electric (50 amp); showers. Fishing, swimming; boat ramp. GPS: N 39-39.6 W 94-12.8

Washington State Park

13041 MO Hwy 104, DeSoto, MO 63020. Phone: (636) 586-5768. Located 9 miles SW of DeSoto on MO 21. 50 sites, 24 with electric; showers; laundry; store. Swimming, fishing. Boat ramp; canoe, raft rentals. Reservable. GPS: N 38-05.1 W 90-41.1

Watkins Mill State Park

26600 Park Rd N, Lawson, MO 64062. Phone: (816) 580-3387. Located off I-35 exit 26, E of Keamey off MO 92, on Hwy RA. (Adjacent to Watkins Woolen Mill State Historic Site.) 96 sites, 74 with electric; showers; laundry. Reservable. Horse trails; fishing, swimming; boat ramp. GPS: N 39-23.0 W 94-15.9

Weston Bend State Park

16600 Hwy 45 N, Weston, MO 64098. Phone: (816) 640-5443. Located 1 mile S of Weston on Missouri River, on MO 45, near Kansas City. 36 sites with electric; showers; laundry. GPS: N 39-23.6 W 95-15.8

MONTANA

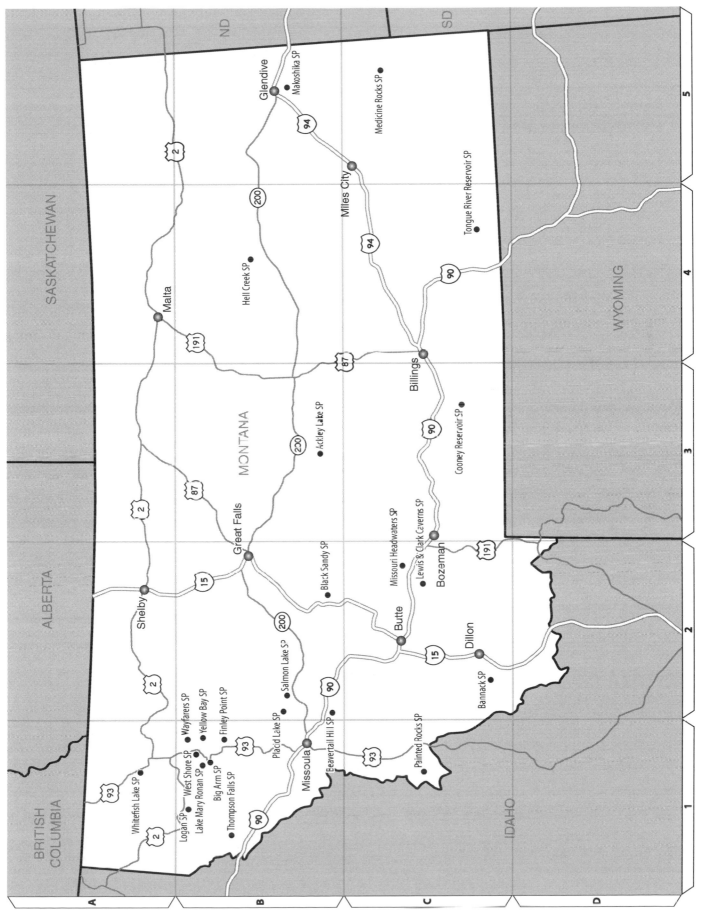

Montana

The Big Sky State offers the RV traveler 24 state parks with facilities. (Five on Flathead Lake.) However, all parks are "dry camp" locations, with water and dump stations available at most. The majority of these parks are in the western and central sections of Montana. Some parks are listed as "primitive" and the campsites are free. Pets are permitted in all parks.

Note: Several Montana parks have mailing addresses different than their physical locations and some parks share the same telephone number. Follow the location directions listed for each park and indicate the park you are calling about, if you call for information. Also, many of these parks are seasonal and may close earlier than usual, depending on weather conditions. Rate group: A.

Montana Fish, Wildlife & Parks
1420 E. 6th Ave.
Helena, MT 69620

Information: (800) 847-4868
Reservations: (855) 922-6768
Internet: www.stateparks.mt.gov

Montana Park Locator

Montana Parks

Ackley Lake State Park

989 Ackley Lake Rd, Hobson, MT 59452. Phone: (406) 454-5840. Located 17 miles SW of Lewistown on Ackley Lake, off US 87 via Secondary 541 or 400. 15 sites. 24-foot limit. Swimming, fishing; boat ramp. GPS: N 46-58.0 W 110-02.1

Bannack State Park

721 Bannack Rd, Dillon, MT 59725. Phone: (406) 834-3413. Remote location SW of Dillon on Grasshopper Creek, off I-15 exit 59, via Secondary 278, 20 miles west. Near Bannack ghost town. 28 sites. 35-foot limit. Horse trails. Fishing. GPS: N 45-09.5 W 112-59.6

Beavertail Hill State Park

29895 Bonita Station Rd, Clinton, MT 59825. Phone: (406) 542-5500. Located off I-90 exit 130, 26 miles E of Missoula, S of freeway on Clark Fork River. 26 sites. 28-foot limit. Seasonal. Fishing, boating. GPS: N 46-43.3 W 113-34.6

Big Arm State Park

28031 Big Arm State Park Rd, Big Arm, MT 59910. Phone: (406) 849-5255. Located on US 93, west side of Flathead Lake, 14 miles N of Polson. 40 sites; showers. 30-foot limit. Swimming, fishing; boat ramp. GPS: N 47-89.9 W 114-18.5

Black Sandy State Park

6563 Hause Dr, Helena, MT 59602. Phone: (406) 495-3260 . Located on Hauser Lake about 7 miles N of Helena from I-15 exit 200 via Secondary 453 and county road; follow signs. 29 sites; dump station. 35-foot limit. Swimming, fishing; boat ramp. GPS: N 46-43.0 W 111-59.9

Cooney Reservoir State Park

86 Lake Shore Rd, Roberts, MT 59070. Phone: (406) 445-2326. Located about 28 miles S of I-90 exit 408 or 434; SW of Billings. 72 sites, some with electric; showers. 30-foot limit. Swimming, fishing; boat ramp. GPS: N 45-26.3 W 109-13.0

Finley Point State Park

31453 Findley Point Rd, Finley Poiny, MT 59860. Phone: (406) 887-2715. Located off MT 35 on SE side of Flathead Lake, 11 miles NE of Polson, on county road; follow signs. 18 sites with electric, water. 40-foot limit. Seasonal. Swimming, fishing; boat ramp. GPS: N 47-42.7 W 114-02.8

Hell Creek State Park

2456 Hell Creek Rd, Jordan, MT 59337. Phone: (406) 234-0900. Remote location on Fort Peck Lake, 25 miles N of Jordan (MT 200 & 59). 55 sites, some with electric; showers; dump station. 35-foot limit. Swimming, fishing; boat ramp. GPS: N 47-32.8 W 106-56.1

Lake Mary Ronan State Park

50623 Lake Mary Ronan Rd, Dayton, MT 59860. Phone: (406) 849-5082. Located near Flathead Lake, NW of Polson off US 93; follow signs from US 93. 22 sites with electric. 35-foot limit. Fishing, swimming; boat launch GPS: N 47-56.6 W 114-23.8

Lewis & Clark Caverns State Park

25 Lewis & Clark Caverns Rd, Whitehall, MT 59759. Phone: (406) 287-3541. Located on MT 2 on Jefferson River, 23 miles W of Three Forks. 40 sites; showers; dump station. No size limit. Cave tours, (fee). Fishing. GPS: N 45-49.3 W 111-50.5

Logan State Park

77518 US 2, Libby, MT 59923. Phone: (406) 293-7190. Located 45 miles SW of Kalispell on Middle Thompson Lake on US 2. 36 sites; showers; dump station. 30-foot limit. Swimming, fishing; boat ramp. GPS: N 48-00.4 W 115-00.3

Makoshika State Park

1301 Snyder, Glendive, MT 59330. Phone: (406) 377-6256. Located in eastern MT in Glendive (I-94 exit 215); follow signs. 16 sites. 40-foot limit. Disc golf. GPS: N 47-05.4 W 104-42.6

Medicine Rocks State Park

1141 MT 7, Ekalaka, MT 59330. Phone: (406) 377-6256. Remote location in eastern MT, 25 miles S of Baker (US 12 & MT 7) on MT 7. 12 sites. 50-foot limit. GPS: N 46-02.7 W 104-27.4

Missouri Headwaters State Park

1585 Trident Rd, Three Forks, MT 59752. Phone: (406) 285-3610. Located 4 miles NE of Three Forks at confluence of Jefferson, Madison and Gallatin rivers, on MT 286 off MT 205, N of I-90 exit 278. 17 sites. 35-foot limit. Fishing; boat ramp. GPS: N 45-55.5 W 111-30.1

Painted Rocks State Park

8809 W Fork Rd, Darby, MT 59829. Phone: (406) 542-5500. Remote location in southwestern Montana on Painted Rocks Reservoir, on MT 473, 23 miles off US 93, 17 miles S of Hamilton. 25 sites; no fee. 25-foot limit. Swimming, fishing; boat ramp. GPS: N 45-42.4 W 114-17.0

Placid Lake State Park

5001 N Placid Lake Rd, Seeley Lake, MT 59868 (mail). Phone: (406) 677-6804. Located on Placid Lake, 47 miles NE of Missoula via MT 200 and MT 83. 40 sites; showers. 30-foot limit. Seasonal. Swimming, fishing; boat ramp. GPS: N 47-08.3 W 113-31.5

Salmon Lake State Park

2329 MT 83N, Seeley Lake, MT 59868. Phone: (406) 542-5500. Located on Salmon Lake, 42 miles NE of Missoula via MT 200 and MT 83. 20 sites with electric; showers; dump station. 25-foot limit. Swimming, fishing; boat ramp. GPS: N 47-05.4 W 113-26.7

Thompson Falls State Park

2220 Blue Slide Rd, Thompson Falls, MT 59873 (406) 827-3110. Located on Clark Fork River in northwestern Montana, 1 mile NW of Thompson Falls on MT 200. 17 sites. 30-foot limit. Swimming, fishing; boat ramp. GPS: N 47-37.8 W 115-32.0

Tongue River Reservoir State Park

290 Campers Point, Decker, MT 59025. Phone: (406) 757-2298. Located on Tongue River Reservoir, N of Sheridan, Wyoming, off MT 314 on county road, 6 miles N of Decker. 150 sites, some electric; dump station. No size limit. Marina, store. Swimming, fishing; boat ramp. GPS: N 45-05.6 W 106-48.3

Wayfarers State Park

8600 MT 35, Big Fork, MT 59911. Phone: (406) 837-4196. Located on MT 35 on NE side of Flathead Lake, 1/2 mile S of Bigfork. 23 sites; showers; dump station. 50-foot limit. Swimming, fishing; boat ramp. GPS: N 48-03.4 W 114-04.8

West Shore State Park

17768 MT 93, Lakeside, MT 59922. Phone: (406) 844-3044. Located on US 93 on NW side of Flathead Lake, 20 miles S of Kalispell. 24 sites. 40-foot limit. Swimming, fishing; boat ramp. GPS: N 47-56.9 W 114-11.3

Whitefish Lake State Park

1615 W Lakeshore, Whitefish, MT 59937. Phone: (406) 862-3991. Located on Whitefish Lake, 1 mile W of Whitefish, off US 93 on county road; follow signs. 25 sites; showers. 40-foot limit. Swimming, fishing; boat ramp. GPS: N 48-25.3 W 114-24.9

Yellow Bay State Park

23861 MT 35, Big Fork, MT 59911. Phone: (406) 982-3034. Located on MT 35 on east side of Flathead Lake, 15 miles N of Polson. 5 sites; showers. 30-foot limit. Marina. Swimming, fishing; boat ramp. GPS: N 47-52.5 W 114.01.6

NEBRASKA

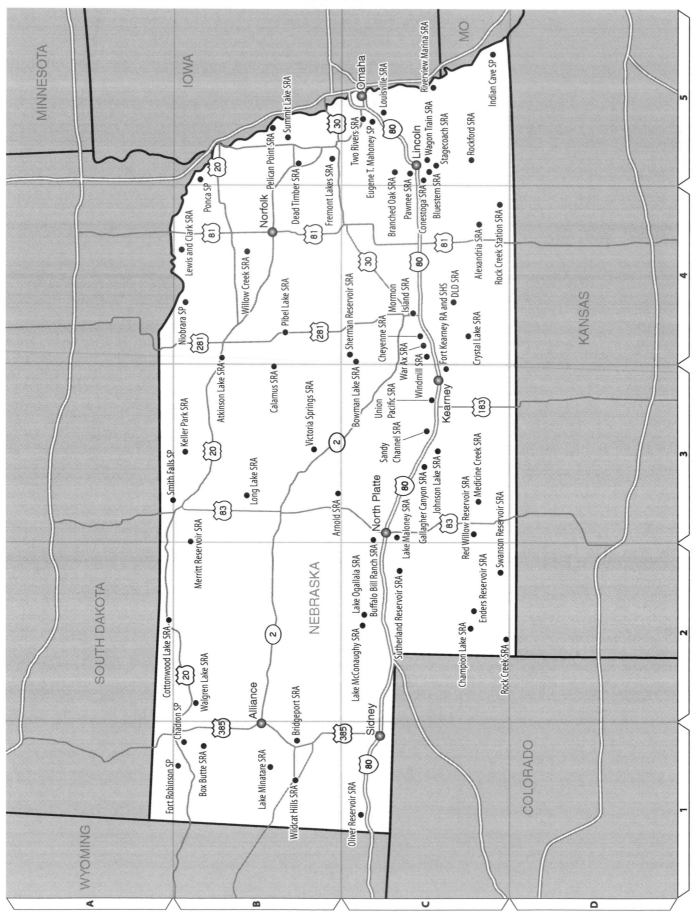

Nebraska

The Cornhusker State has 64 state-owned areas with RV facilities. Some of these areas are state parks, some are state recreation areas. Electric hook-ups are available in more than half of these areas and drinking water is available in all locations. All these areas have non-electric sites in addition to sites with electricity. Pets on leashes are permitted in all parks. Alcoholic beverages are not allowed on state property. Most parks are seasonal; locations that are open in winter do not have showers or water. Nebraska has a new online and telephone reservation system for most parks. (You will have to check the desired park for this service.) Otherwise, parks with reservable sites accept requests directly at the park. Some of the listed telephone numbers are for a district or regional office but will give information on any particular location. All state locations require a daily entrance fee in addition to campground charges. Unless indicated, rig size is not a problem in these locations. Rate groups: A and B, depending on the particular park and services provided. Reservation fees are additional.

Nebraska Game & Parks Commission
2200 N 33rd St.
Lincoln, NE 68503

Information: (402) 471-0641 or
(800) 826-7275 (recorded message)
Reservations: (402) 471-1414
Internet: www.ngpc.state.ne.us

Nebraska Park Locator

Nebraska Parks

Alexandria State Recreation Area

57426 710th Rd, Fairbury, NE 68352. Phone: (402) 729-5777. Located in southeastern Nebraska, 4 miles E of Alexandra, off US 136 and NE 53. 46 sites with electric; dump station. Fishing. (Electric motors only.) GPS: N 40-13.0 W 97-18.0

Arnold State Recreation Area

HC 69 Box 117, Anselmo, NE 68813. Phone: (308) 749-2235. Located in central Nebraska, 38 miles NE of North Platte, outside Arnold on NE 40. 80 sites, 20 with electric; dump station. Fishing, boating (electric motors.) GPS: N 41-24.8 W 100-11.6

Atkinson Lake State Recreation Area

Bassett, NE 68714. Phone: (402) 684-2921. Located on Atkinson Lake in north-central Nebraska outside Atkinson at junction of US 20 & NE 11. 28 sites, 8 with electric. Fishing. (Electric motors only.) GPS: N 42-31.5 W 99-00.2

Bluestem State Recreation Area

Sprague, NE 68503. Phone: (402)796-2362 . Located SW of Lincoln, 2.5 miles W of Sprague (US 77). 219 sites, no electricity; dump station. Swimming, fishing; boat ramp. GPS: N 40-37.0 W 96-48.0

Bowman Lake State Recreation Area

RR 2 Box 117, Loup City, NE 68853. Phone: (308) 745-0230. Located 9 miles SE of Bartlett. 10 sites, no electricity; fishing, boat ramp. GPS: N41-48.0 W98-31.8

Box Butte State Recreation Area

Crawford, NE 69339. Phone: (308) 665-2903. Located 10 miles N of Hemingford. 54 sites,(some electric). Fishing, swimming, boat ramp. GPS: N42-27.6 W103-6.6

Branched Oak State Recreation Area

12000 W Branched Oak Rd, Raymond, NE 68428. Phone: (402) 783-3400. Located in southeastern Nebraska, 16 miles NW of Lincoln on Salt Valley Lake, 2.5 miles N of Malcom. 519 sites, 283 with electric (some 30/50 amp); showers; dump stations. Swimming, fishing; boat ramp. Equestrian area. GPS; N 40-58.9 W 96-54.1

Bridgeport State Recreation Area

Bridgeport, NE 69341. Phone: (308) 436-3777. Located at the north edge of Bridgeport. 13 sites; fishing, swimming; boat ramp. GPS: N41-42.0 W103-06.6

Buffalo Bill Ranch State Recreation Area

2921 Scouts Rest Ranch Rd, North Platte, NE 69101. Phone: (308) 535-8035. Located on Platte River in south-central Nebraska, 2 miles W of North Platte on US 30, next to Buffalo Bill Ranch State Historic Park. 29 sites, 23 with electric (50 amp). Fishing. GPS: N 41-09.6 W 100-47.8

Calamus State Recreation Area

42285 York Point Rd, Burwell, NE 68823. Phone: (308) 346-5666. Located on Calamus Reservoir in central Nebraska, 6 miles NW of Burwell on NE 96. 177 sites, 122 with electric; showers; dump station. Swimming, fishing; boat ramp. GPS: N 41-50.3 W 99-12.2

Chadron State Park

15951 Hwy 385, Chadron, NE 69337. Phone: (308) 432-6167. Located in northwestern Nebraska, 9 miles S of Chadron on US 385. 70 sites with electric (30-amp); showers; dump station. Laundry. Swimming, fishing. Boat rental. GPS: N 42-42.7 W 103-00.5

Champion Lake State Recreation Area

73122 338 Ave, Enders, NE 69027. Phone: (402) 471-1623. Located 1/2 mile W of Champion on Champion Lake. 8 sites, 1 electric; fishing, boating. GPS N40-28.2 W101-45.0

Cheyenne State Recreation Area

Wood River, NE 68832. Phone: (308) 385-6210. Located off I-80, exit 300. 8 sites, no electricity; fishing, boating. GPS: N40-48.1 W96-18.0

Conestoga State Recreation Area

Denton, NE 68524. Phone: (402) 796-2362. Located in southeastern Nebraska, 20 miles SW of Lincoln, 2 miles N of Denton via NE S-55A, off US 6. 57 sites, 25 with electric (30/50 amp); dump station. Fishing; boat ramp. GPS: N 40-48.3 W 95-48.1

Cottonwood Lake State Recreation Area

Merriman, NE 69218. Phone: (308) 684-3428. Located 1/2 mile SE of Merriman. 30 sites, no electricity; fishing, boat ramp. GPS N42-54.6 W101-40.8

Crystal Lake State Recreation Area

7425 S US Hwy 281, Doniphan, NE 68832. Phone: (308) 385-6210. Located on Little Blue River in southern Nebraska, 1.5 miles N of Ayr on NE 74. 70 sites, 20 with electric. Swimming, fishing. (Electric motors only.) GPS: N 40-27.2 W 98-25.8

Dead Timber State Recreation Area

227 County Road & 12 Blvd, Scribner, NE 68057. Phone: (402) 727-2922. Located on Elkhorn River in eastern Nebraska, 11 miles S of West Point on US 275. 17 sites with electric; some primitive sites. Fishing. (Electric motors only.) GPS: N 41-43.2 W 96-42.0

DLD State Recreation Area

Hastings, NE 68832. Phone: (308) 385-6211. Located 5 miles E of Hastings. (Old rest area) 4 sites. GPS: N40-36.0 W98-18.1

Enders Reservoir State Recreation Area

73122 338th Ave, Enders, NE 69027. Phone: (308) 737-6577. Located in southwestern Nebraska near Colorado state line just outside Enders on US 6. 232 sites, 32 with electric; showers; dump station. Fishing, swimming; boat ramp. GPS: N 40-27.3 W 101-33.8

Eugene T. Mahoney State Park

28500 West Park Hwy, Ashland, NE 68003. Phone: (402) 944-2523. Located on Platte River in southeastern Nebraska, I-80 exit 426 near Ashland. 149 sites with electric; showers; laundry; dump station. Marina. Aquatic park; fishing; boat rentals. GPS: N 41-00.8 W 96-18.6

Fort Kearney State Historical Park

1020 V Rd, Kearney, NE 68847. Phone: (308) 865-5305. Located in south-central Nebraska, off I-80 exit 279, on NE 10 near Kearney on Platte River. 220 sites, 75 with electric (30/50 amp); showers; dump station. Eight lakes in park. Swimming, fishing. (Electric motors only.) GPS: N 40-39.1 W 98-59.4

Fort Robinson State Park

Crawford, NE 69339. Phone: (308) 665-2900. Located in northwestern Nebraska, 3 miles W of Crawford on US 20. 100 sites with electric (30/50 amp); showers; dump station. Laundry. Open year-round. Swimming, fishing. (Electric motors.) Equestrian area/trails. GPS: N 42-39.7 W 103-34.1

Fremont Lakes State Recreation Area

4349 W State Lakes Rd, Fremont, NE 68025. Phone: (402) 727-2922. Located in eastern Nebraska, 3 miles W of Fremont on US 30. 812 sites, 212 with electric; numerous primitive sites; showers; dump station. 20 lakes in park. Swimming, fishing; boat ramp. GPS: N 41-27.0 W 96-33.8

Gallagher Canyon State Recreation Area

1 East Park Dr 25A, Elwood, NE 68937. Phone: (308) 785-2685. Remote location in south-central Nebraska. From Cozad go 8 miles S on Hwy 23 to Gallagher Canyon sign. Go E on CR 751 for 2 miles, turn north on CR 422, then W on gravel road. 25 sites, no electricity; fishing, boat ramp. GPS: N40-42.1 W99-58.2

Indian Cave State Park

65296 720 Rd, Shubert, NE 68437. Phone: (402) 883-2575. Located in southeastern Nebraska on the Missouri River, SE of Auburn off NE 67 on NE 64E. 144 sites, 134 with electric (some 50 amp); showers; laundry; dump station. Fishing, boat ramp; horse trails. GPS: N 40-15.8 W 95-35.2

Johnson Lake State Recreation Area

Lexington, NE 68937. Phone: (308) 785-2685. Located in south-central Nebraska, 7 miles S of Lexington on US 283, off I-80 exit 237. 207 sites, 113 with electric; showers; dump station. Swimming, fishing; boat ramp. GPS: N 40-42.1 W 99-48.1

Keller Park State Recreation Area

Long Pine, NE 68714. Phone: (402) 684-2921. Located on Bone Creek in north-central Nebraska, 9 miles NE of Ainsworth, on US 183 off US 20. 35 sites, 25 with electric; dump station. Fishing. (Electric motors.) GPS: N 42-40.2 W 99-46.0

Lake Maloney State Recreation Area

301 E State Farm Rd, North Platte, NE 69101. Phone: (308) 535-8025. Located in south-central Nebraska, 1 mile S of North Platte on US 83, off I-80 exit 177. 256 sites, 56 with electric; showers; dump station. Swimming, fishing; boat ramp. GPS: N 41-04.5 W 100-47.0

Lake McConaughy State Recreation Area

1450 Hwy 61 N, Ogallala, NE 69153. Phone: (308) 284-8800. Located in southwestern Nebraska, 11 miles NE of Ogallala (next to Lake Ogallala SRA) on NE 61. 208 sites with electric (20/30/50 amp); many primitive sites; showers; dump station. Swimming, fishing; boat ramp, rentals. GPS; N 41-15.4 W 101-43.9

Lake Minatare State Recreation Area

Minatare, NE 69356. Phone: (308) 783-2911. Located on Lake Minatare in western Nebraska, 12 miles NE of Scottsbluff, off US 26 on county roads; follow signs. 152 sites, 52 with electric; showers; dump station. Seasonal. Horse trails. Laundry. Swimming, fishing; boat ramp. GPS: N 41-55.8 W 103-31.1

Lake Ogallala State Recreation Area

1450 Hwy 61 N, Ogallala, NE 69153. Phone: (308) 284-8800. Located on McConaughy Reservoir in southwestern Nebraska, 9 miles NE of Ogallala on NE 61 off US 26. 262 sites, 62 with electric (20/30 amp); showers. Fishing, boat ramp, rentals. GPS: N 41-12.2 W 101-40.1

Lewis and Clark State Recreation Area

54731 897 Rd, Crofton, NE 68730. Phone: (402) 388-4169. Located on Missouri River (Lewis & Clark Lake) in northeastern Nebraska on South Dakota state line, 9 miles N of Crofton on NE 121, off US 81. Two areas: 314 sites, 174 with electric (30/50 amp), 140 primitive; showers; dump stations. Marina. Swimming, fishing; boat ramp. Horse trails. GPS: N 42-49.8 W 97-30.3

Long Lake State Recreation Area

Johnstown, NE 68714. Phone: (402) 684-2921. Located 20 miles S of Johnstown, (remote area); 10 sites, no electricity; fishing, boating. GPS N42-17.4 W101-06.2

Louisville State Recreation Area

15810 Hwy 50 Louisville, NE 68037. Phone: (402) 234-6855. Located on Platte River in southeastern Nebraska outside Louisville (30 miles NE of Lincoln), on Hwy 50. 236 sites, 223 with electric; showers; dump station. Five lakes in park. Swimming, fishing. (Electric motors only.) GPS: N 41-00.3 W 96-12.1

Medicine Creek State Recreation Area

40611 Road 728, Cambridge, NE 69022. Phone: (308) 697-4667. Located on Medicine Creek (dam) in southern Nebraska, 9 miles NW of Cambridge off US 34 on county road; follow signs. 318 sites, 68 with electric; showers; dump station. Swimming, fishing; boat ramp. GPS: N 40-22.0 W 100-12.8

Merritt Reservoir State Recreation Area

120 First St, Valentine, NE 69201. Phone: (402) 376-3320. Located on Merritt Reservoir (Snake River) in central Nebraska, 26 miles SW of Valentine. 218 sites, 28 with electric; showers; dump station. Fishing; boat ramp, rentals. GPS: N 42-38.3 W 100-52.1

Mormon Island State Recreation Area

7425 S US Hwy 281, Doniphan, NE 68832. Phone: (308) 385-6211. Located in southeastern Nebraska on the "Chain of Lakes" at I-80 exit 212 (Grand Island exit). 38 sites, 34 with electric (30/50 amp); showers; dump station. Swimming, fishing. (Electric motors only.) GPS: N 40-48.4 W 98-24.1

Niobrara State Park

89261 522 Ave, Niobrara, NE 68760. Phone: (402) 857-3373. Located in northeastern Nebraska near South Dakota state line, 1 mile W of Niobrara on NE 12. 106 sites, 76 with electric. Showers; dump station. Swimming, fishing; boat ramp; (electric motors). Horse trails. GPS: N 42-44.8 W 98-03.0

Oliver Reservoir State Recreation Area

210615 Hwy 71, Gering, NE 69341. Phone: (308) 436-3777. Located in southwestern Nebraska 12 miles W of Kimball on US 30 near Wyoming state line, off I-80 exit 8. 175 sites; no electricity. Swimming, fishing; boat ramp. GPS: N 41-12.9 W 103-51.8

Pawnee State Recreation Area

Emerald, NE 68524. Phone: (402) 796-2362. Located in southeastern Nebraska, 15 miles W of Lincoln, 1.5 miles W of Emerald off US 34. 102 sites, 68 with electric (30/50 amp); showers; dump station. Swimming, fishing; boat ramp. GPS: N 40-48.6 W 96-48.1

Pelican Point State Recreation Area

Fort Calhoun, NE 68023. Phone: (402) 468-5611. Located 8 miles NE of Tekamgh (see Smith Falls SP). 6 sites, no electrcity; fishing, boating. (Remote area.) GPS: N41-48.3 W96-07.0

Pibel Lake State Recreation Area

Bartlett, NE 68862. Phone: (308) 728-3221. Located 9 miles SE of Bartlett. 30 sites, no electricity; fishing, boat ramp. GPS: N41-48.0 W98-31.8

Ponca State Park

88090 Spur 26 E, Ponca, NE 68770. Phone: (402) 755-2284. Located in northeastern Nebraska on Missouri River near South Dakota state line, 2 miles NE of Ponca at junction of Hwys 12 & 9. 167 sites, 92 with electric (30/50 amp); showers; dump station. Swimming, fishing; boat ramp. GPS: N 42-36.0 W 96-42.9

Red Willow Reservoir State Recreation Area

McCook, NE 69001. Phone: (308) 737-6577. Located on Red Willow Creek (dam) in southern Nebraska, 11 miles N of McCook on US 83. 205 sites, 45 with electric; showers; dump station. Marina. Swimming, fishing; boat ramp. GPS: N 40-21.8 W 100-39.6

Riverview Marina State Recreation Area

Nebraska City, NE 68410. Phone: (402) 873-7222. Located on the Missouri River in Nebraska City. 46 sites, 16 with electric (also open camping); showers. Fishing; boat ramp. GPS: N 40-41.4 W 95-51.0

Rock Creek State Recreation Area

73122 338th Ave, Enders, NE 69027. Phone: (308) 737-6577. Located one mile W of Parks. 43 sites, no electricity; fishing, boat ramp (electric motors). GPS: N40-05.6 W101-45.7

Rock Creek Station State Historical Park

57426 710th Rd, Fairbury, NE 68352. Phone: (402) 729-5777. Located in southeastern Nebraska, 6 miles E of Fairbury; follow signs from Fairbury (next to Rock Creek State Historical Park). 35 sites, 25 with electric, (30/50 amp); showers; dump station. GPS: N 40-06.1 W 97-06.0

Rockford State Recreation Area

Beatrice, NE 68503. Phone: (402) 729-5777. Located SE of Beatrice. 30 sites with electric (30/50 amp); fishing, swimming, boat ramp. GPS: N40-12.0 W96-36.1

Sandy Channel State Recreation Area

Elm Creek, NE 68847. Phone: (308) 865-5305. Located off I-80, exit 257. 30 sites, no electricity; fishing, boating. GPS: N40-42.2 W99-18.1

Sherman Reservoir State Recreation Area

79025 Sherman Dam Rd, Loup City, NE 68853. Phone: (308) 745-0230. Located on Oak Creek (Sherman Dam), 5 miles NE of Loup City (NE 92 & 58). 360 sites, no electricity; showers; dump station. Marina. Fishing; boat ramp, rentals. GPS: N 41-17.3 W 98-56.7

Smith Falls State Park

90159 Smith Falls Rd, Valentine, NE 69201. Phone: (402) 468-5611. (State's newest park; remote location.) Located 8 miles NE of Tekamgh. 23 sites, no electricity. Fishing, boating. GPS: N41-48.3 W96-07.0

Stagecoach State Recreation Area

Hickman, NE 68503. Phone: (402) 796-2362. Located in southeastern Nebraska, 21 miles SE of Lincoln, 1 mile SW of Hickman. 72 sites, 22 with electric (30/50 amp). Some open camping. Fishing; boat ramp. GPS: N 40-36.2 W 96-39.5

Summit Lake State Recreation Area

Tekamgh, NE 68023. Phone: (402) 374-1727. Located 2 miles W of Tekamgh. (See Smith Falls SP.) 67 sites, 30 with electric. Dump station; fishing, swimming, boat ramp. GPS: N41-48.1 W96-18.0

Sutherland Reservoir State Recreation Area

301 E State Farm Rd, North Platte, NE 69101. Phone: (308) 535-8025. Located 4 miles S of I-80, exit 158. 85 sites, no electricity; fishing, swimming; boat ramp. GPS: N41-06.1 W101-07.8

Swanson Reservoir State Recreation Area

Stratton, NE 69043. Phone: (308) 737-6577. Located on the Republican River (Swanson Reservoir) in southwestern Nebraska, 25 miles W of McCook on US 34. 204 sites, 54 with electric (20/30 amp); showers; dump stations. Fishing, swimming, boat ramp. GPS: N 40-10.6 W 101-05.5

Two Rivers State Recreation Area

Venice, NE 68069. Phone: (402) 359-5165. Located in eastern Nebraska, 28 miles SW of Omaha on the Platte River near Venice. Five areas: 229 sites, 113 with electric (some with water); showers; dump station. Fishing, swimming. Horse trails. GPS: N 41-13.2 W 96-20.8

Union Pacific State Recreation Area

Odessa, NE 68847. Phone: (308) 865-5305. Located near Kearney. 5 sites; fishing, boating. GPS: N40-42.2 W99-18.1

Victoria Springs State Recreation Area

43400 Hwy S21A, Anselmo, NE 68813. Phone: (308) 749-2235. Located in central Nebraska, 17 miles NW of Broken Bow, off Hwy 2 on Hwy S21A. 81 sites, 21 with electric (30/50 amp); showers; dump station. Fishing. GPS: N 41-36.7 W 99-44.9

Wagon Train State Recreation Area

Hickman, NE 68503. Phone: (402) 471-5566. Located in southeastern Nebraska, 16 miles SE of Lincoln near Hickman on NE 33. 88 sites, 28 with electric (30/50 amp); dump station. Swimming, fishing; boat ramp. GPS: N 40-36.1 W 96-34.3

Walgren Lake State Recreation Area

15951 Hwy 385, Chadron, NE 69337. Phone: (308) 432-6167. Located 2.5 miles SE of Hay. 40 sites; no electricity; fishing, boat ramp. GPS: N42-38.4 W102-37.8

War Ax State Recreation Area

Skelton, NE 68840. Phone: (308) 468-5700. Located off I-80 between exits 291 & 300. 8 sites, no electricity; fishing, boating. GPS: N40-42.1 W98-42.1

Wildcat Hills State Recreation Area

210615 Hwy 71, Gering, NE 69341. Phone: (308) 436-3777. Located in western Nebraska, 10 miles S of Gering (S of Scottsbluff) on NE 71. 5 primitive sites. Nature Center. GPS: N 41-42.1 W 103-40.4

Willow Creek State Recreation Area

54876 852 Rd, Pierce, NE 68767. Phone: (402) 329-4053. Located in northeastern Nebraska, 12 miles NW of Norfolk on NE 13. 102 sites, 84 with electric; showers; dump station. Lake in park. Swimming, fishing; boat ramp. Equestrian area. GPS: N 42-12.5 W 97-36.1

Windmill State Recreation Area

Gibbon, NE 68840. Phone: (308) 468-5700. Located on "Chain of Lakes" off I-80, between exits 285 and 291. 89 sites, 69 with electric (30/50 amp); showers; dump station. Swimming, fishing. (Electric motors only.) GPS: N 40-42.5 W 98-48.2

NEVADA

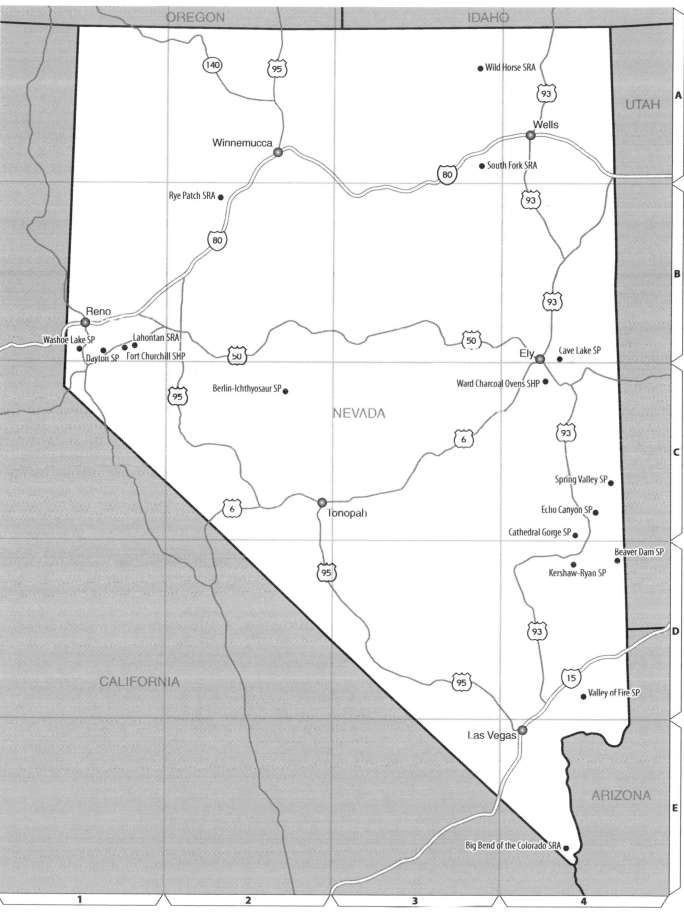

OREGON

IDAHO

UTAH

140

95

● Wild Horse SRA

93

Wells

80

● South Fork SRA

Winnemucca

Rye Patch SRA ●

93

80

93

Reno

50

Washoe Lake SP ●

Lahontan SRA

Ely ●

Cave Lake SP

Dayton SP ● Fort Churchill SHP

50

Ward Charcoal Ovens SHP ●

95

Berlin-Ichthyosaur SP ●

NEVADA

6

93

Spring Valley SP ●

6

Echo Canyon SP ●

Tonopah

Cathedral Gorge SP ●

Beaver Dam SP ●

Kershaw-Ryan SP ●

95

93

CALIFORNIA

95

15

Valley of Fire SP ●

Las Vegas

ARIZONA

Big Bend of the Colorado SRA ●

A

B

C

D

E

1   2   3   4

Nevada

RV-friendly parks or recreation areas in Nevada are located in convenient places throughout the state. There are 17 such locations, all open year-round. User fees are required to enter all Nevada parks and an additional fee is required for campground usage. Because of the altitudes of some parks, winter weather can cause closures. Travelers should contact the respective park to check road and park conditions. You can also check with each park to determine space availability at any time, or to request reservations. (No central reservation system.) Rate group: A. Entrance fee and sites with facilities, boat launch fees extra.

Nevada Division of State Parks
Department of Conservation & Natural Resources
901 S Stewart St
5th Fl, Ste 5005
Carson City, NV 89701

Information: (775) 684-2770 or (800) 638-2328
Internet: www.parks.nv.gov

Nevada Park Locator

Nevada Parks

Beaver Dam State Park

Panaca, NV 89042. Phone: (775) 728-4460. Located about 155 miles N of Las Vegas (NV) via US 93 on Utah state line. Two areas, 34 sites, water. Fishing. 28-foot limit. No trash containers. GPS: N37-30.1 W114-04.2.

Berlin-Ichthyosaur State Park

HC 61, Austin, NV 89310. Phone: (775) 964-2440. Located 23 miles E of Gabbs via NV 844. (Gabbs is located on NV 361, midway between US 50 and US 95.) 14 sites; water; dump station. 25-foot limit. GPS: N 38-53.0 W 117-36.7

Big Bend of the Colorado State Recreation Area

4220 S Needles Hwy, Laughlin, NV 89028. Phone: (702) 298-1859. Located on Colorado River 5 miles S of Laughlin, in town limits, 1 mile S of Casino Drive on Needles Hwy. 24 full hook-up sites (most are pull-through); showers. Swimming, fishing; boat ramp. 60-foot limt. GPS: N 35-04.0 W 114-36.8

Cathedral Gorge State Park

Panaca, NV 89042. Phone: (775) 728-4460. Located 2 miles N of Panaca, just W of US 93. (Panaca is located in SE Nevada, at junction of US 93 & NV 319.) 22 sites with electric; showers; water; dump station. 40-foot limit. GPS: N 37-49.2 W 114-24.5

Cave Lake State Park

Ely, NV 89315. Phone: (775) 296-1505. Located on Cove Lake about 15 miles SE of Ely off US Hwys 6, 50 and 93 and Success Summit Rd. 23 sites; showers; water; dump station. Winter weather may force closings. Fishing; boat ramp. (5 mph. limit on lake.) GPS: N 39-03.9 W 114-41.0

Dayton State Park

US Hwy 50, East Dayton, NV 89403. Phone: (775) 687-5678. Located on US 50, 12 miles E of Carson City on Carson River in the town of Dayton. 10 sites; water available; dump station. 34-foot limit. GPS: N 39-15.2 W 119-35.2

Echo Canyon State Park

HC 74, Pioche NV 89043. Phone: (775) 962-5103. Located 12 miles E of Pioche (southeastern NV at US 93 & NV 322) via NV 322 & 323 and about 12 miles W of Utah/Nevada state line. 33 sites (first-come first-served); water available; dump station. Fishing, swimming; boat ramp. 25-foot limit. GPS: N 37-54.6 W 114-16.4

Fort Churchill State Historic Park

10003 Hwy US 95A, Silver Springs, NV 89429. Phone: (775) 577-2345. Located on US 95A 8.5 miles S of Silver Springs (about 40 miles E of Carson City) at junction of US 50 & 95A. On the Carson River. 20 sites; water available; no hook-ups; dump station. No Reservations. GPS: N 39-17.7 W 119-16.1

Kershaw-Ryan State Park

Caliente, NV 89008. Phone: (775) 726-3564. Located two miles S of Caliente in southeast NV, via US 93 and NV 317. 15 spaces; water. 30-foot limit. GPS: N37-34.8 W114-31.2.

Lahontan State Recreation Area

16799 Lahontan Dam, Fallon, NV 89406. Phone: (775) 867-3500. On the Carson River (on Lahontan Reservoir), 18 miles W of Fallon and 45 miles NE of Carson City, via US 50. Access the park from either US 50 east of Silver Springs or US 95 south of Silver Springs. Silver Springs Beach 7 offers 26 sites with modern restrooms. Showers and water are available. Primitive on-the-beach camping is available in all areas. Dump stations are available near both entrances to the park. Swimming, fishing; boat ramp. 65-foot limit. GPS: N 39-25.9 W 119-09.4

Rye Patch State Recreation Area

2505 Rye Patch Reservoir Rd, Lovelock, NV 89419. Phone: (775) 538-7321. Located on Rye Patch Reservoir, 22 miles N of Lovelock just off I-80 exit 129. 47 sites, 25 improved; showers; water; dump station. Swimming, fishing; boat ramp. GPS: N 40-28.1 W 118-18.2

South Fork State Recreation Area

353 Lower South Fork #8, Spring Creek, NV 89815. Phone: (775) 744-4346. Remote location on NV 228, 16 miles S of Elko (I-80 exit 301) on South Fork Reservoir, on NV 228. 25 sites (open early May to October 15th); water; showers; dump station. Swimming, fishing; boat ramp. 30-foot limit. GPS: N 40-40.8 W 115-44.0

Spring Valley State Park

Pioche, NV 89043. Phone: (775) 962-5102. Located on Eagle Valley Reservoir, 20 miles E of Pioche via NV 322. (Pioche is located in southeastern Nevada at junction of US 93 & NV 322.) Two campgrounds: Horsethief Gulch has 37 sites with water, showers; Ranch Campground has 6 sites with water; dump station. Snow may make winter access difficult. Swimming, fishing; boat ramp. 35-foot limit. GPS: N 38 01.0 W 114-12.3

Valley of Fire State Park

29450 Valley of Fire Rd, Overton, NV 89040. Phone: (702) 397-2088. (Largest state park in Nevada.) Located 6 miles from Lake Mead, 55 miles NE of Las Vegas off I-15 at exit 75. 72 sites with electric, water; showers; dump station. 50-foot limit. GPS: N 36-25.1 W 114-35.8

Ward Charcoal Ovens State Historical Park

Ely, NV 89315. Phone: (775) 289-1693. Located 18 miles S of Ely off US 93 (watch for signs). Willow Creek Campground has 26 sites with two pull-through spaces. 35-foot limit.

Washoe Lake State Park

4855 East Lake Blvd, Carson City, NV 98704. Phone: (775) 687-4319. Located 5 miles N of Carson City and 18 miles S of Reno off US 395 on East Lake Blvd. 49 sites; showers; dump station. Several sites will accept RVs up to 45 feet. Fishing; boat ramp. Equestrian area. GPS: N 39-14.6 W 119-45.6

Wild Horse State Recreation Area

HC 31, Elko, NV 89801. Phone: (775) 385-5939. Remote location on NV 225, 67 miles N of Elko (I-80 exit 301), on Wildhorse Reservoir. 33 sites; showers; water; dump station. Swimming, fishing; boat ramp. 45-foot limit. GPS: N 41-39.7 W 115-46.1

NEW HAMPSHIRE

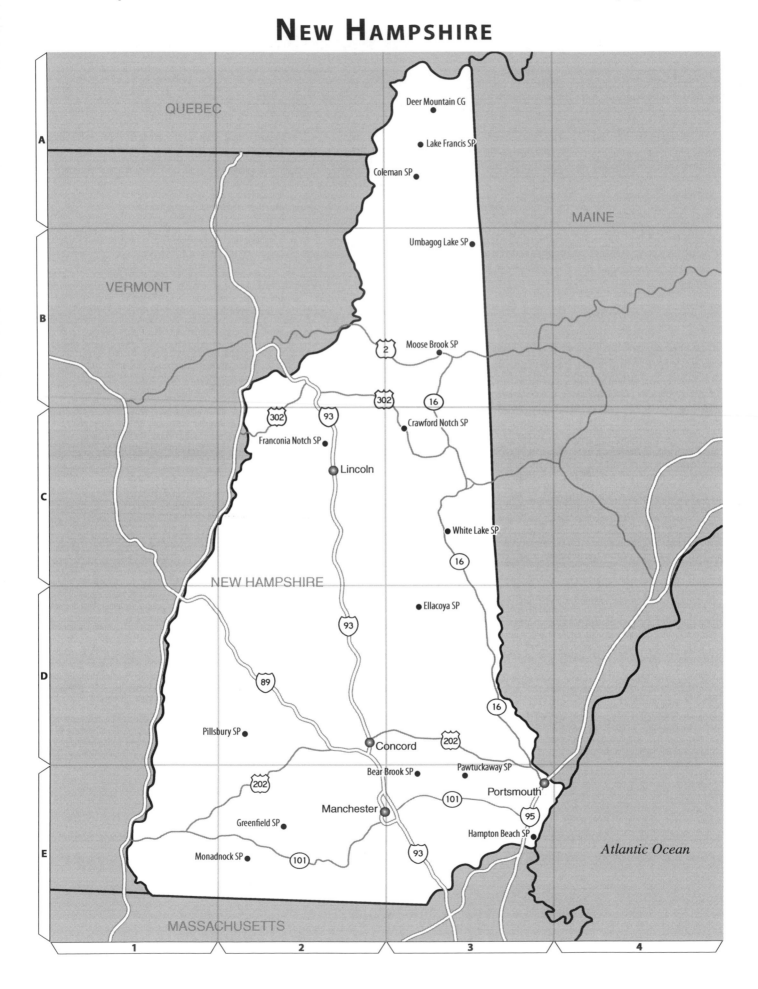

QUEBEC

MAINE

VERMONT

Deer Mountain CG

Lake Francis SP

Coleman SP

Umbagog Lake SP

Moose Brook SP

2

302

16

302

93

Crawford Notch SP

Franconia Notch SP

Lincoln

White Lake SP

16

NEW HAMPSHIRE

Ellacoya SP

93

89

16

Pillsbury SP

202

Concord

Bear Brook SP

Pawtuckaway SP

Portsmouth

202

Manchester

101

95

Greenfield SP

Hampton Beach SP

Monadnock SP

101

93

Atlantic Ocean

MASSACHUSETTS

A

B

C

D

E

1   2   3   4

New Hampshire

Fifteen of New Hampshire's state parks accommodate RVs. Most of these parks do not have site facilities. In all cases you should contact the park you seek to determine space availability and if your rig will fit the space. Several of the parks are open to RVs with the warning that RVs are welcome ("RVs OK") if the rig will fit the site. Most parks hold some spaces out of the reservation "pool" for drive-in travelers, but you must check with the park. Some parks prohibit pets. Credit cards are accepted. Seniors (62+) are eligible for discounts but you must ask at check-in. Most parks are open seasonally; some open as late as mid-June. Rate groups: B and C depending on site utilities.

New Hampshire Division of Parks & Recreation
PO Box 1856
Concord, NH 03302

Information: (800) 386-4664
Reservations: (603) 271-3628
Internet: www.nhparks.state.nh.us

New Hampshire Park Locator

New Hampshire Parks

Bear Brook State Park
157 Deerfield Rd, Allenstown, NH 03275. Phone: (603) 485-9869. Located SE of Concord off NH 28, 5 miles off US 3. 101 sites (RVs "OK"); dump station. Canoe rentals. Two ponds in park. Laundry. Swimming, fishing. Horse trails. GPS: N 43-09.8 W 71-24.3

Coleman State Park
1166 Diamond Pond Rd, Stewartstown, NH 03597. Phone: (603) 237-5382. Remote location off NH 26 at Kidderville on Little Diamond Pond in northern NH. 16 sites; showers; dump station. 35-foot limit. Laundry. Reservations required. Fishing; boat ramp, rentals. GPS: N 44-56.0 W 71-20.0

Crawford Notch State Park
1464 US 302; Harts Location, NH 03812. Phone: (603) 374-2272. Located near North Conway. 19 sites; water available; showers, laundry. GPS: N 44-2.7 W 71-4.4

Deer Mountain Campground
Located in Connecticut Lakes State Forest. 5309 N Main St, Pittsburg, NH 03592. Phone: (603) 538-6965. Located on US 3 near Lake Francis State Park in northern NH, near Canadian border. 25 primitive sites; size limitations in some sites. Fishing. GPS: N 45-03.1 W 71-23.1

Ellacoya State Park
266 Scenic Dr, Gilford, NH 03246. Phone: (603) 293-7821. Located NE of Laconia on Lake Winnipesaukee along NH 11. 37 sites with water, electric; some pull-through; showers; laundry. Seasonal. No pets. Swimming. GPS: N 43 34.3 W 71-21.0

Franconia Notch State Park
9 Franconia Notch Pkwy, Franconia, NH 03580. Phone: (603) 745-8391. Located in White Mountain National Forest between Plymouth and Littleton, off I-93 between exits 34 & 35. 104 sites (two areas); showers; some hook-ups. (Includes Cannon Mountain RV area.) No pets. Fishing, swimming; boat ramp. 35-foot limit. GPS: N 44-11.6 W 71-42.9

Greenfield State Park
133 Beach Rd, Greenfield, NH 03047. Phone: (603) 547-3497. Located in southern NH on Contogcook River, W of Manchester, on NH 136, near Greenfield. 179 sites, 134 by reservation only, (RVs "OK"); showers; laundry; dump station. Swimming, fishing; boat ramp; canoe/kayak rentals. (Limited hours - call.) GPS: N 42-57.0 W 71-52.9

Hampton Beach State Park
160 Ocean Blvd, Hampton, NH 03842. Phone: (603) 926-3784. Located on Atlantic Ocean in southeastern NH on Route 1A, outside Hampton. 28 full hook-up sites; showers; store. Swimming, fishing. No pets. GPS: N 42-54.4 W 70-48.7

Lake Francis State Park
439 River Rd, Pittsburg, NH 03592. Phone: (603) 538-6965. Located in far north NH on Lake Francis, 5 miles E of Pittsburg off US 3. 45 sites, 9 with hook-ups; showers; dump station. Swimming, fishing; boat ramp. GPS: N 45-03.6 W 71-18.2

Monadnock State Park

116 Poole Rd, Jaffrey, NH 03452. Phone: (603) 532-8862. Located in southern NH, northwest of Jaffrey (US 202 & NH 124), off NH 124. 21 sites (suitable for pop-up trailers); showers. 20-foot limit. Open all year. Store. Swimming, fishing; boat ramp. GPS: N 42-50.7 W 72-05.2

Moose Brook State Park

30 Jimtown Rd, Gorham, NH 03581. Phone: (603) 466-3860. Located on Moose Brook, S of Berlin near Gorham, off US 2. 27 sites (RVs "OK"); showers. Swimming, fishing. GPS: N 44-23.5 W 71-13.5

Pawtuckaway State Park

40 Pawtuckaway Rd, Nottingham, NH 03290. Phone: (603) 895-3031. Located NE of Manchester off NH 101, on NH 156. 192 sites (RVs "OK"); showers. No pets. Swimming, fishing; boat ramp, rentals. No alcohol in beach area. GPS: N 43-05.4 W 71-09.8

Pillsbury State Park

100 Pillsbury State Park Rd, Washington, NH 03280. Phone: (603) 863-2860. Located 30 miles W of Concord, 7 miles N of Washington on NH 31. 25 sites, some remote; water available. Four ponds in park. Boat ramp. (No motors.) GPS: N 43-14.2 W 72-07.4

Umbagog Lake State Park

235 E Route 26, Cambridge, NH 03579. Phone: (603) 482-7795. Located on Umbagog Lake in Northern NH, 9 miles SE of Errol (NH 16 & 26), on NH 26. 27 sites with electric; water; dump station. Store. Swimming, fishing; boat ramp, rentals. GPS: N 44-42.8 W 71-04.4

White Lake State Park

94 State Park Rd, Tamworth, NH 03886. Phone: (603) 323-7350. Located in east-central NH on White Lake off NH 16. 80 sites (two areas); dump station; showers. Store. Swimming, fishing. Canoe rentals. GPS: N 43-49.7 W 71-12.6

NEW JERSEY

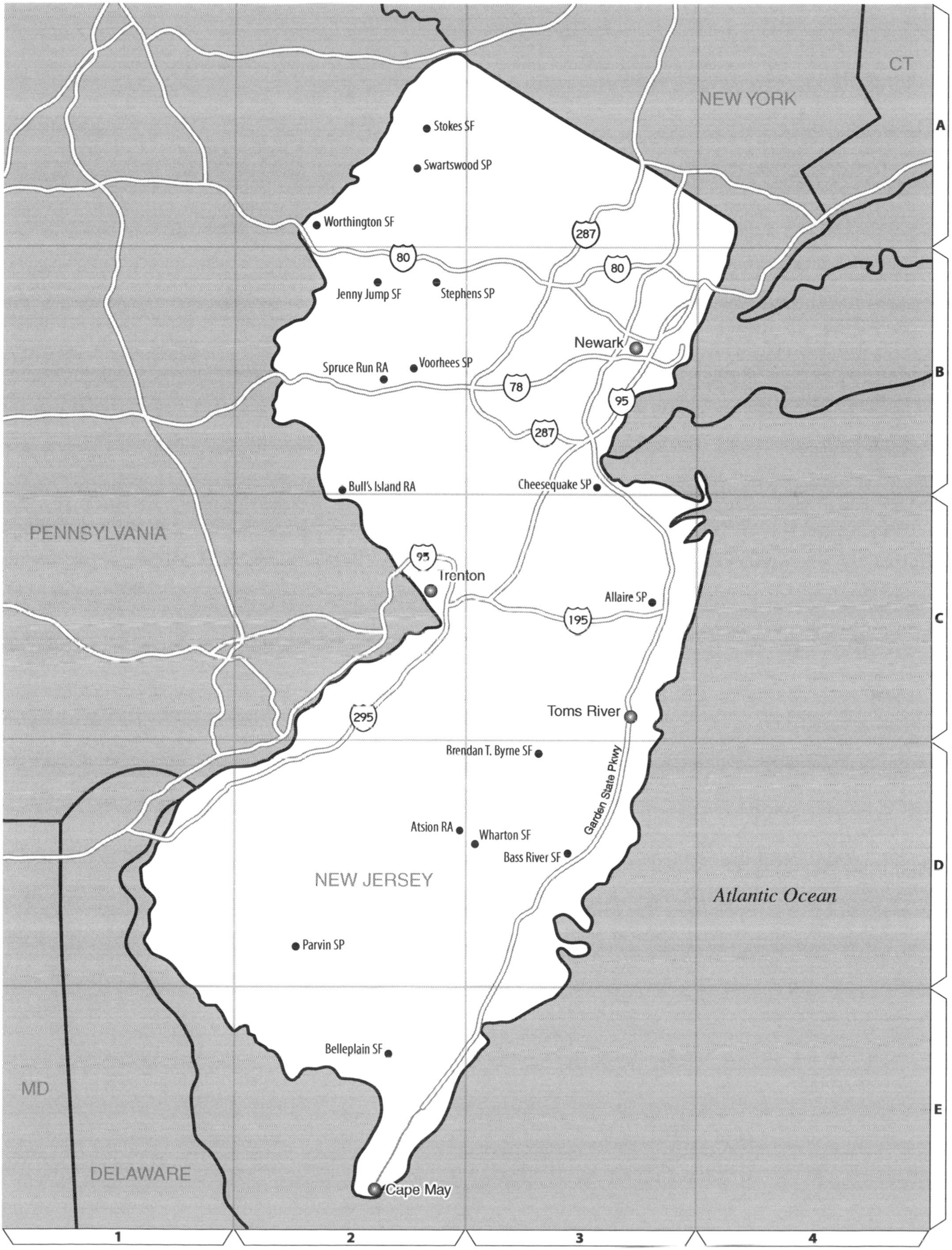

CT

NEW YORK

A

Stokes SF

Swartswood SP

Worthington SF

287

80

80

Jenny Jump SF   Stephens SP

Newark

B

Spruce Run RA   Voorhees SP

78

95

287

Bull's Island RA   Cheesequake SP

PENNSYLVANIA

95

Trenton

Allaire SP

195

C

295

Toms River

Brendan T. Byrne SF

Atsion RA
            Wharton SF
        Bass River SF

Garden State Pkwy

NEW JERSEY

Atlantic Ocean

D

Parvin SP

Belleplain SF

MD

E

DELAWARE

Cape May

| 1 | 2 | 3 | 4 |

New Jersey

The Garden State maintains 16 state parks and forests with RV facilities; however, none have sites with hook-ups. Water is available in all the parks and most have dump stations. Pets are not allowed in overnight campsites. Alcoholic beverages are not permitted in New Jersey campgrounds. Eight of the parks are open year-round. While reservations are accepted in all parks, it is possible to obtain space on a drive-in basis; you should call the particular park to verify space availability. Rate group: B. Entrance fee (in some parks) extra.

New Jersey Dept. of Environmental Protection
Division of Parks and Forestry
PO Box 404
Trenton, NJ 08625

Information & Reservations: (855) 607-3075
(Reserve America)
Internet: www.nj.gov/dep/parksandforests

New Jersey Park Locator

Allaire State Park....................C3
Atsion Recreation Area (Wharton State Forest)....................D2
Bass River State Forest....................D3
Belleplain State Forest....................E2
Brendan T. Byrne State Forest....................D3
Bull's Island Recreation Area....................B2
Cheesequake State Park....................B3
Jenny Jump State Forest....................B2
Parvin State Park....................D2
Spruce Run Recreation Area....................B2
Stephens State Park....................B2
Stokes State Forest....................A2
Swartswood State Park....................A2
Voorhees State Park....................B2
Wharton State Forest....................D3
Worthington State Forest....................A2

New Jersey Parks

Allaire State Park

4265 Atlantic Ave, Farmingdale, NJ 07727. Phone: (732) 938-2371. Located on Manasquam River on NJ 524, 1.5 miles W of Garden State Pkwy exit 98 or I-195 exit 31B. 45 sites; showers; dump station; Fishing; horse trails. GPS: N 40-10.9 W 74-09.3

Atsion Recreation Area (Wharton State Forest)

744 Rt 206, Shamong, NJ 08088. Phone: (609) 268-0444. Located on US 206, 8 miles N of Hammonton. 50 sites; showers; dump station. Seasonal. GPS: N 39-44.6 W 74-43.0

Bass River State Forest

762 Stage Rd, Tuckerton, NJ 08087. Phone: (609) 296-1114. Located on Stage Rd W of Garden State Pkwy exits 50 or 52, 6 miles W of Tuckerton. 176 sites; showers; laundry; dump station. Swimming, fishing; boat ramp. (Electric motors only.) GPS: N 39-39.7 W 74-25.4

Belleplain State Forest

1 Henkinsifkin Rd, Woodbine, NJ 08088. Phone: (609) 861-2404. Located in southern NJ on CR 550, 2 miles W of Woodbine; follow signs. 169 sites; showers; laundry; dump station. Swimming, fishing; boat ramp. (Electric motors only.) GPS: N 39-15.1 W 74-50.7

Brendan T. Byrne State Forest

Rt 72 E, Mile 1, Woodland Township, NJ 08064. Phone: (609) 726-1191. Located southeast of Browns Mills on NJ 72. 79 sites; showers; laundry; dump station. Fishing. GPS: N 39-54.3 W 74-29.7

Bull's Island Recreation Area

2185 Daniel Bray Hwy, Stockton, NJ 08559. Phone: (609) 397-2949. Located on the Delaware River NW of Trenton; on NJ 29, 3 miles NW of Stockton. 44 sites; showers; dump station. Seasonal. No pets. Fishing. GPS: N 40-24.6 W 75-02.6

Cheesequake State Park

300 Gordon Rd, Matawan, NJ 07747. Phone: (732) 566-2161. Located off NJ 34 near junction with US 9, 3 miles NW of Matawan; follow signs. 53 sites; showers; dump station. Seasonal. 11-foot height limit. No pets. Swimming, fishing. GPS: N 40-26.1 W 74-15.8

Jenny Jump State Forest

Hope, NJ 07844. Phone: (908) 459-4366. Located NW of Great Meadow on State Park Rd, 3 miles N of NJ 519. 22 sites; showers. Seasonal. Fishing; boating. GPS: N 40-53.2 W 75-00.4

Parvin State Park

701 Almond Rd, Pittsgrove, NJ 08318. Phone: (856) 358-8616. Located between Centerton and Vineland, near junction of CR 540 and NJ 553 on CR 540. 56 sites; showers; laundry; dump station. No pets. Swimming; fishing. (Electric motors.) GPS: N 39-30.5 W 75-07.7

Spruce Run Recreation Area

68 Van Sykel's Rd, Clinton, NJ 08809. Phone: (908) 638-8572. Located S of Washington off NJ 31 (I-78 exits 15 or 17). 67 sites; showers. Seasonal. Swimming, fishing; boat ramp, rentals. GPS: N 40-39.5 W 74-56.9

Stephens State Park

800 Willow Grove St, Hackettstown, NJ 07840. Phone: (908) 852-3790. Located 2 miles N of Hackettstown off US 46. 40 sites; no facilities. No pets. Seasonal. Fishing; horse trails. GPS: N 40-52.3 W 74-48.2

Stokes State Forest

1 Coursen Rd, Branchville, NJ 07826. Phone: (973) 948-3820. Located on Stoney Lake in northern NJ off US 206, 4 miles NW of Branchville. 50 sites; showers. No pets. Swimming, fishing. GPS: N 41-11.1 W 74-47.8

Swartswood State Park

Swartswood, NJ 07877. Phone: (973) 383-5230. State's first state park. Located on CR 619, 4 miles NW of Newton (US 206), on Swartswood Lake. 65 sites; showers; laundry; dump station. Seasonal. Swimming, fishing; boat ramp; boat/canoe rentals, (electric motors.) GPS: N 41-04.4 W 74-49.1

Voorhees State Park

251 CR 513, Glen Gardner, NJ 08826. Phone: (908) 638-8572. Located on CR 513 near junction with NJ 31 at High Bridge; follow signs. 47 sites; showers; dump station. Fishing. GPS: N 40-41.7 W 74-53.2

Wharton State Forest

31 Batsto Rd, Hammonton, NJ 08037. Phone: (609) 561-0024. Located 8 miles E of Hammonton on NJ 542. Godfrey Bridge Campground: 49 sites; no facilities; 21-foot limit. Also see Atsion Recreation Area. Swimming, fishing; boat ramp. GPS: N 39-38.9 W 74-40.4

Worthington State Forest

Old Mine Rd, Columbia, NJ 07832. Phone: (908) 841-9575. Located on Old Mine Rd, 8 miles N of Delaware Water Gap, near I-80 exit 1. 69 sites; showers. Seasonal. Fishing; boat ramp. (Electric motors only.) GPS: N 40-59.3 W 75-07.4

NEW MEXICO

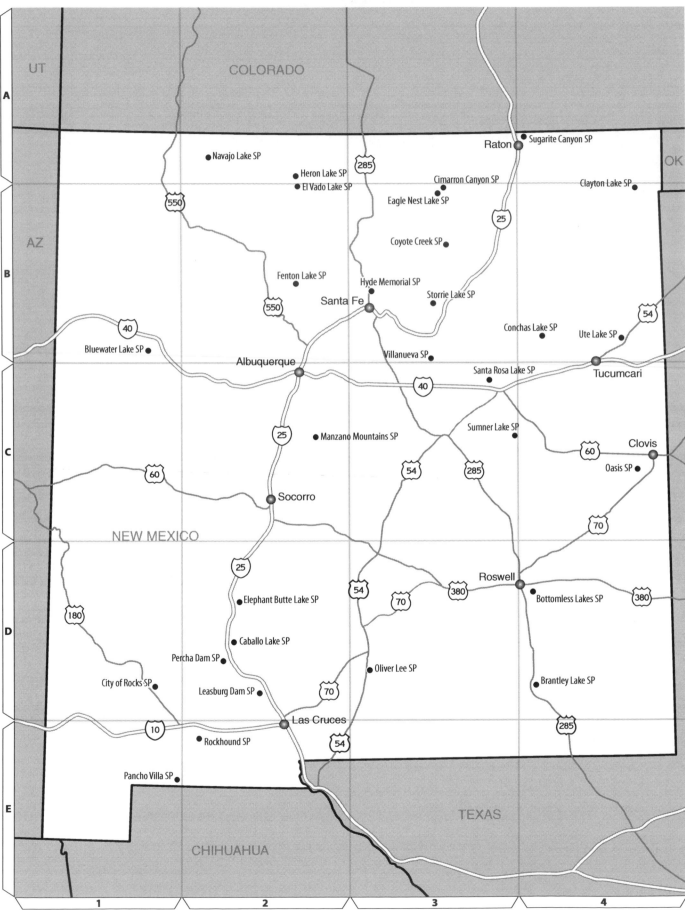

UT

COLORADO

A

● Navajo Lake SP

Raton ● Sugarite Canyon SP

285

● Heron Lake SP
● El Vado Lake SP

Cimarron Canyon SP ●

Clayton Lake SP ●

550

Eagle Nest Lake SP ●

25

AZ

Coyote Creek SP ●

B

Fenton Lake SP ●

Hyde Memorial SP ●

Storrie Lake SP ●

550

Santa Fe ●

54

40

Conchas Lake SP ●

Ute Lake SP ●

Bluewater Lake SP ●

Albuquerque ●

Villanueva SP ●

Santa Rosa Lake SP ●

Tucumcari

40

Sumner Lake SP ●

25

Manzano Mountains SP ●

60

Clovis

54

285

60

C

Oasis SP ●

Socorro ●

70

NEW MEXICO

25

Roswell

Elephant Butte Lake SP ●

54

380

Bottomless Lakes SP ●

380

70

180

D

Caballo Lake SP ●

Percha Dam SP ●

Oliver Lee SP ●

Brantley Lake SP ●

City of Rocks SP ●

Leasburg Dam SP ●

70

10

Las Cruces ●

285

● Rockhound SP

54

Pancho Villa SP ●

E

TEXAS

CHIHUAHUA

| 1 | 2 | 3 | 4 |

New Mexico

The 29 New Mexico state parks suitable for RVs rank highly in facilities and locations. Most have full facilities, will accept large rigs, and are close to major highways or Interstates. Some parks prohibit alcoholic beverages (check by park) and pets must be on leashes. All the parks have developed sites, which means roads are paved or hard gravel, site pads and tables. Other site amenities vary by park. Credit cards are accepted. Rate groups: A and B, depending on site facilities.

New Mexico State Parks Division
1220 S.St. Francis Dr.
Santa Fe, NM 87505

Information: (888) 667-2757
Reservations: (877) 664-7787
Internet: www.nmparks.com
Reservations: www.newmexico.reserveworld.com

New Mexico Park Locator

New Mexico Parks

Bluewater Lake State Park

30 Bluewater State Park Rd, Prewitt, NM 87045. Phone: (505) 876-2391. Located on Bluewater Lake, 28 miles NW of Grants off I-40 exit 63 on NM 412. 149 sites, 14 with electric; showers; dump station. 45-foot limit. Fishing, swimming; boat ramp. GPS: N 35-17.3 W 108-07.5

Bottomless Lakes State Park

545A Bottomless Lake Rd, Roswell, NM 88201. Phone: (575) 624-6058. Located on Lea Lake on NM 409 east of Roswell via US 380. 38 sites, 32 with electric, water; 6 full hook-up; showers; dump station. 50-foot limit. Fishing, swimming; boat ramp. Wi-Fi. GPS: N 33-19.0 W 104-20.0

Brantley Lake State Park

33 E Brantly Lake Rd, Carlsbad, NM 88221. Phone: (575) 457-2384. Located on Brantley Lake, 12 miles N of Carlsbad on Eddy County Road 3, off US 285. 51 sites with electric, water, (three full hook-up); showers; dump station. 50-foot limit. Fishing, swimming; boat ramp. GPS: N 32-32.8 W 104-22.5

Caballo Lake State Park

Hwy 187, Caballo, NM 87931. Phone: (575) 743-3942. Located on Caballo Reservoir, 16 miles S of Truth or Consequences off I-25 exit 59. 170 sites, 115 with electric; showers; dump station. 85-foot limit. Fishing, swimming; boat ramp. Horse trails. GPS: N 32-54.7 W 107-18.9

Cimarron Canyon State Park

28869 Hwy 64, Eagle Nest, NM 87718. Phone: (575) 377-6271. Located NE of Taos in the New Mexico high country (8,000 ft. altitude) on US 64. 94 sites, no hook-ups; showers, dump station. Fishing. Horse trails. GPS: N 36-32.5 W 105-08.5

City of Rocks State Park

327 Hwy 61, Faywood, NM 88034. Phone: (505) 536-2800. Located N of Deming on NM 61, off US 180. 52 sites, 10 with electric; showers. 65-foot limit. GPS: N 32-35.3 W 107-58.4

Clayton Lake State Park

141 Clayton Lake Rd, Clayton, NM 88415. Phone: (575) 374-8808. Located on Clayton Lake, 12 miles NW of Clayton off NM 370. 42 sites, some with electric; showers; water. 45-foot limit. Fishing; boat ramp. GPS: N 36-34.4 W 103-18.1

Conchas Lake State Park

501 Bell Ranch Rd, Conchas Dam, NM 88416. Phone: (575) 868-2270. Located on Conchas Lake, 34 miles NW of Tucumcari off NM 104. 145 sites, 40 with electric, water; showers; dump station. 40-foot limit. Fishing, swimming, boat ramp. Marina. GPS: N 35-22.5 W 104-11.7

Coyote Creek State Park

Hwy 434, Mile 17, Guadalupita, NM 87722. Phone: (575) 387-2328. Located 17 miles N of Mora off NM 434, N of Las Vegas in north-central NM. 47 sites, 34 with electric, 15 with water and electric;

showers; dump station. 38-foot limit. Fishing; boat ramp. Wi-Fi. GPS: N 36-11.3 W 105-14.0

Eagle Nest Lake State Park

42 Marina Way, Eagle Nest, NM 87718. Phone: (575) 377-1594. Located off US 64 on Eagle Nest Lake, NE of Taos. 19 sites, water available. Fishing, swimming; boat ramp. GPS: N 36-35.5 W 105-12.6

El Vado Lake State Park

State Rd 112, Tierra Amarilla, NM 87575. Phone: (575) 588-7247. Located on El Vado Lake, 17 miles SW of Tierra Amarilla (US 64 & 84) on NM 112. 80 sites, 17 with water, electric, 2 full hook-up; showers; dump station. 35-foot limit. Fishing, swimming, boat ramp. GPS: N 36-35.6 W 106-44.0

Elephant Butte Lake State Park

101 Hwy 195, Elephant Butte, NM 87935. Phone: (575) 744-5923. Located on Elephant Butte Reservoir 5 miles N of Truth or Consequences off I-25 exit 83. (Largest lake in New Mexico.) 173 sites, 144 with water, electric, 8 full hook-up; showers; dump station. No length limit. Fishing, swimming; boat ramp. Marina. Wi-Fi. GPS: N 33-09.8 W 107-11.9

Fenton Lake State Park

455 Fenton Lake Rd, Jemez Springs, NM 87025. Phone: (575) 829-3630. Located on Fenton Lake, NW of Santa Fe off NM 126, just E of US 550. 37 sites, 5 with electric, water. 40-foot limit. Equestrian area, trails. Fishing; boat ramp. (Electric motors only.) GPS: N 35-55.6 W 106-44.1

Heron Lake State Park

640 State Rd 95, Los Ojos, NM 87551. Phone: (575) 588-7470. Located on Heron Lake, 11 miles NW of Tierra Amarilla off US 64/84 via NM 95. 250 sites, 54 with electric, water; showers; dump station. 35-foot limit. Fishing, swimming. Boat ramp. Wi-Fi. GPS: N 36-41.5 W 106-39.4

Hyde Memorial State Park

740 Hyde Park Rd, Santa Fe, NM 87501. Phone: (505) 983-7175. Located 8 miles NE of Santa Fe off NM 475. 50 sites, 7 with electric; dump station, water. 53-foot limit. GPS: N 35-44.3 W 105-50.2

Leasburg Dam State Park

12712 State Park Rd, Radium Springs, NM 88054. Phone: (575) 524-4068. Located on the Rio Grande River, 15 miles N of Las Cruces off NM 185 at I-25 exit 19. 31 sites, 16 with water, electric; showers; dump station. 36-foot limit. Swimming, fishing. (No motors.) GPS: N 32-29.4 W 106-55.3

Manzano Mountains State Park

Hwy 131, Mile 3, Mountainair, NM 87036. Phone: (505) 847-2820. Located 16 miles NW of Mountainair (US 60) via NM 55 & 131. 17 sites, 10 with electric; showers; dump station. 40-foot limit. Seasonal. GPS: N 34-39.9 W 106-21.8

Navajo Lake State Park

1448 Hwy 511 #1, Navajo Dam, NM 87419. Phone: (505) 632-2278. Located on Navajo Lake, 25 miles E of Bloomfield off US 64. 244 sites, 56 with electric, water; showers; dump station. 48-foot limit. Fishing, swimming, boating, boat ramp. Marina. GPS: N 36-48.4 W 107-36.6

Oasis State Park

1891 Oasis Rd, Portales, NM 88130. Phone: (575) 356-5331. Located in eastern NM, 6.5 miles NW of Portales via NM 467. 23 sites, 12 with electric; showers; dump station. 80-foot limit. Fishing. GPS: N 34-15.6 W 103-20.7

Oliver Lee State Park

409 Dog Canyon Rd, Alamogordo, NM 88310. Phone: (575) 437-8284. Located 12 miles S of Alamogordo, off US 54. 44 sites, 33 with water, electric; showers; dump station. 38-foot limit. GPS: N 32-44.7 W 105-56.1

Pancho Villa State Park

400 W Hwy 4, Columbus, NM 88029. Phone: (575) 531-2711. Located in Columbus, 35 miles S of Deming via NM 11, near Mexican border. 79 sites, 75 with electric; showers; dump station. 62-foot limit. GPS: N 31-49.7 W 107-18.5

Percha Dam State Park

Hwy 187, Caballo, NM 87931. Phone: (575) 743-3942. Located on the Rio Grande near Caballo Lake State Park south of Truth or Consequences at I-25 exit 59. 50 sites, 30 with water, electric; showers. 85-foot limit. Fishing. GPS: N 32-52.4 W 107-18.5

Rockhound State Park

9880 Stirrup Rd SE, Deming, NM 88030. Phone: (575) 546-6182. Located SE of Deming via NM 11 and NM 141. 29 sites, 23 with electric; showers; dump station. 36-foot limit. GPS: N 32-11.1 W 107-36.8

Santa Rosa Lake State Park

NM Hwy 91, Santa Rosa, NM 88435. Phone: (575) 472-3110. Located on Santa Rosa Lake, 7 miles N of Santa Rosa on NM 91; I-40 exit 272. 75 sites, 25 with electric; showers; dump station. 50-foot limit. Fishing; boat ramp. GPS: N 34-59.3 W 104-39.6

Storrie Lake State Park

Hwy 518, Mile 3.5, Las Vegas, NM 87701. Phone: (505) 425-7278. Located on Storrie Lake, 4 miles N of Las Vegas off NM 518. 45 sites, 22 with electric; showers; dump station. 40-foot limit. Fishing; swimming; boat ramp. GPS: N 35-39.3 W 105-13.9

Sugarite Canyon State Park

211 Hwy 526, Raton, NM 87740. Phone: (575) 445-5607. Located near Colorado state line off I-25 exit 452 to NM 72 and NM 526. 40 sites, 10 with water, electric; showers; dump station. 40-foot limit. Fishing; boat ramp. Horse trails. GPS: N 36-58.4 W 104-20.3

Sumner Lake State Park

32 Lakeview Ln, Sumner Lake, NM 88119. Phone: (575) 355-2541. Located on NM 203 via US 84, NW of Fort Sumner on Sumner Lake. 50 sites, 16 with electric, 16 with water, electric; showers; dump station. 60-foot limit. Fishing, swimming; boat ramp. GPS: N 34-36.4 W 104-23.2

Ute Lake State Park

1800 540 Loop, Logan, NM 88426. Phone: (575) 487-2284. Located on Ute Lake, 3 miles NW of Logan off NM 40. 142 sites, 77 with electric; showers; dump station. 40-foot limit. Marina. Fishing; boat ramp. Wi-Fi. GPS: N 35-20.4 W 103-26.6

Villanueva State Park

135 Dodge Rd, Villanueva, NM 87583. Phone: (575) 421-2957. Located S of Las Vegas, off I-25 exit 323, off NM 3. 33 sites, 12 with electric; showers; dump station. 40-foot limit. Fishing. GPS: N 35-15.6 W 105-22.1

NEW YORK

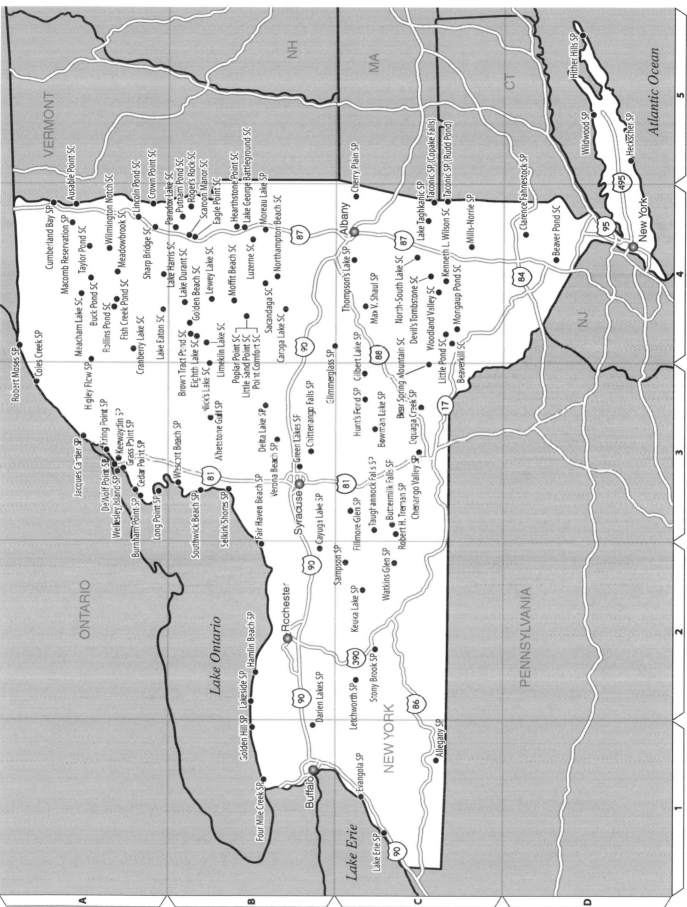

New York

New York *loves* RVers, with 104 state parks and campgrounds equipped for recreational vehicles. These parks stretch from the eastern tip of Long Island to the Empire State's western boundary with Pennsylvania. Many locations are on water, including New York's two Great Lakes, Ontario and Erie, and several are on the picturesque Finger Lakes in western New York. (In most cases if a location is on water, power boating is permitted unless noted.) A large number of campgrounds are in the Adirondack Park and on lakes and ponds in that scenic part of the state. Most parks have sites with water and electricity. Rig size usually is not a problem; if in doubt, call!

Most of the parks and campgrounds are open May through mid-October, but some are year-round; check with the particular park if you're enjoying New York in other times of the year. Reservations are available in all parks and are recommended during the "busy" season and weekends. Reservations must be for a minimum of two nights. However, drive-ins are accepted for a single night, space permitting. Pets on leashes are permitted in some parks and must have proof of current rabies vaccination. You should check the particular park before arrival. Credit cards are accepted. Rate groups: A, B and C (special locations).

New York State Office of Parks, Recreation &
Historic Preservation
Empire State Plaza
Agency Building 1
Albany, NY 12238

Information: (800) 225-5697 or (518) 474-0456
Reservations: (800) 456-2267 (Reserve America)
Internet: www.nysparks.com / www.dec.state.ny.us
Reservations: www.ReserveAmerica.com

New York Park Locator

New York Parks

Allegany State Park

2373 Allegany State Park Rd, Salamanca, NY 14779. Phone: (716) 354-2182. Located in southern NY, bordering PA state line, off NY 17/I-86 exit 19, outside Salamanca. (Two campgrounds.) 189 sites, some with electric; showers; dump station(s). Pets OK. Largest park in NY system. Contact park office for campsite assignment, directions and location. Swimming, fishing; boat ramp, rentals. GPS: N 42-06.4 W 78-46.0

Ausable Point State Campground

3346 Lake Shore Rd, Peru, NY 12972. Phone: (518) 561-7080. Located on Lake Champlain south of Plattsburg along US 9. 115 sites; showers; dump station. Fishing, swimming; boat ramp. GPS: N 44-34.5 W 73-25.4

Bear Spring Mountain State Campground

512 E Trout Brook Rd, Downsville, NY 13755. Phone: (607) 865-6989. Located on Launt Pond, 4 miles SE of Walton off NY 206, on East Trout Brook Rd. 38 sites; dump station. Boat/canoe rentals. Equestrian area. Fishing, swimming; boat ramp. GPS: N 42-07.3 W 75-04.6

Beaver Pond State Campground

700 Kanawauke Rd, Porona, (Stony Point), NY 10970. Phone: (845) 947-2792. Located on Lake Welch, SE of Harriman on NY 106, just E of NYS Thruway. 137 sites; showers; dump station. No pets. Swimming, fishing; boat ramp. No alcohol. GPS: N 41-13.8 W 74-09.2

Beaverkill State Campground

792 Berrybrook Rd Spur, Roscoe, NY 12776. Phone: (845) 439-4281. Located N of Livingston Manor (NY 17 exit 96) off CR 54 on Beaverkill trout stream. 83 sites; showers; dump station. Fishing. GPS: N 41-59.5 W 74-50.9

Bowman Lake State Park

745 Bliven Sherman Rd, Oxford, NY 13830. Phone: (607) 334-2718. Located on Bowman Lake, N of NY 220, 8 miles W of Oxford. 172 sites; showers; dump station. Pets OK. Swimming, fishing; boat ramp, rentals. GPS: N 42-31.0 W 75-40.2

Brown Tract Pond State Campground

Uncas Road, Raquette Lake, NY 13436. Phone: (315) 354-4412. Located SW of Raquette Lake on Brown Tract Pond, off NY 28 on Uncas Rd. 84 sites; dump station. Swimming, fishing; boat ramp, rentals. GPS: N 43-47.5 W 74-43.9

Buck Pond State Campground

1339 CR 60, Onchiota, NY 12989. Phone: (518) 891-3449. Located 13 miles N of Saranac Lake via NY 3 and CR 30. 112 sites; showers; dump station. 30-foot limit. Swimming, fishing; boat ramp, boat/canoe rentals; ramp. GPS: N 44-32.0 W 74-06.9

Burnham Point State Park

340765 Rt 12E, Cape Vincent, NY 13618. Phone: (315) 654-2522. Located on St. Lawrence River, 4 miles E of Cape Vincent on NY 12E. 47 sites, 18 with electric; showers; dump station. Marina; fishing docks; boat ramp. Pets OK. GPS: N 44-09.6 W 76-15.9

Buttermilk Falls State Park

Route 13S, Ithaca, NY 14850. Phone: (607) 273-5761 or (607) 273-3440. Located just S of Ithaca on NY 13. 46 sites; showers. Pets OK. Swimming, fishing. GPS: N 42-20.8 W 76-29.3

Caroga Lake State Campground

3043 Rt 29A, Gloversville, NY 12032. Phone: (518) 835-4241. Located in Adirondack Park, outside Caroga Lake (NY 10 & 29A). 156 sites with showers; dump station. Boat/canoe/kayak rentals; boat ramp. Fishing, swimming. GPS: N 43-08.5 W 74-28.2

Cayuga Lake State Park

2678 Lower Lake Rd, Seneca Falls, NY 13148. Phone: (315) 568-5163. Located on Cayuga Lake, 4 miles S of Seneca Falls on NY 89. 286 sites, 36 with electric; showers; dump station. Pets OK. Swimming, fishing; boat ramp. GPS: N 42-53.9 W 76-45.3

Cedar Point State Park

36661 Cedar Point State Park Dr, Clayton, NY 13624. Phone: (315) 654-2522. Located E of Burnham Point State Park on NY 12E, 6 miles W of Clayton. 165 sites, 55 with electric, 33 with sewer; showers; dump station. Docks. Fishing, swimming. GPS: N 44-12.0 W 76-11.5

Chenango Valley State Park

153 State Park Rd, Chenango Fork, NY 13746. Phone: (607) 648-5251. Located NE of Johnson City off NY 369. 184 sites, 51 with electric; showers; dump station. Golf course. Two lakes in park. Pets OK. Fishing, swimming; boat rentals. GPS: N 42-12.9 W 75-49.6

Cherry Plain State Park

26 State Park Rd, Cherry Plain, NY 12040. Phone: (518) 733-5400. Located S of Cherry Plain near MA state line, off NY 22 and Miller Rd. 10 sites; showers. Fishing, swimming; boat ramp, rentals. GPS: N 43-37.4 W 73-24.6

Chittenango Falls State Park

2300 Rathbun Rd, Cazenovia, NY 13035. Phone: (315) 637-6111. Located on Cazenovia Lake SE of Syracuse along NY 13. 22 sites; showers. Pets OK. Fishing. GPS: N 42-58.8 W 75-50.4

Clarence Fahnestock State Park

1498 Rt 301 W, Carmel, NY 10512. Phone: (845) 225-7207. Located on NY 301, NE of Cold Spring, off Taconic State Pkwy (Rt 301 exit). 77 sites: showers. Swimming, fishing; boat ramp; rentals. GPS: N 41-25.1 W 73-47.7

Coles Creek State Park

Rt 37, Waddington, NY 13694. Phone: (315) 388-5636. Located N of Waddington on NY 37 in far northern NY, on Lake Saint Lawrence. 230 sites, 147 with electric; showers; dump station. Marina. Boat rentals. Fishing, swimming. Pets OK. GPS: N 44-52.4 W 75-10.1

Cranberry Lake State Campground

243 Lone Pine Rd, Cranberry Lake, NY 12927. Phone: (315) 848-2315. Located in Cranberry Lake (village) on Cranberry Lake along NY 3. 167 sites; showers; dump station. Fishing, swimming. GPS: N 44-12.4 W 74-49.9

Crown Point State Campground

754 Bridge Rd, Crown Point, NY 12928. Phone: (518) 597-3603. Located on Lake Champlain about 7 miles SE of Port Henry, along NY 903, E of NY 9N. 63 sites; showers; dump station. Fishing; boat ramp. GPS: N 44-01.6 W 73-25.9

Cumberland Bay State Park

152 Cumberland Head Rd, Plattsburg, NY 12901. Phone: (518) 563-5240. Located on Lake Champlain N of Plattsburg, on NY 314E. 133 sites; showers; dump station. Pets OK. Swimming, fishing; boating. GPS: N 44-43.5 W 73-25.3

Darien Lakes State Park

10289 Harlow Rd, Darien Center, NY 14040. Phone: (585) 547-9242. Located E of Buffalo off US 20, 3 miles W of NY 77. 158 sites with electric, 50 with sewer; showers; dump station. Pets OK. Swimming, fishing; boat rentals. Horse trails. GPS: N 42-54.9 W 78-26.0

Delta Lake State Park

8797 Rt 46, Rome, NY 13440. Phone: (315) 337-4670. Located on Delta Reservoir, N of Rome on NY 46. 101 sites; showers; dump station. Pets OK. Swimming, fishing; boat ramp. GPS: N 43-17.4 W 75-24.9

Devil's Tombstone State Campground

Rt 214, Hunter, NY 12442. Phone: (845) 688-7160. Located SE of Hunter on NY 214, near junction of NY 214 & 23A. 22 sites. GPS: N 42-11.3 W 74-11.2

DeWolf Point State Park

45920 CR 191, Fineview, NY 13640. Phone: (315) 482-2722. Located 2 miles N of Alexandria Bay on Saint Lawrence River, off I-81 exit 51 on Wellesley Island. (Via bridge.) 28 sites; showers; dump station. Boat ramp; docks. Fishing. Pets OK. GPS: N 44-20.0 W 75-59.5

Eagle Point State Campground

8448 Rt 9, Pottersville, NY 12860. Phone: (518) 494-2220. Located on Schroon Lake north of Pottersville on US 9. 69 sites; showers; dump station. Fishing; boat ramp. GPS: N 43-44.4 W 73-48.4

Eighth Lake State Campground

Rt 28, Inlet, NY 13360. Phone: (315) 354-4120. Located on Eighth Lake south of Raquette Lake on NY 28. 116 sites; showers; dump station. 40-foot limit. Swimming, fishing; boat ramp, boat/canoe rentals. GPS: N 43-46.3 W 74-42.0

Evangola State Park

10191 Old Lake Shore Rd, Irving, NY 14081. Phone: (716) 549-1802. Located 27 miles SW of Buffalo on NY 5, outside Farnham, on Lake Erie. 78 sites, 37 with electric; showers; dump station. Pets OK. Swimming, fishing. Disc golf. GPS: N 42-36.1 W 79-05.0

Fair Haven Beach State Park

14985 Rt 104A, Fair Haven, NY 13064. Phone: (315) 947-5205. Located on Lake Ontario, 15 miles SW of Oswego via NY 104A, outside Fair Haven.184 sites, 46 with electric; showers; dump station. Pets OK. Swimming, fishing; boat ramp, rentals. GPS: N 43-19.3 W 76-41.8

Fillmore Glen State Park

1686 Rt 38, Moravia, NY 13118. Phone: (315) 497-0130. Located on NY 38 outside of Moravia, on south end of Owasco Lake. 60 sites, 10 with electric; showers; dump station. Swimming, fishing. GPS: N 42-42.1 W 76-25.2

Fish Creek Pond State Campground

4523 Rt 30, Saranac Lake, NY 12983. Phone: (518) 891-4560. Located NE of Tupper Lake on two ponds, off NY 30. 322 sites; showers; dump station. 40-foot limit. Boat/canoe rentals; ramp. Fishing, swimming. GPS: N 44-17.4 W 74-21.5

Four Mile Creek State Park

1055 Lake Rd, Youngstown, NY 14174. Phone: (716) 745-3802. Located 4 miles E of Youngstown along NY 18F, on Lake Ontario. 266 sites, 131 with electric (10 with 50 amp); showers; laundry; dump station. Pets OK. Fishing. GPS: N 43-16.4 W 78-59.8

Gilbert Lake State Park

18 CCC Rd, Laurens, NY 13796. Phone: (607) 432-2114. Located on Gilbert Lake, N of Oneonta via NY 205 and CR 12. 192 sites, 17 with electric; showers; dump station. Pets OK. Swimming, fishing; boat ramp, rentals (no motors). GPS: N 42-34.5 W 75-07.6

Glimmerglass State Park

1527 CR 31, Cooperstown, NY 13326. Phone: (607) 547-8662. Located on Otsego Lake south of US 20, 8 miles NE of Cooperstown (Baseball Hall of Fame) at East Springfield, on CR 31. 43 sites; showers; dump station. Pets OK. Swimming, fishing. GPS: N 42-47.1 W 74-51.7

Golden Beach State Campground

Rt 28, Raquette Lake, NY 13426. Phone: (315) 354-4230. Located on Raquette Lake, E of Raquette Lake (village) on NY 28. 195 sites; showers; dump station. 40-foot limit. Fishing, swimming. GPS: N 43-49.2 W 74-35.2

Golden Hill State Park

9691 Lower Lake Rd, Barker, NY 14012. Phone: (716) 795-3885. Located on Lake Ontario, N of Barker off NY 269, via NY 18 or 104. 55 sites, 22 with electric; showers; dump station. Fishing; boat ramp. GPS: N 43-21.9 W 78-29.3

Grass Point State Park

42247 Grass Point Rd, Alexandria Bay, NY 13624. Phone: (315) 686-4472. Located 27 miles N of Watertown at I-81 exit 50, on Saint Lawrence River. 73 sites, 17 with electric; showers; dump station. Marina. Fishing, swimming; boat ramp. Pets OK. GPS: N 44-16.7 W 75-59.7

Green Lakes State Park

7900 Green Lakes Rd, Fayetteville, NY 13066. Phone: (315) 637-6111. Located 6 miles E of Syracuse off NY 5. 132 sites, 42 with electric; showers; dump station. Golf course. Two lakes in park. Swimming, fishing; boat rentals. GPS: N 43-03.6 W 78-58.1

Hamlin Beach State Park

1 Camp Rd, Hamlin, NY 14464. Phone: (585) 964-2462. Located on Lake Ontario about 28 miles NW of Rochester off Lake Ontario State Pkwy at Hamlin Beach SP exit. 264 sites; showers; dump station. Pets OK. Swimming, fishing; boat ramp (nearby). GPS: N 43-21.7 W 77-56.7

Hearthstone Point State Campground

Route 9N, 3298 Lakeshore Dr, Lake George, NY 12845. Phone: (518) 668-5193. Located on southwest shore of Lake George, 2 miles N of Lake George (village). 241 sites; showers; dump station. Fishing, swimming. GPS: N 43-28.1 W 73-41.4

Heckscher State Park

Heckscher State Pkwy, East Islip, NY 11730. Phone: (631) 581-2100. Located on south shore of Long Island, S of East Islip, off NY 44. 69 sites; dump station. Swimming pool; boat ramp. GPS: N 40-42.6 W 73-10.2

Higley Flow State Park

442 Cold Brook Dr, Colton, NY 13625. Phone: (315) 262-2880. Located on Raquette River, 14 miles S of Potsdam via NY 56. 128 sites with sewer hookup; 43 with electric; showers; dump station. Swimming, fishing; boat ramp. (Some pet restrictions by site.) GPS: N 44-30.6 W 74-53.3

Hither Hills State Park

164 Old Montauk Hwy, Montauk, NY 11954. Phone: (631) 668-2554. Located at eastern end of Long Island on the Atlantic Ocean, just W of Montauk, off NY 27. 155 sites; showers; dump station. Pet restrictions. Swimming. GPS: N 41-00.5 W 72-00.9

Hunt's Pond State Park

New Berlin, NY 13411. Phone: (607) 859-2249. Remote location S of New Berlin (NY 80 & 8), off CR 28. 18 primitive sites. Fishing; boat ramp (no motors). GPS: N 42-35.5 W 75-22.6

Jacques Cartier State Park

Rt 12, Morristown, NY 13664. Phone: (315) 375-6371. Located on Saint Lawrence River 3 miles SW of Morristown along NY 12. 89 sites, 22 with electric; showers; dump station. Boat rentals; ramp; docks. Swimming, fishing. Pets OK. GPS: N 44-33.4 W 75-40.9

Keewaydin State Park

46165 Rt 12, Alexandria Bay, NY 13607. Phone: (315) 482-3331. Located on Saint Lawrence River, 1 mile W of Alexandria Bay on NY 12. 47 sites; showers. Marina. Fishing, swimming pool; boat ramp, rentals. Pets OK. GPS: N 44-19.4 W 75-55.6

Kenneth L. Wilson State Campground

859 Wittenberg Rd, Mount Tremper, NY 12457. Phone: (845) 679-7020. Located NW of Woodstock off NY 212, on Wittenberg Rd (CR 40). 71 sites; showers; dump station. Fishing; boat rentals. GPS: N 42-00.9 W 74-10.4

Keuka Lake State Park

3370 Pepper Rd, Bluff Point, NY 14478. Phone: (315) 536-3666. Located SE of Branchport off NY 54A, on north end of West Branch Keuka Lake, in New York wine region. 150 sites, 53 with electric; showers; dump station. Pets OK. Swimming, fishing; boat ramp, docks. GPS: N 42-35.5 W 77-07.8

Kring Point State Park

25950 Kring Point Rd, Redwood, NY 13679. Phone: (315) 482-2444.

On Saint Lawrence River NE of Alexandria Bay, off NY 12 on Kring Point Rd. 100 sites, 28 with electric; showers; dump station. Boat ramp; rentals. Fishing, swimming. GPS: N 44-23.1 W 75-51.0

Lake Durant State Campground

Rt 28, Blue Mountain Lake, NY 12812. Phone: (518) 352-7797. Located on Lake Durant just outside of Blue Mountain Lake (village) on NY 28. 56 sites; showers; dump station. Fishing, swimming; boat ramp, (shallow lake.) GPS: N 43-50.3 W 74-22.4

Lake Eaton State Campground

Rt 30, Long Lake, NY 12847. Phone: (518) 624-2641. Located on Lake Eaton, 1.5 miles NW of Long Lake on NY 30. 127 sites; showers; dump station. Fishing, swimming; boat ramp, rentals. GPS: N 44-00.1 W 74-28.5

Lake Erie State Park

5838 NY 5, Brocton, NY 14716. Phone: (716) 792-9214. Located on Lake Erie 5 miles SW of Dunkirk, N of Brocton, on NY 5. 97 sites; showers; dump station. Fishing. GPS: N 42-25.1 W 79-26.0

Lake George Battleground State Campground

2224 Rt 9, Lake George, NY 12845. Phone: (518) 668-3348. Located N of Glens Falls at I-87 exit 21 and 1/4 mile S of Lake George. Historic area; tours. 62 sites; showers; dump station. Fishing, swimming; boat ramp, rentals. GPS: N 43-26.2 W 73-41.1

Lake Harris State Campground

291 Campsite Rd, Newcomb, NY 12852. Phone: (518) 582-2503. Located on Harris Lake outside Newcomb, on NY 28N, next to Adirondack Park Visitor Center. 85 sites; showers; dump station. 40-foot limit. Boat/canoe rentals; ramp. Fishing. GPS: N 43-59.1 W 74-08.6

Lake Taghkanic State Park

1528 Rt 82, Ancram, NY 12502. Phone: (518) 851-3633. Located NW of Ancram on NY 82, off Taconic State Pkwy (Rt 82 exit). 55 sites; showers. No pets. Fishing, swimming, boat ramp; rentals. GPS: N 42-05.5 W 73-41.4

Lakeside State Park

Rt 18, Waterport, NY 14571. Phone: (585) 682-4888. Located on Lake Ontario, N of Waterport on NY 18. 274 sites with electric; showers; dump station. Pets OK. Fishing, disc golf. GPS: N 43-22.0 W 78-14.2

Letchworth State Park

1 Letchworth State Park Rd, Castile, NY 14427. Phone: (585) 493-3600. Located S of Mount Morris on NY 408, spanning Genesee River gorge; "Grand Canyon of the East". 258 sites with electric; showers; dump station. Pets OK. Swimming, fishing. Horse trails. GPS: N 42-41.6 W 77-57.7

Lewey Lake State Campground

4155 Rt 30N, Lake Pleasant, NY 12108. Phone: (518) 648-5266. Located on Lewey Lake, 12 miles N of Speculator along NY 30. 197 sites; showers; dump station. Boat ramp. Fishing, swimming. GPS: N 43-40.0 W 74-23.7

Limekiln Lake State Campground

Limekiln Lake Rd, Inlet, NY 13360. Phone: (315) 357-4401. Located on Limekiln Lake, just S of Inlet off NY 28 via CR 14 (Limekiln Rd). 260 sites; showers; dump station. Boat rentals; ramp. Fishing, swimming. GPS: N 43-42.8 W 74-49.6

Lincoln Pond State Campground

4363 Lincoln Pond Rd, Elizabethtown, NY 12932. Phone: (518) 942-5292. Located on Lincoln Pond, NW of Witherbee (I-87 exit 30) on CR 7. 34 sites; showers; dump station. Fishing, swimming; boat ramp, rentals. GPS: N 44-08.3 W 73-35.0

Little Pond State Campground

549 Little Pond State Campground Rd, Andes, NY 13731. Phone: (845) 439-5480. Located 7 miles NE of Roscoe (NY 17 exit 94) off CR 54. 68 sites; showers; dump station. Fishing, swimming. Boat ramp; rentals. GPS: N 42-02.3 W 74-45.7

Little Sand Point State Campground

CR 24, (Old Piseco Rd), Piseco, NY 12139. Phone: (518) 548-7585. Located 11 miles SW of Speculator on Old Piseco Rd, off NY 8. 74 sites; dump station. Fishing, swimming; boat ramp, boat, canoe rentals. GPS: N 43-25.4 W 74-33.6

Long Point State Park

7495 State Park Rd, Three Mile Bay, NY 13693. Phone: (315) 649-5258. Located on Lake Ontario 3 miles W of Three Mile Bay on Port Peninsula, off NY 12E via CR 57. 80 sites, 19 with electric; showers; dump station. Boat ramp; rentals; docks. Swimming, fishing. Pets OK. (Remote location.) GPS: N 44-01.6 W 76-13.1

Luzerne State Campground

892 Lake Ave, Lake Luzerne, NY 12846. Phone: (518) 696-2031. Located on Fourth Lake, NW of Glens Falls on NY 9N. 165 sites; showers; dump station. Fishing, swimming; boat ramp, rentals. Equestrian sites, trails GPS: N 43-21.8 W 73-49.1

Macomb Reservation State Park

201 Campsite Rd, Schuyler Falls, NY 12985. Phone: (518) 643-9952. Located 2 miles SW of Schuyler Falls on county road, off NY 22B; follow signs. 123 sites (some with electric); showers; dump station. Fishing, swimming; boat ramp. GPS: N 44-37.8 W 73-37.2

Max V. Shaul State Park

Rt 30, Fultonham, NY 12071. Phone: (518) 827-4711. Located 6 miles SW of Middleburgh on NY 30. 30 sites; showers. Fishing. GPS: N 42-32.8 W 74-24.6

Meacham Lake State Campground

119 State Campsite Rd, Duane, NY 12953. Phone: (518) 483-5116. Located on Meacham Lake, 10 miles N of Paul Smiths on NY 30. 219 sites; showers; dump station. Fishing, swimming; boat ramp, rentals. GPS: N 44-33.9 W 74-16.1

Meadowbrook Public Campground

1174 Rt 86, Raybrook, NY 12977. Phone: (315) 891-4351. Located 4 miles W of Lake Placid in Ray Brook on NY 86. 58 sites; showers; dump station. GPS: N 44-17.8 W 74-04.2

Mills-Norrie State Park

Rt 9 (Old Post Rd), Staatsburg, NY 12580. Phone: (845) 889-4646. Located on US 9, outside Staatsburg, on Hudson River. 46 sites; showers; dump station. Golf course. Marina. Fishing; boat ramp. GPS: N 41-51.4 W 73-55.8

Moffit Beach State Campground

Page Street, Speculator, NY 12164. Phone: (518) 548-7102. Located on Scandaga Lake outside Speculator (NY 30 & 8) on NY 8. 248 sites; showers; dump station. Fishing, swimming; boat ramp. GPS: N 43-31.0 W 74-24.3

Mongaup Pond State Campground

231 Mongaup Pond Rd, Livingston Manor, NY 12758. Phone: (845) 439-4233. Located NE of Livingston Manor off NY 17 exit 96 on Mongaup Lake. 154 sites; showers; dump station. Fishing, swimming. GPS: N 41-58.0 W 74-39.2

Moreau Lake State Park

605 Old Saratoga Rd, Gansevoort, NY 12831. Phone: (518) 793-0511. Located on Moreau Lake, 10 miles N of Saratoga Springs off I-87, exit 17. 147 sites; showers; dump station. Fishing, swimming; boat ramp. GPS: N 43-14.8 W 73-42.5

Nick's Lake State Campground

278 Bisby Rd, Old Forge, NY 13420. Phone: (315) 369-3314. Located S of Old Forge off NY 28 on Bisby Rd. 104 sites; showers; dump station. Fishing, swimming; boat ramp. GPS: N 43-41.0 W 75-00.5

North - South Lake State Campground

CR 18, Haines Falls, NY 12436. Phone: (518) 589-5058. Located NE of Haines Falls off NY 23A. 207 sites; showers; dump station. Two lakes in park. Fishing, swimming. Boat/canoe/kayak rentals; boat ramp. GPS: N 42-12.9 W 74-02.7

Northampton Beach State Campground

328 Houseman St, Mayfield, NY 12117. Phone: (518) 863-6000. Located S of Northville in Adirondack Park on NY 30, on Great Scandaga Lake. 158 sites; showers; dump station. Fishing, swimming; boat ramp; rentals. GPS: N 43-11.1 W 74-10.8

Oquaga Creek State Park

5995 CR 20, Bainbridge, NY 13733. Phone: (607) 467-4160. Located E of Binghamton and S of Bennettsville off I-88 exit 8, on CR 20. 90 sites; showers; dump station. Boat rentals (no motors). Swimming, fishing. Pets OK. Disc golf. GPS: N 42-10.3 W 75-26.6

Paradox Lake State Campground

897 Rt 74, Paradox, NY 12858. Phone: (518) 532-7451. Located on Paradox Lake E of Severance (I-87 exit 28) on NY 74, off US 9. 56 sites; showers; dump station. Boat ramp; rentals. Fishing. GPS: N 43-53.1 W 73-42.0

Point Comfort State Campground

1365 CR 24, Piseco, NY 12139. Phone: (518) 548-7586. Located S of Piseco off NY 8, next to Little Sand Point State Campground. 63 sites. Swimming, fishing; boat ramp, boat/canoe rentals; ramp. GPS: N 43-24.4 W 74-34.7

Poplar Point State Campground

CR 24, Piseco, NY 12139. Phone: (518) 548-8031. Located S of Piseco on Old Piseco Rd, off NY 8. 19 sites. Swimming, fishing; boat ramp, boat/canoe rentals. GPS: N 43-26.6 W 74-31.7

Putnam Pond State Campground

763 Putts Pond Rd, Ticonderoga, NY 12883. Phone: (518) 585-7280. Located near Paradox Lake State Campground, on Putnam Pond, W of Ticonderoga (NY 9N) on NY 74. 69 sites; showers; dump station. Boat ramp; rentals. Fishing, swimming. GPS: N 43-50.8 W 73-32.9

Robert H. Treman State Park

105 Enfield Falls Rd, Ithaca, NY 14850. Phone: (607) 273-3440. Located on south end of Cayuga Lake, 5 miles SW of Ithaca on NY 327, near junction with NY 13. 71 sites, 11 with electric; showers; dump station. Pets OK. Swimming, fishing. GPS: N 42-24.1 W 76-32.9

Robert Moses State Park

19 Robertson Bay Rd, Massena, NY 13662. Phone: (315) 769-8663. Located in far northern part of state, 3 miles N of Massena, off NY 37, next to Eisenhower Locks on Saint Lawrence River. 197 sites, 38 with electric; showers; dump station. Marina. Boat ramp. Swimming, fishing. Pets OK. GPS: N 45-00.8 W 74-49.6

Roger's Rock State Campground

9894 Lake Shore Dr, Hague, NY 12836. Phone: (518) 585-6746. Located on Lake George (northern end) about 7 miles S of Ticonderoga on NY 9N. 301 sites; showers; dump station. Boat ramp. Swimming, fishing. GPS: N 43-47.2 W 73-28.8

Rollins Pond State Campground

4523 Rt 30, Saranac Lake, NY 12983. Phone: (518) 891-3239. Located on Rollins Pond NE of Tupper Lake off NY 30 next to Fish Creek Pond. 266 sites; showers; dump station. Boat/canoe/kayak rentals; ramp. Fishing, swimming. GPS: N 44-22.1 W 74-19.6

Sacandaga State Campground

1047 Rt 30, Northville, NY 12134. Phone: (518) 924-4121. Located on Scandaga River, S of Wells on NY 30. 137 sites; showers; dump station. Boat ramp. Fishing. GPS: N 43-21.7 W 74-17.3

Sampson State Park

6096 Rt 96A, Romulus, NY 14541. Phone: (315) 585-6392. Located S of Geneva (I-90 exit 42), east side of Seneca Lake. 309 sites, 245 with electric; showers; dump station. Marina. Swimming, fishing; boat ramp. Pets OK. GPS: N 42-44.2 W 76-54.6

Scaroon Manor State Campground

8728 Rt 9, Pottersville, NY 12860. Phone: (518) 494-2631. Located 4 miles N of Pottersville on US 9. 57 sites; dump station; fishing, swimming; boating. GPS: N43-46.01 W73-47.9

Selkirk Shores State Park

7101 Rt 3, Pulaski, NY 13142. Phone: (315) 298-5737. Located 5 miles W of Pulaski on NY 3; on east shore of Lake Ontario. 143 sites; showers; dump station. Boat ramp. Fishing. Pets OK. GPS: N 43-32.8 W 76-11.4

Sharp Bridge State Campground

4390 Rt 9, North Hudson, NY 12870. Phone: (518) 532-7538. Located on Schroon River, N of North Hudson on US 9. 36 sites; showers; dump station. 20-foot limit. Fishing. GPS: N 44-02.8 W 73-39.5

Southwick Beach State Park

8119 Southwick's Place, Woodville, NY 13650. Phone: (315) 846-5338. Located outside Woodville on NY 3; on east edge of Lake Ontario. 100 sites, 44 with electric; showers; dump station. Swimming, fishing; boat ramp. Pets OK. GPS: N 43-46.0 W 76-11.8

Stony Brook State Park

10820 Rt 36S, Dansville, NY 14437. Phone: (585) 335-8111. Located S of Dansville (I-390 exit 4), on NY 36. 119 sites; showers; dump station. Tennis courts. Pets OK. GPS: N 42-39.6 W 77-41.8

Taconic State Park (Copake Falls)

Rt 344, Copake Falls, NY 12517. Phone: (518) 329-3993. Located on state border just north of CT/MA/NY state lines on NY 344, just outside of Copake Falls. 96 sites; showers; dump station. 30-foot limit. Swimming, fishing. No RVs on Taconic State Pkwy. Use NY 22. GPS: N 42-07.2 W 73-31.2

Taconic State Park (Rudd Pond)

59 Rudd Pond Dr, Millerton, NY 12546. Phone: (518) 789-3059. Located off NY 22 about 2 miles N of Millerton along CR 62. 38 sites; showers. Pets OK in certain campsites. Fishing, swimming; boat ramp; (no motors) rentals. GPS: N 41-59.1 W 73-30.4

Taughannock Falls State Park

2221 Taughannock Rd, Trumansburg, NY 14886. Phone: (607) 387-6739. Located 8 miles N of Ithaca on NY 89; on west side of Cayuga Lake. 68 sites, 16 with electric; showers; dump station. Pets OK. Marina. Swimming, fishing; boat ramp. GPS: N 42-32.8 W 76-36.3

Taylor Pond State Campground

1865 Silver Lake Rd, Ausable Forks, NY 12912. Phone: (518) 647-5250. Remote location 9 miles NW of Ausable Forks (NY 9N) on Taylor Pond. 29 primitive sites, water available. 30-foot limit. Boat rentals; ramp. GPS: N 44-29.2 W 73-49.1

Thompson's Lake State Park

68 Thompson's Lake Rd, East Berne, NY 12059. Phone: (518) 872-1674. Located on Thompson's Lake W of Voorheesville on NY 157. 137 sites; showers; dump station. Swimming, fishing; boat ramp, rentals. GPS: N 42-39.5 W 74-02.5

Verona Beach State Park

6541 Lakeshore Rd S, Verona Beach, NY 13162. Phone: (315) 762-4463. Located N of Oneida (I-90 exit 34) on NY 13; on Barge Canal & Oneida Lake. 43 sites; showers; dump station. Pets OK. Swimming, fishing. Horse trails. GPS: N 43-10.8 W 75-43.5

Watkins Glen State Park

Rt 14 & 414, Watkins Glen, NY 14891. Phone: (607) 535-4511. Located just outside Watkins Glen on NY 14 & 414, south end of Seneca Lake. 283 sites, 54 with electric; showers; dump station. Pets OK. Swimming pool, fishing. GPS: N 42-22.6 W 76-52.3

Wellesley Island State Park

44927 Cross Island Rd, Fineview, NY 13640. Phone: (315) 482-2722. Located on Wellesley Island, I-81 exit 51 on Saint Lawrence River, (via bridge.) 412 sites, 131 with electric, 57 with sewer; showers; dump station. Golf course. Marina. Fishing, swimming; boat ramp, rentals. Pets OK. GPS: N 44-19.0 W 76-01.2

Wescott Beach State Park

12224 Rt 3, Henderson, NY 13650. Phone: (315) 646-2239. Located 3 miles W of Sackets Harbor on NY 3 in Henderson Bay (Lake Ontario). 154 sites, 85 with electric; showers; dump station. Marina. Boat ramp. Fishing, swimming. Pets OK. GPS: N 43-54.0 W 76-07.3

Whetstone Gulf State Park

6065 West Rd, Lowville, NY 13367. Phone: (315) 376-6630. Located about 7 miles S of Lowville on NY 26. 56 sites, 12 with electric; showers; dump station. Pets OK. Fishing, swimming. GPS: N 43-42.1 W 73-49.1

Wildwood State Park

790 Hulse Landing Rd, Wading River, NY 11792. Phone: (631) 929-4314. Located 73 miles E of Manhattan on NY 25A on Long Island Sound North Shore between Wading River and Woodcliff Park off Rt 25A. 314 sites with electric; showers; dump station. No pets. GPS: N 40-57.3 W 72-47.3

Wilmington Notch State Campground

4953 Rt 86, Wilmington, NY 12997. Phone: (518) 946-7172. Located 8 miles NE of Lake Placid on Ausable River, S of Wilmington, on NY 86. 49 sites; showers; dump station. Fishing. GPS: N 44-21.4 W 73-51.1

Woodland Valley State Campground

1319 Woodland Valley Rd, Phoenicia, NY 12464. Phone: (845) 688-7647. Located SW of Mount Tremper off NY 28, on Woodland Valley Rd. 65 sites; showers; dump station. Fishing. GPS: N 42-02.4 W 74-19.2

NORTH CAROLINA

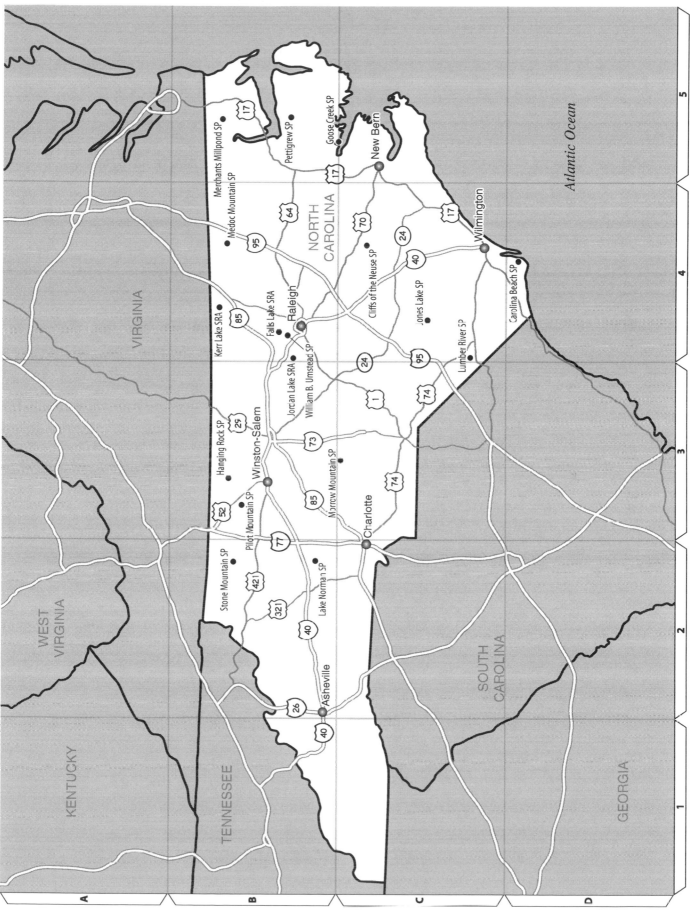

North Carolina

North Carolina has 17 state parks or recreation areas with RV facilities. Most of these parks have dump stations and all have shower facilities within the camping area. Most North Carolina parks are available on a first-come, first-served basis; reservations, if desired, must be made at the particular park. The state has no centralized reservation system. Pets are permitted on leashes. Seniors age 62 or older are eligible for a discount, depending on the published fee for the particular campsite; proof of age is required. Rate groups: A and B, depending upon site amenities. Entrance fee extra.

North Carolina Division of Parks & Recreation
1615 MSC
Raleigh, NC 27699

Information: (919) 733-7275
Internet: www.ncsparks.net
Reservations: (877) 722-6762

North Carolina Park Locator

North Carolina Parks

Carolina Beach State Park
1010 State Park Rd, Carolina Beach, NC 28428. Phone: (910) 458-8206. Located on the Intercoastal Waterway in southeastern NC, off US 421, 10 miles S of Wilmington. 60 sites; dump station. Marina. Fishing; boat ramp. GPS: N 34-02.7 W 77-54.2

Cliffs of the Neuse State Park
240-A Park Entrance Rd, Seven Springs, NC 28578. Phone: (919) 778-6234. Located 11 miles SE of Goldsboro on NC 111. 35 sites; dump station. Swimming, fishing; boat rentals. GPS: N 35-14.4 W 77-54.1

Falls Lake State Recreation Area
13304 Creedmoor Rd, Wake Forest, NC 27587. Phone: (919) 676-1027. Located about 10 miles N of Raleigh and 12 miles E of Durham off US 1 on Falls Lake. 268 sites, 176 (seven areas) with water, electric; dump station. Swimming, fishing. (Electric motors.) GPS: N 36-00.3 W 78-41.2

Goose Creek State Park
2190 Camp Leach Rd, Washington, NC 27889. Phone: (252) 923-2191. Located on the Pamlico River, off US 264, E of Washington. 12 primitive sites. Swimming, fishing, boating. GPS:N 34-28.1 W 76-54.06

Hanging Rock State Park
1790 Hanging Rock Park Rd, Danbury, NC 27016. Phone: (336) 593-8480. Located about 25 miles N of Winston-Salem on NC 89. 73 sites. Lake in park. Horse trails. Swimming, fishing; boat ramp, boat/ canoe rentals. GPS: N 36-24.8 W 80-15.29

Jones Lake State Park
4117 Hwy 242N, Elizabethtown, NC 28337. Phone: (910) 588-4550. Located on Jones Lake, 4 miles N of Elizabethtown on NC 242. 20 sites. Swimming, fishing; boat ramp, boat/canoe rentals. GPS: N 34-42.3 W 78-36.5

Jordan Lake State Recreation Area
280 State Park Rd, Apex, NC 27523. Phone: (919) 362-0586. Located on Jordan Lake, about 21 miles W of Raleigh along US 64. Nine areas, 1,000 sites, 620 with electric; showers, dump station. Swimming, fishing; boat ramp. GPS: N 35-44.2 W 78-59.8

Kerr Lake State Recreation Area
6254 Satterwhite Point Rd, Henderson, NC 27537. Phone: (252) 438-7791. Located N of Henderson near VA state line on Kerr Lake, off NC 39. 709 sites; 260 with electric, water; dump station. Swimming, fishing; boat ramp. Marina. GPS: N 36-26.6 W 78-22.2

Lake Norman State Park
159 Inland Sea Lane, Troutman, NC 28166. Phone: (704) 528-6350. Located on Lake Norman about 7 miles W of I-77 exit 42 via US 21, NC 1301, and NC 1321. 33 sites; dump station. Swimming, fishing; boat ramp, boat/canoe rentals. GPS: N 35-38.4 W 80-55.9

Lumber River State Park

2819 Princess Ann Rd, Orrum, NC 28369. Phone: (910) 628-4564. Located on the Lumber River, SE of Lumberton off NC 72 (remote location) 22 primitive sites; water available. Fishing, boating. GPS: N34-23.4 W79-00.1

Medoc Mountain State Park

1541 Medoc State Park Rd, Hollister, NC 27844. Phone: (252) 586-6588. Located W of I-95 between exits 150 & 160 off NC 48. 34 sites, 12 with electric; showers. Fishing. GPS: N 36-16.8 W 77-52.7

Merchants Millpond State Park

176 Millpond Rd, Gatesville, NC 27938. Phone: (252) 357-1191. Located in northeastern NC, outside Sunbury on NC 32. 20 sites; showers; water available. Canoe rentals. Fishing. GPS: N 36-27.0 W 76-41.9

Morrow Mountain State Park

49104 Morrow Mountain Rd, Albemarle, NC 28001. Phone: (704) 982-4402. Located on Lake Tillery, 6 miles E of Albemarle (US 52) off NC 740. 84 sites, 22 with electric; showers; water available; dump station. Swimming, fishing; boat ramp, rentals. GPS: N 35-22.4 W 80-04.6

Pettigrew State Park

2252 Lake Shore Rd, Creswell, NC 27928. Phone: (252) 797-4475. Located on Phelps Lake in eastern NC, 7 miles S of Creswell, off US 64; follow signs from Creswell and Cherry. 13 sites; showers. Fishing; boat ramp. GPS: N 35-48.7 W 76-25.8

Pilot Mountain State Park

1792 Pilot Knob Park Rd, Pinnacle, NC 27043. Phone: (336) 325-2355. Located about 24 miles NW of Winston-Salem, off US 52 at Pinnacle exit. 49 primitive sites; showers; water available. Fishing. GPS: N 36-20.5 W 80-28.8

Stone Mountain State Park

3042 Frank Pkwy, Roaring Gap, NC 28668. Phone: (336) 957-8185. Located NW of Winston-Salem and W of I-77 exits 83 or 93, off US 21 and John P. Frank Pkwy. 88 sites, some with water, electric; dump station. Fishing. GPS: N 36-20.7 W 81-01.3

William B. Umstead State Park

8801 Glenwood Ave, Raleigh, NC 27612. Phone: (919) 571-4170. Located between Raleigh and Durham, off US 70 via I-540. 28 sites; showers. Horse trails. Fishing; boat ramp, rentals. GPS: N 35-51.6 W 78-43.8

North Dakota

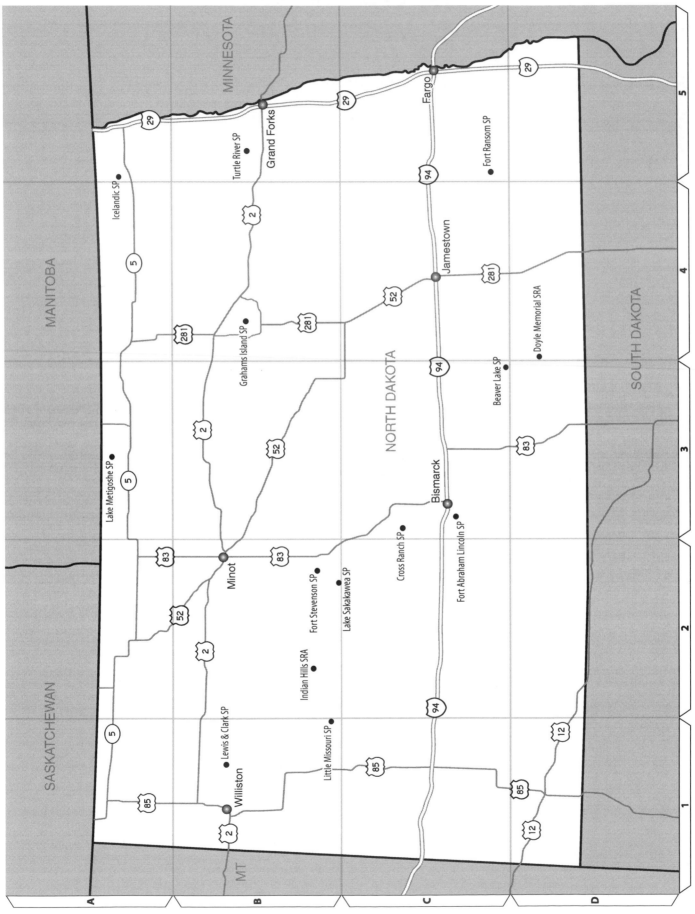

North Dakota

North Dakota has 14 state parks with RV camping spaces and facilities. These parks have more than 1,300 sites, most of which are available through the toll-free state reservation number or online. All parks require a valid entrance permit (daily or annual) plus daily camping fees. Some sites offer 50-amp electrical service; most are 30-amp. Off-season fees (September 30 through late May) are less than in-season. All locations have drinking water. Rate group: A. Entrance and equestrian fees extra.

North Dakota Parks & Recreation Dept.
1600 East Century Ave., Ste. 3
Bismarck, ND 58503

Information: (701) 328-5357
Reservations: (800) 807 4723
Internet: www.parkrec.nd.gov/

North Dakota Park Locator

North Dakota Parks

Beaver Lake State Park

3850 70th St SE, Wishek, ND 58495. Phone: (701) 452-2752. Located off ND 3, 17 miles SE of Napoleon (ND 3 & 34). 25 sites with electric (some 50 amp); showers; dump station. Fishing, swimming; boat ramp. GPS: N 46-24.1 W 99-37.0

Cross Ranch State Park

1403 River Rd, Center, ND 58530. Phone: (701) 794-3731. Located on Missouri River, 12 miles SE of Hensler, off ND 200A (exit US 83 at Washburn). 70 sites, some with electric, water; showers; dump station. 35-foot limit. Fishing, canoe rentals. GPS: N 47-11,1 W 100-59.9

Doyle Memorial State Recreation Area

Wishek, ND 58495. Phone: (701) 452-2351. Located on Green Lake, 7 miles SE of Wishek, off ND 3 & 13. 12 sites with electric; showers; dump station. Boat ramp; fishing. GPS: N 46-14.2 W 99-33.9

Fort Abraham Lincoln State Park

4480 Fort Lincoln Rd, Mandan, ND 58003. Phone: (701) 667-6340. Located 7 miles S of Mandan (SW of Bismark) on ND 1806 (I-94 exit 147). 95 sites with electric; showers; dump station. Equestrian area. Site of Lt. Col. George A. Custer historic home. GPS: N 46-46.3 W 100-50.9

Fort Ransom State Park

5981 Walt Hjelle Pkwy, Fort Ransom, ND 58033. Phone: (701) 973-4331. Located 2 miles N of Fort Ransom, off ND 32, about 25 miles S of I-94 exit 302. 30 sites with electric; showers; dump station. Equestrian area, trails. Canoe/kayak rentals; fishing. GPS: N 46-32.7 W 97-55.5

Fort Stevenson State Park

1252A 41st Ave NW, Garrison, ND 58540. Phone: (701) 337-5576. Located on Lake Sakakawea, 3 miles S of Garrison. (Exit US 83 at ND 37 to Garrison.) 120 sites, 105 with electric (some 50 amp, some with sewer); showers; dump station. Swimming, fishing; two marinas, boat ramp. GPS: N 47-35.6 W 101-25.2

Grahams Island State Park (Devils Lake)

152 S Duncan Dr, Devils Lake, ND 58301. Phone: (701) 766-4015. There are 3 areas on Devils Lake. Located 10 miles SW of Devils Lake off ND 19. 107 sites with electric (some 50 amp); showers; dump station. Boat ramp; fishing, swimming. GPS N 48-07.3 W 99-04.2

Icelandic State Park

13571 Hwy 5, Cavalier, ND 58220. Phone: (701) 265-4561. Located on Lake Renwick, 5 miles W of Cavalier on Hwy 5 (about 19 miles W of I-29 exit 203; watch for direction signs for campground entrance). 160 sites with electric; showers; dump station. Boat ramp; fishing, swimming. GPS: N 48-46,4 W 97-44.2

Indian Hills State Recreation Area

7302 14th St NW, Garrison, ND 58540. Phone: (701) 743-4122. Located 31 miles W of Garrison via ND 37 and ND 1804; on Lake Sakakawea. 63 sites with electric; showers; dump station. Marina; fishing, swimming. GPS: N 47-38.2 W 102-07.2

Lake Metigoshe State Park

#2 Lake Metigoshe State Park, Bottineau, ND 58318. Phone: (701) 263-4651. Located on Lake Metigoshe, 14 miles NE of Bottineau on ND 43, off ND 14. 129 sites with electric (30 amp); showers; dump station. Boat ramp; fishing, swimming. GPS: N 48-58.8 W 100-19.6

Lake Sakakawea State Park

Riverdale, ND 58565. Phone: (701) 487-3315. Located on Lake Sakakawea, 1 mile N of Pick City off ND 200 about 16 miles W of US 83. 192 sites with electric some (50 amp); showers, dump station. Store. Boat ramp, rentals; fishing, swimming. Marina. GPS: N 47-30.7 W 101-27.0

Lewis & Clark State Park

4904 119th Rd NW, Epping, ND 58843. Phone: (701) 859-3071. Located on Lake Sakakawea, 19 miles SE of Williston (US 2 & 85) on ND 1804. 73 sites with electric; showers; dump station. Boat ramp; fishing, swimming. Marina. Store. Wi-Fi. GPS: N 48-07.0 W 103-14.5

Little Missouri State Park

Hwy 22, Killdeer, ND 58640 (satellite of Cross Ranch State Park). Phone: (701) 764-5256 or (701) 794-3731 (winter). Located 17 miles N of Killdeer (ND 22 & 200) off ND 22. 30 sites with electric. Contact park for reservations. Equestrian area, trails. GPS N 47-34.6 W 102-45.9

Turtle River State Park

3084 Park Ave, Arvilla, ND 58214. Phone: (701) 594-4445. Located 22 miles W of Grand Forks and I-29 on US 2. 125 sites, 74 with electric; showers; dump station. Fishing. GPS N 47-55.9 W 97-30.3

OHIO

MICHIGAN

ONTARIO

Lake Erie

PA

Geneva SP · 90

Harrison Lake SP · 80/90 Toledo · Maumee Bay SP · Pymatuning SP ·

South Bass Island SP · Kelleys Island SP · Punderson SP

East Harbor SP · Cleveland

IN · Mary Jane Thurston SP · Mosquito Lake SP

24 · 80/90

Van Buren SP · Findley SP · Akron · 80 · West Branch SP · B

30 · 71 · 76

30 · Portage Lakes SP · Guilford Lake SP

Lima · 30 · 30 · 77 · Beaver Creek SP

Grand Lake St. Mary's SP · 75 · Malabar Farm SP

Mt. Gilead SP · Mohican SP

Lake Loramie SP · Indian Lake SP · Jefferson Lake SP

Delaware SP · OHIO

33

Kiser Lake SP · Muskingum River SP · Salt Fork SP · 70

Buck Creek SP · 70 · Alum Creek SP · Dillon SP · Barkcamp SP · C

John Bryan SP · Columbus · 70 · Blue Rock SP · Wolf Run SP

Deer Creek SP · A.W. Marion SP · 77

Hueston Woods SP · 71 · 33

Ceasar Creek SP · 75 · Burr Oak SP

Cowan Lake SP · Great Seal SP · Athens

Stonelick SP · Paint Creek SP · Tar Hollow SP · Hocking Hills SP · Strouds Run SP

Rocky Fork SP · Scioto Trail SP · Lake Hope SP

Cincinnati · Pike Lake SP · Lake Alma SP · Forked Run SP · D

Lake White SP · 32

East Fork SP · 32

Jackson Lake SP

Shawnee SP · Portsmouth

WEST VIRGINIA

E

KENTUCKY

1 · 2 · 3 · 4

Ohio

Ohio boasts 56 RV friendly state parks, many of which are on lakes or waterways. Most of these parks have electric hook-ups (some 50-amp) and dump stations. Eight parks have sewer and water at the sites. Most of the parks are open year-round but some of the facilities are curtailed in cold months. Dump stations are free to campers and $10 per use for non-campers. Campsites are available on a first-come basis but one can call ahead for same day rentals. Major credit cards are accepted. Pets are permitted in campgrounds. No alcohol is allowed in the parks. Six parks (Deer Creek, Hueston Woods, Maumee Bay, Punderson, Salt Fork and Shawnee) have golf courses. Rate groups: B and C depending upon site facilities; winter rates are less. No entrance fees.

Ohio Department of Natural Resources
Division of Parks and Recreation
2045 Morse Road, Bldg C
Columbus. OH 43299

Information: (614) 265-6561
Reservations: (866) 644-6727 or call park
Internet: www.ohiostateparks.org

Ohio Park Locator

Ohio Parks

A.W. Marion State Park

7317 Warner-Huffer Rd, Circleville, OH (mail: c/o Deer Creek State Park, 20635 Waterloo Rd, Mt. Sterling, OH 43143). Phone: (740) 869-3124. Located 6 miles NE of Circleville via US 22 and Ringold Southern Rd. Hargus Lake in park. 60 sites, 29 with electric (50 amp); dump station. 35-foot limit. Fishing; boat ramp, rentals. GPS: N 39-38.0 W 82-53.1

Alum Creek State Park

3615 S Old State Rd, Delaware, OH 43015. Phone: (740) 548-4631. Located between US 23 & I-71, 15 miles N of Columbus on Alum Creek Reservoir. 289 sites, 3 full service, 286 with electric (50 amp); showers; laundry; dump station. 35-foot limit. 30 equestrian sites. Swimming, fishing; marina, boat ramp, rentals. GPS: N 40-13.6 W 82-57.4

Barkcamp State Park

65330 Barkcamp Rd, Belmont, OH 43718. Phone: (740) 484-4064. Located near Belmont off I-70 exit 208, between Wheeling, WV and Cambridge, OH. 150 sites with electric (50 amp); showers; dump station. 35-foot limit. 27 equestrian sites. Swimming, fishing; boat ramp. GPS: N 40-02.8 W 81-01.9

Beaver Creek State Park

12021 Echo Dell Rd, East Liverpool, OH 43920. Phone: (330) 385-3091. Located N of East Liverpool, off OH 7, about 6 miles N of OH 11. 53 sites, 7 with electric; dump station. 35-foot limit. 59 equestrian sites, (equestrian camp - 12816 Sprucevale Rd.) Fishing. GPS: N 40-42.6 W 80-35.8

Blue Rock State Park

7924 Cutler Lake Rd, Blue Rock, OH 43720. Phone: (740) 453-4377. Located SE of Zanesville off OH 60. Cutler Lake in park. 97 sites; showers; dump station. 40-foot limit. Swimming, fishing; boat ramp, (electric motors only); horse trails. GPS: N 39-50.5 W 81-51.5

Buck Creek State Park

1901 Buck Creek Ln, Springfield, OH 45502. Phone: (937) 322-5284. Located E of Springfield on Brown Reservoir, off OH 4. 112 sites, 89 with electric; showers; laundry; dump station. 35-foot limit. Marina. Swimming, fishing; boat ramp, rentals. GPS: N 39-58.8 W 83-43.8

Burr Oak State Park

10220 Burr Oak Lodge Rd, Glouster, OH 45732. Phone: (740) 767-3570. Located on Burr Oak Reservoir between Athens and New Lexington, off OH 13. 99 sites, 16 with electric; showers; laundry; dump station. 30-foot limit. Swimming, fishing; boat ramp, rentals. GPS: N 39-30.9 W 82-01.6

Caesar Creek State Park

8570 E State Rt 73, Waynesville, OH 45068. Phone: (513) 897-3055. Located on Caesar Creek Lake along OH 73, W of I-71 exit 45. 241 sites, with electric; showers; laundry; dump station. 40-foot limit. 30 equestrian sites. Swimming, fishing, boating; boat ramp. GPS: N 39-30.9 W 84-02.2

Cowan Lake State Park

1750 Osborn Rd, Wilmington, OH 45177. Phone: (937) 383-3751. Located on Cowan Lake, SW of Wilmington, off US 68 and OH 350. 254 sites, 237 with electric (50 amp); showers; laundry; dump station. 35-foot limit. Swimming, fishing, marina; boating (10 hp limit); boat rentals. GPS: N 39-22.5 W 83-54.6

Deer Creek State Park

20635 Waterloo Rd, Mt. Sterling, OH 43143. Phone: (740) 869-3508 or (740) 869-3124. Located on Deer Creek Reservoir S of Mt. Sterling, off OH 207. 227 sites with electric; showers; laundry; dump station. 40-foot limit. 3 equestrian sites. Golf course. Swimming, (pool and beach) fishing, marina; boat rentals. GPS: N 39-38.7 W 83-13.2

Delaware State Park

5202 US 23 N, Delaware, OH 43015. Phone: (740) 363-4561. Located on Delaware Lake about 8 miles N of Delaware on US 23. 211 sites; showers; laundry; dump station. 35-foot limit. Marina. Swimming, fishing, boating, boat ramp, rentals. GPS: N 40-22.7 W 83-03.4

Dillon State Park

5265 Dillon Hills Dr, Nashport, OH 43830. Phone: (740) 453-4377. Located on Dillon Lake between Newark and Zanesville, off OH 146. 195 sites, 183 with electric (50 amp); showers; laundry; dump station. Wi-Fi. 40-foot limit. Disc golf. Swimming, fishing, boating, boat ramp, rentals. Store. GPS: N 40-01.3 W 82-07.6

East Fork State Park

3294 Elklick Rd, Bethel, OH 45106. Phone: (513) 734-4323. Located on East Fork Lake, SE of Cincinnati off OH 133, between OH 32 & 125. 389 sites, 384 with electric, 5 full hook-up; showers; laundry; dump station. 30-foot limit. 17 equestrian sites. Swimming, fishing, boating, boat ramp. GPS: N 39-00.2 W 84-07.8

East Harbor State Park

1169 N Buck Rd, Lakeside-Marblehead, OH 43440. Phone: (419) 734-5857. Located on Lake Erie east of Port Clinton on OH 269, off US 2. 570 sites, 374 with electric (50 amp); showers; laundry; dump station. 40-foot limit. Marina. Wi-Fi. Disc golf; swimming, fishing, boating, boat ramp. Seasonal. GPS: N 41-32.8 W 82-48.2

Findley State Park

25381 State Rt 58, Wellington, OH 44090. Phone: (440) 647-4490. Located 3 miles S of Wellington on OH 58. 271 sites, 90 with electric; showers; laundry; dump station. 40-foot limit. Lake in park. Disc golf. Swimming, fishing, boating (electric motors only), boat ramp, rentals. GPS: N 41-08.0 W 82-13.1

Forked Run State Park

63300 State Rt 124, Reedsville, OH 45772. Phone: (740) 378-6206. Located on the Ohio River, SE of Athens, S of Reedsville, on OH 124. 155 sites, 81 with electric; showers; laundry; dump station. 30-foot limit. Swimming, fishing, boating (10 hp limit), boat ramp. GPS: N 39-05.1 W 81-46.2

Geneva State Park

4499 Padanarum Rd, Geneva, OH 44041. Phone: (440) 466-8400. On Lake Erie, N of Geneva and I-90 exit 218 via OH 534. 100 sites, 89 with electric, 4 full hook-up; showers; laundry; dump station. 40-foot limit. Marina. Golf course. Swimming, fishing; boat ramp. GPS: N 41-50.7 W 80-58.5

Grand Lake St. Mary's State Park

834 Edgewater Dr, St. Mary's, OH 45885. Phone: (419) 394-2774. Located on Grand Lake St. Mary's west of St. Mary's (I-75 exit 110) on OH 703. 204 sites, 166 with electric; showers; laundry; dump station. 35-foot limit. Wi-Fi. Swimming, fishing, boating, boat ramp, rentals. GPS: N 40-31.5 W 84-28.2

Great Seal State Park

635 Rocky Rd, Chillicothe, OH 45601. Phone: (740) 887-4818 (Tar Hollow SP). Located outside Chillicothe, off US 23 (follow signs). 15 sites; 5 equestrian sites; trails. Disc golf. (Also see Scioto Trail SP.) GPS: N 39-22.9 W 82-56.3

Guilford Lake State Park

6835 E Lake Rd, Lisbon, OH 44432. Phone: (330) 222-1712. Located in northeastern Ohio on Little Beaver Creek, off OH 172 between Canton and OH 11. 41 sites with electric (50 amp); showers; dump station. 35-foot limit. Swimming, fishing, boating (10 hp limit), boat ramp. GPS: N 40-47.7 W 80-52.7

Harrison Lake State Park

26246 Harrison Lake Rd, Fayette, OH 43521. Phone: (419) 237-2593. Located on Harrison Lake, 5 miles SW of Fayette via US 20 and CR 27. 173 sites, 150 with electric (50 amp); showers; laundry; dump station. 35-foot limit. Swimming, fishing, boating, boat ramp. GPS: N 41-38.5 W 84-22.3

Hocking Hills State Park

19852 State Rt 664 S, Logan, OH. Phone: (740) 385-6842. Located SW of Logan on OH 664 in Hocking State Forest. 168 sites, 156 with electric (some 50 amp); showers; laundry; dump station. 50-foot limit. Swimming, fishing. GPS: N 39-25.9 W 82-32.3

Hueston Woods State Park

6301 Park Office Rd, College Corner, OH 45003. Phone: (513) 523-1060. Located near Indiana state line, NW of Oxford, off US 27. Acton Lake in park. 488 sites, 252 with electric; showers; laundry; dump station. Wi-Fi. 35-foot limit. 28 equestrian sites. Golf course. Swimming, fishing; boat ramp, rentals. GPS: N 39-34.4 W 84-42.9

Indian Lake State Park

12774 State Rt 235 N, Lakeview, OH 43331. Phone: (937) 843-3553. Located on Indian Lake, about 12 miles NW of Bellefontaine via US 33. 452 sites, 13 full service, 440 with electric (some 50 amp); showers; laundry; dump station. 35-foot limit. Swimming, fishing, boating, boat ramp. GPS: N 40-29.6 W 83-52.8

Jackson Lake State Park

35 Tommy Been Rd, Oak Hill, OH 45656. Phone: (740) 682-6197 or (740) 596-5253 (Lake Hope SP). Located on Jackson Lake, S of Jackson via OH 93 and OH 279. 34 sites with electric (50 amp); dump station. 35-foot limit. Swimming, fishing, boating (10 hp limit), boat ramp. GPS: N 38-53.6 W 82-35.8

Jefferson Lake State Park

501 Township Rd 261-A, Richmond, OH 43944. Phone: (740) 765-4459 or (330) 222-1712. Located 5 miles NW of Richmond via OH 43 and CR 54. 53 sites; dump station. 35-foot limit. 5 equestrian sites. Swimming, fishing, boating (4 hp electric motors max.), boat ramp. GPS: N 40-27.7 W 80-48.4

John Bryan State Park

3790 State Rt 370, Yellow Springs, OH 45387. Phone: (937) 767-1274. Located on Little Miami River, on OH 370, NE of Dayton, off OH 343, near Clifton. 60 sites, 10 with electric (50 amp); dump station. 40-foot limit. Disc golf; Canoe boating; Fishing. GPS: N 39-47.5 W 83-51.1

Kelleys Island State Park

920 Division St, Kelleys Island, OH 43438. Phone: (419) 746-2546. Located on Lake Erie, on Kelleys Island NE of Port Clinton. (Access by ferry only, RVs OK.) 127 sites, some with electric (50 amp); showers; dump station. 35-foot limit. (Also see South Bass Island State Park.) Swimming, fishing, boating, boat ramp. GPS: N 41-36.8 W 82-42.0

Kiser Lake State Park

4889 N State Rt 235, Conover, OH 45317. Phone: (937) 362-3565. Located on Kiser Lake on OH 235 between Urbana and Sidney, N of US 36. 78 sites, 10 with electric; dump station. 40-foot limit. Swimming, fishing, boat ramp, rentals (no motors). GPS: N 40-11.6 W 83-57.9

Lake Alma State Park

422 Lake Alma Rd, Wellston, OH 45692. Phone: (740) 384-4474. (Off season: Lake Hope SP - (740) 597-4938). Located on Little Raccoon River, N of Wellston, off OH 32/124; follow signs. 64 sites with electric (some 50 amp); dump station. 40-foot limit. Swimming, fishing, boating (electric motors only), boat ramp, rentals. GPS: N 39-08.6 W 82-30.9

Lake Hope State Park

27331 State Rt 278, McArthur, OH 45651. Phone: (740) 596-4938. Located in Zaleski State Forest, NE of McArthur, off US 50 on OH 278. 187 sites, 46 with electric (50 amp); showers; laundry; dump station. 35-foot limit. 16 equestrian sites. Lake in park. Swimming, fishing; boating (electric motors), boat ramp, rentals. GPS: N 39-20.1 W 82-21.3

Lake Loramie State Park

4401 Ft. Loramie Swanders Rd, Minster, OH 45865. Phone: (937) 295-3900. Located on Lake Loramie, E of Minster off OH 363. 161 sites with electric; showers; laundry; dump station. 40-foot limit. Swimming, fishing, boating, boat ramp. Bicycle/canoe rentals. GPS: N 40-22.3 W 84-21.2

Lake White State Park

2767 State Rt 551, Waverly, OH 45690. Phone: (740) 947-4059 or (740) 492-2212 (Pike Lake SP). Located on Lake White, SW of Waverly via US 23 and OH 104. 10 sites. 35-foot limit. GPS: N 39-06.5 W 83-01.5

Malabar Farm State Park

4050 Bromfield Rd, Lucas, OH 44843. Phone: (419) 892-2784. Located SE of Mansfield and I-71 exits 165 or 169; follow signs. Louis Bromfield home site in park. 15 sites. Primitive. No size limit. Wagon tours of farm. Equestrian area. Fishing. GPS N 40-38.7 W 82-23.0

Mary Jane Thurston State Park

1466 State Rt 65, McClure, OH 43534. Phone: (419) 832-7662. Located on Maumee Lake on OH 65 between US 6 & 24, E of Napoleon. 35 sites; dump station. Marina; boat ramp; canoe rentals. 35-foot limit. GPS: N 41-24.6 W 83-52.9

Maumee Bay State Park

1400 State Park Rd, Oregon, OH 43618. Phone: (419) 836-8828. Located on Lake Erie, 7 miles NE of Oregon via OH 2 and Norden Rd. 370 sites with electric; water available; showers; laundry; dump station. 60-foot limit. Golf course. Swimming, fishing; marina; boat ramp. GPS: N 41-41.9 W 83-21.5

Mohican State Park

3116 State Rt 3, Loudonville, OH 44842. Phone: (419) 994-4290. Located SE of Mansfield on OH 3, near Loudonville. 286 sites, 118 with electric (50 amp), 33 full hook-up; some pull-through; showers; laundry; dump station. 40-foot limit. Two swimming pools. Fishing; canoeing. GPS: N 40-36.1 W 82-16.7

Mosquito Lake State Park

1439 State Rt 305, Cortland, OH 44410. Phone: (330) 638-5700. Located on Mosquito Lake, N of Warren on OH 305. 234 sites, 218 with electric (50 amp); showers; laundry; dump station. Wi-Fi. Disc golf. 35-foot limit. Swimming, fishing; boating, boat ramp, dock/boat rentals. GPS: N 41-21.5 W 80-44.5

Mt. Gilead State Park

4119 State Rt 95, Mt. Gilead, OH 43338. Phone: (419) 946-1961. (In season.) Located outside Mt. Gilead on OH 95, off US 42. 60 sites with electric (50 amp); dump station. 45-foot limit. Two lakes in park. Fishing; boating (electric motors); boat ramp. GPS: N 40-32.7 W 82-48.9

Muskingum River State Park

1390 Ellis Dam Rd, Zanesville, OH 43701. Phone: (740) 674-4794 or (740) 453-4377 (Dillon SP). Located on Muskingum River, N of Zanesville, off OH 60. 20 sites. Fishing, boating, boat ramp. GPS: N 40-02.5 W 81-58.6

Paint Creek State Park

280 Taylor Rd, Bainbridge, OH 45612. Phone: (937) 981-7061. Located on Paint Creek Lake, NW of Bainbridge, off US 50. 197 sites with electric (20 amp); showers; laundry; dump station. 50-foot limit. Swimming, fishing; boat ramp, rentals. GPS: N 39-15.7 W 83-23.8

Pike Lake State Park

1847 Pike Lake Rd, Bainbridge, OH 45612. Phone: (740) 493-2212. Located 7 miles S of Bainbridge via county roads. 80 sites with electric (50 amp); dump station. 35-foot limit. Lake in park. Disc golf. Store. Swimming, fishing; boating (electric motors), boat rentals. GPS: N 39-09.7 W 83-13.2

Portage Lakes State Park

5031 Manchester Rd, Akron, OH 44319. Phone: (330) 644 2220. Located on Nimisila Reservoir, (8 lakes) SE of Barberton off OH 93 near OH 619. 74 sites; dump station. 35-foot limit. Swimming, fishing; boating, boat ramp, rentals. GPS: N 40-58.2 W 81-32.9

Punderson State Park

11755 Kinsman Rd, Newbury, OH 44065. Phone: (440) 564-1195. Located on Punderson Lake, 15 miles E of Beachwood and I-271 exit 29 via OH 87. 178 sites with electric, 5 full hook-up; showers; laundry; dump station. 35-foot limit. Golf course, disc golf. Wi-Fi. Swimming, fishing; boating (electric motors), boat ramp, rentals. GPS: N 41-27.3 W 81-12.6

Pymatuning State Park

7514 Pymatuning Lake Rd, Andover, OH 44003. Phone: (440) 293-6684. Located on Pymatuning Reservoir N of Andover, off OH 85. 388 sites, 18 full service, 331 with electric; showers; laundry; dump station. Store. 35-foot limit. Swimming, fishing; boat/dock rentals, (20 hp limit) ramp. GPS: N 41-34.9 W 80-29.5

Rocky Fork State Park

9800 North Shore Dr, Hillsboro, OH 45133. Phone: (937) 393-4284. Located on Rocky Fork Lake, E of Hillsboro, off US 50. 171 sites, 44 full service, 96 with electric (50 amp); store; showers; laundry; dump station. 35-foot limit. Wi-Fi. Three marinas. Swimming, fishing; boat ramp, rentals. GPS: N 39-11.4 W 83-29.9

Salt Fork State Park

14755 Cadiz Rd, Lore City, OH 43755. Phone: (740) 432-1508. Located on Salt Fork Reservoir NE of Cambridge and I-77 exit 47 via US 22. (State's largest park.) 212 sites, 20 full service, 192 with electric (50 amp); showers; laundry; dump station. 20 equestrian sites. Golf course. Swimming, fishing; boating, boat ramp, marinas, boat/dock rentals. GPS: N 40-07.9 W 81-29.6

Scioto Trail State Park

144 Lake Rd, Chillicothe, OH 45601. Phone: (740) 887-4818 (Tar Hollow SP). Located about 7 miles S of Chillicothe, off US 23. 73 sites, 40 with electric (50 amp); dump station. 35-foot limit. Store. (Also see Great Seal SP.) Swimming, fishing; boat ramp. GPS: N 39-17.8 W 82-55.4

Shawnee State Park

4404 State Rt 125, Portsmouth, OH 45663. Phone: (740) 858-4561. Located in Shawnee State Forest, W of Portsmouth on Roosevelt Lake along OH 125. 107 sites, 101 with electric (some 20 amp, some 50 amp); showers; laundry; dump station. Store. 35-foot limit. 38 equestrian sites. Golf course. Swimming, fishing, boating; ramp, rentals. GPS: N 38-43.0 W 83-13.4

South Bass Island State Park

1523 Catawba Ave, Put-In-Bay, OH 43456. Phone: (419) 285-2112. Located on South Bass Island in Lake Erie, N of Port Clinton; only accessible by ferry. 127 sites, 82 with electric (50 amp); showers; dump station. 35-foot limit. Swimming, fishing, boating, ramp. GPS: N 41-38.2 W 82-50.1

Stonelick State Park

2895 Lake Dr, Pleasant Plain, OH 45162. Phone: (513) 734-4323 (East Fork SP). Located on Stonelick Lake, NE of Cincinnati, off OH 727. 115 sites, 108 with electric (50 amp); showers; laundry; dump station. 35-foot limit. Swimming, fishing; boat ramp. GPS: N 39-13.5 W 84-04.1

Strouds Run State Park

11661 State Park Rd, Athens, OH 45701. Phone: (740) 594-2628 (Burr Oak SP). Located off US 50, just E of Athens. 80 sites; dump station. 35-foot limit. Dow Lake in park. Swimming, fishing; boating (10 hp limit) boat ramp, rentals. GPS: N 39-21.1 W 82-02.1

Tar Hollow State Park

16396 Tar Hollow Rd, Laurelville, OH 43135. Phone: (740) 887-4818. Located E of Chillicothe via US 50 and OH 327. 83 sites, 71 with electric (50 amp); showers; dump station. 35-foot limit. Pine Lake in park. Swimming, fishing, boating (electric motors). GPS: N 39-21.3 W 82-46.4

Van Buren State Park

12259 Township Rd 218, Van Buren, OH 45889. Phone: (419) 832-7662. (Mary Jane Thurston SP.) Located N of Findlay at I-75 exit 164 and OH 613. 65 sites, 8 with electric; dump station. Disc golf (own discs). 35-foot limit. Horse trails. Fishing; boat ramp. GPS: N 41-07.8 W 83-38.1

West Branch State Park

5708 Esworthy Rd, Ravenna, OH 44266. Phone: (330) 296-3239 (Lake Milton SP). Located on Kerwin Reservoir, E of Akron, off OH 5. 197 sites, 29 full service, 155 with electric (50 amp); showers; laundry; dump station. 35-foot limit. 10 equestrian sites. Swimming, fishing; marina, boat ramp, rentals. GPS: N 41-08.9 W 81-08.8

Wolf Run State Park

16170 Wolf Run Rd, Caldwell, OH 43724. Phone: (740) 732-5035. Located on Wolf Run Lake, E of Belle Valley and I-77 exit 28 via OH 821 and OH 215. 140 sites, 71 with electric (50 amp); showers; laundry; dump station. 35-foot limit. Swimming, fishing; boating (10 hp limit), ramp. GPS: N 39-47.1 W 81-32.4

OKLAHOMA

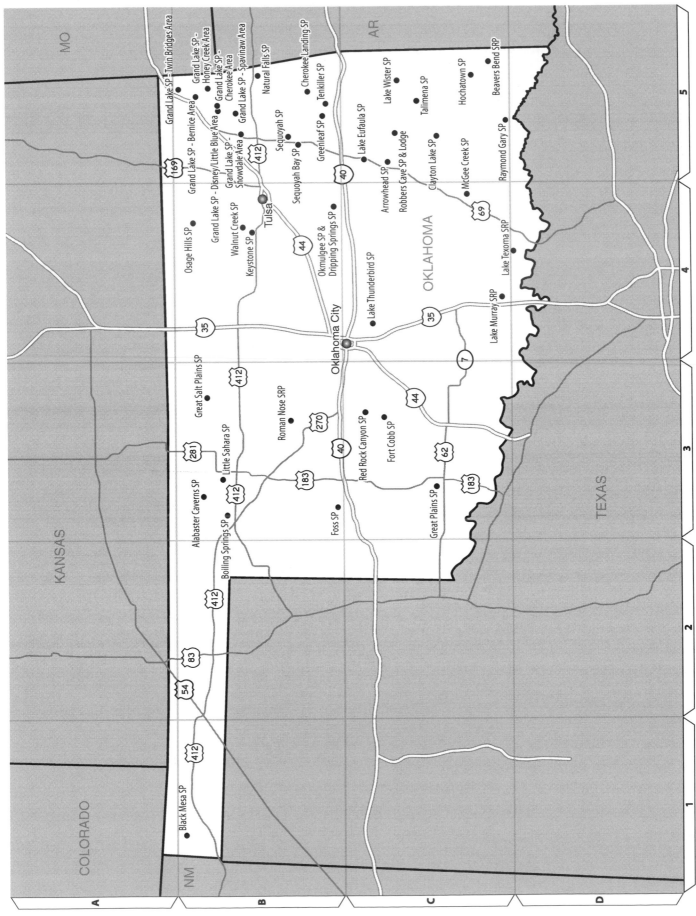

Oklahoma

When it comes to state parks with RV facilities, The Sooner State takes a back seat to no one! Oklahoma offers the RVer 41 state parks and/or resorts, all of which have some campground sites equipped with an electric hook-up. Many parks have numerous full hook-up sites and all have drinking water in the respective park, if not at the site. Rig size is not a problem in any of the listed parks. All are open year-round and they accept major credit cards. Reservations are accepted at some parks, so the traveler should check with the particular park. Senior discounts are available to anyone over age 62. (Ask!) Proof of age is required. Pets on leashes are OK. Rate group: B. No additional entrance fee.

Oklahoma Tourism & Recreation Dept.
Travel & Tourism Division
PO Box 52002
Oklahoma City, OK 73152

Information: (800) 652-6552
Reservations: (800) 654-8240
Internet: www.oklahomaparks.com

Oklahoma Park Locator

Oklahoma Parks

Alabaster Caverns State Park

217036 SH 50A, Freedom, OK 73842. Phone: (580) 621-3381. Located in northern OK between US 64 & 412, on OK 50. 23 sites, 11 with electric and water, 12 primitive; showers; dump station. Cave tours available, (fee charged). GPS: N 36-41.8 W 99-09.0

Arrowhead State Park

3995 Main Park Rd, Canadian, OK 74425. Phone: (918) 339-2204. Located in eastern OK on Lake Eufaula 18 miles N of McAlester off US 69. 234 sites, 40 full hook-ups, 61 with electric and water, 133 primitive; showers; dump station. Golf course. Equestrian area. Marina. Swimming, fishing. GPS: N 35-10.1 W 95-38.4

Beavers Bend State Resort Park

Hwy 259A, Broken Bow, OK 74728. Phone: (580) 494-6538. Located on Broken Bow Lake in southeastern OK, 11 miles NE of Broken Bow on US 259 and 259A. 393 sites, 15 full hook-ups, 15 with electric and water, 39 primitive; showers; dump station. Swimming, fishing. GPS: N 34-07.7 W 94-41.5

Black Mesa State Park

CR 325, Kenton, OK 73946. Phone: (580) 426-2222. Located in west tip of the "Panhandle," on Lake Carl Etling, 27 miles NW of Boise City. 64 sites, 34 with electric and water, 30 primitive; showers; dump station. Equestrian area/sites. Fishing, boat ramp. GPS: N 36-51.3 W 102-53.2

Boiling Springs State Park

207745 Boiling Springs Rd, Woodward, OK 73801. Phone: (580) 256-7664. Located in northern OK, 8 miles NE of Woodward on OK 34C. 49 sites, 10 full hook-up, 29 with electric and water, 12 primitive; showers; dump station. Swimming pool. Golf course next to park. GPS: N 36-27.1 W 99-17.0

Cherokee Landing State Park

28610 Park 20, Park Hill, OK 74451. Phone: (918) 457-5716. Located on Lake Tenkiller in eastern OK, 14 miles S of Tahlequah on OK 82. 138 sites, 93 with electric and water, some pull-through; showers; dump station. Disc golf. Wi-Fi. Swimming, fishing; boat ramp. GPS: N 35-42.9 W 94-55.9

Clayton Lake State Park

Hwy 271, Clayton, OK 74536. Phone: (918) 569-7981. Located on Clayton Lake in southeastern OK, 5 miles S of Clayton on US 271. 30 sites, some with electric and water, 33 primitive; showers; dump station. Swimming, fishing; boating, boat rentals. GPS: N 34-32.7 W 95-18.4

Fort Cobb State Park

27022 Copperhead Rd, Fort Cobb, OK 73038. Phone: (405) 643-2249. Located on Fort Cobb Lake in west-central OK, 25 miles S of I-40, 6 miles N of Fort Cobb. 299 sites with electric and water. Golf course. Marina. Swimming, fishing. Boat rentals. GPS: N 35-12.2 W 98-27.9

Foss State Park

10252 Hwy 44, Foss, OK 73647. Phone: (580) 592-4433. Located on Foss Lake in western OK, 7 miles N of I-40 exit 53, off OK 44; follow signs. 6 campgrounds with 110 sites, 100 with electric and water, 10 full hook-up, some pull-through; showers; dump stations. Equestrian area. Marina. Swimming, fishing; boat rentals. Bison herd in park. GPS: N 35-31.6 W 99-11.2

Grand Lake State Park - Bernice Area

54101 E Hwy 85A, Bernice, OK 74331. Phone: (918) 257-8330. Located on Grand Lake, 1/2 mile E of Bernice in northeastern OK, off OK 85A. ("Crappie Capital of the World") 30 sites with electric, water; showers; dump station. Swimming, fishing; boat ramp. GPS: N 36-39.1 W 94-50.7

Grand Lake State Park - Cherokee Area

N 4475 Road, Langley, OK 74350 Phone: (918) 435-2101. Located in NE Oklahoma, NE of Tulsa, off OK 28, on Grand Lake. 12 sites (no utilities). Swimming, fishing. GPS: N 36-36.2 W 94-54.7

Grand Lake State Park - Disney/Little Blue Area

232 Cliff Heights, Disney, OK 74340. Phone: (918) 435-8066. Located on Grand Lake in northeastern OK, outside Langley on OK 82 at OK 28. 49 full hook-up sites; showers; dump station. Golf course. Swimming, fishing; boat ramp. GPS: N 36-28.5 W 95-01.2

Grand Lake State Park - Honey Creek Area

901 State Park Rd, Grove, OK 74344. Phone: (918) 786-9447. Located in northeastern OK on Grand Lake, S of Grove off US 59. 150 sites, 52 with electric and water, 53 primitive; showers; dump station. Swimming, fishing, boating. GPS: N 36-35.2 W 94-47.1

Grand Lake State Park - Snowdale Area

501 S 439, Salina, OK 74361. Phone: (918) 434-2651. Located on Lake Hudson in northeastern OK, 8 miles E of Pryor via OK 20. 17 sites with electric and water; showers; dump station. Swimming, fishing; boat ramp. GPS: N 36-18.4 W 95-11.9

Grand Lake State Park - Spavinaw Area

555 S Main, Spavinaw, OK 74366. Phone: (918) 435-8066. Located on Spavinaw Lake in northeastern OK, 14 miles E of Pryor on OK 20. 26 sites with electric and water; dump station. Swimming, fishing. GPS: N 36-23.2 W 95-03.2

Grand Lake State Park - Twin Bridges Area

14801 S Hwy 137, Fairland, OK 74343. Phone: (918) 542-6969. Located in far northeastern OK, 6 miles NE of Fairland at OK 137/US 60. 63 sites with electric and water; showers; dump station. Lake in park. Fishing; boat ramp. GPS: N 36-48.3 W 94-45.5

Great Plains State Park

22487 E 1566 Rd, Mountain Park, OK 73559. Phone: (580) 569-2032. Located in southwestern OK on Lake Tom Steed, 6 miles N of Snyder via US 183. 56 sites, 14 full hook-up, 42 with electric and water; showers; dump station. Store. Swimming, fishing; boat ramp. GPS: N 34-43.8 W 98-59.1

Great Salt Plains State Park

23280 S Spillway Dr, Jet, OK 73749. Phone: (580) 626-4731. Located NW of Enid on Great Salt Plains Lake, 8 miles N of Jet (US 64) on OK 38. 170 sites, 64 with electric and water, 106 primitive; showers; dump station. Equestrian area. Swimming, fishing; canoes/kayaks only. GPS: N 36-45.2 W 98-09.0

Greenleaf State Park

Hwy 10 S, Braggs, OK 74423. Phone: (918) 487-5196. Located on Greenleaf Lake in eastern OK, 17 miles SE of Muskogee via US 62 and OK 10. 98 sites, 22 full hook-up, 76 with electric and water, some pull-through; showers; dump station. Laundry. Marina. Swimming, fishing; boat/bicycle/canoe rentals. GPS: N 35-37.3 W 95-10.8

Hochatown State Park

Hwy 259A, Broken Bow, OK 74728. Phone: (580) 494-6538. Located on Broken Bow Lake, in Beavers Bend State Resort Park, on US 259, 11 miles NE of Broken Bow. 202 sites, 24 full hook-ups, 27 with electric and water, 151 primitive; showers; dump station. Golf course. Swimming, fishing. GPS: N 34-11.7 W 94-45.3

Keystone State Park

1926 Hwy 151, Sand Springs, OK 74063. Phone: (918) 865-4991. Located on Lake Keystone, 16 miles W of Tulsa via US 64/412 (Keystone Expwy) and OK 151. 72 full hook-up sites; showers; dump station. Marina. Swimming, fishing; boat rentals. ATV area nearby. GPS: N 36-08.4 W 96-15.7

Lake Eufaula State Park

Hwys 69 & 150, Checotah, OK 74426. Phone: (918) 689-5311. Located on Lake Eufaula (largest man-made lake in state), 14 miles SW of Checotah off I-40 exit 259 and OK 150. 198 sites, 34 full hook-up, 59 with electric and water, 105 primitive; showers; dump station. Disc golf. Golf course nearby. Marina. Swimming, fishing; boat ramp. GPS: N 35-24.9 W 95-37.7

Lake Murray State Resort Park

13528 Hwy 77, Ardmore, OK 73401. Phone: (580) 223-4044. Located on Lake Murray, S of Ardmore in southern OK, E of I-35 exit 24. 450 sites (9 areas); 56 full hook-up, 295 with electric and water, 99 primitive; showers; dump station. Store. Disc golf and golf course. Marina. ATV area. Equestrian area. Swimming, fishing; boat ramp; boat/bicycle/PWC rentals. GPS: N 34-09.3 W 97-07.3

Lake Texoma State Resort Park

11500 Park Office Rd, Kingston, OK 73439. Phone: (580) 564-2566. Located on Lake Texoma (stripped bass hotspot) in southern OK near TX state line, 5 miles E of Kingston on US 70. 517 sites, 153 full hook-up, 117 with electric and water, 247 primitive; showers; dump station. Store. Two golf courses. Marina. Swimming, fishing; boat ramp. GPS: N 33-59.9 W 96-39.1

Lake Thunderbird State Park

13101 Alameda Dr, Norman, OK 73026. Phone: (405) 360-3572. Located E of Norman on Lake Thurnderbird in central OK, 15 miles E of I-35 exit 108A via OK 9. 200+ sites, 30 full hook-up (50 amp), 189 primitive; showers; dump station. Wi-Fi. Marinas. Equestrian area & rental stables. Swimming, fishing; boat ramp; canoe, paddleboat rentals. GPS: N 35-13.9 W 97-14.8

Lake Wister State Park

25567 US 270, Wister, OK 74966. Phone: (918) 655-7212. Located on Lake Wister, 2 miles S of Wister in SE OK, on US 270. 182 sites, 16 full hook-up, 86 with electric and water, 80 primitive; showers; dump station. Swimming, fishing; boat ramp. GPS: N 34-56.0 W 94-42.5

Little Sahara State Park

101 Main St, Waynoka, OK 73860. Phone: (580) 824-1471. Located in northwestern OK, 4 miles S of Waynoka, between US 412 & 64 on US 281. 88 sites with electric (30 & 50 amp) and water, 10 primitive; showers. Off-road vehicle trails, dunes. GPS: N 36-32.0 W 98 53.5

McGee Creek State Park

576 A.S. McGee Creek Lake Rd, Atoka, OK 74525. Phone: (580) 889-5822. Located on McGee Creek Lake, SE of Atoka via OK 3, N of Farris. 41 sites with electric and water; showers; dump station. Horse trails. Fishing; boat ramp. GPS: N 34-19.2 W 95-54.4

Natural Falls State Park

Hwy 412 W, West Siloam Springs, OK 74338. Phone: (918) 422-5802. Located in northeastern OK near Arkansas state line, 3 miles W of West Siloam Springs on US 412. 44 sites with electric and water; showers; dump station. Fishing. GPS: N 36-09.6 W 94-41.1

Okmulgee State Park & Dripping Springs State Park

16830 Dripping Springs Rd, Okmulgee, OK 74447. Phone: (918) 756-5971. Two parks, 3 miles apart on two lakes. Located S of Tulsa in eastern OK, 6 miles W of Okmulgee, off US 75, on OK 56. 297 sites in 5 campgrounds, 75 with electric and water, some pull-through; showers; dump stations. Swimming, fishing; boat ramp. GPS: N 35-37.1 W 96-03.8

Osage Hills State Park

2131 Osage Hills State Park Rd, Pawhuska, OK 74056. Phone: (918) 336-4141. Located in northeastern OK on US 60, 9 miles W of Bartlesville. 55 sites, 20 with electric and water; showers; dump station. Swimming pool; boat rentals. GPS: N 36-45.1 W 96-10.7

Raymond Gary State Park

US Hwy 70, Fort Towson, OK 74735. Phone: (580) 873-2307. Located in southeastern OK, near TX state line; 15 miles E of Hugo on US 70; on Lake Raymond Gary. 120 sites, 10 full hook-up, 9 with electric and water, 101 primitive; showers; dump station. Swimming, fishing; boat ramp, rentals. GPS: N 33-59.9 W 95-15.2

Red Rock Canyon State Park

116 Red Rock Canyon Rd, Hinton, OK 73047. Phone: (405) 542-6344. Located W of Oklahoma City, 5 miles S of I-40 exit 101 via US 281. 52 sites, 5 full hook-up, 47 with electric and water; showers; dump station. Swimming, fishing. GPS: N 35-27.4 W 98-21.5

Robbers Cave State Park & Lodge

Hwy 2 N, Wilburton, OK 74578. Phone: (918) 465-2562. Located in southeastern OK, 5 miles N of Wilburton on OK 2, north off US 270. 122 sites, 19 full hook-up, 62 with electric and water, 41 primitive; showers; dump station. Store. Disc golf. Equestrian area, sites, rentals. Swimming, fishing; boat rentals (limited hp). GPS: N 34-57.7 W 95-21.3

Roman Nose State Resort Park

3236 S Hwy 8A, Watonga, OK 73772. Phone: (580) 623-7281. Located NW of Oklahoma City, 4 miles N of Watonga, off US 270/281 on OK 8A. 93 sites, 32 full hook-up, 61 primitive; showers; dump station. Golf course. Lake Watonga in park. Wi-Fi. Equestrian area. Swimming, fishing; boat rentals. GPS: N 35-55.7 W 98-25.4

Sequoyah Bay State Park

6237 E 100th St N, Wagoner, OK 74467. Phone: (918) 683-0878. Located on Fort Gibson Reservoir in eastern OK, 4 miles S of Wagoner on OK 16, follow signs. 71 sites with electric (30/50 amp) and water; showers; dump station. Marina; boat ramp. Swimming, fishing. GPS: N 35-52.6 W 95-17.4

Sequoyah State Park / Western Hills Guest Ranch

17131 Park 10, Hulbert, OK 74441. Phone: (918) 772-2545. Located on Fort Gibson Lake in eastern OK, 8 miles E of Wagoner, off US 69 on OK 51. 425 sites, 28 full hook-up, 149 with electric and water, 248 primitive; showers; dump station. Golf course. Equestrian area. Marina. Swimming, fishing; boat ramp, rentals. GPS: N 35-55.7 W 95-15.9

Talimena State Park

50884 Hwy 271, Talihina, OK 74571. Phone: (918) 567-2052. Located in southeastern OK, 7 miles N of Talihina on US 271. 10 full hook-up sites; showers; dump station. ATV trails. GPS: N 34-46.0 W 94-57.8

Tenkiller State Park

Hwy 100, Vian, OK 74962. Phone: (918) 489-5641. Located on Lake Tenkiller in eastern OK, off I-40 exit 297 (Vian), 10 miles N on OK 82 to OK 100; follow signs. 240 sites, 37 full hook-up, 50 with electric and water, 153 primitive; showers; dump station. Marina. Swimming, fishing; boat ramp. GPS: N 35-36.0 W 95-02.0

Walnut Creek State Park

209 West Ave, Prue, OK 74060. Phone: (918) 865-4991. Located on Keystone Lake northwest of Tulsa off US 412 (Cimarron Turnpike), 13 miles N on 209th West Ave; follow signs. 78 full hook-up sites, showers; dump station. Equestrian area. Swimming, fishing; boat ramp. GPS: N 36-13.6 W 96-22.0

OREGON

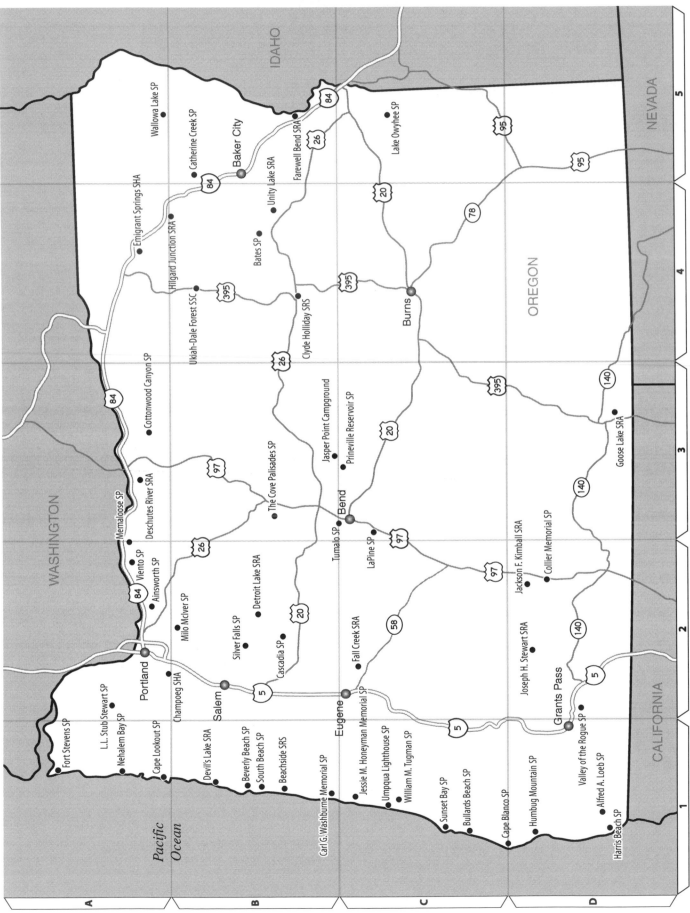

Oregon

There are 49 state parks or recreation areas in Oregon with RV facilities. Many parks are on the Pacific Ocean and several are on the Columbia River, near world-class wind surfing areas. About half of Oregon locations accept reservations, however, space permitting, all will accept campers on a "first-come" basis. Travelers on the Oregon Coast should be aware that this area is very popular in late Spring through early Autumn and sites are often hard to procure. The reservation system requires two days notice. There is a 14-day limit at all parks. RVers should always call these reservable locations before stopping. Most Oregon parks have campsites with electric hook-ups and a good number feature full hook-up sites. Parks with primitive sites do have water in the park. Unless otherwise noted, all parks are open year-round. "Seasonal" means closed from late October until late March. Discovery Season, October 1 through April 30, offers lower camping fees and smaller crowds. Rate groups: B and C depending on site facilities/season.

Oregon Parks & Recreation Dept.
State Parks
725 Summer Street NE, Ste C
Salem, OR 97301

Information: (800) 551-6949 or (503) 986-0707
Reservations: (800) 452-5687
Internet: www.oregonstateparks.org

Oregon Park Locator

Oregon Parks

Ainsworth State Park

Hood River, OR 97031. Phone: (503) 695-2261. Located in northwestern OR, 35 miles E of Portland on Historic Columbia River Hwy, off I-84 exit 35. 43 full hook-up sites, some pull-thru; showers; dump station. 60-foot limit. No reservations. Seasonal. GPS: N 45-35.7 W 122-03.2

Alfred A Loeb State Park

Brookings, OR 97415. Phone: (541) 469-2021. Located in southwestern OR, 10 miles NE of Brookings off US 101, on Chetco River; follow signs from 101. 45 sites with electric, water; showers. 50-foot limit. No reservations. Fishing, swimming, boating. GPS: N 42-06.8 W 124-11.3

Bates State Park

Austin Junction, OR 97817. Phone: (541) 448-2585. Located on Middle Fork of John Day River, 30 miles E of John Day, off US 26 on CR 20 (off OR 7.) 28 primitive sites. GPS: N44-36.0 W118-30.6

Beachside State Recreation Site

Waldport, OR 97394. Phone: (541) 867-7451. Located on central OR coast, 3 miles S of Waldport on US 101. 32 sites with electric, water; showers. 30-foot limit. Seasonal. Fishing. GPS: N 44-22.9 W 124-05.3

Beverly Beach State Park

Newport, OR 97365. Phone: (541) 265-9278. Located on central OR coast, 7 miles N of Newport on US 101. 128 sites, 53 full hook-ups, (25 with cable TV), 75 with electric, water; showers; dump station. 65-foot limit. Fishing. GPS: N 44-36.6 W 124-03.4

Bullards Beach State Park

Bandon, OR 97411. Phone: (541) 347-2209. Located on southern OR coast, 2 miles N of Bandon on US 101, at mouth of Coquille River. 185 sites, 104 full hook-ups, 82 with electric, water; showers; dump station. Equestrian area (8 sites). 65-foot limit. Fishing, boating. GPS: N 43-09.1 W 124-23.7

Cape Blanco State Park

Sixes, OR 97476. Phone: (541) 332-2973. Located on southern OR coast outside Sixes, 9 miles N of Port Orford off US 101. 53 sites with electric; showers; dump station. 65-foot limit. Equestrian area, sites. No reservations. Lighthouse tours. Fishing. GPS: N 42-49.6 W 124-31.5

Cape Lookout State Park

Tillamook, OR 97141. Phone: (503) 842-4981. Located in northwestern OR off US 101 on Three Capes Scenic Loop, 12 miles SW of Tillamook; follow signs from 101. 38 full hook-up sites, one with electric, water; showers; dump station. 60-foot limit. Fishing. GPS: N 45-22.0 W 123-57.7

Carl G. Washburne Memorial State Park

Florence, OR 97439. Phone: (541) 547-3416. Located on central OR coast (not on the ocean), 14 miles N of Florence on US 101, near Heceta Head Lighthouse. 58 sites, 50 full hook-up, 8 with electric and water; showers; dump station. 45-foot limit. No reservations. Seasonal. GPS: N 44-08.5 W 124-07.0

Cascadia State Park

Detroit, OR 37342. Phone: (541) 367-6021. Located in central OR, 14 miles E of Sweet Home (I-5 exits 216 or 233) on US 20. 25 sites with water. 35-foot limit. No reservations. Seasonal. Swimming, fishing. GPS: N 44-23.8 W 122-28.6

Catherine Creek State Park

Union, OR 97883. Phone: (541) 983-2277. Located in northeastern OR, 8 miles SE of Union on OR 203. 20 primitive sites, water available. 50-foot limit. Seasonal. Fishing. GPS: N 45-08.9 W 117-44.0

Champoeg State Heritage Area

St. Paul, OR 97137. Phone: (503) 678-1251, Ext 221. Located in western OR on Willamette River about 18 miles S of Portland and 5 miles W of I-5 exit 278. 79 sites in two campgrounds, 8 full hook-up, 67 with electric and water, some pull-thrus; showers; dump station. 60-foot limit. Historic site where Oregon's first provisional government was formed. Disc golf course. Fishing. Boat dock. GPS: N 45-14.9 W 122-53.6

Clyde Holliday State Recreation Site

Mount Vernon, OR 97865. Phone: (541) 932-4453. Located in central OR, 8 miles W of John Day on US 26, near US 395. 31 sites with electric, water; showers; dump station. 60-foot limit. No reservations. Seasonal. Fishing. GPS: N 45-08.9 W 117-44.0

Collier Memorial State Park

Chiloquin, OR 97624. Phone: (541) 783-2471. Located in southern OR, 30 miles N of Klamath Falls on US 97. 17 full hook-up sites; showers; laundry; dump station. Equestrian area, sites; 60-foot limit. Seasonal. GPS: N 42-39.9 W 121-52.3

Cottonwood Canyon State Park

Moro, OR 97039. Phone: (541) 394-0002. Located on Hwy 206 between Condon and Wasco on John Day River. 21 primitive sites. 75 foot limit. Equestrian area, trails. Fishing, boat ramp. GPS: N 45-30.7 W 120-30.3

Deschutes River State Recreation Area

Wasco, OR 97065. Phone: (541) 739-2322. Located in northwestern OR, 17 miles E of The Dalles, off I-84 exit 97, on Deschutes & Columbia Rivers. 59 sites, 34 with electric, water; 25 primitive. Equestrian area. 50-foot limit. Fishing, boating. GPS: N 45-38.6 W 120-51.7

Detroit Lake State Recreation Area

Detroit, OR 97342. Phone: (503) 854-3346. Located on Detroit Lake in west-central OR, 50 miles E of Salem on OR 22. 176 sites, 106 full hook-ups, 69 with electric; showers. 60-foot limit. Marina. Reservations recommended. Swimming, fishing; boat ramp. GPS: N 44-43.1 W 122-11.4

Devil's Lake State Recreation Area

Lincoln City, OR 97367. Phone: (541) 994-2002. Located in northwestern OR along the coast off US 101, outside Lincoln City, on Devil's Lake. 33 sites, 28 full hook-ups (all with TV cable), 5 with electric; showers. 62-foot limit. Year-round. Fishing; boat ramp. GPS: N 44-57.9 W 123-59.7

Emigrant Springs State Heritage Area

Meacham, OR 97859. Phone: (541) 983-2277. Located in northeastern OR, 26 miles SE of Pendelton off I-84 exits 228 or 238, (in Blue Mountains). 19 sites, 18 full hook-up, 1 with electric; showers. 60-foot limit. Equestrian area. GPS: N 45-32.6 W 118-27.8

Fall Creek State Recreation Area

Lowell, OR 97452. Phone: (541) 973-1173. Located in western OR on Fall Creek Reservoir, 27 miles SE of Eugene-Springfield (I-5 exit 186), N of Lowell off OR 58. 39 primitive sites. 45-foot limit. No reservations. Seasonal. Swimming, fishing; boat ramp. GPS: N 43-55.8 W 122-49.0

Farewell Bend State Recreation Area

Huntington, OR 97907. Phone: (541) 869-2365 or (800) 551-6949. Located in eastern OR, 25 miles NW of Ontario, 1 mile N of I-84 exit 353 on the Snake River. 94 sites with electric, water; showers;

dump station. 56-foot limit. Fishing; boat ramp. GPS: N 44-19.1 W 117-14.5

Fort Stevens State Park

Hammond, OR 97121. Phone: (503) 861-3170, Ext 21. Located in northwestern OR off US 101, 10 miles W of Astoria at the mouth of the Columbia River. 477 sites, 174 full hook-ups, 302 sites with electric, water; showers; dump station. Equestrian area. 50-foot limit. Year-round. Swimming, boating. GPS: N 46-12.1 W 123-57.7

Goose Lake State Recreation Area

New Pine Creek, OR 97635. Phone: (541) 783-2471. Located on Goose Lake in southern OR at CA/OR state line on US 395, S of Lakeview, 1 mile W of New Pine Creek. 47 sites with electric, water; showers; dump station. 50-foot limit. No reservations. Seasonal. Fishing; boat ramp. GPS: N 41-59.6 W 120-19.2

Harris Beach State Park

Brookings, OR 97415. Phone: (541) 469-2021. Located on southern OR coast, north side of Brookings, on US 101. 86 sites, 36 full hook-ups, 50 with electric, water; some sites w/cable TV; showers; dump station. 50-foot limit. Wi-Fi. Fishing. GPS: N 42-04.0 W 124-18.3

Hilgard Junction State Recreation Area

LaGrande, OR 97850. Phone: (541) 983-2277. Located in northeastern OR, 8 miles W of LaGrande off I-84 exit 252, on Grande Ronde River. 18 primitive sites; water available. 30-foot limit. No reservations. Seasonal. Fishing. GPS: N 45-20.4 W 118-14.3

Humbug Mountain State Park

Port Orford, OR 97465. Phone: (541) 332-6774. Located on southern OR coast, 6 miles S of Port Orford on US 101. 40 sites with electric, water; showers; dump station. 55-foot limit. Fishing. GPS: N 42-41.2 W 124-26.8

Jackson F. Kimball State Recreation Area

Chiloquin, OR 97624. Phone: (541) 783-2471. Located in southern OR near Crater Lake National Park, 3 miles N of Fort Klamath on OR 62, off US 97. 10 primitive sites; no water. 45-foot limit. No reservations. GPS: N 42-44.2 W 121-58.7

Jasper Point Campground (Prineville Reservoir)

Prineville, OR 97754. Phone: (541) 447-4363. Located in central OR, 14 miles SE of Prineville off US 26. 30 sites with electric, water. 35-foot limit. Seasonal. Swimming, fishing; boat ramp. GPS: N 44-16.9 W 120-39.9

Jessie M. Honeyman Memorial State Park

Westlake, OR 97493. Phone: (541) 997-3851. Located on central OR coast, 3 miles S of Florence on US 101, next to Oregon Dunes National Recreation Area. 167 sites, 47 full hook-ups, 120 with electric and water; showers; dump station. 60-foot limit. ATVs OK. Swimming, fishing; boat ramp. GPS: N 43-56.0 W 124-06.4

Joseph H. Stewart State Recreation Area

Trail, OR 97541. Phone: (541) 560-3334. Located in southern OR on Lost Creek Reservoir, 35 miles NE of Medford on OR 62. 151 sites with electric, water; showers; dump station. 80-foot limit. Seasonal. Marina. Swimming, fishing; boat ramp, rentals. GPS: N 42-40.2 W 122-38.5

Lake Owyhee State Park

Nyssa, OR 97913. Phone: (541) 339-2331 or (800) 551-6949. Located in eastern OR, 33 miles SW of Nyssa (I-84 exit 374), off OR 201; follow signs. Two campgrounds. 29 sites with electric, water; showers; dump station. 55-foot limit. Seasonal. Fishing; boat ramp. GPS: N 43-37.7 W 117-13.9

L.L.Stub Stewart State Park

Buxton, OR 97109. Phone: (503) 324-0606. Located on OR 47 (Nehalem Hwy), 35 miles W of Portland. 75 full hook-up sites; Equestrian area with 13 full hook-up sites; showers. Disc golf. GPS N 45-43.9 W 123-06.9

LaPine State Park

LaPine, OR 97739. Phone: (541) 536-2428. Located in central OR, 27 miles SW of Bend, off US 97. 128 sites, 80 full hook-ups, 48 with electric, some pull-thrus; showers; dump station. Store. 85-foot limit. Fishing; boat ramp. GPS: N 42-45.4 W 121-29.8

Memaloose State Park

Hood River, OR 97031. Phone: (541) 478-3008. Located on Columbia River in northwestern OR, 11 miles W of The Dalles on I-84 (Westbound access only, at rest area. Eastbound I-84 travelers should use exit 76 and return westbound 3 miles on Interstate 84.) 44 full hook-up sites; showers; dump station. 60-foot limit. Seasonal. Wind surfing. GPS: N 45-41.8 W 121-20.6

Milo McIver State Park

Estacada, OR 97023. Phone: (503) 630-7150. Located in northwestern OR on the Clackamas River, 4 miles W of Estacada, off OR 211, via OR 224 off I-205; follow signs from OR 224. 44 sites with electric, water; showers; dump station. 50-foot limit. Disc golf. Horse trails. Seasonal. Fishing; boat ramp. GPS: N 45-18.0 W 122-22.8

Nehalem Bay State Park

Manzanita, OR 97130. Phone: (503) 368-5154. Located in northwestern OR, 3 miles S of Manzanita junction, off US 101 on Nehalem Bay. 265 sites with electric, water; showers; dump station. 60-foot limit. Equestrian area (17 sites with corrals). Fishing, boating. GPS: N 45-42.6 W 123-55.9

Prineville Reservoir State Park

Prineville, OR 97754. Phone: (541) 447-4363. Located in central OR, 14 miles SE of Prineville off US 26. 44 sites, 22 full hook-ups, 22 with electric; showers. 50-foot limit. Swimming, fishing; boat ramp. GPS: N 44-08.7 W 120-44.3

Silver Falls State Park (Resort)

Silverton, OR 97381. Phone: (503) 873-8681. Located in western OR, 25 miles E of Salem on OR 214, off OR 22 from I-5 exit 253. (Largest park in state.) 52 sites with electric, water; showers; dump station. Equestrian area. 60-foot limit. Swimming, fishing. GPS: N 44-53.3 W 122-37.6

South Beach State Park

Newport, OR 97366. Phone: (541) 867-7451. Located on central OR coast, 2 miles S of Newport on US 101. 228 sites, 227 with electric, water; showers; dump station. 60-foot limit. Fishing. (South Jetty, adjacent to park-wind surfing; horse access to beach.) Fishing. GPS: N 44-35.9 W 124-03.6

Sunset Bay State Park

Coos Bay, OR 97420. Phone: (541) 888-3778. Located on southern OR coast, 12 miles SW of Coos Bay off US 101; follow signs. 65 sites, 30 full hook-ups, 35 with electric; showers. 47-foot limit. Golf course nearby. Swimming, fishing; boat ramp. GPS: N 43-20.4 W 124-21.7

The Cove Palisades State Park

Culver, OR 97734. Phone: (541) 546-3412. Located in central OR, 15 miles SW of Madras off US 97 on Lake Billy Chinook. 173 sites in two areas, 82 full hook-up, 91 with electric and water; showers; dump station. Marina. 60-foot limit. Swimming, fishing; boat ramp, rentals. GPS: N 44-33.0 W 121-15.6

Tumalo State Park

Bend, OR 97701. Phone: (541) 388-6055. Located in central OR, 5 miles NW of Bend off US 20 on Deschutes River. 23 full hook-up sites; showers. 44-foot limit. Swimming, fishing. GPS: N 44-05.2 W 121-18.5

Ukiah-Dale Forest State Scenic Corridor

Ukiah, OR 97880. Phone: (541) 983-2277. Remote location SW of LaGrande on US 395. 27 primitive sites, water nearby. Fishing. GPS: N 45-06.3 W 118-57.3

Umpqua Lighthouse State Park

Lakeside, OR 974. Phone: (541) 271-4118. Located on south-central OR coast, 6 miles S of Reedsport on US 101, near mouth of Winchester Bay. 10 full hook-up sites, nine with electric, water; showers. In Oregon Dunes National Recreation Area. ATVs OK. 45-foot limit. Fishing, boat ramp. GPS: N 43-40.2 W 124-11.0

Unity Lake State Recreation Area

Unity, OR 97. Phone: (541) 446-3470. Located in eastern OR, 50 miles E of John Day off US 26 on OR 245. 35 sites with electric (30/50 amp), water; showers; dump station. 40-foot limit. No reservations. Fishing; boat ramp. GPS: N 44-29.6 W 118-11.3

Valley of the Rogue State Park

Gold Hill, OR 97525. Phone: (541) 582-1118. Located in southwestern OR, 12 miles E of Grants Pass at I-5 exit 45B. 147 sites, 88 full hook-ups, 59 with electric, water; showers; dump station. 75-foot limit. Fishing, boat ramp. GPS: N 42-24.7 W 123-07.8

Viento State Park

Hood River, OR 97031. Phone: (541) 374-8811. Overlooks the Columbia River in northern OR, 8 miles W of Hood River at I-84 exit 56. 56 sites with electric, water; showers. 30-foot limit. No reservations. Seasonal. Wind surfing area. Fishing. GPS: N 45-41.8 W 121-40.1

Wallowa Lake State Park

Joseph, OR 97846. Phone: (541) 432-4185. Located on Wallowa Lake in northeastern OR, 6 miles S of Joseph off OR 82, at the foot of the Wallowa Mountains. 121 full hook-up sites, some pull-thru; showers; dump station. 90-foot limit. Swimming, fishing; boat ramp. Marina. GPS: N 45-16.8 W 117-12.4

William M. Tugman State Park

Lakeside, OR 97449. Phone: (541) 759-3604. Located on southern OR coast, 8 miles S of Reedsport, off US 101 on Eel Lake. 94 sites with electric, water; showers; dump station. 50-foot limit. Swimming, fishing; boat ramp. GPS: N 43-37.4 W 124-10.9

PENNSYLVANIA

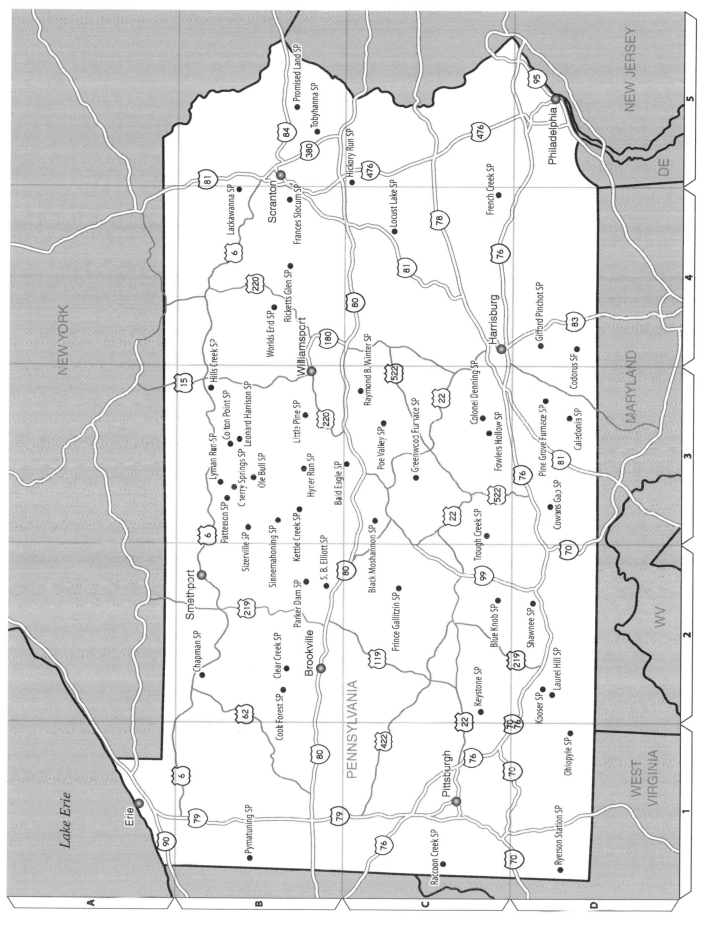

NEW JERSEY

NEW YORK

Lake Erie

WEST VIRGINIA

MARYLAND

WV

DE

PENNSYLVANIA

Erie

Scranton

Williamsport

Smethport

Brookville

Harrisburg

Pittsburgh

Philadelphia

Promised Land SP

Tobyhanna SP

Hickory Run SP

Locust Lake SP

French Creek SP

Lackawanna SP

Frances Slocum SP

Ricketts Glen SP

Worlds End SP

Gifford Pinchot SP

Codorus SF

Hills Creek SP

Raymond B. Winter SP

Colonel Denning SP

Pine Grove Furnace SP

Caledonia SP

Little Pine SP

Greenwood Furnace SP

Fowlers Hollow SP

Cowans Gap SP

Lyman Run SP

Cotton Point SP

Leonard Harrison SP

Ole Bull SP

Hyner Run SP

Bald Eagle SP

Poe Valley SP

Cherry Springs SP

Patterson SP

Sizerville SP

Kettle Creek SP

S. B. Elliott SP

Black Moshannon SP

Trough Creek SP

Sinnemahoning SP

Parker Dam SP

Chapman SP

Clear Creek SP

Prince Gallitzin SP

Blue Knob SP

Shawnee SP

Laurel Hill SP

Cook Forest SP

Keystone SP

Kooser SP

Ohiopyle SP

Pymatuning SP

Raccoon Creek SP

Ryerson Station SP

Pennsylvania

The Commonwealth of Pennsylvania is one of the richest states in number of RV sites, with nearly 7,000 spread among 49 state parks. While none of the parks offer sewer or water hook-ups, most have electric connections (not at all sites in every park) and drinking water is available in all the parks. (Not all parks are equipped to provide holding tank water because of hand pump delivery.) As a rule, Pennsylvania parks do not allow pets in camping areas, however there are some exceptions; call to verify. Also, alcoholic beverages are not allowed in these parks. While most of the parks are open from Spring through late Autumn, parks open year-round are often closed because of snow during winter months. Reservations require a 48-hour advance notice. Several parks do not accept reservations—call to verify. Seniors (62 & older) are eligible for a discount on all park rates. Major credit cards are accepted and there are resident and non-resident fees. Rate group: B, depending upon site type and day of the week; weekend fees are usually higher.

Pennsylvania Dept. of Conservation &
Natural Resources
Bureau of State Parks
PO Box 8551
Harrisburg, PA 17105

Information & Reservations: (888) 727-2757
Internet: www.dcnr.state.pa.us

Pennsylvania Park Locator

Pennsylvania Parks

Bald Eagle State Park

149 Main Park Rd, Howard, PA 16841. Phone: (814) 625-2775. Located in north-central PA on PA 150, 10 miles N of Milesburg and I-80 exit 158 on Foster Joseph Sayers Reservoir. 35 sites with electric (some 50 amp); showers; dump station. Marina. Swimming, fishing; boat ramp, rentals. Seasonal. GPS: N 41-02.5 W 77-38.6

Black Moshannon State Park

4216 Beaver Rd, Philipsburg, PA 16866. Phone: (814) 342-5960. Located in central PA on PA 504, 9 miles E of Philipsburg on Black Moshannon Lake. 80 sites with electric; showers; dump station. Swimming, fishing; boat ramp, rentals. Seasonal. GPS: N 40-54.9 W78-03.5

Blue Knob State Park

124 Park Rd, Imler, PA 16655. Phone: (814) 276-3576. Located in southwestern PA 9 miles W of I-99 exit 7 near Imler, via PA 869. 45 sites, 25 with electric; showers; dump station. Equestrian trails. Swimming, fishing. Seasonal. GPS: N 40-15.9 W 79-35.1

Caledonia State Park

40 Rocky Mountain Rd, Fayetteville, PA 17222. Phone: (717) 352-2161. Located in south-central PA on US 30 at PA 233, midway between Gettysburg (US 15) and Chambersburg (I-81). Two campgrounds; 175 sites, some with electric; showers; dump station. Golf course. Swimming, fishing. GPS: N 39-54.3 W 77-28.7

Chapman State Park

4790 Chapman Dam Rd, Clarendon, PA 16313. Phone: (814) 723-0250. Located in northwestern PA off US 6 near Clarendon, next to Allegheny National Forest. 82 sites, some with electric; water available; dump station. Lake Chapman in park. Swimming, fishing; boat ramp, canoe/kayak rentals. GPS: N 41-45.5 W 79-10.2

Cherry Springs State Park

c/o Lyman Run, Galeton, PA 16922. Phone: (814) 435-5010. Located in north-central PA in Susquehannock State Forest, in Cherry Springs on PA 44, S of US 6. 30 sites (rustic); dump station. GPS: N 41-39.6 W 77-46.1

Clear Creek State Park

38 Clear Creek State Park Rd, Sigel, PA 15860. Phone: (814) 752-2368. Located in northwestern PA on Clear Creek on PA 949; I-80 exit 73 (PA 949) or I-80 exit 78 (PA 36), N about 12 miles. 53 sites, some with electric; dump station. Seasonal. Swimming, fishing. GPS: N 41-19.9 W 79-06.0

Codorus State Park

1066 Blooming Grove Rd, Hanover, PA 17331. Phone: (717) 637-2816. Located in southeastern PA, on PA 216, 3 miles SE of Hanover. 198 sites, many with electric; 50-foot limit; showers; dump station. Lake Marburg in park. Swimming pool. Disc golf course. Seasonal. Horse trails. Fishing; boat ramp, rentals. GPS: N 39-47.0 W 76-54.5

Colonel Denning State Park

1599 Doubling Gap Rd, Newville, PA 17241. Phone: (717) 776-5272. Located in south-central PA on PA 233, 8 miles N of Newville; 9 miles S of Landisburg. 52 sites, some with electric; dump station. Lake in park. Seasonal. Swimming, fishing. GPS: N 40-16.9 W 77-25.0

Colton Point State Park

c/o Leonard Harrison SP, 4797 Rt 660, Wellsboro, PA 16901. Phone: (570) 724-3061. Located in north-central PA on west rim of Grand Canyon of Pennsylvania, opposite Leonard Harrison SP, 5 miles S of US 6 at Ansonia, SW of Wellsboro. 25 sites (rustic); dump station. Fishing. Seasonal. GPS: N 41-42.7 W 77-27.9

Cook Forest State Park

Cooksburg, PA 16217. Phone: (814) 744-8407. Located in northwestern PA near Cooksburg; I-80 exit 60 (PA 66) or I-80 exit 60 (PA 36), N about 15 miles. 226 sites, some with electric; showers; dump station; laundry. Horse trails. Swimming, fishing; canoe launch ramp. GPS: N 41-20.0 W 79-12.6

Cowans Gap State Park

6235 Aughwick Rd, Fort Loudon, PA 17224. Phone: (717) 485-3948. Located in south-central PA off PA 75 between Chambersburg and McConnellsburg; N of US 30 at Fort Loudon. Two areas: 224 sites, some with electric; showers; dump station. Cowens Gap Lake in park. Swimming, fishing; boat ramp, rentals (electric motors only). Seasonal. GPS: N 39-59.4 W 77-55.7

Fowlers Hollow State Park

5700 Fowler Hollow Rd, Blair, PA 17241. Phone: (717) 776-5272. Located in south-central PA, W of Harrisburg, off PA 274. (Remote location; no easy access.) 12 sites with electric; dump station. Horse trails. Fishing. GPS: N 40-16.4 W 77-34.8

Frances Slocum State Park

565 Mount Oilivet Rd, Wyoming, PA 18644. Phone: (570) 696-3525. Located in northeastern PA 10 miles NW of Wilkes-Barre; 5 miles E of Dallas; off US 11 to PA 309. 100 sites, some with electric; showers; dump station. Francis Slocum Lake in park. Swimming, fishing; boat ramp, boat/canoe rentals (electric motors only). GPS: N 41-20.4 W 75-55.1

French Creek State Park

843 Park Rd, Elverson, PA 19520. Phone: (610) 582-9680. Located in southeastern PA off PA 345, SW of Pottstown and NE of I-76 exit 298. 201 sites, 65 with electric; showers; dump station. Two lakes in park. Horse trails. Swimming, fishing; boat ramp, rentals (electric motors only). GPS: N 40-12.5 W 75-47.0

Gifford Pinchot State Park

2200 Rosstown Rd, Lewisberry, PA 17339. Phone: (717) 292-4112 or (717) 432-5011. Located in southeastern PA on PA 177 between Rossville and Lewisberry, S of Harrisburg; I-83 exit 35. 339 sites, some with electric; showers; dump station. Pinchot Lake in park. Equestrian trails. Disc golf course. Seasonal. Swimming, fishing; boat ramp, rentals (electric motors only). GPS: N 40-05.2 W 76-53.3

Greenwood Furnace State Park

15795 Greenwood Rd, Huntingdon, PA 16652. Phone: (814) 667-1800. Located in central PA on PA 305, NW of Belleville; SE of State College. 51 sites, 46 with electric (30/50 amp); showers; dump station. Lake in park. Swimming, fishing. Seasonal. GPS: N 40-39.0 W 77-45.4

Hickory Run State Park

White Haven, PA 18661. Phone: (570) 443-0400. Located in northeastern PA in Pocono Mts., on PA 534, S of I-80/I-476 junction. 381 sites, some with electric; showers; dump station. Lake in park. Pets OK. Disc golf course. Swimming, fishing. Seasonal. No alcohol. GPS: N 41-02.1 W 75-44.2

Hills Creek State Park

111 Spillway Rd, Wellsboro, PA 16901. Phone: (570) 724-4246. Located in north-central PA between Wellsboro and Mansfield, off US 6 via PA 287 at Tioga. 85 sites, some with electric; showers; dump station. Hills Creek Lake in park. Swimming, fishing; boat ramp, boat/canoe/kayak rentals. Seasonal. GPS: N 41-49.0 W 77-12.4

Hyner Run State Park

864 Hyner Park Rd, North Bend, PA 17760. Phone: (570) 923-6000. Located in north-central PA on PA 120, 6 miles E of Renovo; 3 miles N of Hyner. 30 sites (rustic); showers; dump station. Swimming, fishing. Seasonal. GPS: N 41-21.5 W 77-37.5

Kettle Creek State Park

97 Kettle Creek Park Ln, Renovo, PA 17764. Phone: (570) 923-6004. Located in central PA, on Kettle Creek Reservoir, on PA 4001, 7 miles NW of Westport (PA 120). 68 sites, 48 with electric; water available; dump station. Horse trails. Swimming, fishing; boat ramp (electric motors only). Seasonal. GPS: N 41-22.6 W 77-55.8

Keystone State Park

1150 Keystone Park Rd, Derry, PA 15627. Phone: (724) 668-2939. Located in southwestern PA, about 45 miles E of Pittsburgh, off US 22 at New Alexandria. 100 sites, some with electric; showers; dump station. Lake in park. Swimming, fishing; boat ramp (electric motors only). Seasonal. GPS: N 40-22.5 W 79-22.7

Kooser State Park

943 Glades Pike, Somerset, PA 15501. Phone: (814) 445-8673. Located in southwestern PA on PA 31 between Donegal and Somerset (I-76/70 exits 91 & 110). 47 sites, 14 with electric (20/30/50 amp), some pull throughs; dump station. Swimming, fishing. Seasonal. GPS: N 40-03.8 W 79-14.0

Lackawanna State Park

Dalton, PA 18414. Phone: (570) 945-3239. Located in northeastern PA on PA 407 west of I-81 exit 199; US 6/11 use PA 438 to PA 407. 92 sites, 61 with electric (50 amp); showers; dump station. Lake in park. Swimming, fishing; boat ramp, rentals. Horse trails. Seasonal. GPS: N 41-34.5 W 75-42.7

Laurel Hill State Park

1454 Laurel Hill Park Rd, Somerset, PA 15501. Phone: (814) 445-7725. Located in southwestern PA south of PA 31 between Donegal and Somerset (I-76/70 exits 91 & 110), follow signs to Trent Rd. 264 sites, 149 with electric; showers; dump station. Laurel Hill Lake in park. Swimming, fishing; boat ramp, boat/canoe rentals. Seasonal. GPS: N 39-59.1 W 79-14.1

Leonard Harrison State Park

4797 Rt 660, Wellsboro, PA 16901. Phone: (570) 724-3601. Located in north-central PA on PA 660, on rim of Grand Canyon of Pennsylvania. 10 miles SW of Wellsboro. 30 sites, some with electric; dump station. Fishing. Seasonal. GPS: N 41-41.8 W 77-27.2

Little Pine State Park

4205 Little Pine Creek Rd, Waterville, PA 17776. Phone: (570) 753-6000. Located in north-central PA, about 25 miles NW of Williamsport (US 15 & 220) via PA 287 to English Center, follow signs. 99 sites, most with electric; showers; dump station. 30-foot limit. Little Pine Lake in park. Swimming, fishing; boat ramp, boat/canoe rentals. Seasonal. GPS: N 41-22.3 W 77-21.6

Locust Lake State Park

c/o Tuscarora, Barnesville, PA 18214. Phone: (570) 467-2404. Located in east-central PA, 3 miles SW of Mahanoy City, 2 miles from PA 54 and I-81 interchange. 88 sites with electric; showers; dump station. Locust Lake in park. Swimming, fishing; boat ramp (electric motors only). Pets OK. GPS: N 40-46.7 W 76-08.7

Lyman Run State Park

454 Lyman Run Rd, Galeton, PA 16922. Phone: (814) 435-5010. Located in north-central PA off US 6, 15 miles E of Coudersport; 7 miles W of Galeton. 35 sites with electric; dump station. Lyman Run Lake in park. Swimming, fishing; boat ramp (electric motors only). ATV trails. Seasonal. GPS: N 41-43.5 W 77-45.7

Ohiopyle State Park

124 Main St, Ohiopyle, PA 15470. Phone: (724) 329-8591. Located on Youghiogheny River in southwestern PA, SE of Uniontown, off PA 381. RVs should use US 40 and PA 381 (PA 2019 is very steep). 199 sites, some with electric; showers; dump station. Whitewater rafting section. Equestrian trails. Fishing. Seasonal. GPS: N 39-52.4 W 79-30.6

Ole Bull State Park

21 Valhalla Ln, Cross Fork, PA 17729. Phone: (814) 435-5000. Located in north-central PA on Kettle Creek on PA 144, 18 miles S of Galeton (US 6). 43 sites with electric; dump station. Swimming, fishing. No pets. GPS: N 41-32.6 W 77-42.6

Parker Dam State Park

28 Fairview Rd, Penfield, PA 15849. Phone: (814) 765-0630. Located in west-central PA on Parker Lake, off PA 153, 8 miles N of I-80 exit 111; follow signs. 110 sites, 80 with electric; showers; dump station. Swimming, fishing; boat ramp, boat/canoe rentals (electric motors only). Seasonal. GPS: N 41-12.2 W 78-30.3

Patterson State Park

c/o Lyman Run, Galeton, PA 16922. Phone: (814) 435-5010. Located in north-central PA on PA 44, 6.5 miles S of Sweden Valley (US 6). 10 sites (rustic); no facilities. Seasonal. GPS: N 41-43.0 W 77-51.2

Pine Grove Furnace State Park

1100 Pine Grove Rd, Gardners, PA 17324. Phone: (717) 486-7174. Located in south-central PA, SW of Harrisburg on PA 233, 8 miles S of I-81 exit 37. 71 sites, some with electric; dump station; store. Laurel Lake in park. Swimming, fishing; boat ramp, rentals; (electric motors only). Seasonal. GPS: N 40-02.0 W 77-18.3

Poe Valley State Park

c/o Reeds Gap, Milroy, PA 17063. Phone: (814) 349-2460. Located in central PA in Bald Eagle State Forest (near Poe Paddy State Park), E of State College, 12 miles E of Potters Mills (US 322) via state forest roads; follow signs. 67 sites, 32 with electric; dump station. Poe Lake in park. Swimming, fishing; boat ramp, rentals (electric motors only). Seasonal. GPS: N 40-43.4 W 77-28.5

Prince Gallitzin State Park

966 Marina Rd, Patton, PA 16668. Phone: (814) 674-1000. Located in south-central PA, northwest of Altoona via PA 36 and PA 53. Remote campground. 401 sites, some with electric; showers; laundry; store; dump station. Glendale Lake in park. Equestrian area. Marina. Swimming, fishing; boat ramp, rentals. Seasonal. GPS: N 40-40.2 W 78-34.5

Promised Land State Park

100 Lower Lake Rd, Greentown, PA 18426. Phone: (570) 676-3428. Located in northeastern PA in Delaware State Forest on PA 390, S of I-84 exits 20 or 26. 232 sites (four areas), some with electric; showers; dump station. Equestrian area. Two lakes in park.

Swimming, fishing; boat/canoe/kayak rentals (electric motors only). Seasonal. GPS: N 41-18.8 W 75-12.6

Pymatuning State Park

2660 Williams Field Rd, Jamestown, PA 16134. Phone: (724) 932-3141. Located on Pymatuning Reservoir in northwestern PA off US 322, 1.5 miles N of Jamestown. (Largest park in the state; four areas.) 339 sites with electric; showers; laundry; dump station. Three marinas. Swimming, fishing; boat ramp, rentals (20 h.p. limit). Seasonal. GPS: N 41-32.6 W 80-29.1

Raccoon Creek State Park

3000 State Rt 18, Hookstown, PA 15050. Phone: (724) 899-2200. Located in southwestern PA, west of Pittsburgh on PA 18, off US 22 or 30. 172 sites, some with electric; showers; dump station. Horse trails. Swimming, fishing; boat ramp, boat/canoe/kayak rentals (electric motors only). Seasonal. GPS: N 40-30.2 W 80-25.5

Raymond B. Winter State Park

17215 Buffalo Rd, Mifflinburg, PA 17844. Phone: (570) 966-1455. Located in central PA in Bald Eagle State Forest on PA 192, 18 miles W of Lewisburg. 59 sites, some with electric; showers; dump station. Halfway Lake in park. Swimming, fishing. Seasonal. GPS: N 40-59.5 W 77-12.0

Ricketts Glen State Park

695 State Rt 487, Benton, PA 17814. Phone: (570) 477-5675. Located in northeastern PA on PA 487, 30 miles N of Bloomsburg between Williamsport and Wilkes-Barre. 120 sites (rustic); showers; dump station. RV access recommended via Dushore (US 220 to PA 487) because of very steep road from Red Rock. Lake Jean in park. Swimming, fishing; boat ramp, boat/canoe/kayak rentals (electric motors only). Equestrian trails. GPS: N 41-20.1 W 76-18.1

Ryerson Station State Park

361 Bristoria Rd, Wind Ridge, PA 15380. Phone: (724) 428-4254. Located off PA 21, 3 miles W of Wind Ridge (southwestern PA, near WV state line). 48 sites, 16 with electric; showers; dump station. Swimming pool. Duke Lake in park. Fishing; boat ramp (electric motors only). Seasonal. GPS: N 39-53.5 W 80-27.0

S.B. Elliott State Park

c/o Parker Dam, Penfield, PA 15849. Phone: (814) 765-0630. Located in west-central PA on PA 153 just off I-80 exit 111, NW of Clearfield. 25 sites (rustic); dump station. Fishing. Seasonal. GPS: N 41-07.1 W 78-32.1

Shawnee State Park

132 State Park Rd, Schellsburg, PA 15559. Phone: (814) 733-4218. Located in south-central PA, southeast of Johnstown at junction of US 30 and PA 96. 293 sites, 65 with electric; showers; dump station. Shawnee Lake in park. Swimming, fishing; boat ramp (electric motors only). Seasonal. GPS: N 40-02.3 W 78-38.7

Sinnemahoning State Park

8288 First Fork Rd, Austin, PA 16720. Phone: (814) 647-8401. Located in north-central PA on Sinnemahoning Creek (Geo. B. Stevenson Reservoir), on PA 872, 8 miles N of PA 120; 35 miles S of Coudersport (US 6). 35 sites, some with electric; showers; dump station. Fishing (electric motors only). Seasonal. GPS: N 41-27.0 W 78-03.3

Sizerville State Park

199 E Crowley Run Rd, Emporium, PA 15834. Phone: (814) 486-5605. Located in north-central PA in Elk State Forest, on PA 155, 6 miles N of Emporium (PA 120). 23 sites with electric; shower; dump station. Swimming, fishing. Seasonal. GPS: N 41-37.4 W 78-11.7

Tobyhanna State Park

Tobyhanna, PA 18466. Phone: (570) 894-8336. Located in northeastern PA, southeast of Scranton, 2 miles N of Tobyhanna on PA 423 (I-380 is 2.5 miles S of park). 140 sites; hand pump water; dump station. Tobyhanna Lake in park. Swimming, fishing; boat ramp, rentals (electric motors only). Pets OK. Seasonal. GPS: N 41-12.8 W 75-23.0

Trough Creek State Park

16362 Little Valley Rd, James Creek, PA 16657. Phone: (814) 658-3847. Located in south-central PA on Great Trough Creek, on PA 994, SE of Entriken (off PA 26). 29 sites with electric; dump station. Fishing. Seasonal. GPS: N 40-18.7 W 78-07.9

Worlds End State Park

82 Cabin Bridge Rd, Forksville, PA 18616. Phone: (570) 924-3287. Located on Loyalsock Creek, in northeastern PA, northeast of Williamsport on PA 154 about 7 miles NW of US 220. 70 sites, 35 with electric; showers; dump station. Swimming, fishing; whitewater boating. GPS: N 41-28.3 W 76-35.2

RHODE ISLAND

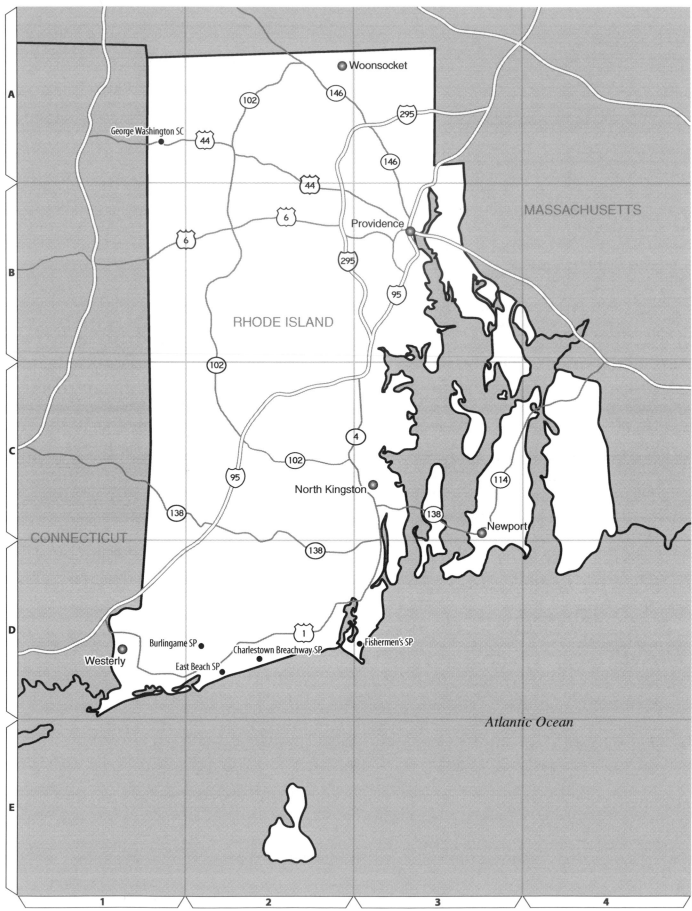

Woonsocket

George Washington SC

MASSACHUSETTS

Providence

RHODE ISLAND

North Kingston

Newport

CONNECTICUT

Westerly

Burlingame SP

Charlestown Breachway SP

Fishermen's SP

East Beach SP

Atlantic Ocean

Rhode Island

Rhode Island has only five state parks with RV spaces; four are located along the south shore, on or near the Atlantic Ocean. Pets on leashes are permitted at some parks. You should contact the respective park for site availability and rules regarding pets (and alcohol use) at that park. All state parks operate on a seasonal basis. Seniors (65+) are eligible for discounts. Rate groups: B (RI residents), C (non-residents). Entrance fee extra.

Rhode Island Division of Parks & Recreation
2321 Hartford Ave.
Johnston, RI 02919

Reservations: (877) 742-2675 (Reserve America)
Information: (401) 222-2632
Internet: www.riparks.com

Rhode Island Park Locator

Rhode Island Parks

Burlingame State Park

Sanctuary Rd (US 1), Charlestown, RI 02813. Phone: (401) 322-8910. Located near Watchaug Pond, just N of US 1, W of Charlestown. (Huge campground.) Six areas. 755 sites, no utilities, water available; showers; 2 dump stations. Fishing, swimming; boat ramp. Call park for instructions, area directions. GPS: N 41-22.0 W 71-42.7

Charlestown Breachway State Park

Charlestown Beach Rd, Charlestown, RI 02813. Phone: (401) 364-7000 or 322-8910. Located S of Charlestown, off US 1 on Block Island Sound. 75 sites, no utilities; showers. No pets. Fishing, swimming; boat ramp. GPS: N 41-21.8 W 71-37.3

East Beach State Park

(Off) East Beach Rd, Charlestown, RI 02813. Phone: (401) 322-0450 or 328-8910. Located on Block Island Sound, SW of Charlestown. 20 sites; showers. No pets or alcohol. Fishing, swimming; boat ramp. GPS: N 41-21.5 W 71-39.1

Fishermen's (Memorial) State Park

State Rt 108, 1011 Point Judith Rd, Narragansett, RI 02882. Phone: (401) 789-8374. Located near the end of RI 108, S of US 1 and Narragansett. 40 full hook-up sites, 107 sites with water and electric; showers. Note: In season minimum stay of 5 nights may be required, check with park. Fishing, swimming (nearby). GPS: N 41-22.8 W 71-29.3

George Washington State Campground

Putnam Pike, Glouster, RI 02814. Phone: (401) 568-6700. Located in NW RI, off RI 100, on Bowdish (Wilson) Reservoir. 45 sites, no utilities; water available. Swimming, fishing, boating. GPS: N42-05.3 W 71-07.2

SOUTH CAROLINA

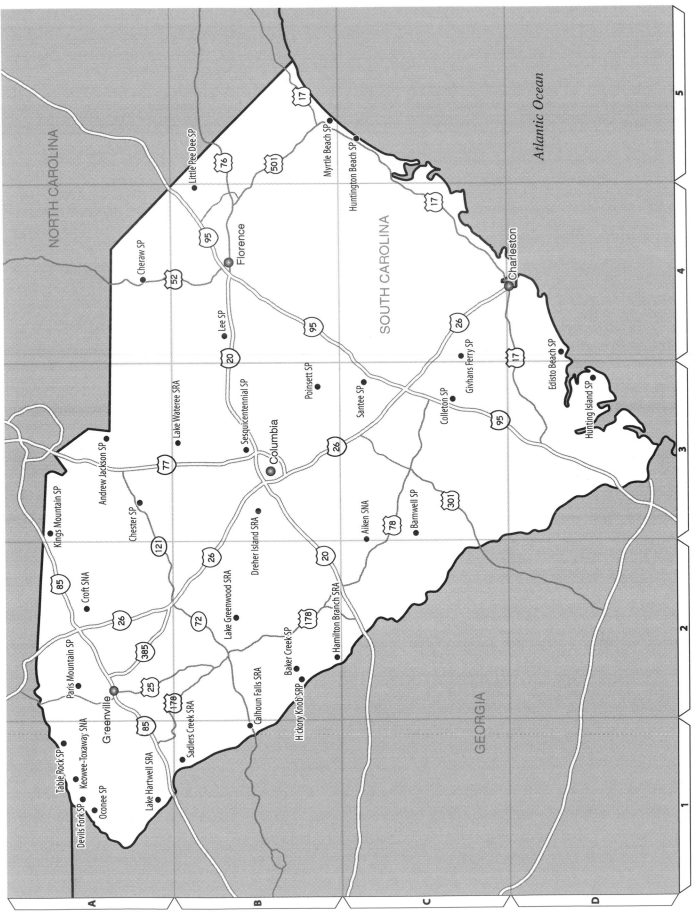

NORTH CAROLINA

Atlantic Ocean

SOUTH CAROLINA

GEORGIA

Little Pee Dee SP

Myrtle Beach SP

Huntington Beach SP

Charleston

Cheraw SP

Florence

Lee SP

Poinsett SP

Santee SP

Givhans Ferry SP

Colleton SP

Edisto Beach SP

Hunting Island SP

Lake Wateree SRA

Sesquicentennial SP

Columbia

Andrew Jackson SP

Kings Mountain SP

Chester SP

Aiken SNA

Barnwell SP

Croft SNA

Dreher Island SRA

Lake Greenwood SRA

Hamilton Branch SRA

Baker Creek SP

Calhoun Falls SRA

Paris Mountain SP

Hickory Knob SRP

Greenville

Sadlers Creek SRA

Table Rock SP

Keowee-Toxaway SNA

Oconee SP

Lake Hartwell SRA

Devils Fork SP

South Carolina

South Carolina has 32 state parks with RV facilities. Unless otherwise noted, these facilities include water and electric at each site, showers nearby and at least one dump station in the park. Most parks have a limited number of pull-through sites (check with the particular park to ascertain availability). All parks but Edisto Beach accept reservations. Reservations made through the central reservation number require three days processing time and a minimum two-night stay. Otherwise, contact the particular park directly. Most of the parks have rig size limitations; see listings. Pets on leashes are OK. Rate groups: A, B and C depending on park location.

South Carolina Dept. of Parks, Recreation & Tourism
1205 Pendelton St.
Columbia, SC 29202

Information: (888) 887-2757 or (866) 224-9339
Reservations: (866) 345-7275
Internet: www.SouthCarolinaParks.com

South Carolina Park Locator

South Carolina Parks

Aiken State Natural Area

1145 State Park Rd, Windsor, SC 29856. Phone: (803) 649-2857. Located 16 miles E of Aiken (US 1 & 78) off SC 302 & 4; on South Edisto River. 25 sites. Four lakes in park. 35-foot limit. Store. Fishing; boat ramp, rentals. GPS: N 33-32.9 W 81-29.4

Andrew Jackson State Park

196 Andrew Jackson Park Rd, Lancaster, SC 29720. Phone: (803) 285-3344. Located SE of Rock Hill, off US 521 at SC/NC state line. Andrew Jackson Museum in park. 25 sites, 5 pull-thru. 36-foot limit. Fishing; boat rentals. (Electric motors.) GPS: N 34.50.2 W 80-48.5

Baker Creek State Park

863 Baker Creek Rd, McCormick, SC 29835. Phone: (864) 443-2457. Located on Lake Thurmond, SW of McCormick, off US 378 & SC 28. 50 sites. 40-foot limit. Swimming, fishing; boat ramp, rentals. GPS: N 33-52.9 W 82-20.9

Barnwell State Park

223 State Park Rd, Blackville, SC 29817. Phone: (803) 284-2212. Located off SC 3, SW of Blackville (US 78 & SC 3). 25 sites, 8 full hook-up. Two lakes in park. 36-foot limit. Fishing; boat rentals; no motors. GPS: N 33-19.8 W 81-18.0

Calhoun Falls State Recreation Area

46 Maintenance Shop Rd, Calhoun Falls, SC 29628. Phone: (864) 447-8267. Located on Lake Russell in Calhoun Falls on SC 72, about 3 miles from GA state line. 86 sites. 40-foot limit. Laundry, store. Marina. Horse trails. Swimming, fishing; boat ramp. GPS: N 34-06.7 W 82-36.2

Cheraw State Park

100 State Park Rd, Cheraw, SC 29520. Phone: (843) 537-9656. Located on Lake Juniper near junction of US 1 & 52, about 5 miles S of Cheraw. 17 sites. Golf course. Store. Equestrian area. 40-foot limit. Swimming, fishing; boat ramp, rentals (10 h.p. limit). GPS: N 34-38.5 W 79-55.7

Chester State Park

759 State Park Dr, Chester, SC 29706. Phone: (803) 385-2680. Located 2 miles SW of Chester via SC 72. 25 sites, 5 pull-through. Lake in park. 33-foot limit. Disc golf. Fishing; boat rentals (electric motors only). GPS: N 34-41.0 W 81-15.0

Colleton State Park

147 Wayside Ln, Walterboro, SC 29488. Phone: (843) 538-8206. Located on Edisto River, on SC 15 near Colleton, off I-95 exit 68 via SC 61. 25 sites. 40-foot limit. Store. Fishing; boat rentals. GPS: N 33-03.8 W 80-36.8

Croft State Natural Area

450 Croft State Park Rd, Spartanburg, SC 29302. Phone: (864) 585-1283. Located 17 miles SE of Spartanburg (I-26 & I-85) off US 176. 50 sites. Two lakes in park. 40-foot limit. Equestrian area. Fishing; boat ramp, rentals, (electric motors only). GPS: N 34-53.5 W 81-52.6

Devils Fork State Park

161 Holcombe Circle, Salem, SC 29676. Phone: (864) 944-2639. Located on Lake Jocassee, off SC 11 near SC/GA/NC state lines. 59 sites. 36-foot limit. Swimming, fishing; boat ramp. Wi-Fi. GPS: N 34-58.1 W 82-58.7

Dreher Island State Recreation Area

3677 State Park Rd, Prosperity, SC 29127. Phone: (803) 364-4152. Located on Lake Murray, off US 76 about 30 miles W of Columbia. From I-26 exit 91, follow signs. From US 378, take SC 391 north and follow signs. 97 sites. 45-foot limit. Store. Swimming, fishing; boat ramp. GPS: N 34-05.7 W 81-24.9

Edisto Beach State Park

8377 State Cabin Rd, Edisto Island, SC 29438. Phone: (843) 869-2156. Located in Edisto Beach at end of SC 174, off US 17, on the Atlantic Ocean. 111 sites. 40-foot limit. Fishing; boat ramp.Wi-Fi. GPS: N 32-30.3 W 80-18.6

Givhans Ferry State Park

746 Givhans Ferry Rd, Ridgeville, SC 29472. Phone: (843) 873-0692. Located on Edisto River, off SC 61 near Givhans (I-26 exit 187). 25 sites. 40-foot limit. Store. Fishing; boat ramp. Equestrian area. GPS: N 33-01.5 W 80-23.2

Hamilton Branch State Recreation Area

111 Campground Rd, Plum Branch, SC 28845. Phone: (864) 333-2223. Located on Strom Thurmond Lake on SC 28 midway between McCormick, SC and Augusta, GA. 173 sites (most on the lake). Swimming, fishing; boat ramp. 40-foot limit. Store. GPS: N 35-45.4 W 82-12.1

Hickory Knob State Resort Park

1591 Resort Dr, McCormick, SC 29835. Phone: (864) 391-2450. Located on Strom Thurmond Lake, off US 378 on SC 7, about 6 miles SW of McCormick, at GA state line. 44 sites, (21 on waterfront). 30-foot limit. Golf course. Store. Swimming, fishing; boat ramp, rentals. Wi-Fi. GPS: N 33-53.0 W 82-24.8

Hunting Island State Park

2555 Sea Island Pkwy, Hunting Island, SC 29920. Phone: (843) 838-2011. Located at end of US 21, SE of Beaufort, on the Atlantic Ocean. Most popular park in SC system. 171 sites. 40-foot limit. Store. Swimming, fishing; boat ramp. Equestrian trails (open Dec to Feb). Wi-Fi. GPS: N 32-21.6 W 80-27.1

Huntington Beach State Park

16148 Ocean Hwy, Murrells Inlet, SC 29576. Phone: (843) 237-4440. Located about 18 miles SW of Myrtle Beach, off US 17, on the Atlantic Ocean. 107 standard sites, 24 full hook-up. 40-foot limit. Store. Swimming, fishing; boat ramp. Wi-Fi. GPS: N 33-30.2 W 79-04.9

Keowee-Toxaway State Natural Area

108 Residence Dr, Sunset, SC 29685. Phone: (864) 868-2605. Located off SC 288 about 18 miles NW of Greenville. 10 sites. 40-foot limit. Swimming, fishing, boating. (Ramp is five miles from park). GPS: N 34-55.8 W 82-53.4

Kings Mountain State Park

1277 Park Rd, Blacksburg, SC 29702. Phone: (803) 222-3209. Located near NC state line, about 8 miles W of Clover via SC 55 and SC 161; adjacent to Kings Mountain National Military Park. 115 sites. Equestrian area (15 sites). Store. 40-foot limit. Boat/canoe rentals. GPS: N 35-06.8 W 81-23.6

Lake Greenwood State Recreation Area

302 State Park Rd, Ninety-Six, SC 29666. Phone: (864) 543-3535. Located on Lake Greenwood, 16 miles E of Greenwood, off SC 34 & 702. 125 sites. 40-foot limit. Swimming, fishing; boat ramp. GPS: N 34-11.1 W 81-57.0

Lake Hartwell State Recreation Area

19138-A Hwy 11S, Fair Play, SC 29643. Phone: (864) 972-3352. Located on Tugaloo River (Lake Hartwell), N of I-85 exit 1 via SC 11. 115 sites. Store. Swimming, fishing; boat ramp. Wi-Fi. GPS: N 34-33.0 W 83-03.0

Lake Wateree State Recreation Area

881 State Park Rd, Winnsboro, SC 29180. Phone: (803) 482-6401. Located on Lake Wateree Reservoir off US 21 near I-77, midway between Columbia and Rock Hill. Follow signs from US 21. 72 sites: 5 pull-through, five waterfront. 40-foot limit. Store. Swimming, fishing; boat ramp. GPS: N 34-25.5 W 80-52.1

Lee State Park

487 Loop Rd, Bishopville, SC 29010. Phone: (803) 428-5307. Located off I-20 exit 123, NE of Wisacky on Lynches River. 25 sites. 36-foot limit. Equestrian area with 23 sites, electric and water. Fishing. GPS: N 34-12.3 W 80-10.5

Little Pee Dee State Park

1298 State Park Rd, Dillon, SC 29536. Phone: (843) 774-8872. Located on Little Pee Dee River off SC 57 about 11 miles SE of Dillon (I-95 exit 193). 32 sites. Store. Swimming, fishing; boat rentals (electric motors only). GPS: N 34-19.8 W 79-17.0

Myrtle Beach State Park

4401 S Kings Hwy, Myrtle Beach, SC 29575. Phone: (843) 238-5325. Located on Bus. US 17 about 3 miles SW of Myrtle Beach, on the Atlantic Ocean. 270 sites, (66 full hook-up). 40-foot limit. Laundry. Swimming (ocean). Pier fishing. Equestrian area; (Horses on beach allowed Nov to Feb with permit.) Wi-Fi. GPS: N 33-39.0 W 78-56.3

Oconee State Park

624 State Park Rd, Mountain Rest, SC 29664. Phone: (864) 638-5353. Located off SC 107, NW of Clemson. 140 sites. Two lakes in park. 35-foot limit. Store. Swimming, fishing. Boat rentals (no private boats allowed). Wi-Fi. GPS: N 34-51.9 W 83-06.6

Paris Mountain State Park

2401 State Park Rd, Greenville, SC 29609. Phone: (864) 244-5565. Located off US 25 about 14 miles N of Greenville. 26 sites. Lake in park. 40-foot limit. Swimming, fishing; boat rentals (no private boats allowed). GPS: N 34-55.5 W 82-21.9

Poinsett State Park

6660 Poinsett Park Rd, Wedgefield, SC 29168. Phone: (803) 494-8177. Located off SC 261 about 20 miles SW of Sumter. 24 sites. Lake in park. 40-foot limit. Store. Fishing; boat rentals (13-foot limit; electric motors only). Wi-Fi. GPS: N 33-48.3 W 80-30.4

Sadlers Creek State Recreation Area

940 Sadlers Creek Park Rd, Anderson, SC 29626. Phone: (864) 226-8950. Located on Lake Hartwell on SC 187 via US 29, about 13 miles SW of Anderson. 52 sites. 40-foot limit. Swimming, fishing; boat ramp. GPS: N 34-25.5 W 82-49.7

Santee State Park

251 State Park Rd, Santee, SC 29142. Phone: (803) 854-2408. Located on Lake Marion, 1 mile W of Santee, on SC 6 near I-95 exit 98. 158 sites. 40 foot limit. Laundry; store. Fishing; boat ramp, rentals. GPS: N 33-29.5 W 80-29.6

Sesquicentennial State Park

9564 Two Notch Rd, Columbia, SC 29223. Phone: (803) 788-2706. Located off US 1 (Two Notch Rd), 4 miles NE of Columbia. 84 sites, 14 pull-through. 35-foot limit. Store. Fishing; boat rentals (no ramp; electric motors only). GPS: N 34-06.1 W 80-54.7

Table Rock State Park

158 E Ellison Ln, Pickens, SC 29671. Phone: (864) 878-9813. Located 12 miles N of Pickens via US 178 and SC 11. 89 sites. Two lakes in park. 40-foot limit. Swimming, fishing; boat ramp, rentals. GPS: N 35-01.3 W 82-42.6

SOUTH DAKOTA

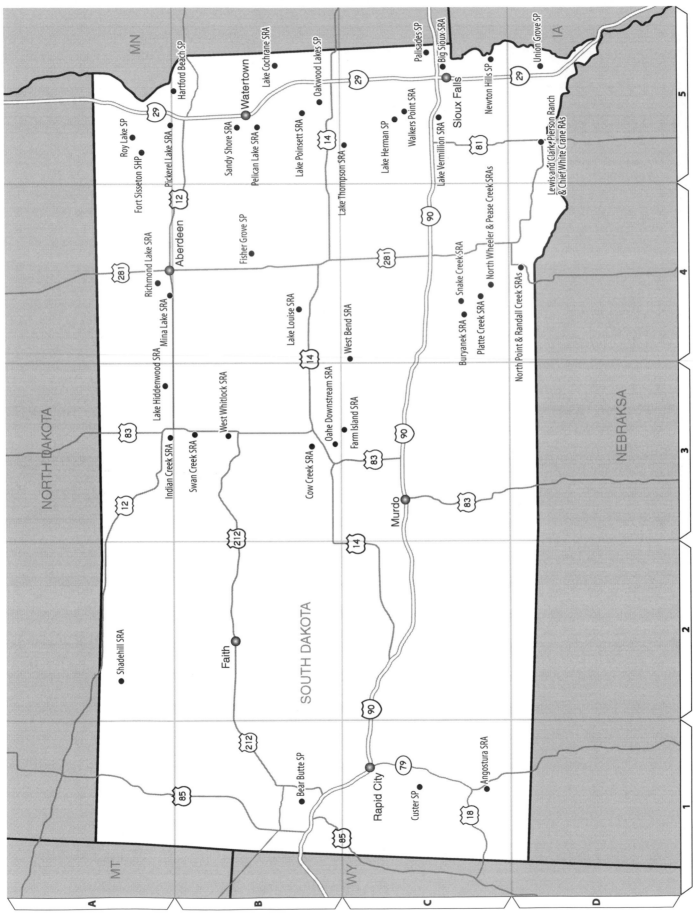

MN

IA

Hartford Beach SP

Lake Cochrane SRA

Palisades SP

Big Sioux SRA

Union Grove SP

Oakwood Lakes SP

Newton Hills SP

Watertown

Roy Lake SP

Pickerel Lake SRA

Sandy Shore SRA

Pelican Lake SRA

Lake Poinsett SRA

Lake Thompson SRA

Walkers Point SRA

Lake Herman SP

Lake Vermillion SRA

Sioux Falls

Lewis and Clark, Pierson Ranch & Chief White Crane RAs

Fort Sisseton SHP

Richmond Lake SRA

Aberdeen

Fisher Grove SP

North Wheeler & Pease Creek SRAs

Mina Lake SRA

Lake Louise SRA

West Bend SRA

Buryanek SRA

Snake Creek SRA

Platte Creek SRA

North Point & Randall Creek SRAs

Lake Hiddenwood SRA

West Whitlock SRA

Oahe Downstream SRA

Farm Island SRA

Indian Creek SRA

Swan Creek SRA

Cow Creek SRA

Murdo

NORTH DAKOTA

NEBRAKSA

Shadehill SRA

Faith

SOUTH DAKOTA

Bear Butte SP

Angostura SRA

Rapid City

Custer SP

MT

WY

South Dakota

South Dakota has 11 state parks and 28 recreation areas that will accommodate RVs. These parks and recreation areas are part of the state-wide reservation system. All these areas require a daily (or annual) license fee in addition to the fees charged for campsite usage. A number of areas are controlled by other locations and these parks are identified. While you cannot use the address other than for mail or telephone contact, the GPS coordinates are for actual locations. Sites are divided into three categories: *Preferred* campgrounds (most popular state campgrounds) have restrooms with showers and some sites with electric hook-ups. *Modern* campgrounds also have restrooms with showers and some sites with electric hook-ups. *Basic* campgrounds have vault toilets, no showers and few sites with electric hookups. All the parks have water available. Some facilities are limited in winter months when water systems are shut down. Credit cards are accepted. Pets on a leash are OK. Rate group: A, admission fee extra.

South Dakota Dept. of Game, Fish and Parks
523 East Capitol Ave
Pierre, SD 57501

Information: (605) 773-3391
Reservations: (800) 710-2267
Internet: southdakotastateparks.com
Reservations: www.CampSD.com

South Dakota Park Locator

South Dakota Parks

Angostura State Recreational Area

13157 N Angostura Rd, Hot Springs, SD 57747. Phone: (605) 745-6996. Located on Angostura Reservoir, 10 miles SE of Hot Springs, off US 18 & 385. (Four areas.) 169 sites, 150 with electric; showers; dump station. Marina. Swimming, fishing; boat ramp. Disc golf. GPS: N 43-21.1 W 103-25.4

Bear Butte State Park

20250 E Hwy 79, Sturgis, SD 57785. Phone: (605) 347-5240. Located off SD 79, 6 miles NE of Sturgis, I-90 exit 30. 15 sites. Fishing; boat ramp (25 hp limit). Equestrian trails. GPS: N 44-27.6 W 103-26.0

Big Sioux State Recreation Area

410 Park Ave, Brandon, SD 57005. Phone: (605) 582-7243. Located on Big Sioux River, 4 miles SW of Brandon, off I-90 exit 406 (Sioux Falls area). 43 sites with electric; showers; dump station. Disc golf course. Fishing; canoe ramp. GPS: N 43-34.4 W 96-35.7

Buryanek State Recreation Area

27450 Buryanek Rd, Burke, SD 57523. Phone: (605) 337-2587. Located 20 miles N of Platte, off SD 44. 43 sites (some electric). Swimming, fishing, boating, ramp. GPS: N43-25.2 W99-10.2

Cow Creek State Recreation Area

28229 Cow Creek Rd, Fort Pierre, SD 57532. Phone: (605) 223-7722. Located on Missouri River, off SD 1804, about 17 miles NW of Pierre.

30 sites; showers. Swimming, fishing; boat ramp. No Reservations. GPS: N 44-28.3 W 100-23.1

Custer State Park

13329 US 16A, Custer, SD 57730. Eight campgrounds in Custer State Park complex. Located near Mt. Rushmore, junction US 16 & 385. Reservations recommended; call information number for space availability: (605) 255-4515; Reservations (800) 710-2267. Equestrian area. Most locations have (some) electric hook-ups. Bison herd in park. GPS: N 43-46.2 W 103-26.4

   a. Blue Bell State Park Campground, 35 sites; showers.
   b. Game Lodge State Park Campground, 58 sites (designed for big rigs); showers; dump station.
   c. Legion Lake State Park Campground, 25 sites; showers.
   d. Sylvan Lake State Park Campground, 39 sites; showers.
   e. Center Lake State Park Campground, 71 sites, no hook-ups; showers.
   f. Stockade Lake State Park Campground (North and South): 69 sites; showers.
   g. Grace Coolidge State Park Campground, 26 sites. No reservations.
   h. French Creek State Park Horse Camp - horse campers only; showers.

Farm Island State Recreation Area

1301 Farm Island Rd, Pierre, SD 57501. Phone: (605) 773-2885. Located on Lake Sharpe, 4 miles E of Pierre via SD 34. 90 sites with electric; showers; dump station. Swimming, fishing; boat ramp. Bicycle rentals. GPS: N 44-21.0 W 100-16.5

Fisher Grove State Park

17290 Fishers Ln, Frankfort, SD 57440. Phone: (605) 472-1336. Located on James River off US 212, 7 miles E of Redfield (junction US 212 & 281). 22 sites with electric; showers; dump station. Fishing. Canoe launch area. GPS: N 44-52.7 W 98-21.4

Fort Sisseton State Historic Park

11907 434th Ave, Lake City, SD 57247. Phone: (605) 448-5474. Located 10 miles SW of Lake City off US 10. 10 sites with electric; showers. Fishing; boat ramp, rentals. Restored 1864 army base in park. Wi-Fi. GPS: N 45-40.4 W 97-31.1

Hartford Beach State Park

13672 Hartford Beach Rd, Corona, SD 57227. Phone: (605) 432-6374. Located on Big Stone Lake, 15 miles N of Milbank via SD 15. 43 sites, 36 with electric; showers; dump station. Disc golf course. Swimming, fishing; boat ramp. GPS: N 45-23.9 W 96-40.1

Indian Creek State Recreation Area

12905 288th Ave, Mobridge, SD 57601. Phone: (605) 845-7112. Located on Lake Oahe off US 12, 2 miles SE of Mobridge in north-central SD. 123 sites with electric; showers; dump station. Swimming; fishing; boat ramp. Marina. GPS: N 45-31.1 W 100-23.3

Lake Cochrane State Recreation Area

3454 Edgewater Dr, Gary, SD 57237. Phone: (605) 882-5200. Located between two lakes, 10 miles E of Clear Lake, off SD 22 (I-29 exit 164). 30 sites with electric; showers. Dump station. Swimming, fishing; boat ramp. GPS: N 44-43.1 W 96-27.2

Lake Herman State Park

23409 State Park Dr, Madison, SD 57042. Phone: (605) 256-5003. Located on Lake Herman, 2 miles W of Madison (US 81 & SD 34) off SD 34. 68 sites with electric; showers; dump station. Swimming, fishing; boat ramp; canoe/kayak rentals. GPS: N 43-59.6 W 97-09.6

Lake Hiddenwood State Recreation Area.

Selby, SD 57601. Phone: (605) 845-7112. Located on Lake Hiddenwood, 5 miles NE of Selby, off US 12 & 83. 13 sites, 7 with electric. Swimming, fishing; boat ramp. No reservations. GPS: N45-33.1 W 99-59.2

Lake Louise State Recreation Area

35250 191st St, Miller, SD 57362. Phone: (605) 853-2533. Located on Lake Louise off US 14, 14 miles NW of Miller (junction US 14 & SD 45). 33 sites with electric; showers; dump station. Swimming, fishing; boat ramp. GPS: N 44-35.8 W 99-08.3

Lake Poinsett State Recreation Area

45617 S Poinsett Dr, Arlington, SD 57212. Phone: (605) 983-5085. Located on Lake Poinsett, 14 miles N of Arlington, off US 81. 114 sites, 106 with electric; showers; dump station. Swimming, fishing; boat ramp. Disc golf. GPS: N 44-32.1 W 97-05.0

Lake Thompson State Recreation Area

21176 Flood Club Rd, Lake Preston, SD 57249. Phone: (605) 847-4893. Located on Lake Thompson off US 14, 6 miles SW of Lake Preston. 103 sites, 97 with electric; showers; dump station. Swimming, fishing; boat ramp. GPS: N 44-19.6 W 97-28.3

Lake Vermillion State Recreation Area

26140 451st Ave, Canistota, SD 57012. Phone: (605) 296-3643. Located on Lake Vermillion, 5 miles S of I-90 exit 374. 90 sites, 62 with electric; showers; dump station. Swimming, fishing; boat ramp; canoe, kayak rentals. GPS: N 43-36.1 W 97-11.3

Lewis and Clark, Pierson Ranch & Chief White Crane Recreation Areas

43349 SD Hwy 52, Yankton, SD 57078. Phone: (605) 668-2985. Located on Lewis & Clark Lake, about 6 miles W of Yankton (US 81 at NE/SD state line) on SD 52. 270 sites with electric, 35 prime sites; showers; dump station. Equestrian area (8 sites with electric). Marina. Disc golf course. Swimming; fishing; boat ramp. Wi-Fi. GPS: N 42-49.8 W 97.31.3

Mina Lake State Recreation Area

402 Park Ave, Mina, SD 57451. Phone: (605) 626-3488. Located on Mina Lake, 11 miles W of Aberdeen off US 12. 37 sites with electric; showers; dump station. Swimming, fishing; boat ramp. Reservations are accepted. GPS: N 45-26.4 W 98-45.2

Newton Hills State Park

28767 482nd Ave, Canton, SD 57013. Phone: (605) 987-2263. Located on Lake Lakota, 6 miles S of Canton, off US 18 (I-90 exit 62) and CR 135. 111 sites, 108 with electric; showers; dump station. Equestrian area (10 sites with electric). Swimming, fishing; boat ramp. GPS: N 43-13.1 W 96-34.2

North Point & Randall Creek State Recreation Areas

38180 297th St, Lake Andes, SD 57356. Phone: (605) 487-7046. Located on Missouri River, off US 281 & US 18, 1 mile NW of Pickstown. 111 sites with electric; showers; dump station. Swimming, fishing; boat ramp, rentals. Golf course. Marina. Reservations accepted. GPS: N 43-02.9 W 98-34.3

North Wheeler & Pease Creek State Recreation Areas

29084 N Wheeler Rd, Geddes, SD 57342 Phone: (605) 487-7046. Located on Lake Francis Case off SD 1804, 16 miles S of Platte (junction of SD 44 & 45). 25 sites, 15 with electric; Pease Creek has showers. Fishing; boat ramp. No Reservations. GPS: N 43-23.1 W 99-02.0

Oahe Downstream State Recreation Area

20439 Marina Loop Rd, Fort Pierre, SD 57532. Phone: (605) 224-7722. Located on Lake Sharpe off SD 1806, below Oahe Dam, 5 miles N of Fort Pierre. 205 sites with electric; showers; dump station. Swimming, fishing; boat ramp. Shooting range. Disc golf. Wi-Fi. GPS: N 44-27.6 W 100-23.5

Oakwood Lakes State Park

20247 Oakwoood Dr, Bruce, SD 57220. Phone: (605) 627-5441. Located off US 14, 7 miles N and 3 miles W of Volga (I-29 exit 140). 136 sites, 130 with electric; showers; dump station. Equestrian area - 10 sites with electric. Swimming, fishing; boat ramp. Canoe/kayak rentals. GPS: N 44-27.3 W 96-59.4

Palisades State Park

25495 485th Ave, Garretson, SD 57030. Phone: (605) 594 3824. Located on Split Rock Creek south of Garretson, about 10 miles N of I-90 exit 406. 26 sites, 22 with electric; showers. Golf course. Fishing. Reservations accepted. GPS: N 43-41.3 W 96-31.0

Pelican Lake State Recreation Area

17450 450th Ave, Watertown, SD 57201. Phone: (605) 882-5200. Located on Pelican Lake, 9 miles SW of Watertown in eastern SD, off US 212. 76 sites with electric; showers; dump station. Swimming, fishing; boat ramp. Equestrian area, 6 sites. GPS: N 44-52.0 W 97-13.7

Pickerel Lake State Recreation Area

12980 446th Ave, Grenville, SD 57239. Phone: (605) 486-4753. Located on Pickerel Lake in northeastern SD, 10 miles N of Waubay off US 12. 72 sites with electric; showers; dump station. Swimming; fishing; boat ramp, rentals. GPS: N 45-29.8 W 97-17.3

Platte Creek State Recreation Area

35910 282nd St, Platte, SD 57369. Phone: (605) 337-2587. Located off SD 54, 8 miles W and 10 miles S of Platte (junction of SD 44 & 45). 37 sites with electric; showers; dump station. Fishing; boat ramp. GPS: N 43-19.7 W 98-55.7

Richmond Lake State Recreation Area

37908 Youth Camp Rd, Aberdeen, SD 57401. Phone: (605) 626-3488. Located on Richmond Lake, 10 miles NW of Aberdeen off US 281. 24 sites with electric; showers. Swimming, fishing; boat ramp. Disc golf. GPS: N 45-32.7 W 98-35.9

Roy Lake State Park

11545 Northside Dr, Lake City, SD 57247. Phone: (605) 448-5701. Located on Roy Lake, 3 miles SW of Lake City off SD 10. 102 sites, 88 with electric; showers; dump station. Swimming, fishing; boat ramp. Disc golf. GPS: N 45-42.2 W 97-24.5

Sandy Shore State Recreation Area

1100 S Lake Dr, Watertown, SD 57201. Phone: (605) 882-5200. Located on Lake Kampeska, off US 212, 5 miles W of Watertown (I-29 exit 177). 19 sites, 15 with electric; showers. Swimming, fishing; boat ramp. GPS: N 44-53.6 W 97-14.4

Shadehill State Recreation Area

19150 Summerville Rd, Shadehill, SD 57653. Phone: (605) 374-5114. Located off SD 73, 14 miles S of Lemmon in northwestern SD on North Fork Grand River (Shadehill Reservoir). 54 sites with electric; showers; dump station. Swimming, fishing; boat ramp. Horse trails. GPS: N 45-45.3 W 102-22.4

Snake Creek State Recreation Area

35316 SD Hwy 44, Platte, SD 57369. Phone: (605) 337-2587. Located on Lake Francis Case (Missouri River) off SD 44, 14 miles W of Platte. 127 sites, 111 with electric; showers; dump station. Swimming, fishing; boat ramp. Resort. Marina. Reservations accepted. GPS: N 43-23.4 W 99-07.2

Swan Creek State Recreation Area

c/o West Whitlock SRA, 16157A W Whitlock Rd, Gettysburg, SD 57442. Phone: (605) 765-9410. Located on Lake Oahe 9 miles W of Akaska in north-central SD off US 83. 22 sites with electric; showers; dump station. Fishing; boat ramp. GPS: N 45-20.0 W 100-16.9

Union Grove State Park

30828 471st Ave, Beresford SD 57004. Phone: (605) 987-2263. Located 11 miles S of Beresford off I-29 exit 38. 19 sites with electric; showers. Equestrian area (4 sites with electric). GPS: N 42-55.3 W 96-47.1

Walkers Point State Recreation Area

6431 Walkers Point Dr, Madison, SD 57042. Phone: (605) 256-5003. Located on Lake Madison, 9 miles SE of Madison, off SD 19, and CR 44. 42 sites with electric; showers; dump station. Swimming, fishing; boat ramp; canoe/kayak rentals. GPS: N 43-54.9 W 97-03.0

West Bend State Recreation Area

22154 West Bend Rd, Harrold, SD 57536. Phone: (605) 773-2885. Located on Missouri River, off SD 34, 35 miles E and 9 miles S of Pierre. 127 sites with electric; (some on lakeshore); showers; dump station. Swimming, fishing; boat ramp. Wi-Fi. GPS: N 44-10.3 W 99-14.1

West Whitlock State Recreation Area

16157 W Whitlock Rd, Gettysburg, SD 57442. Phone: (605) 765-9410. Located on Lake Oahe off US 212, 18 miles W of Gettysburg in north-central SD. 101 sites with electric; showers; dump station. Swimming, fishing; boat ramp. GPS: N 45-04.0 W 100-16.5

TENNESSEE

Tennessee

There are 32 Tennessee state parks with RV sites. Most offer water and electric hook-ups; several with 50-amp service. Many have laundry facilities and most have dump stations. Tennessee has no central reservation system. All the parks with campgrounds operate on a first-come, first-served basis except Meeman-Shelby and Rock Island (see listings). It is wise to contact the particular park to check for space before proceeding there. All the parks are very busy during the summer months. Many are open year-round and you should check for facilities in autumn and winter months. Unless specified in the listings, there are no rig size limitations. Pets on a leash are OK. Only Tennessee residents are eligible for senior citizen discounts. Rate group: B, depending on site facilities. (Winter rates are less if park's bath house is closed.)

Tennessee State Parks
401 Church Street
L & C Tower, 7th Fl
Nashville, TN 37243

Information: (888) 867-2757
Internet: www.tnstateparks.com

Tennessee Park Locator

Tennessee Parks

Big Ridge State Park

1015 Big Ridge Rd, Maynardville, TN 37807. Phone: (865) 992-5523. Located on Norris Reservoir, about 35 miles N of Knoxville. From I-75 exit 122, follow TN 61 east about 12 miles to park. 50 sites with water, electric; showers. Swimming, fishing; boat ramp, rentals. (Electric motors only.) GPS: N 36-14.5 W 83-55.8

Bledsoe Creek State Park

400 Zieglers Ford Rd, Gallatin, TN 37066. Phone: (615) 452-3706. Located on Old Hickory Reservoir, 7 miles E of Gallatin on TN 25 (northeast Nashville, via US 31E). 57 sites with water, electric; showers; dump station. Fishing; boat ramp. GPS: N 36-22.7 W 86-21.4

Cedars of Lebanon State Park

328 Cedars Forest Rd, Lebanon, TN 37090. Phone: (615) 443-2769. Located 31 miles E of Nashville; 6 miles S of I-40 on US 231. 87 sites with water, electric; showers; dump station; store, laundry. Horse trails. Swimming. GPS: N 36-05.6 W 86-20.1

Chicksaw State Park

20 Cabin Ln, Henderson, TN 38340. Phone: (731) 989-5141. Located on Lake Placid, 8 miles W of Henderson (on US 45) on TN 100. 52 sites with water, electric; dump station. Equestrian area (rental horses available) -32 sites with electric. Golf course. Swimming, fishing; boat rentals, (no personal boats). GPS: N 35-23.6 W 88-46.3

Cove Lake State Park

110 Cove Lake Ln, Caryville, TN 37714. Phone: (423) 566-9701. Located on Cove Lake, 30 miles NW of Knoxville on US 25W at I-75 exit 134 in Caryville. 106 sites with water, electric; showers; dump station. Boat rentals (electric motors only, no private boats). Swimming, fishing. GPS: N 36-18.3 W 84-12.6

Cumberland Mountain State Park

24 Office Dr, Crossville, TN 38555. Phone: (931) 484-6138. Located on Byrd Lake on US 127 about 4.5 miles SE of Crossville. 145 sites with water, electric; showers. Golf course. Boat/canoe rentals, (no private boats). Swimming, fishing. GPS: N 35-53.9 W 84-59.7

David Crockett State Park

1400 W Gaines, Lawrenceburg, TN 38464. Phone: (931) 762-9408. Located on Shoal Creek off US 64, 1/2 mile W of Lawrenceburg. 107 sites with water, electric; showers; dump station. Boat rentals (no personal boats; electric motors only). Swimming. Crockett museum. GPS: N 35-14.6 W 87-21.3

Davy Crockett Birthplace State Park 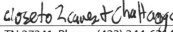 *close to 2 caves + KY*

1245 Davy Crockett Park Rd, Limestone, TN 37681. Phone: (423) 257-2167; Campground: (423) 257-4500. Located on Nolichucky River on US 11E & 321, SW of Johnson City. 88 sites with water and electric (40 with full hook-ups); showers; dump station. Swimming, fishing; boat ramp. Davy Crockett Museum in park. GPS: N 36-13.3 W 82-39.6

Edgar Evins State Park

1630 Edgar Evins State Park Rd, Silver Point, TN 38582. Phone: (931) 858-2246 or (800) 250-8619. Located on Center Hill Reservoir between Cookeville and Lebanon, 60 miles E of Nashville; I-40 exit 268 (TN 56). 60 sites with water, electric (some 50 amp); showers; dump station; laundry. 30-foot limit. Marina. Swimming, fishing; boat rentals. GPS: N 36-06.2 W 85-49.1

Fall Creek Falls State Park

2009 Village Camp Rd, Pikeville, TN 37367. Phone: (423) 881-5298 or (800) 250-8611 (reservations). Located on Fall Creek Lake 18 miles NW of Pikeville via TN 30 and TN 284. Five areas, 222 sites with water, electric (some with sewers); showers; dump station. Lake in park. Golf course. Fishing; boat rentals - electric motors only. (No personal boats.) GPS: N 35-40.6 W 85-20.3

Harrison Bay State Park *close to 2 caves + Chattooga*

8411 Harrison Bay Rd, Harrison, TN 37341. Phone: (423) 344-6214. Located on Chickamauga Lake, northeast of Chattanooga via TN 58. 128 sites with water, electric; showers; dump station. (Some sites 65-feet plus.) Marina. Golf course. Swimming, fishing; boat ramp. GPS: N 35-10.6 W 85-06.9

Henry Horton State Park

4358 Nashville Hwy, Chapel Hill, TN 37034. Phone: (931) 364-2222 or (800) 250-8612. Located on Duck River on US 31-A, 40 miles S of Nashville; or I-65 exit 46, follow signs. 56 sites with water, electric; showers; dump station. Resort. Trap and skeet range. Golf course. Disc golf. Swimming, fishing. GPS: N 35-35.7 W 86-41.9

Hiwassee & Ocoee Rivers State Park *closest to Lost Sea*

404 Spring Creek Rd, Delano, TN 37325. Phone: (423) 263-0050. Located on Ocoee River, 6 miles N of Benton on TN 30, off US 411. 47 primitive sites (also overflow area); showers. White water rafting area in park. Fishing. Horse trails nearby. GPS: N 35-14.1 W 84-31.4

Indian Mountain State Park

143 State Park Circle, Jellico, TN 37762. Phone: (423) 784-7958. Located near Jellico at KY state line; I-75 exit 160 to US 25W, follow signs. 47 sites with water, electric; showers; dump station. Two lakes in park. Swimming, fishing. Pedal boat rentals. (Electric motors only.) GPS: N 36-35.0 W 84-08.4

Meeman-Shelby Forest State Park

910 Riddick Rd, Millington, TN 38053. Phone: (901) 876-5215 or (800) 471-5293 (reservations). Located on the Mississippi River, 18 miles N of Memphis. I-40 exit on to US 51 to Millington; follow signs. 49 sites with water, electric; showers; dump station. Two lakes in park. Boat rentals (electric motors only on lakes). Swimming, fishing; boat ramp; horse trails. GPS: N 35-20.2 W 90-01.7

Montgomery Bell State Park/Resort

1020 Jackson Hill Rd, Burns, TN 37029. Phone: (615) 797-9052 or (800) 250-8613. Located on Lake Acorn on US 70, 7 miles E of Dickson; I-40 exit 182. 80 sites with water, electric (30 & 50 amp); 40 sites with sewer hookups; showers; dump station. (Some sites will accept only pop-up campers; call if in doubt.) Golf course. Boat rentals; electric motors only. Swimming, fishing. GPS: N 36-06.4 W 87-16.1

Mousetail Landing State Park

3 Campground Rd, Linden, TN 37096. Phone: (731) 847-0841. Located on Tennessee River on TN 438, near junction with US 412. 25 sites, 19 with water and electric; showers; laundry; dump station. Swimming, fishing; boat ramp. GPS: N 35-39.3 W 87-59.6

Natchez Trace State Park

24845 Natchez Trace Rd, Wildersville, TN 38388. Phone: (800) 250-8616 or (731) 968-3742. Located on Pin Oak Lake, 6 miles NE of Lexington off I-40 exit 116, between Nashville and Memphis. 208 sites (50 amp), 77 full hook-up; showers; laundry; store. Resort. Equestrian trails. Wi-Fi. Pistol range. Swimming, fishing; boat ramp, rentals. Wi-Fi. GPS: N 35-50.4 W 88-15.2

Nathan Bedford Forrest State Park

1825 Pilot Knob Rd, Eva, TN 38333. Phone: (731) 584-6356. Located on Kentucky Lake near Eva on local roads. I-40 exit 126 (US 641) N to Camden (US 70); follow signs. 37 sites with water, electric (50 amp), also one primitive area; showers; dump station. Fishing; boat ramp. GPS: N 36-05.3 W 87-58.8

Norris Dam State Park

125 Village Green Circle, Lake City, TN 37769. Phone: (865) 426-7461. Located on Norris Reservoir on US 441, 2.5 miles S of I-75 exit 128. 75 sites in two areas with water and electric; showers; laundry; dump station. Horse trails. Marina. Swimming, fishing; boat ramp, rentals. GPS: N 36-14.1 W 84-07.6

Old Stone Fort State Park

732 Stone Fort Dr, Manchester, TN 37855. Phone: (931) 723-5073. Located off US 41 in Manchester; use I-24 exit 111, follow signs. 51 sites with water, electric; showers; dump station (summer only). Fishing; boat ramp GPS: N 35-29.4 W 86-06.0

Panther Creek State Park

2010 Panther Creek Park Rd, Morristown, TN 37814. Phone: (423) 587-7046. Located on Cherokee Reservoir, 6 miles W of Morristown, off US 11E. 50 sites with water, electric; dump station. Swimming, fishing; boat ramp. Horse trails nearby. GPS: N 36-12.8 W 83-24.7

Paris Landing State Park

16055 Hwy 79N, Buchanan, TN 38222. Phone: (731) 641-4465 or (800) 250-8614. Located on the Tennessee River, 18 miles NE of Paris, on US 79. 45 sites with water, electric; showers; dump station. 38-foot limit. Laundry. Resort. Golf course. Marina. Swimming, fishing; boat ramp. GPS: N 36-26.1 W 88-04.8

Pickett State Park

4605 Pickett Park Hwy, Jamestown, TN 38556. Phone: (931) 879-5821. Located on TN 154, NE of Jamestown (US 127), in Upper Cumberland Mountains. 32 sites with water and electric; showers; dump station. Lake in park. Equestrian area. Swimming, fishing; boat/canoe rentals (no personal boats). GPS: N 36-32.3 W 84-48.1

Pickwick Landing State Park/Resort

Park Rd, Pickwick Dam, TN 38365. Phone: (731) 689-3129 or (800) 250-8615. Located on the Tennessee River on TN 57, S of Savannah (US 64); follow TN 128 to TN 57. 48 sites with water, electric (some 50 amp, 31 sites 20 amp); showers; dump station. Marina. Golf course. Swimming, fishing; boat ramp. GPS: N 35-03.0 W 88-14.4

Reelfoot Lake State Park

2595 SR 21E, Tiptonville, TN 38079. Phone: (731) 253-9652 or (800) 250-8617. Located in northwestern TN on Reelfoot Lake, on TN 21 & 22. From US 51 follow TN 22 from Union City to park; or TN 183 from Obion to park. 86 sites with water, electric; showers; laundry; dump station. Swimming, fishing; boat ramp. GPS: N 36-24.9 W 89-25.6

Roan Mountain State Park

1015 Hwy 143, Roan Mountain, TN 37681. Phone: (423) 772-0190 or (800) 250-8620. Located in NE Tennessee about 25 miles SE of Johnson City on TN 143, near NC state line. 87 sites with water, electric; showers; dump station. Swimming, fishing (exceptional trout fishing). GPS: N 36-10.3 W 82-05.4

Rock Island State Park

82 Beach Rd, Rock Island, TN 38581. Phone: (931) 686-2471. Located at confluence of Collins and Caney Fork rivers on TN 287 between McMinnville and Crossville; off US 70S at Campaign. 60 sites with water, electric; showers; laundry; dump station. Two lakes in park. Swimming, fishing; boat ramp. Reservations accepted. GPS: N 35-48.6 W 85-38.5

Standing Stone State Park

1647 Standing Stone Park Hwy, Hilham, TN 38568. Phone: (931) 823-6347 or (800) 713-5157. Located on TN 52, 9 miles NW of Livingston (TN 111 & 52). 36 sites with water, electric; showers; dump station. Seasonal. Standing Stone Lake in park; boat rentals (no personal boats, electric motors only). Swimming, fishing. 45-foot limit. GPS: N 36-27.5 W 85-26.2

T.O. Fuller State Park

1500 Mitchell Rd, Memphis, TN 38109. Phone: (901) 543-7581. Located in West Memphis; I-55 exit 9 (Mitchell Rd); follow signs. 45 sites with water, electric; showers; dump station. Golf course. Swimming. GPS: N 35-04.5 W 90-06.8

Tims Ford State Park

570 Tims Ford Dr, Winchester, TN 37398. Phone: (931) 962-1183. Located on Tims Ford Reservoir on TN 82, NW of Winchester. Two campgrounds: Tims Ford has 52 sites with water and electric (30 amp); showers; dump station; laundry. 40-foot limit. Fairview has 88 sites (30 full hook-up, 38 with water and electric (30 amp), and 20 with water only); showers. Fairview Campground is undergoing renovation from fall 2014 through spring 2015; dump station. Golf course (Nicklaus designed). Marina. Swimming, fishing; boat rentals. GPS: N 35-13.3 W 86-15.4

Warrior's Path State Park

490 Hemlock Rd, Kingsport, TN 37663. Phone: (423) 239-8531. Located on Patrick Henry Reservoir, off TN 36; I-81 exit 59. 134 sites, 94 with water and electric; showers; dump station. Marina. Golf course. Disc golf. Equestrian area (rentals available). Swimming, fishing; boat ramp. GPS: N 36-20.2 W 82-28.9

TEXAS

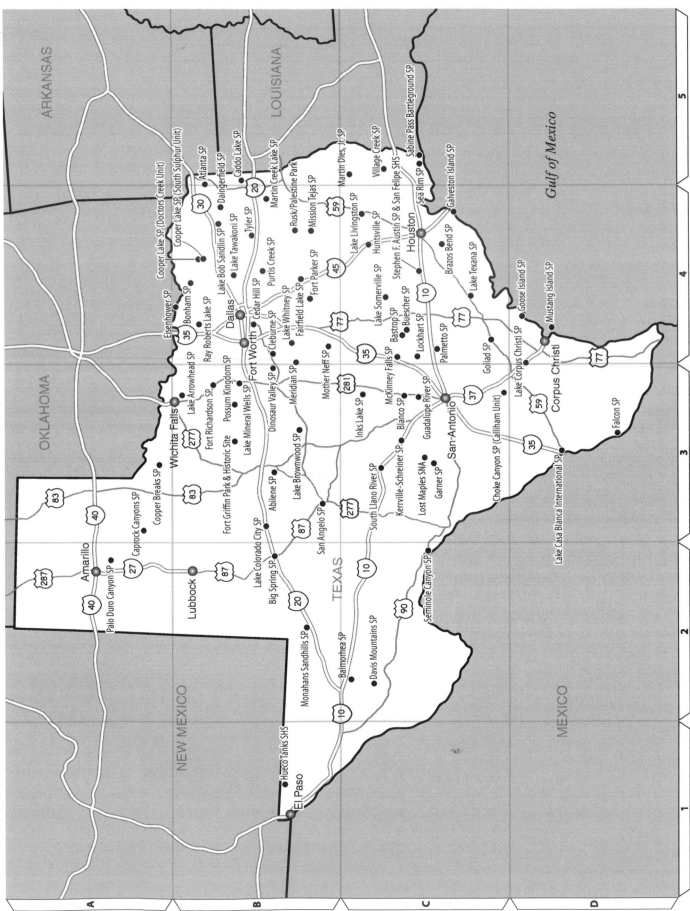

Texas

Texas offers the RVer 71 locations with facilities, ranging from primitive to full hook-up. Many parks are on lakes and near major highways. Some offer "specials," which usually require multiple nights stay. While only Texas residents qualify for fee discounts, all the parks accept major credit cards. Many parks have overflow parking areas that offer traveling RVers a dry camp site for one night at a reduced price. It is necessary when calling a particular park to inquire about these areas and if they are available. Several parks with overflow areas also have water nearby. Most parks have reservable sites. Reservations require 48 hours advance request; for same day reservations, call the park directly. Rate groups: A, B, and C depending upon site utilities and park location. Winter rates are less. Entrance fees (in some parks) are $2 to $5 extra.

Note: Most of the parks are reachable via a road designated as "FM" followed by a number. This abbreviation means Farm to Market Road. Some of these roads are paved, some are gravel. All are marked with the appropriate number.

Texas Parks & Wildlife Dept.
4200 Smith School Road
Austin, TX 78744

Information: (800) 792-1112
Reservations: (512) 389-8900
Internet: www.tpwd.state.tx.us/state-parks/

Texas Park Locator

Texas Parks

Abilene State Park

150 Park Rd 32, Tuscola, TX 79562. Phone: (325) 572-3204. Located SW of Abilene on Park Rd 32, off US 83, near junction with US 84. 76 sites with water and electric, 3 full hook-up; showers; dump station. Swimming, fishing. GPS: N 32-14.6 W 99-52.8

Atlanta State Park

927 Park Rd 42, Atlanta, TX 75551. Phone: (903) 796-6476. Located on Lake Wright Patman Dam, 11 miles NW of Atlanta, near Arkansas state line, off US 59. 58 sites, 14 full hook-up, 44 with water and electric; showers; dump station. Swimming, fishing; boat ramp; rentals. GPS: N 33-13.8 W 94-15.0

Balmorhea State Park

Toyahvale, TX 79786. Phone: (432) 375-2370. Located 4 milies SW of Balmorhea on TX 17. I-10 westbound use exit 206; I-10 eastbound, exit 192. Follow signs to Ranch Rd 3078. 34 sites, 28 with water and electric (some with TV cable), 6 water only; showers; dump station. Swimming. GPS: N 30-56.8 W 103-47.1

Bastrop State Park

100 Park Rd 1A, Bastrop, TX 78602. Phone: (512) 321-2101. Located 30 miles SE of Austin, 1 mile E of Bastrop on Lake Bastrop, near junction of TX 71 & 21. 70 sites, 35 full hook-up (some pull-through), 19 with water and electric, 16 water only; showers; dump station. Golf course. Boating; canoe rentals. Swimming pool. Wi-Fi. GPS: N 30-06.6 W 97-17.4

Big Spring State Park

1 Scenic Dr, Big Spring, TX 79720. Phone: (432) 263-4931. Located in Big Spring (junction of I-20 & US 87). 2 sites with water and electric. GPS: N 32-13.8 W 101-28.9

Blanco State Park

101 Park Rd 23, Blanco, TX 78606. Phone: (830) 833-4333. Located on S side of Blanco on the Blanco River, 40 miles N of San Antonio on US 281 (SW of Austin - US 290 to 281). 29 sites, 17 full hook-up, 12 with water and electric; showers; dump station. Swimming, fishing. (Electric motors only.) GPS: N 30-05.6 W 98-25.4

Bonham State Park

1363 State Park Rd 24, Bonham, TX 75418. Phone: (903) 583-5022. Located NE of Dallas and 1.5 miles SE of Bonham. Use TX 78 to FM 271, follow signs. 14 sites with water and electric; also dry sites; showers; dump station. Lake in park. Swimming, fishing; boat ramp (5 mph limit). GPS: N 33-32.6 W 96-09.0

Brazos Bend State Park

21901 FM 762, Needville, TX 77461. Phone: (979) 553-5102. Located on Brazos River, SW of Houston off FM 1462, from TX 288 at Rosharon. 88 sites, 73 with water and electric, 15 primitive; dump station. 19 primitive equestrian sites. Fishing. GPS: N 29-22.4 W 95-38.4

Buescher State Park

100 Park Rd 1E, Smithville, TX 78957. Phone: (512) 237-2241. Located 2 miles NW of Smithville and about 20 miles E of Austin via TX 71 to FM 153, follow signs. 57 sites, 32 with water and electric, 25 water only; showers; dump station. Swimming, fishing. GPS: N 30-04.4 W 97-10.6

Caddo Lake State Park

245 Park Rd 2, Karnack, TX 75661. Phone: (903) 679-3351. Located on Caddo Lake, 15 miles NE of Marshall off TX 43 and FM 2198. 46 sites, 8 full hook-up, 18 with water and electric (some 50 amp), 20 water only; showers; dump station. Lake (boat) tours. Swimming, fishing; boat ramp, canoe rentals. GPS: N 32-40.8 W 94-10.5

Caprock Canyons State Park

Quitaque, TX 79255. Phone: (806) 455-1492. Located 100 miles SE of Amarillo on FM 1065, 3.5 miles N of Quitaque, off TX 86. 56 sites with water and electric; several dry camp sites; showers; dump station. 12 equestrian sites. Swimming, fishing; boat ramp, rentals. GPS: N 34-24.4 W 101-02.9

Cedar Hill State Park

1570 W FM 1382, Cedar Hill, TX 75104. Phone: (972) 291-3900. Located on Joe Pool Reservoir, 10 miles SW of Dallas between I-20 and US 67. 355 sites with water and electric, 30 primitive; showers; dump station. Wi-Fi. Marina. Swimming, fishing; boat ramp. GPS: N 32-37.3 W 96-58.8

Choke Canyon State Park (Calliham Unit)

Calliham, TX 78007. Phone: (361) 786-3868. Located on Choke Canyon Reservoir, 12 miles W of Three Rivers on TX 72. 40 sites with water and electric (50 amp); showers; dump station. Equestrian area. Fishing; boat ramp. Operated by Texas Historical Commission. GPS: N 28-27.7 W 98-21.4

Cleburne State Park

5800 Park Rd 21, Cleburne, TX 76033. Phone: (817) 645-4215. Located about 40 miles SW of Fort Worth and 10 miles SW of Cleburne off US 67 on Park Rd. 58 sites, 27 full hook-up, 31 water and electric; showers; dump station. Swimming, fishing; boat ramp (no wake). GPS: N 32-15.8 W 97-33.6

Cooper Lake State Park (Doctors Creek Unit)

1664 FM 1529 S, Cooper, TX 75432. Phone: (903) 395-3100. Located on NE side of Cooper Lake near Cooper about 18 miles N of I-30 exit 122 on TX 19 to FM 1529; follow signs. 42 sites with water and electric; showers; dump station. Swimming, fishing; boat ramp. No reservations. GPS: N 33-20.9 W 95-42.8

Cooper Lake State Park (South Sulphur Unit)

1690 FM 3505, Sulphur Springs, TX 75482. Phone: (903) 945-5256. Located on south side of Cooper Lake, about 13 miles N of 1-30 exit 122 via TX 19 to TX 71 to FM 3505. 87 sites with water and electric (some pull-thru), some dry-camp sites; showers; dump station. 15 site equestrian area. Swimming, fishing; boat ramp. GPS: N 33-19.5 W 95-45.0

Copper Breaks State Park

777 Park Rd 62, Quanah, TX 79252. Phone: (940) 839-4331. Located 12 miles S of Quanah, off TX 6 between US 70 & 287. 31 sites, 24 with water and electric, 8 water only; showers; dump station. Equestrian area (10 sites). Swimming, fishing; boat ramp. GPS: N 34-06.7 W 99-44.5

Daingerfield State Park

455 Park Rd 17, Daingerfield, TX 75638. Phone: (903) 645-2921. Located on TX 49 east of Daingerfield. Accessible via I-30 to Mt. Pleasant, S on TX 49. 58 sites, 40 full hook-up, (10 pull-through), 18 water only; showers; dump station. Lake in park. Swimming, fishing; boat ramp, rentals (5 mph limit). GPS: N 33-00.7 W 94-41.5

Davis Mountains State Park

Fort Davis, TX 79734. Phone: (432) 426-3337. Located 4 miles NW of Fort Davis. Follow TX 17 from Fort Davis N to TX 118, W to park entrance. 94 sites, 33 water only, 34 with water and electric, 27 full hook-up; showers; dump station. Equestrian area (6 sites). GPS: N 30-36.0 W 103-55.8

Dinosaur Valley State Park

Glen Rose, TX 76043. Phone: (254) 897-4588. Located on FM 205, 4 miles NW of Glen Rose, off US 67. 46 sites with water and electric; showers; dump station. Horse trails. (Dinosaur tracks in river.) Swimming, fishing. GPS: N 32-15.0 W 97-48.9

Eisenhower State Park

50 Park Rd 20, Denison, TX 75020. Phone: (903) 465-1956. Located off FM 1310 on Lake Texoma, NW of Denison (US 75, exit 72 to TX 91 to FM 1310). 142 sites, 50 full hook-up, 45 with water and electric, 47 water nearby; showers; dump station. Marina. Swimming, fishing; boat ramp, rentals. GPS: N 33-48.6 W 96-36.0

Fairfield Lake State Park

123 State Park Rd 64, Fairfield, TX 75840. Phone: (903) 389-4514. Located on Fairfield Lake, 6 miles NE of Fairfield (I-45 exit 197) on FM 3285; follow signs. 131 sites, 96 with water and electric, 35 water only; showers; dump station. Horse trails. Swimming, fishing, boat ramp. GPS: N 31-45.9 W 96-05.0

Falcon State Park

Falcon Heights, TX 78545. Phone: (956) 848-5327. Located between Zapata and Roma on Falcon Reservoir (about 90 miles SE of Laredo) on FM 2098, off US 83. 98 sites, 31 full hook-up, 31 with water and electric, (all 50 amp & pull-through), 36 primitive; showers; dump station. Swimming, fishing; boat ramp. GPS: N 26-35.0 W 99-08.6

Fort Griffin Park & Historic Site

1701 N US 283, Albany, TX 76430. Phone: (325) 762-3592. Located 15 miles N of Albany (NE of Abilene) on US 283/183. 15 sites with water and electric, 2 full hook-up, 25 dry sites; showers; dump station. 35 equestrian sites. (Operated by Texas Historical Commission.) GPS: N 32-55.5 W 99-13.2

Fort Parker State Park

194 Park Rd 28, Mexia, TX 76667. Phone: (254) 562-5751. Located 7 miles S of Mexia on TX 14. 35 sites, 25 with water and electric, 10 water nearby; showers; dump station. Swimming, fishing; boat ramp, rentals. GPS: N 31-35.6 W 96-31.5

Fort Richardson State Park

228 State Park Rd 61, Jacksboro, TX 76458. Phone: (940) 567-3506. Located NW of Fort Worth on Lost Creek Reservoir off US 281/380, about 2.5 miles S of Jacksboro. Historical site. 41 sites, 37 with water and electric, 4 full hook-up; showers; dump station. Horse trails. Swimming, fishing. GPS: N 33-12.3 W 98-09.6

Galveston Island State Park

14901 FM 3005, Galveston, TX 77554. Phone: (409) 737-1222. Located in Galveston near I-45 exit 1A on Seawall Blvd on Gulf of Mexico. 56 sites with water and electric (some 50 amp, some beach side); showers; dump station. Swimming, fishing, boat ramp. GPS: N 29-11.8 W 94-57.4

Garner State Park

234 RR 1050, Concan, TX 78838. Phone: (830) 232-6132. Located on the Frio River, 31 miles N of Uvalde, on US 83. 286 sites, 172 with water and electric, 124 water only; showers; dump station. Miniature golf. Swimming, fishing; boat rentals. GPS: N 29-35.2 W 99-44.8

Goliad State Park

108 Park Rd 6, Goliad, TX 77963. Phone: (361) 645-3405. Located 1/4 mile S of Goliad on US 183 & 77A on San Antonio River. 58 sites, 24 with water and electric, 14 water only, 20 full hook-up; overflow area; showers; dump station. Swimming, fishing. GPS: N 28-39.4 W 97-23.0

Goose Island State Park

202 S Palmetto St, Rockport, TX 78382. Phone: (361) 729-2858. Located next to the IC Waterway on St. Charles & Aransas bays, 10 miles NE of Rockport, off TX 35. Accessable by bridges. 102 sites with water and electric; some dry-camp sites (overflow); showers; dump station. Fishing, boat ramp. GPS: N 28-08.0 W 96-59.1

Guadalupe River State Park

3350 Park Rd 31, Spring Branch, TX 78070. Phone: (830) 438-2656. Located on the Guadalupe River, 30 miles N of San Antonio on US 281. 89 sites, 4 full hook-up, 48 with water and electric, 37 water only; showers; dump station. Horse trails. Swimming, fishing. GPS: N 29-50.5 W 98-30.9

Hueco Tanks State Historic Site

6900 Hueco Tanks Rd 1, El Paso, TX 79938. Phone: (915) 857-1135. Located 32 miles E of El Paso; US 62/180 east to Ranch Rd 2775. 20 sites, 3 water only, 17 with water and electric; showers; dump station. Wi-Fi. GPS: N 31-55.6 W 106-02.7

Huntsville State Park

Huntsville, TX 77342. Phone: (936) 285-5644. Located 6 miles SW of Huntsville, off I-45 exit 103. 175 sites, 77 with water and electric, 60 water only, 23 full hook-up, 30 with water, electric and screened shelters; showers; dump station. Horse rentals. Swimming, fishing; boat ramp (low speed limits). GPS: N 30-38.2 W 95-30.8

Inks Lake State Park

3630 Park Rd 4 W, Burnet, TX 78611. Phone: (512) 793-2223. Located on Inks Lake (Colorado River), 9 miles W of Burnet off TX 29. 172 sites, 123 with water and electric, 49 water only; showers; dump station. Wi-Fi. Golf course. Swimming, fishing; boat ramp, rentals. GPS: N 30-44.3 W 98-22.0

Kerrville-Schreiner State Park

2385 Bandera Hwy, Kerrville, TX 78028. Phone: (830) 257-5392 or (830) 257-CAMP. Located 3 miles SW of Kerrville on TX 173. 147 sites, 42 full hook-up, 42 with water and electric, 58 water only, 7 primitive; showers; dump station. Swimming, fishing; boat ramp. Park operated by City of Kerrville. GPS: N 30-00.5 W 99-07.1

Lake Arrowhead State Park

229 Park Rd 63, Wichita Falls, TX 76310. Phone: (940) 528-2211. Located on Lake Arrowhead off FM 1954, 14 miles SE of Wichita Falls. Access FM 1954 from US 281 or US 287. 67 sites, 48 with water and electric, 19 dry-camp sites (water nearby); showers; dump

station. 4 equestrian sites. Disc golf course. Swimming, fishing; boat ramp. GPS: N 33-45.5 W 98-23.7

Lake Bob Sandlin State Park

341 State Park Rd, Pittsburg, TX 75686. Phone: (903) 572-5531. Located on Lake Bob Sandlin, 12 miles SE of Mount Pleasant and I-30 exit 146 via TX 37 and FM 21. 75 sites with water and electric; showers; dump station. Swimming, fishing; boat ramp. GPS: N 33-03.4 W 95-06.3

Lake Brownwood State Park

200 State Hwy Park Rd 15, Brownwood, TX 76801. Phone: (325) 784-5223. Located on Lake Brownwood, 16 miles N of Brownwood (US 67 & 377) off TX 279. 78 sites, 46 with water and electric (some 50 amp), 20 full hook-up; showers; dump station. Swimming, fishing; boat ramp. GPS: N 31-51.4 W 99-01.3

Lake Casa Blanca International State Park

5102 Bob Bullock Loop, Laredo, TX 78044. Phone: (956) 725-3826. Located on Lake Casa Blanca, 3 miles E of Laredo on US 59. 66 sites, 56 with water and electric, 10 full hook-up; showers; dump station. Swimming, fishing; boat ramp. GPS: N 27-32.5 W 99-26.0

Lake Colorado City State Park

4582 FM 2836, Colorado City, TX 79512. Phone: (325) 728-3931. Located on the Colorado River on FM 2836, off I-20 exit 213, 11 miles SW of Colorado City. 112 sites, 69 with water and electric, 34 water only, (9 pull-through sites); showers; dump station. Swimming, fishing; boat ramp, (canoes/kayaks only). GPS: N 32-18.8 W 100-55.5

Lake Corpus Christi State Park

Mathis, TX 78368. Phone: (361) 547-2635. Located on Lake Corpus Christi, 35 miles NW of Corpus Christi, 4 miles SW of Mathis off TX 359; I-37 exit 34. 108 sites, 23 with water and electric, 25 full hook-up; showers; dump station. Swimming, fishing, boat ramp. GPS: N 28-03.6 W 97-52.1

Lake Livingston State Park

300 State Park Rd 65, Livingston, TX. Phone: (936) 365-2201. Located on Lake Livingston, 1 mile S of Livingston on US 59. 153 sites, 78 full hook-up, 59 with water and electric, 16 water only; showers; dump station. Swimming (pool and lake), fishing; boat ramp. Horse rentals (personal horses not allowed). GPS: N 30-39.7 W 95-00.3

Lake Mineral Wells State Park

100 Park Rd 71, Mineral Wells, TX 76067. Phone: (940) 328-1171. Located on Lake Mineral Wells, 4 miles E of Mineral Wells on US 180. 88 sites, 77 with water and electric, (some 50-amp), 11 water only; showers; dump station. 20 equestrian sites. Swimming, fishing; boat ramp, (low speed limits in lake). GPS: N 32-48.8 W 98-02.6

Lake Somerville State Park (Birch Creek Unit)

14222 Park Rd 57, Somerville, TX 77879. Phone: (979) 535-7763. Located on Lake Somerville, NW of Brenham, via TX 36 & 60 to PR 57. 88 sites, 77 with water and electric, 11 water only; showers; dump station. 20 equestrian sites. Swimming, fishing; boat ramp. Horse trails. (Birch Creek connected to Nails Creek Unit via tramway.) GPS: N 30-18.8 W 96-37.7

Lake Tawakoni State Park

10822 FM 2475, Wills Point, TX 75169. Phone: (903) 560-7123. Located on Lake Tawakoni (Reservoir), 50 miles E of Dallas via TX 47 off I-20 exit 516, north through Wills Point. 78 sites: 62 with water and electric, 16 full hook-up; showers; dump station. Swimming, fishing; boat ramp. GPS: N 32-50.5 W 96-00.6

Lake Texana State Park

46 Park Rd 1, Edna, TX 77957. Phone: (361) 782-5718. Located 6.5 miles E of Edna (US 59) on TX 111. 141 sites, 86 with water and electric, 55 with water; showers; dump station. Swimming, fishing; boat ramp. (For reservations call park office.) GPS: N 28-57.2 W 96-34.0

Lake Whitney State Park

Whitney, TX 76692. Phone: (254) 694-3793. Located on Lake Whitney, 3 miles W of Whitney on FM 1244, via TX 22, off I-35 exit 368A. 137 sites; 31 with water and electric, 63 water only, 43 full hook-up, some pull-through sites; showers; dump station. Swimming, fishing; boat ramp. Landing strip. GPS: N 31-55.8 W 97-21.7

Lockhart State Park

4179 State Park Rd, Lockhart, TX 78644. Phone: (512) 398-3479. Located S of Lockhart, off FM 20, via US 183. 20 sites: 10 full hook-up, 10 with water and electric; showers; dump station. Golf course; swimming pool. Fishing. GPS: N 29-51.5 W 97-41.9

Lost Maples State Natural Area

37221 FM 187, Vanderpool, TX 78885. Phone: (830) 966-3413. Located on the Sabinal River, 5 miles N of Vanderpool and about 70 miles NW of San Antonio on FM 187 (off US 83). 30 sites with water and electric; showers; dump station. Swimming, fishing. GPS: N 29-48.4 W 99-34.2

Martin Creek Lake State Park

9515 CR 2181 D, Tatum, TX 75691. Phone: (903) 836-4336. Located on Martin Creek Lake, 20 miles SE of Longview; I-20 exit 589 to US 259 to TX 43. 58 sites with water and electric (some 50 amp); showers; dump station. Swimming, fishing; boat ramp, rentals. GPS: N 32-17.3 W 94-34.6

Martin Dies, Jr. State Park

634 Park Rd 48 S, Jasper, TX 75951. Phone: (409) 384-5231. Located on Steinhagen Reservoir on US 190 between Jasper and Livingston. 176 sites: 122 with water and electric, 33 with water; showers; dump station. Swimming, fishing; boat ramp, rentals. GPS: N 30-51.2 W 94-10.0

McKinney Falls State Park

5808 McKinney Falls Pkwy, Austin, TX 78744. Phone: (512) 243-1643. Located 13 miles S of Austin, between US 183 and I-35 exit 228. 81 sites with water and electric; showers; dump station. Wi-Fi. Swimming. GPS: N 30-10.8 W 97-43.3

Meridian State Park

173 Park Rd 7, Meridian, TX 76665. Phone: (254) 435-2536. Located on Meridian Lane, 3 miles SW of Meridian off TX 22. 31 sites, 7 with water and electric, 8 full hook-up, 8 water only; showers; dump station. Swimming, fishing; boat ramp, (no wake). GPS: N 31-53.6 W 97-41.8

Mission Tejas State Park

120 State Park Rd 44, Grapeland, TX 75844. Phone: (936) 687-2394.

Located 22 miles NE of Crockett on TX 21. 17 sites: 5 full hook-up, 10 with water and electric, 2 water only; showers; dump station. Fishing. GPS: N 31-32.5 W 95-13.9

Monahans Sandhills State Park

Monahans, TX 79756. Phone: (432) 943-2092. Located 31 miles W of Odessa, I-20 exit 86, follow signs to Park Rd 41. 26 sites with water and electric; dump station. Horse trails. GPS: N 31-38.1 W 102-48.9

Mother Neff State Park

1680 TX 236, Moody, TX 76557. Phone: (254) 853-2389. Located on Leon River, 16 miles W of I-35 exit 315, W of Moody, off FM 107. 21 sites, 6 with water and electric, 15 with water in area; showers; dump station. Fishing. GPS: N 31-19.0 W 97-28.3

Mustang Island State Park

17047 State Hwy 361, Port Aransas, TX 78373. Phone: (361) 749-5246. Located on the Gulf of Mexico SE of Corpus Christi; access via JFK Causeway to TX 361. 48 sites with water and electric (50 amp), 300 primitive sites (on Gulf, subject to high tides); showers; dump station. Swimming, fishing. GPS: N 27-40.6 W 97-10.4

Palmetto State Park

78 Park Rd 11S, Gonzales, TX 78629. Phone: (830) 672-3266. Located on San Marcos River, off FM 1586 via US 183. 37 sites, 17 with water and electric, 19 with water, one full hook-up; showers; dump station. Overflow area. Swimming, fishing; boat ramp, rentals. GPS: N 29-36.1 W 97-35.8

Palo Duro Canyon State Park

11450 Park Rd 5, Canyon, TX 79015. Phone: (806) 488-2227. Located in northern Panhandle, 12 miles E of Canyon (I-27 exit 106) on TX 217. 79 sites with water and electric (some 50 amp); showers; dump station. 10 equestrian sites. GPS: N 34-59.1 W 101-42.1

Possum Kingdom State Park

Caddo, TX 76429. Phone: (940) 549-1803. Located on Possum Kingdom Lake NW of Mineral Wells off US 180 at Caddo to FM 33, follow signs. 116 sites, 61 with water and electric, 55 water only; over-flow sites available; showers; dump station. Swimming, fishing; boat ramp. GPS: N 32-52.7 W 98-33.7

Purtis Creek State Park

14225 FM 316, Eustace, TX 75124. Phone: (903) 425-2332. Located on Purtis Creek, 3.5 miles N of Eustace via US 175. 59 sites with water and electric; showers; dump station. Overflow area. Swimming, fishing; boat/canoe/kayak rentals. GPS: N 32-21.1 W 95-59.8

Ray Roberts Lake State Park (Two Units)

a. Isle du Bois Unit, 100 PW 4137, Pilot Point, TX 76258. Phone: (940) 686-2148. Located on Ray Roberts Lake off FM 455, 10 miles E of I-35, off US 377. 115 sites with water and electric; showers; dump station. 14 equestrian sties. Swimming, fishing; boating. Wi-Fi. GPS: N 33-26.7 W 96-55.6

b. Johnson Branch Unit, 100 PW 4153, Valley View, TX 76272. Phone: (940) 637-2294. Located on Ray Roberts Lake, off FM 3002, 7 miles E of I-35, exit 487. 104 sites with water and electric; showers; dump station. Horse trails. Marina. GPS: N 33-22.8 W 97-06.4

Rusk/Palestine Park (2 areas)

Rusk, TX 75785. Phone: (903) 683-5126. Rusk area is located 3 miles W of Rusk, TX, off US 84; Palestine area is located 3 miles E of Palestine, TX, on US 84. Both adjacent to Texas State Railroad. (Parks are located several miles apart.) 71 sites: 32 full hook-up, 22 electric and water; showers; dump station. Call for site availability. Operated by American Heritage Railway. GPS: N 31-48.1 W 95-11.5

Sabine Pass Battleground State Park

FR 3322, Sabine Pass, TX 77655. Phone: (409) 971-2559. Located on the Gulf of Mexico, 15 miles S of Port Arthur near Sabine Pass on TX 87. 17 sites with water and electric, 10 primitive sites; dump station. Operated by Texas Historical Commission. GPS: N 29-43.6 W 93-52.7

San Angelo State Park

3900-2 Mercedes Rd, San Angelo, TX 76901. Phone: (325) 949-4757. Located on O.C. Fisher Reservoir, just W of San Angelo on FM 2288, off US 67 or US 87 (two entrances). 134 sites, 71 with water and electric; showers; dump station. 10 equestrian sites. Swimming, fishing. (Drought has adversely affected Fisher Lake). GPS: N 31-27.2 W 100-29.5

Sea Rim State Park

19335 S Gulfway Dr, Sabine Pass, TX 77655. Phone: (409) 971-2559. Located on TX 87, on Gulf of Mexico, 20 miles S of Port Arthur. 20 sites with water and electric, 10 water only; primitive sites on the beach; showers; dump station. Swimming, fishing; boat ramp, rentals. GPS: N 29-41.7 W 93-57.7

Seminole Canyon State Park

Comstock, TX 78837. Phone: (432) 292-4464. Located 9 miles W of Comstock (about 30 miles NW of Del Rio) on US 90. 46 sites, 8 water only, 23 water and electric, 15 primitive; showers; dump station. Wi-Fi. GPS: N 29-43.6 W 101-14.6

South Llano River State Park

1927 Park Rd 73, Junction, TX 76849. Phone: (325) 446-3994. Located on South Llano River, 7 miles SW of Junction (I-10 exit 456) on US 377. 58 sites with water and electric; showers; dump station. Swimming, fishing. GPS: N 30-26.7 W 99-48.2

Stephen F. Austin SP & San Felipe State Historic Site

Park Road 38, San Felipe, TX 77473. Phone: (979) 885-3613. Located on Brazos River, W of Houston, I-10 exits 718 or 723, off TX 36 to FM 1458. 80 sites: 40 full hook-up, 40 water only; showers; dump station. Golf course adjacent. Fishing. GPS: N 29 47.6 W 96 08.8

Tyler State Park

789 Park Rd 16, Tyler, TX 75706. Phone: (903) 597-5338. Located N of Tyler on FM 14, off I-20 exit 562. 114 sites: 57 full hook-up, 20 with water and electric, 37 water only; showers; dump station. Lake in park. Swimming, fishing; boat rentals (5 mph limit). GPS: N 32-28.9 W 95-16.9

Village Creek State Park

Lumberton, TX 77657. Phone: (409) 755-7322. Located on Village Creek, 10 miles N of Beaumont off US 69/96. 25 sites with water and electric; showers; dump station. No big rigs. Swimming, fishing; boat rentals. GPS: N 30-17.9 W 94-10.1

UTAH

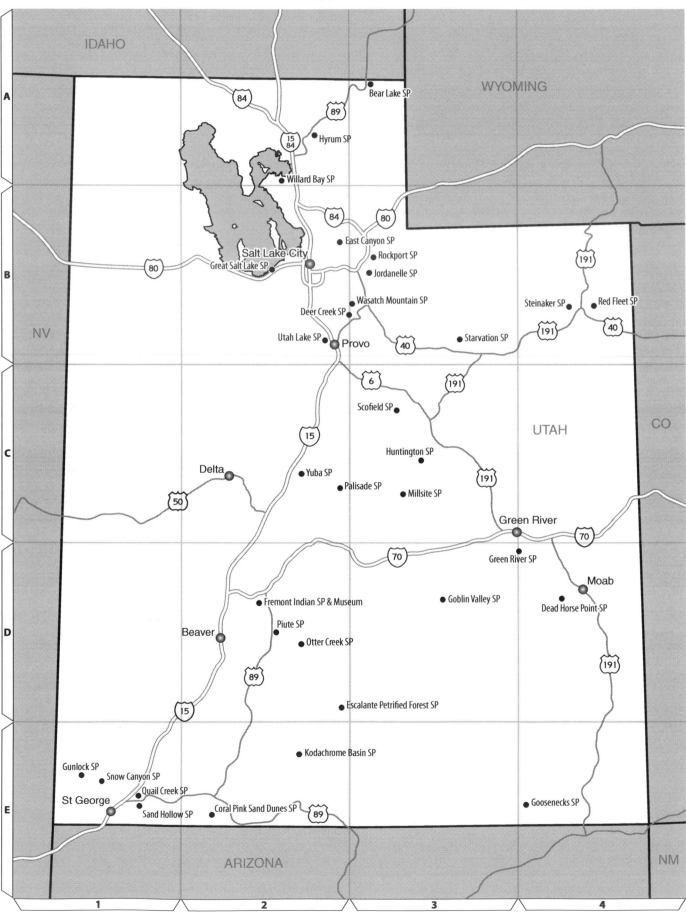

Utah

The Beehive State has 33 state parks with RV sites or facilities. While all the parks offer drinking water, two locations, Dead Horse Point and Goblin Valley, have limited water supplies. RVers should fill their water tanks ahead of time, just to be sure. All the parks charge a day-use fee in addition to the camping fee. Most of the parks are open year-round, however many close the shower facilities in winter. If traveling to any park in winter months, you should call ahead to verify road conditions and status. Most parks, especially those on lakes or reservoirs, are very busy from May through September and require reservations. Senior discounts for Utah residents are available — ask! Summer travelers should call ahead to verify site availability. Rate groups: A and B, depending on site facilities.

Utah State Parks
1594 W North Temple
Salt Lake City, UT 84114

Information: (801) 538-7220
Reservations: (800) 322-3770
Internet: www.stateparks.utah.gov

Utah Park Locator

Utah Parks

Antelope Island State Park
4528 W1700 S, Syracuse, UT 84075. Phone: (801) 773-2941. Located in the Great Salt Lake (via Causeway) W of Ogden off I-15, on Antelope Island. 26 sites; 65-foot limit; showers; dump station. Swimming, boat ramp. Horse trails. Marina. GPS: N 41-05.4 W 112-07.0

Bear Lake State Park
940 N Bear Lake Blvd, Garden City, UT 84028. Phone: (435) 946-3343. Two locations on Bear Lake located at UT/ID state line. Some areas seasonal. Bear Lake Marina is located on US 89, 2 miles N of Garden City and Bear Lake Rendezvous Beach, on the south shore, near Laketown on UT 30. 130 sites, 101 full hook-up, 29 water and electric; showers; dump stations. Marina, swimming, fishing; boat ramp. GPS: N 41-57.9 W 111-24.0

Coral Pink Sand Dunes State Park
Kanab, UT 84741. Phone: (435) 648-2800. Located in southern UT, northwest of Kanab off US 89, follow signs. 22 sites; 45-foot limit; showers; dump station. Water available. Off-road vehicle trails. GPS: N 37-03.9 W 112-42.3

Dead Horse Point State Park
Moab, UT 84532. Phone: (435) 259-2614. Located W of Moab on UT 313, 18 miles off US 191. 21 sites with electric, (20 amp); showers; dump station. Limited water. 46-foot limit. GPS: N 38-28.2 W 109-44.2

Deer Creek State Park
Midway, UT 84049. Phone: (435) 654-0171. Located on Deer Creek on US 189 between Heber City and Provo, on Deer Creek Reservoir. 65 sites, 35 full hook-up; showers; dump station. Swimming, fishing, boat ramp. Marina. Seasonal. 70-foot limit. GPS: N 40-27.2 W 111-28.7

East Canyon State Park
5535 S Hwy 66, Morgan, UT 84050. Phone: (801) 829-6866. Located NE of Salt Lake City on UT 65 & 66; off I-80 & I-84. 31 sites; 35-foot limit; showers; dump station. Seasonal. Swimming, fishing; boat ramp. GPS: N 40-53.6 W 111-35.0

Escalante Petrified Forest State Park

710 N Reservoir Rd, Escalante, UT 84726. Phone: (435) 826-4466. Located on Wide Hollow Reservoir on UT 12. 26 sites, 4 with electric, water; showers, dump station. 40-foot limit. Swimming, fishing; boat ramp. GPS: N 37-47.0 W 111-37.8

Fremont Indian State Park & Museum

3820 W Clear Creek Canyon Rd, Sevier, UT 84766. Phone: (435) 527-4631. Located 21 miles SW of Richfield on I-70 exit 17. 31 sites; dump station. 45-foot limit. ATV trails near-by. Fishing. GPS: N 38-34.6 W 112-20.8

Goblin Valley State Park

Green River, UT 84525. Phone: (435) 275-4584. Located between Hanksville and Green River (I-70 exit 158), off UT 24. 24 sites; showers; dump station. Limited water. Off-road vehicle area adjacent to park. 30-foot limit. GPS: N 38-34.7 W 110-42.9

Goosenecks State Park

Blanding, UT 84511. Phone: (435) 678-2238. Located southwest of Blanding near Mexican Hat (US 163), 4 miles off UT 261. 4 primitive sites; no facilities. No fee. 30-foot limit. GPS: N 37-10.5 W 109-55.6

Great Salt Lake State Park

324 W 200, Salt Lake City, UT 84116. Phone: (801) 250-1898. Located in Salt Lake City, on The Great Salt Lake. 35 sites with water and electric. GPS: N 41-06.5 W 112-01.9

Green River State Park

405 S Green River Blvd, Green River, UT 84525. Phone: (435) 564-3633. Located on the Green River in Green River City off I-70 exit 158. 40 sites, no hook-ups; showers; dump station. Golf course. Off-road vehicle trails nearby. 45-foot limit. Swimming, fishing; boat ramp. GPS: N 38-59.7 W 110-09.4

Gunlock State Park

Gunlock Road, Gunlock, UT 84733. Phone: (435) 680-0715. Located on Gunlock Reservoir, NW of St. George off UT 18. 18 sites; dump station. Swimming, fishing; boat ramp. GPS: N 37-15.9 W 113-46.2

Huntington State Park

Huntington, UT 84528. Phone: (435) 687-2491. Located on Huntington Reservoir, 2 miles NE of Huntington on UT 10. 22 sites, no hook-ups. Showers, dump station. Swimming, fishing, boating. GPS: N 39-20.7 W 110-56.3

Hyrum State Park

405 W 300 S, Hyrum, UT 84319. Phone: (435) 245-6866. Located on Hyrum Lake in Hyrum, 8 miles S of Logan. 40 sites; showers. Dump station. Water available. 40-foot limit. ATV area nearby. Swimming, fishing; boat ramp. 65-foot limit. GPS: N 41-37.6 W 111-52.3

Jordanelle State Park

SR 319, Heber City, UT 84032. Phone: (435) 649-9540. Located on Jordanelle Reservoir near Heber City, SE of Salt Lake City, off US 40. 103 sites (six areas) with water and electric; showers; dump station; laundry. Marina; swimming, fishing; boat ramp, rentals. 48-foot limit. GPS: N 40-37.3 W 111-25.7

Kodachrome Basin State

Cannonville, UT 84718. Phone: (435) 679-8562. Located 9 miles S of UT 12 and Cannonville, E of Bryce Canyon National Park. 25 sites; 45-foot maximum; showers; dump station. Horse trails. GPS: N 37-30.1 W 111-59.6

Millsite State Park

Huntington, UT 84528. Phone: (435) 384-2552. Located on Millsite Reservoir, 4 miles W of UT 10 (I-70 exit 89), NW of Ferron. 20 sites with electric; showers; dump station. 35-foot limit. Fishing; boat ramp. Golf nearby. GPS: N 39-05.9 W 111-11.0

Otter Creek State Park

Antimony, UT 84712. Phone: (435) 624-3268. Located on Otter Creek (lake), 4 miles from Antimony on UT 22; about 12 miles E of US 89 at Kingston. 53 sites (some with electric); water; showers; dump station. ATV trails in park. 45-foot limit. Swimming, fishing; boat ramp. GPS: N 38-10.0 W 112-01.3

Palisade State Park

2200 E Palisade Rd, Sterling, UT 84665. Phone: (435) 835-7275. Located on Palisade Lake, off US 89, SE of Manti. 70 sites (some full hook-up, some pull-thru); showers; dump station. Golf course. Off-highway trails nearby. 75-foot limit. GPS: N 39-12.1 W 111-40.0

Piute State Park

Antimony, UT 84712. Phone: (435) 674-3268. Located off US 89, 5 miles N of Junction. 35 primitive sites. Fishing (trout!). GPS: N 38-18.1 W 112-07.6

Quail Creek State Park

472 N 5300 W, Hurricane, UT 84737. Phone: (435) 879-2378. Located on Quail Creek Reservoir, 3 miles E of I-15 exit 16, on UT 9. Near Zion National Park. 23 sites; no facilities. Off-highway trails nearby. 35-foot limit. Swimming, fishing; boat ramp. GPS: N 37-10.9 W 113-23.8

Red Fleet State Park

8750 N Hwy 191, Vernal, UT 84078. Phone: (435) 789-4432. Located on Red Fleet Reservoir in NE corner of UT, 13 miles N or Vernal, off US 191. 29 sites (some full hook-up); dump station. Off-highway trails nearby. 30-foot limit. Swimming, fishing; boat ramp. GPS: N 40-33.7 W 109-29.1

Rockport State Park

9040 N Hwy 302, Peoa, UT 84061. Phone: (435) 336-2241. Located on Rockport Reservoir, 45 miles E of Salt Lake City near Wanship, on UT 32. 36 sites, some hook-ups; showers; dump station. 45-foot limit. Swimming, fishing; boat ramp, rentals. ATV trails nearby. GPS: N 40-45.1 W 111-22.0

Sand Hollow State Park

3351 S Sand Hollow Rd, Hurricane, UT 84737. Phone: (435) 680-0715. Located 4 miles E of I-15 exit 16 and 1 mile S of UT 9 on Turf Sod Rd. 50 sites with full hook-ups; showers; dump station. Off-highway trails in park. Horse trails. Swimming, fishing; boat ramp. GPS: N 37-08.4 W 113-28.7

Scofield State Park

Price, UT 84501. Phone: (435) 448-9449 or (435) 687-2491. Located on Scofield Reservoir W of Helper, off US 6, on UT 96. Two areas: Scofield Mountain View, located 6 miles N of Scofield. 34 sites; showers; dump station. 30-foot limit. Scofield Madsen Bay, located on north end of Reservoir. 40 sites (no hook-ups either area); dump station. Off-highway vehicle area nearby. 35-foot limit. Both areas seasonal. Swimming, fishing; boat ramp. GPS: N 39-49.5 W 111-08.2

Snow Canyon State Park

1002 N Snow Canyon Dr, Ivins, UT 84738. Phone: (435) 628-2255. Located 11 miles NW of St. George, on UT 18. 31 sites, 17 with water and electric, 21 no hook-ups; showers; dump station. 35-foot limit. Horse trails. GPS: N 37-11.0 W 113-39.7

Starvation State Park

Duchesne, UT 84021. Phone: (435) 738-2326. Located on Strawberry River, 4 miles NW of Duchesne (US 40 & 191) on US 40. 54 primitive sites (narrow), one developed campground; showers; water available; dump station. 40-foot limit. ATV area near-by. Swimming, fishing; boat ramp. GPS: N 40-10.4 W 110-29.5

Steinaker State Park

4335 N Hwy 191, Vernal, UT 84078. Phone: (435) 789-4432. Located on Steinaker Reservoir, 7 miles N of Vernal, off US 191. 31 sites, some full hook-ups; dump station. 35-foot limit. Off highway vehicle area nearby. Swimming, fishing; boat ramp. GPS: N 40-32.1 W 109 31.3

Utah Lake State Park

4400 W Center St, Provo, UT 84601. Phone: (801) 375-0731. Located on Utah Lake (freshwater), 5 miles W of Provo, off I-15. 54 sites with electric, water, some full hook-ups; showers; dump station. 47-foot limit. Seasonal. Swimming, fishing; boat ramp. GPS: N 40-14.2 W 111-44.0

Wasatch Mountain State Park

Midway, UT 84049. Phone: (435) 654-1791. Located near Heber City, off US 40/189. Four campgrounds. 139 sites with water and electric; 35 full hook-up sites; showers; dump station. Golf course. 35-foot limit. Swimming, fishing. Horse trails. ATVs Okay. GPS: N 40-28.7 W 111-31.2

Willard Bay State Park

900 W 650 N #A, Willard, UT 84340. Phone: (435) 734-9494. Located on Willard Reservoir, NW of Ogden. Two locations:

a. Willard Bay North, located 12 miles N of Ogden, off I-15 exit 360. 62 sites, 39 full hook-ups; showers; dump station. Swimming, fishing, boat ramp. Marina. 30-foot limit. GPS: N 41-25.1 W 112-03.2

b. Willard Bay South, located 8 miles N of Ogden, off I-15 exit 354. 30 sites; showers. 35-foot limit. Swimming, fishing, boat ramp. Marina. GPS: N 41-21.1 W 112-04.2

Yuba State Park

Levan, UT 84639. Phone: (435) 758-2611. Located on Sevier Bridge Reservoir 25 miles S of Nephi, off I-15 exits 188 or 202. 68 sites in two camping areas, some hook-ups; showers; dump station. Marina. Off-highway vehicle area nearby. Swimming, fishing; boat ramp. Zip lines. GPS: N 39-22.5 W 112-01.8

VERMONT

QUEBEC

Lake Carmi SP

Brighton SP

Maidstone SP

Grand Isle SP

Smugglers Notch SP

Elmore SP

Burlington

Little River SP

New Discovery SP

Big Deer SP

Stillwater SP

Ricker Pond SP

Montpelier

Button Bay SP

NEW HAMPSHIRE

D.A.R. SP

VERMONT

Branbury SP

Silver Lake SP

Half Moon Pond SP

Gifford Woods SP

Bomoseen SP

Quechee Gorge SP

Coolidge SP

Lake St. Catherine SP

Ascutney SP

Wilgus SP

Emerald Lake SP

NEW YORK

Jamaica SP

Townshend SP

Brattleboro

Woodford SP

Molly Stark SP

Fort Summer SP

MASSACHUSETTS

1   2   3   4

Vermont

Thirty of Vermont's 52 state parks can accommodate RVs. However, none of the parks have hook-ups. If a park indicates "no big rigs" you should call to verify size limit. All but two parks have dump stations and all have showers. All offer drinkable water. The parks accept Visa and MasterCard. Parks are open in the Spring-Summer season only; many close after Labor Day. It is wise to call ahead to (1) check available space and; (2) if open. The reservation system requires 14 days advance request. There is a fee for reservations. Rate groups: A and B.

Vermont State Parks
103 South Main St.
Waterbury, VT 05671

Information: (802) 241-3655
Reservations: (888) 409-7579
Internet: www.vtstateparks.com

Vermont Park Locator

Ascutney State Park....D3
Big Deer State Park....B3
Bomoseen State Park....C1
Branbury State Park....C2
Brighton State Park....A3
Button Bay State Park....B1
Coolidge State Park....D2
D.A.R. State Park....C1
Elmore State Park....B2
Emerald Lake State Park....D2
Fort Dummer State Park....E2
Gifford Woods State Park....C2
Grand Isle State Park....A1
Half Moon Pond State Park....C1
Jamaica State Park....E2
Lake Carmi State Park....A2
Lake St. Catherine State Park....D1
Little River State Park....B2
Maidstone State Park....A4
Molly Stark State Park....E2
New Discovery State Park....B3
Quechee Gorge State Park....C3
Ricker Pond State Park....B3
Silver Lake State Park....C2
Smugglers Notch State Park....B2
Stillwater State Park....B3
Townshend State Park....E2
Wilgus State Park....D3
Woodford State Park....E2

Vermont Parks

Ascutney State Park

1826 Back Mtn Rd, Windsor, VT 05089. Phone: (802) 674-2060. Located off VT 44A (US 5; I-91 exit 8) near Windsor. 39 sites; showers; dump station. GPS: N 43-26.3 W 72-26.4

Big Deer State Park

1467 Boulder Beach Rd, Groton, VT 05046. Phone: (802) 584-3822. Located off VT 232 about 19 miles NW of Groton, via US 302 and VT 232. 23 sites; showers; dump station (Check in at Stillwater State Park). No big rigs. GPS: N 44-17.3 W 72-16.1

Bomoseen State Park

22 Cedar Mtn Rd, Fair Haven, VT 05743. Phone: (802) 265-4242. Located 4 miles N of Hydeville, off VT 4A. 56 sites; some pull-through; showers; dump station. Lake in park. Swimming, fishing. Boat rentals. GPS: N 43-38.8 W 73-14.6

Branbury State Park

3570 Lake Dunmore Rd Rt 53, Salisbury, VT 05733. Phone: (802) 247-5925. Located 9 miles N of Brandon on Rt 53 off US 7, on Lake Dunmore. 37 sites; showers; dump station. Swimming, fishing; boat/canoe rentals. GPS: N 43-54.3 W 73-04.1

Brighton State Park

102 State Park Rd, Island Pond, VT 05846. Phone: (802) 723-4360. Located off VT 105 on Spectacle Pond, 2 miles E of Island Pond (VT 105 & 111). 61 sites; showers; dump station. Swimming; boat rentals. GPS: N 44-47.9 W 71-51.7

Button Bay State Park

118 Button Bay State Park Rd, Ferrisburgh, VT 05491. Phone: (802) 475-2377. Located on Lake Champlain, 6.5 miles W of Vergennes (VT 22A & US 7). 60 sites; showers; dump station. Swimming, fishing; boat rentals. GPS: N 44-11.0 W 73-21.5

Coolidge State Park

855 Coolidge State Park Rd, Plymouth, VT 05056. Phone: (802) 672-3612. Located off VT 100A, NE of Plymouth Notch; 6 miles SW of Bridgewater Corners (US 4). 26 sites; showers; dump station. GPS: N 43-33.2 W 72-42.0

D.A.R. State Park

6750 State Rt 17 W, Addison, VT 05491. Phone: (802) 759-2354. Located on Lake Champlain, 7 miles W of Addison via VT 17 (off VT 22 A). 46 sites; showers; dump station. Swimming, fishing. GPS: N 44-03.5 W 73-24.6

Elmore State Park

856 State Rt 12, Lake Elmore, VT 05657. Phone: (802) 888-2982. Located on Lake Elmore on VT 12, 5 miles SE of Morrisville (VT 100 & 15). 45 sites; showers; dump station. Swimming, fishing; boat/canoe/kayak rentals. GPS: N 44-32.6 W 72-32.0

Emerald Lake State Park

65 Emerald Lake Ln, East Dorset, VT 05253. Phone: (802) 362-1655. Located in East Dorset on Emerald Lake on US 7 about 9 miles N of Manchester. 67 sites; showers; dump station. Swimming, fishing; boat rentals; no motors in lake. GPS: N 43-17.0 W 73-00.2

Fort Dummer State Park

517 Old Guilford Rd, Brattleboro, VT 05301. Phone: (802) 254-2610. Located off I-91 exit 1 off US 5 south of Brattleboro. 50 sites; showers; dump station. GPS: N 42-49.5 W 72-34.0

Gifford Woods State Park

34 Gifford Woods, Killington, VT 05751. Phone: (802) 775-5354. Located near Killington at US 4 and VT 100 junction. 22 sites; showers; dump station. GPS: N 43-40.6 W 72-48.6

Grand Isle State Park

36 East Shore Rd S, Grand Isle, VT 05458. Phone: (802) 372-4300. Located on Lake Champlain, 20 miles N of Burlington via US 2. (Most visited park in VT.) 117 sites, some pull-through; showers; dump station. Swimming, fishing; boat ramp, boat/kayak rentals. GPS: N 44-41.4 W 73-18.5

Half Moon Pond State Park

1621 Black Pond Rd, Hubbardton, VT 05743. Phone: (802) 273-2848. Located about 5 miles S of Hubbardton, off VT 30 on marked roads. 52 sites; showers; dump station. Half Moon Pond in park. Boat rentals; no motors in lake. No big rigs. Swimming, fishing; boat/canoe/kayak rentals. GPS: N 43-41.5 W 73-12.9

Jamaica State Park

285 Salmon Hole Ln, Jamaica, VT 05343. Phone: (802) 874-4600. Located on the West River, off VT 30 outside Jamaica. (8-ton weight limit on bridge leading to park.) 41 sites; showers. Swimming, fishing. GPS: N 43-06.6 W 72-46.3

Lake Carmi State Park

460 Marsh Farm Rd, Enosburg Falls, VT 05450. Phone: (802) 933-8383. Located on Lake Carmi off VT 236, about 9 miles NW of Enosburg Falls (VT 105 & 108). 140 sites; showers; dump station. Swimming, fishing; boat rentals. GPS: N 44-57.1 W 72-52.6

Lake St. Catherine State Park

3034 VT 30 S, Poultney, VT 05764. Phone: (802) 287-9158. Located about 3 miles S of Poultney on VT 30. 50 sites; showers; dump station. Swimming, fishing; boat rentals. GPS: N 43-29.0 W 73-12.1

Little River State Park

3444 Little River Rd, Waterbury, VT 05676. Phone: (802) 244-7103. Located in Mansfield State Forest on Little River, about 6 miles N of Waterbury (I-89 exit 10) off US 2; follow signs. (Very popular park.) 81 sites; showers; dump station. Swimming, fishing; boat ramp. GPS: N 44-23.0 W 72-46.1

Maidstone State Park

5956 Maidenstone Lake Rd, Guildhall, VT 058905. Phone: (802) 676-3930. (Most remote park in VT system.) Located on Maidstone Lake near NH state line, 5 miles N of Maidstone off VT 102 to marked State Forest Hwy. 34 sites; showers; dump station. No big rigs. Swimming, fishing. GPS: N 44-38.1 W 71-38.2

Molly Stark State Park

705 Rt 9 E, Wilmington, VT 05363. Phone: (802) 464-5460. Located about 4 miles E of Wilmington on VT 9 in southern Vermont. 23 sites; showers. GPS: N 42-51.3 W 72-48.9

New Discovery State Park

4239 VT 232, Marshfield, VT 05658. Phone: (802) 426-3042. Located 23 miles NE of Montpelier on VT 232 via US 2. 46 sites; showers; dump station. Equestrian area (7 sites). GPS: N 44-19.0 W 72-17.4

Quechee Gorge State Park

5800 Woodstock Rd, Hartford, VT 05047. Phone: (802) 295-2990. Located off US 4 in Quechee (I-89 exit 1). 45 sites; showers; dump station. GPS: N 43-38.2 W 72-24.3

Ricker Pond State Park

18 Ricker Pond Campground Rd, Groton, VT 05046. Phone: (802) 584-3821. Located on Ricker Pond off VT 232, 5 miles NW of Groton (US 302). 27 sites; showers; dump station. Swimming, fishing; boat ramp; canoe/kayak rentals. GPS: N 44-14.7 W 72-15.2

Silver Lake State Park

20 State Park Beach Rd, Barnard, VT 05031. Phone: (802) 234-9451. Located on Silver Lake, 1 mile N of Barnard on VT 12. 40 sites; showers; dump station. Swimming, fishing; boat/canoe rentals. GPS: N 43-43.9 W 72-37.0

Smugglers Notch State Park

6443 Mountain Rd, Stowe, VT 05672. Phone: (802) 253-4014. Located about 10 miles NW of Stowe on VT 108. 20 sites; showers; dump station. No big rigs. GPS N 44-31.6 W 72-46.8

Stillwater State Park

44 Stillwater Rd, Groton, VT 05046. Phone: (802) 584-3822. Located NW of Groton, via US 302 and VT 232. 62 sites; showers; dump station. Swimming, fishing; boat ramp. GPS: N 44-16.5 W 72-16.4

Townshend State Park

2755 State Forest Rd, Townshend, VT 05353. Phone: (802) 365-7500. Located in Townshend, off VT 30 on the West River. 30 sites; showers. No big rigs. GPS: N 43-02.4 W 72-41.4

Wilgus State Park

3985 Rt 5, Weathersfield, VT 05156. Phone: (802) 674-5422. Located on Connecticut River off US 5, SW of Ascutney (I-91 exit 8). 17 sites; showers. Canoe/kayak rentals. GPS: N 43-23.4 W 72-24.4

Woodford State Park

142 State Park Rd, Woodford, VT 05201. Phone: (802) 447-7169. Located on Adams Reservoir on VT 9 about 10 miles E of Bennington. 83 sites; showers; dump station. Swimming; boat/canoe rentals. GPS: N 42-53.7 W 73-02.3

VIRGINIA

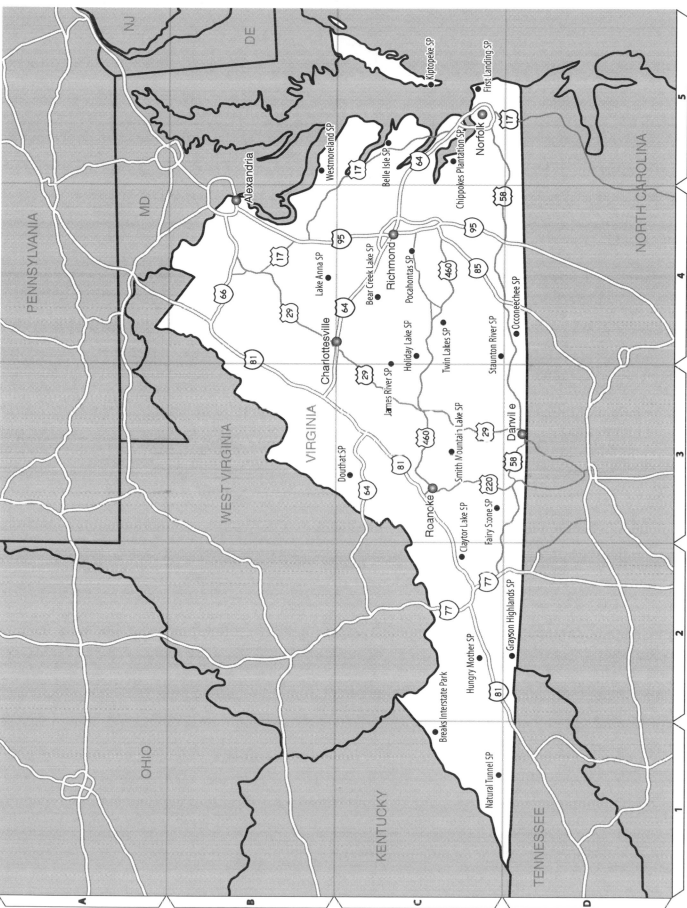

Virginia

Virginia has 21 state parks with RV accessibility. All listed parks have dump stations. Most locations have water and electricity at the sites, several with 50-amp service. Sites listed as "standard" have no hook-ups. Individual parks cannot take reservations (except Breaks Interstate Park) but you can check availability by calling a park. The state-wide reservation service requires 48 hours advance notice and is not open on weekends. The parks charge a fee for each pet and all pets must have current rabies vaccination papers. Rate groups: B and C depending on site facilities; Kiptopeke State Park is considered a premium park.

Virginia Dept. of Conservation and Recreation
203 Governor St., Ste. 213
Richmond, VA 23219

Information: (804) 786-1712
Reservations: (800) 933-7275
Internet: www.dcr.virginia.gov/state-park/
Reservations: www.ReserveAmerica.com

Virginia Park Locator

Virginia Parks

Bear Creek Lake State Park

22 Bear Creek Lake Rd, Cumberland, VA 23040. Phone: (804) 492-4410. Located in Cumberland State Forest off VA 622 (via US 60) 4 miles N of Cumberland. 37 sites with water, electric (23 sites with 20-foot limit; 6 sites with 35-foot limit); showers. Lake in park. Swimming, boat ramp, rentals (electric motors). GPS: N 37-32.0 W 78-16.5

Belle Isle State Park

1632 Belle Isle Rd, Lancaster, VA 22503. Phone: (804) 462-5030. Located on Rappahannock River in eastern VA, off VA 683. 28 sites with electric, water; showers. Laundry. 45-foot limit. Fishing; boat ramp. Horse trails. GPS: N 37-46.9 W 76-34.9

Breaks Interstate Park

627 Commission Cir, Breaks, VA 24607. Phone: (800) 982-5122 or (540) 865-4413. Located in VA on VA/KY state line, off VA-KY 80. 122 sites with electric; showers. No size limit. Equestrian area. Swimming, fishing. Golf privileges (nearby). No reservations. GPS: N 37-18.0 W 82-18.5

Chippokes Plantation State Park

695 Chippokes Park Rd, Surry, VA 23883. Phone: (757) 294-3625. Located NW of Norfolk on the James River, off VA 10. 50 sites with water, electric; showers. 50-foot limit. Swimming, fishing. GPS: N 37-08.6 W 76-44.8

Claytor Lake State Park

6620 Ben H. Bolen Dr, Dublin, VA 24084. Phone: (540) 643-2500. Located northeast of Pulaski at I-81 exit 101; east to park. 110 sites: 40 with water, electric, 70 standard; showers. 35-foot limit. Swimming, fishing; boat ramp, rentals. GPS: N 37-03.5 W 80-37.4

Douthat State Park

14239 Douthat State Park Rd, Millboro, VA 24460. Phone: (540) 862-8100. Located 5 miles N of Clifton Forge and I-64 exit 27 via VA 629. 74 sites, 68 with water and electric, 19 standard; showers. 40-foot limit. Swimming, fishing; boat ramp (electric motors only). GPS: N 37-54.3 W 79-47.9

Fairy Stone State Park

967 Fairy Stone Lake Dr, Stuart, VA 24171. Phone: (276) 930-2424. Located on VA 346 about 24 miles NW of Martinsville via US 58 or VA 57 & 623. 50 sites with water, electric; showers. 30-foot limit. Lake in park. Equestrian area (10 sites); trails. Swimming, fishing, boat ramp, rentals (electric motors only). GPS: N 36-47.5 W 80-07.1

First Landing State Park

2500 Shore Dr, Virginia Beach, VA 23451. Phone: (757) 412-2300. Located on US 60 at Cape Henry in Virginia Beach. 188 sites, 107 with water and electric, 81 standard; showers. (Length limits vary by site type; call ahead.) Swimming, fishing; boat ramp. Bicycles rentals. GPS: N 36-54.7 W 76-00.1

Grayson Highlands State Park

829 Grayson Highland Ln, Mouth of Wilson, VA 24363. Phone: (276) 579-7092. Located 34 miles S of Marion and I-81 exit 45 via

VA 16, US 58, and VA 362. 37 sites with water, electric; 32 standard; showers. 40-foot limit. Three creeks in park. Equestrian area, 90 sites, 23 with electric, water. Fishing. GPS: N 36-36.7 W 81-29.3

Holiday Lake State Park

2759 S Park Rd, Appomattox, VA 24522. Phone: (434) 248-6308. Located off VA 24 in the Appomattox-Buckingham State Forest E of Appomattox; access from VA 636, 640 or 692. 36 sites with water, electric; showers. 38-foot limit; some sites less; call ahead. Lake in park. Swimming, fishing; boat ramp, boat/canoe rentals (electric motors only). GPS: N 37-24.3 W 78-38.7

Hungry Mother State Park

2854 Park Blvd, Marion, VA 24354. Phone: (276) 781-7400. Located on VA 16, 4 miles N of Marion (I-81 exit 47). 72 sites with water, electric (some sewer); showers. 35-foot limit. Swimming, fishing; boat ramp, rentals. (Electric motors.) GPS: N 36-52.9 W 81-31.5

James River State Park

104 Green Hill Dr, Gladstone, VA 24533. Phone: (434) 933-4355. Located on James River on VA 605, NE of Lynchburg on VA 647 via US 29 & VA 655. 40 sites with water, electric; 26 standard sites; showers; dump station. 40-foot limit. Equestrian area (21 sites); trails. Fishing, boat ramp. GPS: N 37-38.7 W 78-48.6

Kiptopeke State Park

35540 Kiptopeke Dr, Cape Charles, VA 23310. Phone: (757) 331-2267. Located on eastern shore of Chesapeake Bay, 3 miles N of Chesapeake Bay Bridge Tunnel on VA 704, via US 13. Tunnel has high toll fees. 86 sites: 54 with water and electric, 32 full hook-up; 40-foot limit. Swimming, fishing; boat ramp. GPS: N 37-10.4 W 75-58.6

Lake Anna State Park

6800 Lawyers Rd, Spotsylvania, VA 22553. Phone: (540) 854-5503. Located 25 miles SW of Fredericksberg, off VA 208. 46 sites, 23 with electric, water, 23 standard; showers. Swimming, fishing; boat ramp. GPS: N 38-07.7 W 77-49.6

Natural Tunnel State Park

1420 Natural Tunnel Pkwy, Duffield, VA 24244. Phone: (276) 940-2674. Located on VA 871 about 13 miles NW of Gate City via US 23. 34 sites with water, electric; showers. 38-foot limit. Tunnel tours. Swimming; fishing (nearby). GPS: N 36-42.2 W 82-44.6

Occoneechee State Park

1192 Occoneechee Park Rd, Clarksvillle, VA 23927. Phone: (434) 374-2210. Located on Buggs Island Lake, 1.5 miles E of Clarksville on US 58, near junction with US 15. 48 sites, 33 with water and electric, 15 standard; (12 sites with lake view); showers. Equestrian area, (11 sites.) 30-foot limit. Fishing, boat ramp, rentals. GPS: N 36-38.1 W 78-31.8

Pocahontas State Park

10301 State Park Rd, Chesterfield, VA 23838. Phone: (804) 796-4255. Located on VA 655 about 20 miles SW of Richmond. From I-95, take exit 61 and go W on VA 10 to VA 655. 114 sites with water, electric; showers. Laundry. 40-foot limit. Swimming, fishing; boat ramp, rentals. Horse trails. GPS: N 37-22.0 W 77-34.4

Smith Mountain Lake State Park

1235 State Park Rd, Huddleston, VA 24104. Phone: (540) 297-6066. Located on Smith Mountain Lake, SE of Roanoke off VA 626. 24 sites with water, electric, (19 sites with 30-foot limit; 5 pull-through sites with 50-foot limit); showers. Swimming, fishing; boat ramp, rentals. GPS: N 37-05.4 W 79-35.3

Staunton River State Park

1170 Staunton Trail, Scottsburg, VA 24589. Phone: (434) 572-4623. Located on Buggs Island Lake, 18 miles E of South Boston via US 360 and VA 344. 34 sites with water, electric (6 sites with 20-foot limit; some to 45-foot limit); showers. Swimming, fishing; boat ramp. GPS: N 36-42.1 W 78-40.7

Twin Lakes State Park

788 Twin Lakes Rd, Green Bay, VA 23942. Phone: (434) 392-3435. Located on VA 629, 5 miles SW of Burkeville via US 360 and VA 613. 33 sites with water, electric; showers. 36-foot limit; 9 sites 25-foot limit. Two lakes in park. Swimming, fishing; boat ramp, boat/canoe rentals (electric motors only). GPS: N 37-10.7 W 78-15.9

Westmoreland State Park

1650 State Park Rd, Montross, VA 22520. Phone: (804) 493-8821. Located on Potomac River, 6 miles NW of Montross via VA 3 and VA 347. 116 sites, 42 with water and electric, 74 standard; showers. 40-foot limit. Swimming, fishing; boat ramp, rentals. GPS: N 38-09.5 W 76-52.2

WASHINGTON

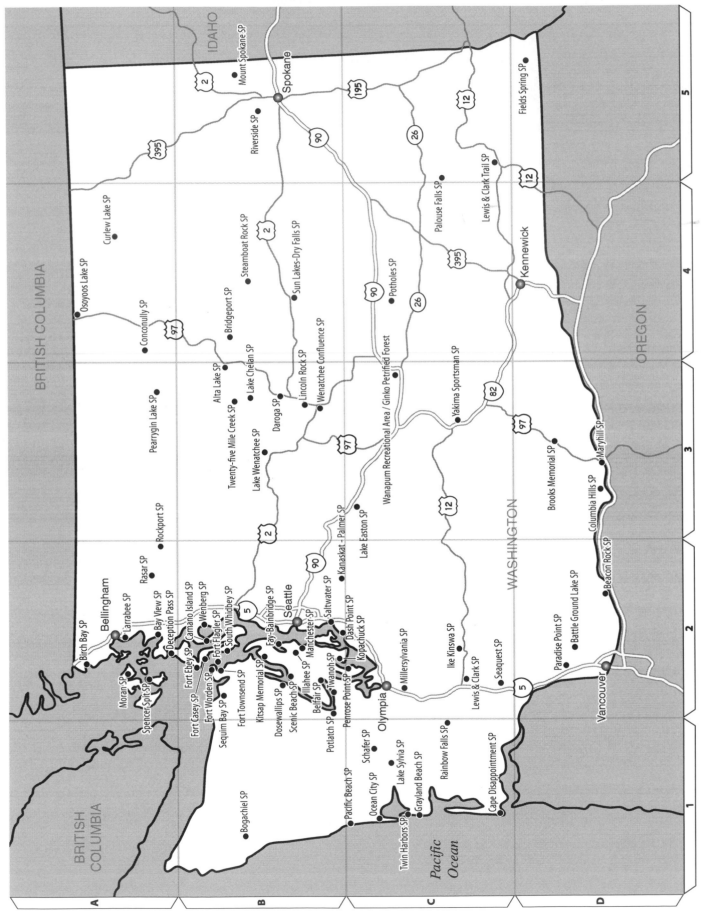

BRITISH COLUMBIA

IDAHO

Mount Spokane SP

Spokane

Fields Spring SP

Riverside SP

Curlew Lake SP

Osoyoos Lake SP

Conconully SP

Steamboat Rock SP

Sun Lakes-Dry Falls SP

Palouse Falls SP

Lewis & Clark Trail SP

Kennewick

Potholes SP

Bridgeport SP

Lake Chelan SP

Wenatchee Confluence SP

Lincoln Rock SP

Alta Lake SP

Daroga SP

Pearrygin Lake SP

Twenty-five Mile Creek SP

Lake Wenatchee SP

Wanapum Recreational Area / Ginko Petrified Forest

Yakima Sportsman SP

OREGON

Rockport SP

Rasar SP

Brooks Memorial SP

Columbia Hills SP

Maryhill SP

WASHINGTON

Kanaskat - Palmer SP

Lake Easton SP

Beacon Rock SP

Bellingham

Birch Bay SP

Larrabee SP

Bay View SP

Deception Pass SP

Camano Island SP

Wenberg SP

South Whidbey SP

Fort Flagler SP

Seattle

Fay-Bainbridge SP

Saltwater SP

Dash Point SP

Battle Ground Lake SP

Paradise Point SP

Moran SP

Spencer Spit SP

Fort Ebey SP

Fort Casey SP

Fort Worden SP

Sequim Bay SP

Fort Townsend SP

Kitsap Memorial SP

Dosewallips SP

Scenic Beach SP

Illahee SP

Manchester SP

Belfair SP

Twanoh SP

Kopachuck SP

Penrose Point SP

Millersylvania SP

Ike Kinswa SP

Seaquest SP

Vancouver

Potlatch SP

Olympia

Schafer SP

Lake Sylvia SP

Rainbow Falls SP

Lewis & Clark SP

Bogachiel SP

Pacific Beach SP

Ocean City SP

Grayland Beach SP

Cape Disappointment SP

Twin Harbors SP

Pacific Ocean

BRITISH COLUMBIA

Washington

There are 73 RV-friendly state parks in Washington with some 6,000 sites (in all categories). Many of these parks offer sites with full hook-ups and only a few are classified as "primitive." Almost every Washington park has some primitive sites in addition to the other listed sites. In the listings, "standard sites" means the campsites have no utilities but have showers and drinking water nearby. The park listing will indicate the number of standard sites, plus the sites that have utilities and their type. Some parks accept reservations but all sites are available on a first-come basis. The reservation system requires 48 hours advance request. Two listings are parks in Washington's San Juan Islands. *These parks are accessible only via the Washington Ferry System.* Numerous parks in the system are located on the islands in Puget Sound, as indicated. These islands are connected to the mainland by bridges and do not require ferry access.

Many Washington parks are located on water, either salt or fresh, and these parks have boat launch ramps. In most cases, fishing in parks on salt water includes crabbing, clamming and oysters. Fishing, commercial and recreational, is a very important part of the state's life. (The crabs in Washington waters are Dungeness crabs, found only in the Pacific Ocean from Northern California to the coast and islands of Washington.) Salt water parks with swimming facilities often have salt water beaches and could be quite cold. Rate groups: A and B depending on site location, utilities or park.

Washington State Parks & Recreation Commission
7150 Cleanwater Drive SW
PO Box 42650
Olympia, WA 98504

Information: (360) 902-8844
Reservations: (888) 226-7688
Internet: www.parks.wa.gov

Washington Park Locator

Washington Parks

Alta Lake State Park

1 B Otto Rd, Paternos, WA 98846. Phone: (509) 923-2473. Located on Alta Lake, 4 miles SW of Paternos on WA 153 near junction of US 97. 91 standard sites, 32 with electric and water; dump station. 38-foot limit. No reservations. Horse trails. Seasonal. Swimming, fishing. Boat ramp. GPS: N 48-01.9 W 119-56.1

Battle Ground Lake State Park

18002 NE 249th St, Battle Ground, WA 98604. Phone: (360) 687-4621. Located on Battle Ground Lake, 21 miles NE of Vancouver on WA 503. 31 full hook-up sites; dump station. 35-foot limit. Reservations accepted. Equestrian area. Swimming, fishing, boating (no motors). GPS: N 45-48.2 W 122-29.5

Bay View State Park

10901 Bay View-Edison Rd, Mt. Vernon, WA 98273. Phone: (888) 226-7688. Located on Padillo Bay (Puget Sound) in northern WA, 7 miles W of Burlington off WA 20; I-5 exit 231, west to park. 30 standard sites, 1 full hook-up, 29 with electric and water. 60-foot limit. Reservations accepted. Swimming, fishing. Boat ramp nearby. GPS: N 48-29.3 W 122-28.8

Beacon Rock State Park

34841 WA 14, Skamania, WA 98648. Phone: (509) 427-8265. Located on Columbia River in southern WA, 35 miles E of Vancouver on WA 14. Also accessible from Oregon I-84 via Cascade Locks exit and toll bridge to WA 14. 26 standard sites, 5 full hook-up; dump station. Equestrian area. 40-foot limit. Fishing, boat ramp/docks. GPS: N 45-37.2 W 122-01.8

Belfair State Park

3151 NE WA 300, Belfair, WA 98528. Phone: (360) 275-0668. Located in Hood Canal, 3 miles W of Belfair on WA 300. From I-5, exit in Tacoma onto WA 16, N to WA 3 in Bremerton then W to WA 300. 120 standard sites, 47 full hook-up; dump station. 60-foot limit. Reservations accepted. Swimming, fishing. GPS: N 47-25.9 W 122-52.9

Birch Bay State Park

5105 Helweg Rd, Blaine, WA 98230. Phone: (360) 371-2800. Located on Strait of Georgia in northwestern WA, 8 miles S of Blaine on WA 58, near Canadian border; I-5 exits 260, 263 or 274 to WA 68. 20 sites with electric and water; dump station. 60-foot limit. Reservations accepted. Swimming, fishing. GPS: N 48-54.2 W 122-45.5

Bogachiel State Park

185983 US 101, Forks, WA 98331. Phone: (360) 374-6356. Located on Bogachiel Reservoir on Olympic Peninsula, 6 miles S of Forks on US 101. 26 standard sites, 6 with electric and water; dump station. 40-foot limit. GPS: N 47-53.7 W 124-21.8

Bridgeport State Park

235A Half Sun Way, Bridgeport, WA 98813. Phone: (509) 686-7231. Located on Rufus Woods Lake in central WA, 3 miles NE of Bridgeport near Chief Joseph Dam on the Columbia River; accessible from US 97 or WA 174. 20 sites with electric and water; dump station. 45-foot limit. Swimming, fishing; boat ramp. GPS: N 48-00.5 W 119-40.4

Brooks Memorial State Park

2465 US 97, Goldendale, WA 98620. Phone: (509) 773-4611. Located in southern WA, 13 miles N of Goldendale on US 97; accessible from WA 14 or Oregon I-84 exit 104 to US 97. 23 full hook-up sites; dump station. 30-foot limit. Fishing. GPS: N 45-57.0 W 120-39.9

Camano Island State Park

2269 S Lowell Point Rd, Camano Island, WA 98282. Phone: (360) 387-3031. Located on Puget Sound in northwestern WA, 14 miles SW of Stanwood (I-5 exit 212) on WA 532. 88 standard sites; dump station. 40-foot limit. Golf course nearby. Swimming, fishing, boat ramp. GPS: N 48-07.9 W 122-30.2

Cape Disappointment State Park

244 Robert Gray Dr, Ilwaco, WA 98640. Phone: (360) 642-3078. Located on Pacific Ocean in southwestern WA near mouth of the Columbia River, outside Ilwaco off US 101. 152 standard sites, 83 with electric and water; dump station. 45-foot limit. Reservations accepted. Fishing, boat ramp. GPS: N 46-17.9 W 124-03.1

Columbia Hills State Park

85 US 97, Dallasport, WA 98617. Phone: (509) 767-1159. Located on Columbia River in southern WA, 28 miles SW of Goldendale on WA 14. 4 standard sites, 8 with electric and water; dump station. 60-foot limit. Swimming, fishing, boat ramp, (no motors). GPS: N 45-38.9 W 121-07.0

Conconully State Park

119 Broadway St, Conconully, WA 98819. Phone: (509) 826-7408. Remote location in north-central WA on Conconully Reservoir, 22 miles NW of Omak, off US 97 on marked county roads. 20 standard sites; dump station. 60-foot limit. Swimming, fishing; boat ramp. GPS: N 48-33.3 W 119-45.0

Curlew Lake State Park

62 State Park Rd, Republic, WA 99166. Phone: (509) 775-3592. Located in northeastern WA on WA 21, on Curlew Lake, 8 miles N of Republic via US 97 or WA 20. 35 full hook-up sites; dump station. 40-foot limit. Swimming, fishing, boat ramp. GPS: N 48-43.1 W 118-39.3

Daroga State Park

1 S Daroga Park Rd, Orondo, WA 98843. Phone: (509) 784-0229. Located in central WA on Columbia River, 18 miles N of East Wenatchee on US Alt 97. 28 sites with electric and water; dump station. 45-foot limit. Swimming, fishing, boat ramp. GPS: N 47-42.3 W 120-11.8

Dash Point State Park

5700 SW Dash Point Rd, Federal Way, WA 98023. Phone: (360) 902-8844. Located in western WA on Puget Sound (in Federal Way), 5 miles NE of Tacoma on WA 509. From I-5 exit 143 west to 47th Ave, follow signs. 114 standard sites, 27 with electric and water; dump station. 45-foot limit. Reservations accepted. Swimming, fishing. GPS: N 47-19.1 W 122-24.9

Deception Pass State Park

41020 WA 20, Oak Harbor, WA 98277. Phone: (360) 675-3767. Located on Deception Pass in western WA on Whidbey Island (bridge access), 9 miles N of Oak Harbor on WA 20. 143 sites with electric and water; dump station. 60-foot limit. Reservations accepted. Swimming, fishing (fresh and saltwater), boat ramp. GPS: N 48-23.5 W 122-38.8

Dosewallips State Park

306996 US 101, Brinnen, WA 98320. Phone: (360) 796-4415. Located on Hood Canal on Olympic Peninsula, 1 mile S of Brinnon on US 101. Access from Olympia via I-5 exit 104, 50 miles N on US 101. 65 sites: 55 full hook-up, 10 water and electric; dump station. 60-foot limit. Reservations accepted. Swimming, fishing, (fresh and saltwater). GPS: N 47-41.1 W 122-54.0

Fay-Bainbridge State Park

15446 Sunrise Dr, Bainbridge Island, WA 98110. Phone: (206) 842-3931. Located in Puget Sound, northeastern end of Bainbridge Island, near WA 305. Not easily accessible, mostly for boat camping; requires ferry from Seattle or via WA 104 from the north. 26 sites with water; dump station. 30-foot limit. Swimming, fishing. GPS: N 47-42.2 W 122-30.6

Fields Spring State Park

992 Park Rd, Anatone, WA 99401. Phone: (509) 256-3332. Remote location in southeastern WA, 30 miles S of Clarkson on WA 129. 20 standard sites; dump station. 30-foot limit. GPS: N 46-05.3 W 117-10.4

Fort Casey State Park

1280 Engle Rd, Coupeville, WA 98239. Phone: (360) 902-8844. Located on Puget Sound (Admirality Inlet) on Whidbey Island (bridge access), 3 miles S of Coupeville on WA 20. 21 standard sites, 14 with water and electric; 40-foot limit. Fishing. GPS: N 48-09.6 W 122-40.3

Fort Ebey State Park

400 Hill Valley Dr, Coupeville, WA 98239. Phone: (360) 902-8844. Located on Whidbey Island (bridge access), on the Strait of Juan de Fuca, 8 miles S of Oak Harbor on WA 20. 40 standard sites, 10 with electric and water. 100-foot limit. Reservations accepted. Fishing (freshwater). GPS: N 48-13.3 W 122-45.7

Fort Flagler State Park

10541 Flagler Rd, Nordland, WA 98358. Phone: (360) 385-1259. Located on northeastern tip of Olympic Peninsula on Puget Sound, 8 miles NE of Port Hadlock off WA 20. 114 sites, 57 standard, 57 with electric and water; dump station. 50-foot limit. Reservations accepted. Swimming, fishing, boat ramp. GPS: N 48-05.1 W 122-42.1

Fort Townsend State Park

1370 Old Port Townsend Rd, Port Townsend, WA 98368. Phone: (360) 385-3595. Located on northern Olympic Peninsula, 4 miles S of Port Townsend on Port Townsend Bay off WA 20. 40 standard sites; dump station. 40-foot limit. Fishing, boating. GPS: N 48-04.7 W 122-48.3

Fort Worden State Park

200 Battery Way, Nordland, WA 98358. Phone: (360) 344-4431. Located on northern end Olympic Peninsula, just N of Port Townsend on Puget Sound, off WA 20. 80 sites in two campgrounds, 50 full hook-up sites, 30 with electric and water; dump station. 60-foot limit. Reservations accepted. Swimming, fishing; boat ramp, moorage, rentals. GPS: N 48-07.9 W 122-46.1

Grayland Beach State Park

925 Cranberry Beach Rd, Grayland, WA 98547. Phone: (360) 267-4301. Located on Washington coast, 5 miles S of Westport on WA 105, 6 miles N of Wallapa Bay. 38 sites with electric and water, 58 full hook-up sites; dump station. 40-foot limit. Equestrian area. Reservations accepted. Fishing. GPS: N 46-47.5 W 124-05.3

Ike Kinswa State Park

873 WA 122, Silver Creek, WA 98585. Phone: (360) 983-3402. Located on Mayfield Lake, 18 miles E of I-5 exit 68 via US 12 and WA 122. 31 standard sites, 41 full hook-up, 31 with electric and water; dump station. 60-foot limit. Swimming, fishing, boat ramp. GPS: N 46-33.3 W 122-32.2

Illahee State Park

3540 NE Bahia Vista Dr, Bremerton, WA 98310. Phone: (360) 478-6460. Located in Puget Sound on Port Orchard Bay, 3 miles N of Bremerton on WA 303, about 9 miles E of WA 16. 23 standard sites, 2 full hook-up; dump station. 40-foot limit. Swimming, fishing, boat ramp. GPS: N 47-35.7 W 122-35.8

Kanaskat - Palmer State Park

32101 Kanaskat-Cumberland Rd, Ravendale, WA 98051. Phone: (360) 902-8844. Located on the Green River in western WA, southeast of Seattle, 11 miles NE of Enumclaw. From I-5 exit 143 to Auburn then WA 164 to Enumclaw, follow signs. 25 standard sites, 19 with electric and water; dump station. 50-foot limit. Reservations accepted. Swimming, fishing, white water kayaking. GPS: N 47-18.7 W 121-53.9

Kitsap Memorial State Park

202 NE Park St, Poulsbo, WA 98370. Phone: (360) 779-3202. Located on Hood Canal in western WA in Puget Sound, SW of Seattle, on WA 3 off WA 104, 4 miles S of Hood Canal Bridge. 21 standard sites, 18 with electric and water; dump station. 40-foot limit. Swimming,

fishing. (Boat ramp 4 miles away.) GPS: N 47-48.9 W 122-38.7

Kopachuck State Park

10712 56th St NW, Gig Harbor, WA 98335. Phone: (253) 265-3606. Located in Puget Sound on Henderson Bay, NW of Tacoma on WA 16, 5 miles W of Gig Harbor. From I-5, exit at WA 16 in Tacoma, N on WA 16 to park. 41 standard sites; dump station. 35-foot limit. Swimming, fishing. GPS: N 47-18.5 W 122-40.8 Note: The campground was closed indefinitely in 2014 but could reopen at any time. Call park to check status.

Lake Chelan State Park

7544 S Lakeshore Rd, Chelan, WA 98816. Phone: (509) 687-3710. Located in central WA on Lake Chelan, 9 miles W of Chelan, off US 97 on WA 971. 109 standard sites, 17 full hook-up, 18 with electric and water; dump station. 30-foot limit. Reservations accepted. Store. Swimming, fishing, boat ramp. GPS: N 47-52.2 W 120-11.6

Lake Easton State Park

150 Lake Easton State Park Rd, Easton, WA 98925. Phone: (509) 656-2230. Located on Lake Easton in central WA, 15 miles W of Cle Elum off I-90 exit 71. 90 standard sites, 45 full hook-up; dump station. 60-foot limit. Reservations accepted. Swimming, fishing, boating (no motors). GPS: N 47-15.0 W 121-11.5

Lake Sylvia State Park

1812 Lake Sylvia Rd, Montesano, WA 98563. Phone: (360) 249-3621. Located on Lake Sylvia in western WA, 1 mile N of Montesano, off US 12 between Olympia and Aberdeen. 31 standard sites, 4 water and electric; dump station. 30-foot limit. Reservations accepted. Swimming, fishing, boat ramp (Electric motors.) GPS: N 46-59.7 W 123-36.0

Lake Wenatchee State Park

21588 WA 207, Leavenworth, WA 98826. Phone: (509) 763-3101. Located on Lake Wenatchee and the Wenatchee River in central WA, 18 miles N of Leavenworth, off US 2 on WA 207. 155 standard sites, 42 with electric and water (many pull-thrus); dump station. Store. Equestrian area (rentals). 60-foot limit. Reservations accepted. Swimming, fishing, boat ramp. White water kayaking. GPS: N 47-48.7 W 120-43.0

Larrabee State Park

245 Chuckanut Dr, Bellingham, WA 98225. Phone: (360) 902-8844. Located in northwestern WA on Samish Bay, 6 miles S of Bellingham off WA 11, next to I-5. 51 standard sites, 26 full hook-up; dump station. 60-foot limit. Two lakes in park. Reservations accepted. Fishing (fresh and saltwater). Boat ramp. (Watch tidal chart for depth.) GPS: N 48-39.3 W 122-29.4

Lewis & Clark State Park

4583 Jackson Hwy, Winlock, WA 98596. Phone: (360) 864-2643. Located in southwestern WA, 12 miles SE of Chehalis on US 12, just off I-5 exit 68. 25 standard sites, 5 full hook-up; equestrian sites/area. 60-foot limit. GPS: N 46-31.6 W 122-49.1

Lewis & Clark Trail State Park

36149 WA 12, Dayton, WA 99328. Phone: (509) 337-6457. Located in southeastern WA on the Touchet River, 25 miles NE of Walla Walla on US 12. 24 standard sites; dump station. 28-foot limit. Swimming, fishing. GPS: N 46-17.2 W 118-03.7

Lincoln Rock State Park

13252 WA 2E, East Wenatchee, WA 98801. Phone: (509) 884-8702. Located in central WA on the Columbia River (Lake Entiat), 7 miles N of East Wenatchee on US 2/97. 27 standard sites, 32 full hook-up, 35 with electric and water; dump station. 65-foot limit. Reservations accepted. Swimming, fishing, boat ramp. GPS: N 47-32.1 W 120-16.9

Manchester State Park

7767 E Hilldale, Port Orchard, WA 98366. Phone: (360) 871-4065. Located on Puget Sound on Olympic Peninsula, 6 miles NE of Port Orchard on WA 16. 35 standard sites, 15 with electric and water; dump station. 60-foot limit. Reservations accepted. Fishing, boating. GPS: N 47-34.7 W 122-33.0

Maryhill State Park

50 US 97, Goldendale, WA 98620. Phone: (509) 723-5007. Located on Deep Lake in southern WA on US 97 and WA 14, on the Columbia River, 12 miles S of Goldendale. 20 standard sites, 50 full hook-up; dump station. 60-foot limit. Swimming, fishing, boat ramp. GPS: N 45-41.0 W 120-49.9

Millersylvania State Park

12245 Tilley Rd S, Olympia, WA 98512. Phone: (360) 753-1519. Located 10 miles S of Olympia in southwestern WA on WA 121 near I-5 exit 95. 120 standard sites, 48 with electric and water; dump station. 60-foot limit. Reservations accepted. Swimming, fishing, boat ramp, rentals (5 mph limit). GPS: N 46-54.6 W 122-54.4

Moran State Park

Olga, WA 98279. Phone: (360) 376-2326. Located on Orcas Island (San Juan Islands) 5 miles S of Eastsound. 151 standard sites; dump station. Access by Washington State ferry. Reservations recommended. Horse trails. Swimming, fishing, clams, crabs; boat rentals (electric motors). GPS: N 48-39.0 W 122-50.9

Mount Spokane State Park

N 26107 Mount Spokane Park Dr, Mead, WA 99021. Phone: (509) 238-4258. Remote location in eastern WA, 25 miles NE of Spokane off US 2 on county roads, follow signs. 8 standard sites. Equestrian area. No reservations. 30-foot limit. GPS: N 47-53.0 W 117-08.0

Ocean City State Park

148 WA 115, Ocean Shores, WA 98569. Phone: (360) 289-3553. Located on Washington coast at intersection of WA 109 & 115, 1.5 miles N of Ocean Shores. 149 standard sites, 29 full hook-up; dump station. 50-foot limit. Reservations accepted. Swimming, fishing (fresh and saltwater). GPS: N 47-02.1 W 124-09.5

Osoyoos Lake State Park

2207 Juniper, Oroville, WA 98844. Phone: (509) 476-3321. Located on Osoyoos Lake in north-central WA near Canadian border, outside Oroville on US 97. 86 standard sites, 1 with electric and water; dump station. 45-foot limit. Reservations accepted. Swimming, fishing, boat ramp. GPS: N 48-57.0 W 119-26.0

Pacific Beach State Park

49 Second St, Pacific Beach, WA 98571. Phone: (360) 276-4297. Located on Washington coast, in Pacific Beach on WA 109. 22 standard sites, 42 with water and electric; dump station; water available. 60-foot limit. Reservations accepted. Swimming, fishing. GPS: N 47-12.4 W 124-12.1

Palouse Falls State Park

Palouse Falls Rd, Palouse, WA 99354. Phone: (509) 646-9218. Remote location in southeastern WA on Palouse River, about 35 miles N of Walla Walla, off WA 262. 11 standard sites; pit toilets. 40-foot limit. GPS: N 46-39.8 W 118-13.7

Paradise Point State Park

33914 NW Paradise Park Rd, Ridgefield, WA 98642. Phone: (360) 263-2350. Located on Lewis River in southwest WA, 6 miles S of Woodland, at I-5 exit 16. 58 standard sites, 18 with electric and water; dump station. 40-foot limit. Reservations accepted. Swimming, fishing. GPS: N 45-53.5 W 122-42.4

Pearrygin Lake State Park

561 Bear Creek Rd, Winthrop, WA 98862. Phone: (509) 996-2370. Located on Pearygin Lake in north-central WA, 4 miles NE of Winthrop on WA 20. 76 standard sites, 50 full hook-up, 27 water and electric; dump station. 60-foot limit. Reservations accepted. Swimming, fishing, boat ramp. GPS: N 48-29.8 W 120-08.8

Penrose Point State Park

321 158th Ave KPS, Lakebay, WA 98349. Phone: (253) 884-2514. Located on Puget Sound (Mayo Cove) on Olympic Peninsula, 3 miles N of Longbranch on WA 302. 82 standard sites; dump station. 35-foot limit. Reservations accepted. Swimming, fishing, boat ramp nearby. GPS: N 47-15.5 W 122-44.9

Potholes State Park

6762 Hwy 262 E, Othello, WA 99344. Phone: (509) 346-2759. Located in east-central WA on Potholes (O'Sullivan) Reservoir, 17 miles SW of Moses Lake (I-90 exit 179) on WA 262, via WA 17. 61 standard sites, 60 full hook-up; dump station. 50-foot limit. Reservations accepted. Swimming, fishing, boat ramp. GPS: N 46 58.2 W 119-21.1

Potlatch State Park

21020 US 101, Shelton, WA 98584. Phone: (360) 877-5361. Located on Hood Canal on Olympic Peninsula NW of Olympia, 12 miles N of Shelton on US 101. 38 standard sites, 35 full hook-up; dump station. 60-foot limit. Swimming, fishing. GPS: N 47-21.8 W 123-09.5

Rainbow Falls State Park

4008 WA 6, Chehalis, WA 98532. Phone: (360) 291-3767. Located on Chehalis River in southwestern WA, 17 miles W of Chehalis off I-5 exit 77, on WA 6. 39 standard sites, 8 water and electric; dump station. Equestrian area (3 sites). 60-foot limit. Swimming, fishing. GPS: N 46-37.8 W 123-14.1

Rasar State Park

38730 Cape Horn Rd, Concrete, WA 98237. Phone: (360) 902-8844. Located in northwestern WA on Skagit River, 17 miles E of Sedro Woolley (I-5 exit 229) on WA 20. 18 standard sites, 20 with electric and water; dump station. 40-foot limit. Reservations accepted. Fishing. GPS: N 48-31.4 W 121-53.6

Riverside State Park

9711 W Charles Rd, Nine Mile Falls, WA 99026. Phone: (509) 465-5064. Located in eastern WA on Spokane and Little Spokane rivers in NW Spokane, off Aubrey White Pkwy. Two campgrounds: 37 standard sites, 16 with electric and water; dump station. Equestrian area (10 sites with corrals). 45-foot limit. Fishing, boat ramp, white water kayaking. GPS: N 47-44.4 W 117-31.3

Rockport State Park

52095 US 20, Rockport, WA 98283. Phone: (360) 902-8844. Located in northwestern WA, 40 miles E of Burlington (I-5 exit 229) on WA 20. 50 full hook-up sites; dump station. 38-foot limit. Fishing, white water kayaking. GPS: N 48-29.3 W 121-36.1 Note: In 2014 campground was closed because of dangerous trees in the old-growth forest. Check with park for availability of camp sites.

Saltwater State Park

25205 8th Place Des Moines, WA 98198. Phone: (360) 902-8844. Located in northwestern WA south of Seattle on Puget Sound, 2 miles S of Des Moines (I-5 exit 149) on WA 509. 47 standard sites; dump station. Fishing. No alcohol. 60-foot limit. GPS: N 47-22.6 W 122-19.4

Scenic Beach State Park

9565 Scenic Beach Rd, Seabeck, WA 98380. Phone: (360) 830-5079. Located on Hood Canal on the Olympic Peninsula, 9 miles SW of Silverdale on WA 300. 52 standard sites (some pull-through); dump station. 60-foot limit. Reservations accepted. Swimming, fishing, boat ramp nearby. GPS: N 47-38.6 W 122-50.5

Schafer State Park

1365 W Schafer Park Rd, Elma, WA 98541. Phone: (360) 482-3852. Located on the Olympic Peninsula on the Satsop River, 12 miles N of Elma off US 12, on WA 102. 41 standard sites, 9 with electric and water; dump station. 40-foot limit. Swimming, fishing. GPS: N 47-05.8 W 123-27.8

Seaquest State Park

3030 Spirit Lake Hwy, Castle Rock, WA 98611. Phone: (360) 274-8633. Located in southwestern WA on Silver Lake, 6 miles E of Castle Rock (I-5 exit 49, near Mt. St. Helens Visitor Center). 55 standard sites, 33 with electric and water; dump station. 32-foot limit. Reservations accepted. GPS: N 46-17.8 W 122-49.3

Sequim Bay State Park

269035 US 101, Sequim, WA 98261. Phone: (360) 683-4235. Located on northern Olympic Peninsula on Puget Sound, 4 miles E of Sequim on US 101. 60 standard sites, 16 full hook-up; dump station. 45-foot limit. Reservations accepted. Swimming, fishing, boat ramp. GPS: N 48-02.4 W 123-01.9

South Whidbey Island State Park

4128 Smugglers Cove Rd, Freeland, WA 98249. Phone: (360) 331-4559. Located on Puget Sound (Admirality Inlet) on Whidbey Island (bridge access), 3 miles S of Greenbank on WA 525. 46 standard sites, 8 with electric and water; dump station. 50-foot limit. Closed Dec/Jan. Reservations accepted. Swimming, fishing. GPS: N 48-03.4 W 122-35.5

Spencer Spit State Park

521A Bakerview Rd, Lopez Island, WA 98261. Phone: (360) 902-8844. Located on Lopez Island (San Juan Islands; ferry acess only), S from ferry landing. 37 standard sites; dump station. Fishing. Washington State ferry access. Reservations recommended. Fishing, clams, crab. GPS: N 48-31.9 W 122-52.1

Steamboat Rock State Park

51052 WA 155, Electric City, WA 99123. Phone: (509) 633-1304. Located in east-central WA, 16 miles SW of Grand Coulee on WA 155, on Banks Lake. 26 standard sites, 136 water and electric; dump station. 50-foot limit. Reservations accepted. Swimming, fishing, boat ramp. GPS: N 47-50.9 W 119-06.9

Sun Lakes-Dry Falls State Park

34875 Park Lake Rd NE, Coulee City, WA 99115. Phone: (509) 632-5583. Located in east-central WA, 7 miles N of Coulee City on WA 17. 152 standard sites, 39 full hook-up; dump station. 65-foot limit. Reservations accepted. Swimming, fishing, boat ramp. GPS: N 47-35.8 W 119-23.3

Twanoh State Park

12190 WA 106 E, Union, WA 98592. Phone: (360) 275-2222. Located on Hood Canal on the Olympic Peninsula, 19 miles SW of Bremerton on WA 106, off WA 3. 25 standard sites, 22 full hook-up. 35-foot limit. Swimming, fishing, boat ramp. GPS: N 47-22.7 W 122-58.4

Twenty-five Mile Creek State Park

20530 Lakeshore Rd, Chelan, WA 98816. Phone: (509) 687-3610. Remote location in central WA on Lake Chelan, 19 miles NW of Chelan via US 97A, WA 971, and South Lakeshore Rd. 46 standard sites, 13 full hook-up, 8 with electric and water; dump station. 30-foot limit. Reservations accepted. Swimming, fishing, boat ramp. GPS: N 47-59.5 W 120-15.2

Twin Harbors State Park

3120 WA 105, Westport, WA 98595. Phone: (360) 268-9717. Located in western WA, just S of Grays Harbor on central WA coast, 3 miles S of Westport on WA 105. 219 standard sites, 49 full hook-up; dump station. 35-foot limit. Reservations accepted. Fishing. Park is near Willapa Bay, famous for oysters. GPS: N 46-51.5 W 124-06.3

Wanapum Recreational Area /Ginko Petrified Forest

4511 Huntzinger Rd, Vantage, WA 98950. Phone: (509) 856-2700. Located on Wanapum River in south-central WA, 3 miles S of Vantage (I-90 exit 136) on the Columbia River. 50 full hook-up sites. 60-foot limit. Reservations accepted. Swimming, fishing, boat ramp. GPS: N 46-55.6 W 119-59.5

Wenatchee Confluence State Park

333 Olds Station Rd, Wenatchee, WA 98801. Phone: (509) 664-6373. Located in central WA in Wenatchee at confluence of Wenatchee and Columbia rivers on US 97/2. 51 full hook-up, 8 standard sites; dump station. 65-foot limit. Reservations accepted. Fishing, boat ramp. GPS: N 47-26.6 W 120-19.6

Wenberg State Park

15430 E Lake Goodwin Rd, Stanwood, WA 98292. Phone: (425) 388-6600. Located in northwestern WA, 18 miles NW of Everett on Lake Goodwin, off I-5 exit 199 west, follow signs. 45 standard sites, 30 with electric and water; dump station. 50-foot limit. No alcohol. Fishing, boat ramp. GPS: N 48-08.2 W 122-17.0

Yakima Sportsman State Park

904 University Pkwy, Yakima, WA 98901. Phone: (509) 575-2774. Located in south-central WA, 3 miles E of Yakima off I-82 exit 34. 30 standard, 37 full hook-up sites; dump station. 60-foot limit. Reservations accepted. Fishing. GPS: N 46-35.5 W 120-27.2

WEST VIRGINIA

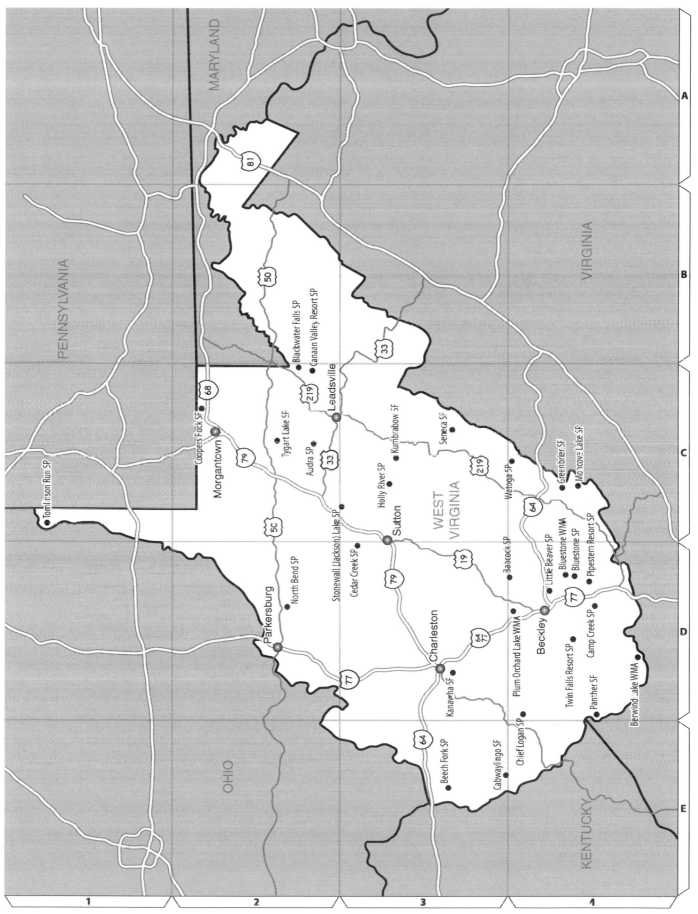

West Virginia

West Virginia maintains 29 parks or wildlife management areas with RV facilities. These locations are well appointed with facilities but most are "off the beaten track" as far as access to major highways. Most are open only seasonally. Four locations (Canaan, Stonewall, Pipestem and Twin Falls) are resorts with exceptional amenities. Senior discounts are available with proof of age but you must request this discount. Pets on leashes are allowed. Alcohol is prohibited in some parks. Credit cards are accepted in most locations. All parks accept reservations, which require a 48-hour advance request and have a reservation fee in addition to the campsite charge. Campsites are listed as "Standard" (with some or full hook-ups) or "Rustic" (no site facilities). All the parks have water available. Unless noted, there are no rig size limitations. Rate groups: A and B depending on site facilities. (Resorts: group C.)

West Virginia State Parks & Forests
1900 Kanawha Blvd East
State Capital Complex, Bldg #3
Charleston, WV 25305

Information: (304) 558-2764 or 800-225-5982
Reservations: (800) 225-5982
Internet: www.wvstateparks.com/

West Virginia Park Locator

West Virginia Parks

Audra State Park
Buckhannon, WV 26201. Phone: (304) 457-1162. Located 15 miles NE of Buckhannon between US 119 & US 250. 67 sites; showers; laundry; dump station. Swimming. GPS: N 39-02.5 W 80-04.0

Babcock State Park
486 Babcock Rd, Clifftop, WV 25831. Phone: (304) 438-3004. Located NE of Beckley on WV 41 at Clifftop, 2 miles S of US 60. 52 sites, some with electric; showers; laundry; dump station. No alcohol. Lake in park. Marina. Boat/canoe rentals. Seasonal. Swimming, fishing. Horse rentals. GPS: N 37-58.9 W 80-56.3

Beech Fork State Park
5601 Long Branch Rd, Barboursville, WV 25504. Phone: (304) 528-5794. Located in western WV, 12 miles S of Huntington, off WV 152 (I-64 exits 8 or 11). 275 sites (some 50 amp), 49 full hook-up; showers; dump station; laundry, store. Open year-round. Swimming, fishing; boat ramp, rentals. (Electric motors.) GPS: N 38-18.5 W 82-21.3

Berwind Lake Wildlife Management Area
Warriormine, WV 24894. Phone: (304) 875-2577. Located on Berwind Lake in southern WV, near VA state line, SE of War (W of Bluefield), off WV 16. 8 sites, 2 with electric. Swimming, fishing; boat ramp (electric motors only). GPS: N 37-17.5 W 81-43.7

Blackwater Falls State Park
1584 Blackwater Lodge Rd, Davis, WV 26260. Phone: (304) 259-5216. Located on Blackwater River near Davis in eastern WV off US 219. 65 sites, 30 with electric (30-amp); showers; laundry; dump station. Lake in park. Seasonal. Swimming, fishing. GPS: N 39-06.7 W 79-29.5

Bluestone State Park
Hinton, WV 25951. Phone: (304) 466-2805. Located on Bluestone Lake, 5 miles S of Hinton on WV 20. 123 sites, 22 with electric; showers; dump station.Marina. Swimming, fishing, boat rentals. GPS: N 37-37.0 W 80-56.0

Bluestone Wildlife Management Area

Indian Mills, WV 24935. Phone: (304) 466-3398. Located on WV 20 near Bluestone State Park, SE of Hinton on Bluestone Lake. Follow signs from Hinton. 330 rustic sites. No alcohol. Fishing. Equestrian area. Fishing, boat ramp. GPS: N 37-32.0 W 80-51.8

Cabwaylingo State Forest

4279 Cabwaylingo Park Rd, Dunlow, WV 25511. Phone: (304) 385-4255. Remote location 27 miles S of Huntington on Twelvepole Creek off WV 152, near KY state line. 21 sites, 6 with electric; showers. Swimming pool, fishing. Seasonal. GPS: N 37-59.2 W 82-21.9

Camp Creek State Park

2390 Camp Creek Rd, Camp Creek, WV 25820. Phone: (304) 425-9481. Located on Camp Creek, 2 miles off I-77 exit 20 in southern WV, next to Camp Creek State Forest. 39 sites (2 areas), 26 with utilities (some full hook-up), 13 rustic; showers; laundry. Equestrian area. Fishing. Wi-Fi. GPS: N 37-30.8 W 81-08.7

Canaan Valley Resort State Park

230 Main Lodge Rd, Davis, WV 26260. Phone: (304) 866-4121 or (800) 622-4121. Located SW of Davis on WV 72, off US 219 or WV 32 in northern WV. 34 sites with full hook-ups; showers. Golf course. Swimming. GPS: N 39-01.0 W 79-26.7

Cedar Creek State Park

2947 Cedar Creek Rd, Glenville, WV 26351. Phone: (304) 462-7158. Located 25 miles W of I-79 exit 79 in central WV, south of Glenville off US 33/119. 65 sites, 58 with electric and water; showers; laundry. Three lakes in park. Swimming pool, fishing. Boat rentals. Seasonal. GPS: N 38-52.9 W 80-51.2

Chief Logan State Park

376 Little Buffalo Creek Rd, Logan, WV 25601. Phone: (304) 792-7125. Located in southwestern WV, 4 miles N of Logan between US 119 & WV 10. 26 sites, 14 full hook-ups, 12 with electric and water; showers. Swimming fishing; miniature golf. GPS: N 37-53.6 W 82-00.5

Coopers Rock State Forest

61 County Lane Dr, Bruceton Mills, WV 26525. Phone: (304) 594-1561. Located on Cheat Lake in northern WV, 13 miles NE of Morgantown, off I-68 exit 15; follow signs. 25 sites with electric; showers. Seasonal. Fishing. GPS: N 39-39.9 W 79-42.8

Greenbrier State Forest

Caldwell, WV 24925. Phone: (304) 536-1944. Located near White Sulphur Springs in southeastern WV near I-64 exit 175. 16 sites with electric; showers. Seasonal. Swimming, fishing. GPS: N 37-45.8 W 80-19.3

Holly River State Park

680 State Park Rd, Hacker Valley, WV 26222. Phone: (304) 493-6353. Remote location in central WV, south of Buckhannon, 22 miles E of I-79 exit 67, on WV 20. 88 sites with electric; showers; laundry; dump station. Swimming pool. GPS: N 38-39.1 W 80-23.2

Kanawha State Forest

7500 Kanawha State Forest Rd, Charleston, WV 24314. Phone: (304) 558-3500. Located 7 miles S of Charleston. From I-64 exit 58A, follow signs. 46 sites, 25 with electric and water; showers; laundry; dump station. Swimming pool, fishing; shooting range. GPS: N 38-18.6 W 81-40.1

Kumbrabow State Forest

Huttonsville, WV 26273. Phone: (304) 335-2219. Remote location in central WV, 24 miles S of Elkins off WV 55 via US 219. 13 rustic sites; showers; laundry. 20-foot limit. Fishing. GPS: N 38-37.7 W 80-06.5

Little Beaver State Park

1402 Grandview Rd, Beaver, WV 25813. Phone: (304) 763-2494. Newest WV park. Located in S West Virginia on WV 307, two miles S of US 64, Exit 129A. 46 sites, 30 with water and electric, 16 electric only; showers; laundry; store. 40-foot limit. Fishing, boat rentals. Wi-Fi. GPS: N 37-42.5 W 81-05.0

Moncove Lake State Park

Gap Mills, WV 24941. Phone: (304) 772-3450. Located on Moncove Lake in southeastern WV, southwest of White Sulphur Springs, off US 219 or WV 3 on CR 8 near Union, follow signs. 48 sites, 25 with electric; showers; dump station. Swimming, fishing; boat ramp, rentals (5 h.p limit). No reservations. GPS: N 37-37.2 W 80-21.2

North Bend State Park/Resort

202 North Bend Park Rd, Cairo, WV 26337. Phone: (304) 643-2931. Located on Hughes River SE of Parkersburg, via US 50 & WV 31, SE of Cairo; follow signs. 77 sites, 28 water and electric, 26 with electric. Swimming, fishing, boat ramp, rentals; (9.9 h.p. maximum). GPS: N 39-13.2 W 81-06.2

Panther State Forest

Panther Creek Rd, Panther, WV 24872. Phone: (304) 938-2252. Located in southwestern WV, near VA/KY state line, off US 52 at Iaeger, follow signs. 6 sites with electric. Swimming, fishing. GPS: N 37-27.4 W 81-57.4

Pipestem Resort State Park

3405 Pipestem Dr, Pipestem, WV 25979. Phone: (304) 466-1800. Located in southern WV, 12 miles S of Hinton on WV 20. 82 sites, 31 full hook-up, 19 with electric; showers; laundry. Two golf courses. Swimming, fishing, disc golf; horse trails, rentals, RC race track. Wi-Fi. GPS: N 37-32.5 W 80-58.8

Plum Orchard Lake Wildlife Management Area

1156 Plum Orchard Lake Rd, Scarbro, WV 25917. Phone: (304) 469-9905. Located on Plum Orchard Creek off I-77 exits 54 or 60, near Moss and Pax, on CR 23. 38 rustic sites; water available. Fishing, boat ramp, rentals. Shooting range. GPS: N 37-56.0 W 81-11.5

Seneca State Forest

10135 Browns Creek Rd, Dunmore, WV 24934. Phone: (304) 799-6213. Remote location in eastern WV in Monongahela National Forest on Greenbrier River, on WV 28, 4 miles S of Dunmore. 10 rustic sites; showers (nearby); laundry. No reservations. Golf course nearby. Swimming, fishing; boat rentals. GPS: N 38-20.8 W 79-56.4

Stonewall (Jackson) Lake State Park/Resort

940 Resort Dr, Roanoke, WV 26447. Phone: (304) 269-7400. Located in central WV on Stonewall Jackson Lake off US 19 at I-79 exit 91; follow signs. 40 full hook-up sites; showers. Two swimming pools.

Marina. Houseboat rentals. Golf course; spa. Wi-Fi. GPS: N 38-55.8 W 80-28.9

Tomlinson Run State Park

84 Osage Rd, New Manchester, WV 26056. Phone: (304) 564-3651. Located at the northern tip of WV "Panhandle," 19 miles N of Weirton on WV 2, on Ohio River. 54 sites, 39 with electric; showers; laundry; dump station. Swimming, fishing; boat rentals; miniature golf; disc golf. GPS: N 40-33.0 W 80-35.7

Twin Falls Resort State Park

Mullens, WV 25882. Phone: (304) 294-4000. Located in southwestern WV, southwest of Beckley on WV 97, off I-77 exits 28 or 42; follow signs. 50 sites, 25 with electric; showers; laundry; dump station. Swimming pool. Golf course. ATV trails. GPS: N 37-37.4 W 81-27.5

Tygart Lake State Park

Grafton, WV 26354. Phone: (304) 265-6144. Located on Tygart Lake in northern WV, S of Grafton (17 miles E of Clarksburg) on US 250. 40 sites, 14 with electric; showers; water available; dump station. Marina; boat rentals. Seasonal. Golf course nearby (5 minutes.) Fishing, swimming. GPS: N 39-14.9 W 80-01.3

Watoga State Park

4800 Watoga Park Dr, Marlinton, WV 24954. Phone: (304) 799-4087. Located in southeastern WV, 14 miles S of Marlinton on WV 28, off US 219. Two campgrounds with 88 sites, 50 with electric; showers; laundry. Seasonal. Swimming, fishing; boat rentals. GPS: N 38-07.3 W 80-09.3

WISCONSIN

Lake Superior

MINNESOTA

MICHIGAN

Big Bay SP

Amnicon Falls SP

Pattison SP

Copper Falls SP

WISCONSIN

Northern Highland/American Legion SF-Crystal Lake

Northern Highland/American Legion SF-Clear Lake

Interstate SP

Brunet Island SP

Council Grounds SP

Peninsula SP

Willow River SP

Lake Wissota SP

Wausau

Potawatomi SP

Eau Claire

Green Bay

Merrick SP

Black River SF

Hartman Creek SP

Point Beach SF

Perrot SP

High Cliff SP

Roche-A-Cri SP

Mill Bluff SP

Kohler-Andrae SP

Wildcat Mountain SP

Kettle Moraine SF - Northern Unit

Rocky Arbor SP

Mirror Lake SP

Harrington Beach SP

Devil's Lake SP

Lake Michigan

Kettle Moraine SF - Pike Lake Unit

Blue Mound SP

Tower Hill SP

Madison

Milwaukee

Governor Dodge SP

Wyalusing SP

Kettle Moraine SF - Southern Unit

Lake Kegonsa SP

Nelson Dewey SP

New Glarus Woods SP

Yellowstone Lake SP

Big Foot Beach SP

Richard Bong SRA

IOWA

ILLINOIS

1   2   3   4

Wisconsin

There are 41 Wisconsin state parks, forests or recreation areas with RV facilities. Some of the parks are seasonal (Spring/Summer) and are noted in the listings; otherwise the park is open year around. No parks offer site water, however, drinking water is available at all parks. Most have dump stations and limited electric hook-up sites. The State reservation system requires 48 hours advance contact and there is an additional reservation fee. You should contact the particular state park on the day of an intended stay to verify available space. No park can hold space except through the state-wide system. Each park charges a daily admission fee in addition to the campground fee. Non-residents pay more for camping fees than Wisconsin residents. Visa and MasterCard accepted. Sunday-Thursday and off season rates are less. Rate group: B, plus entrance fee.

Wisconsin Dept. of Natural Resources
101 South Webster St.
Madison, WI 53703

Information: (608) 266-2181 or (800) 432-8747
Reservations: (888) 947-2757
Internet: www.wiparks.net

Wisconsin Park Locator

Wisconsin Parks

Amnicon Falls State Park
4279 CR U, South Range, WI 54874 (Mail). Phone: (715) 398-3000 or 399-3111. Located 10 miles E of Superior, off US 2. 36 sites; water available. GPS: N 46-36.2 W 91-53.6

Big Bay State Park
2402 Hagen Rd, LaPointe, WI 54850. Phone: (715) 747-6425. Located on Madeline Island (Apostle Island group) in Lake Superior, via ferry from Bayfield. 53 sites with electric; dump station. Swimming, fishing, GPS: N46-07.0 W90-06.0

Big Foot Beach State Park
1550 Lake Shore Dr, Lake Geneva, WI 53147. Phone: (262) 248-2528. Located on Lake Geneva off WI 120, 2 miles S of Lake Geneva. 61 sites with electric; showers; dump station. No alcohol. Swimming, fishing, boat rentals. GPS: N 42-34.0 W 88-26.2

Black River State Forest
W10325 WI 12, Black River Falls, WI 54615. Phone: (715) 284-4103. Located on the Black River on WI 54, I-94 exit 116, E about 12 miles. 97 sites, 50 with electric; showers; dump station. Equestrian area (12 sites). Fishing, boat ramp. ATV trails. GPS: N 44-16.4 W 90-49.8

Blue Mound State Park

4350 Mounds Park Rd, Blue Mounds, WI 53517. Phone: (608) 437-5711. Located about 25 miles W of Madison, off US 18 at CR K. 44 sites with electric; showers; dump station. Swimming pool. GPS: N 43-01 W 89-50.5

Brunet Island State Park

23125 255th St, Cornell, WI 54732. Phone: (715) 239-6888. Located on Chippewa & Fisher rivers (bridge access), 1 mile NW of Cornell (WI 27 & 64) about 25 miles E of US 53. 69 sites, 24 with electric; showers; dump station. Swimming, fishing; boat ramp. GPS: N 45-10.6 W 91-09.7

Capital Springs State Park

3101 Lake Farm Rd, Madison, WI 53711. Phone: (608) 224-3730. Located in Madison on Lake Waubesa, off West Beltline Hwy. 54 sites, 39 with electric; showers, dump station. Fishing; boat ramp. GPS: N 43-01.7 W 89-20.7

Copper Falls State Park

36764 Copper Falls Rd, Mellen, WI 54546. Phone: (715) 274-5123. Located on Bad River, 2 miles N of Mellen, off WI 169. 24 sites with electric; showers; dump station. Swimming, fishing, boat ramp. GPS: N 46-21.9 W 90-39.2

Council Grounds State Park

N1895 Council Grounds Dr, Merrill, WI 54452. Phone: (715) 536-8773. Located on the Wisconsin River, 4 miles W of Merrill via WI 64 and WI 107. 55 sites, 19 with electric; showers; dump station. Swimming, fishing; boat ramp. GPS: N 45-11.3 W 89-44.0

Devil's Lake State Park

S5975 Park Rd, Baraboo, WI 53913. Phone: (608) 356-8301. Located on Devil's Lake about 3 miles S of Baraboo, E of US 12. State's busiest campground; reservations strongly recommended. 423 sites, 106 with electric; showers; dump station. Swimming, fishing; boat ramp, rentals, (electric motors only). GPS: N 43-25.8 W 89-41.7

Governor Dodge State Park

4175 Hwy 23 N, Dodgeville, WI 53533. Phone: (608) 935-2315. Located about 3 miles N of Dodgeville (US 18 & WI 23) on WI 23. 269 sites, 80 with electric; showers; dump station. Equestrian area, 11 sites. Two lakes in park. Swimming, fishing; boat/canoe rentals. GPS: N 43-01.4 W 90-08.5

Harrington Beach State Park

531 CR D, Belgium, WI 53004. Phone: (262) 285-3015. Located 35 miles N of Milwaukee, off I-43, exit 107. 69 sites, 31 with electric; dump station. Swimming, fishing, boating; horse trails. GPS: N43-29.6 W87-48.1

Hartman Creek State Park

N2480 Hartman Creek Rd, Waupaca, WI 54981. Phone: (715) 258-2372. Located N of Madison on Hartman Creek, about 4 miles SW of Waupaca on WI 22 (off US 10). 78 sites, 24 with electric; showers; dump station. Swimming, fishing, boat rentals. GPS: N 44-19.2 W 89-11.7

High Cliff State Park

N7630 State Park Rd, Sherwood, WI 54169. Phone: (920) 989-1106. Located on Lake Winnebago, 9 miles E of Menasha on WI 114. 112 sites, 32 with electric; showers; dump station. Marina. Swimming, fishing; boat ramp; horse trails. GPS: N 44-10.0 W 88-17.5

Interstate State Park

851 Hwy 35, St. Croix Falls, WI 54024. Phone: (715) 483-3747. Located in western WI, on Lake O'the Dalles (St. Croix Waterway), on WI 35, S of US 8. 57 sites, 22 with electric; showers; dump station. Fishing; boat ramp. Seasonal. GPS: N 45-23.8 W 92-38.2

Kettle Moraine State Forest - Northern Unit

N1765 Hwy G, Campbellsport, WI 53010. Phone: (262) 626-2116. Located E of Madison, near junction of US 45 & WI 67. 135 sites, 51 with electric; showers; dump station. Equestrian area, (22 sites.) Two lakes in park. GPS: N 43-38.7 W 88-11.2

Kettle Moraine State Forest - Pike Lake Unit

3544 Kettle Moraine Rd, Hartford, WI 53027. Phone: (262) 670-3400. Located about 45 miles E of Hartford, off WI 60 at US 41. 32 sites, 11 with electric; showers; dump station. Seasonal. Swimming, fishing. GPS: N 43-19.2 W 88-19.2

Kettle Moraine State Forest - Southern Unit

S59 W36530 County ZZ, Dousman, WI 53118. Phone: (262) 594-6200. Located SE of Madison, about 3 miles W of Eagle on WI 59. 201 sites, 49 with electric; showers; dump station. Ottawa Lake in park. Equestrian area (19 sites.) Boat ramp, fishing. GPS: N 42-52.7 W 88-31.4

Kohler-Andrae State Park

1020 Beach Park Ln, Sheboygan, WI 53081. Phone: (920) 451-4080. Located on Lake Michigan about 6 miles S of Sheboygan, off I-43 exit 120. 137 sites, 52 with electric; showers; dump station. Swimming, fishing; horse trails. GPS: N 43-39.5 W 87-43.8

Lake Kegonsa State Park

2405 Door Creek Rd, Stoughton, WI 53589. Phone: (608) 873-9695. Located SE of Madison on Lake Kegonsa, N off US 51 at Stoughton. Seasonal. 96 sites, 29 with electric; showers; dump station. Swimming, fishing. GPS: N 42-58.6 W 89-13.8

Lake Wissota State Park

18127 CR O, Chippewa Falls, WI 54729. Phone: (715) 382-4574. Located on Lake Wissota off WI 178, NE of Eau Claire. Seasonal. 116 sites, 58 with electric; showers; dump station. Swimming, fishing; boat ramp. GPS: N 44-58.9 W 91-18.8

Merrick State Park

S 2965 WI 35, Fountain City, WI 54629. Phone: (608) 687-4936. Located on Mississippi River, 7 miles S of Cochrane along WI 35. 65 sites, 22 with electric; showers; dump station. Fishing; boat ramp, rentals. GPS: N 44-09.2 W 91-44.7

Mill Bluff State Park

15818 Funnel Rd, Camp Douglas, WI 54618. Phone: (608) 337-4775. Located off US 12, near I-90/94 between exits 48 & 55. 21 sites, 6 with electric; showers; dump station. Swimming. GPS: N 43-56.5 W 90-19.1

Mirror Lake State Park

E 10320 Fern Dell Rd, Baraboo, WI 53913. Phone: (608) 254-2333.

Located on Mirror Lake on WI 33, NW of Baraboo near Wisconsin Dells, off I-90/94 exit 89. 151 sites, 47 with electric; showers; dump station. Swimming, fishing, boat ramp. GPS: N 43-32.1 W 89-48.3

Nelson Dewey State Park

12190 CR VV, Cassville, WI 53806. Phone: (608) 725-5374. Located 3 miles NW of Cassville off WI 133, along CR W. 45 sites, 18 with electric; showers; dump station. Fishing. GPS: N 42-44.3 W 91-01.8

New Glarus Woods State Park

W 5446 CR NM, New Glarus, WI 53574. Phone: (608) 527-2335. Located in southern Wisconsin, W of New Glarus, off WI 92. 20 sites, 1 electric; showers, dump station. GPS: N 42-47.2 W 89-37.9

Northern Highland/American Legion SF - Clear Lake

8282 Woodruff Rd, Woodruff, WI 54568. Phone: (715) 542-3923. Located outside Woodruff (US 51, N of Wausau). Swimming, fishing; boat ramp. GPS: N45-51.9 W89-38.9

Northern Highland/American Legion SF - Crystal Lake

10200 Hwy N, Boulder Junction, WI 54512. Phone: (715) 542-3923. This is a 225,000-acre state forest in northern Wisconsin along US 51. 220 sites, 2 electric; showers; dump station. Lake in park. Swimming. GPS: N 46-00.1 W 89-37.3

Pattison State Park

6294 S State Rd 35, Superior, WI 54880. Phone: (715) 399-3111. Located on WI 35 about 15 miles S of Superior. 59 sites, 18 with electric; showers; dump station. Lake in park. Swimming, fishing. GPS: N 46-32.3 W 92-07.2

Peninsula State Park

9462 Shore Rd, Fish Creek, WI 54212. Phone: (920) 868-3258. Located in WI Upper Peninsula on Lake Michigan, between Fish Creek and Ephraim along WI 42. (5 areas); 468 sites, 163 with electric; showers. Store. Golf course. Swimming, fishing; boat ramp. (Most popular park in Wisconsin.) GPS: N 45-08.0 W 87-12.8

Perrot State Park

W26247 Sullivan Rd, Trempealeau, WI 54661. Phone: (608) 534-6409. Located on the Mississippi River off WI 93, NW of I-90 at La Crosse. 102 sites, 38 with electric; showers; dump station. Fishing, boat ramp. GPS: N 44-00.7 W 91-27.8

Point Beach State Forest

9400 CR O, Two Rivers, WI 54241. Phone: (920) 794-7480. Located on Lake Michigan between Two Rivers and Kewaunee on WI 42. 127 sites, 70 with electric; showers; dump station. Swimming, fishing, boat ramp. GPS: N 44-12.0 W 87-31.4

Potawatomi State Park

3740 CR CD, Sturgeon Bay, WI 54235. Phone: (920) 746-2890. Located on Sturgeon Bay in Upper Peninsula off WI 57 near Sturgeon Bay (city). 123 sites, 40 with electric; showers; dump station. Fishing, boat ramp. GPS: N 44-51.1 W 87-25.6

Richard Bong State Recreation Area

26313 Burlington Rd, Kansasville, WI 53139. Phone: (262) 878-5600. Located 8 miles SE of Burlington on WI 142. 217 sites, 54 with electric; showers; dump station. Horse and ATV trails. Swimming, fishing. GPS: N 42-38.2 W 88-07.5

Roche-A-Cri State Park

1767 Hwy 13, Friendship, WI 53934. Phone: (608) 339-6881. Located on Carter Creek on WI 13 in Friendship about 19 miles W of I-39 exit 124. 33 sites, 4 with electric; showers; dump station. Fishing. GPS: N 43-59.8 W 89-48.7

Rocky Arbor State Park

State Hwy 16, Baraboo, WI 53913. Phone: (608) 254-8001 or 254-2333. Located near junction of US 12 and WI 16, 1.5 miles from Wisconsin Dells. 89 sites, 18 with electric; showers; dump station. Seasonal. Fishing. GPS: N 43-38.9 W 89- 48.5

Tower Hill State Park

5808 CR C, Spring Green, WI 53588. Phone: (608) 588-2116. Located S of Spring Green (US 14), on Wisconsin River. 11 sites; no reservations. Seasonal. Dump station. Fishing. GPS: N 43-08.8 W 90-02.7

Wildcat Mountain State Park

E13660 WI 33, Ontario, WI 54651. Phone: (608) 337-4775. Located on the Kickapoo River, about 38 miles SE of La Crosse, near Ontario, on WI 33. 25 sites; showers; dump station. Equestrian area (24 sites). Fishing, boat rentals. GPS: N 43-41.3 W 90-34.0

Willow River State Park

1034 CR A, Hudson, WI 54016. Phone: (715) 386-5931. Located E of St. Paul, MN, northeast of Hudson on the Little Falls Lake, about 4 miles N of I-94 exit 4 via US 12 and CR A. 80 sites, 25 with electric; showers; dump station. Fishing, boat ramp. GPS: N 45-01.1 W 92-40.4

Wyalusing State Park

13081 State Park Ln, Bagley, WI 53801. Phone: (608) 996-2261. Located on the Mississippi River, off US 18, W of Bridgeport. 109 sites, 33 with electric; showers; dump station. Fishing, boat ramp. GPS: N 42-58.3 W 91-06.7

Yellowstone Lake State Park

8495 Lake Rd, Blandchardville, WI 53516. Phone: (608) 523-4427. Located on Yellowstone Lake, W of Blandchardville off WI 78, SW of Madison. 128 sites, 38 with electric; showers; dump station. Fishing, boat ramp. GPS: N 42-46.6 W 89-59.6

WYOMING

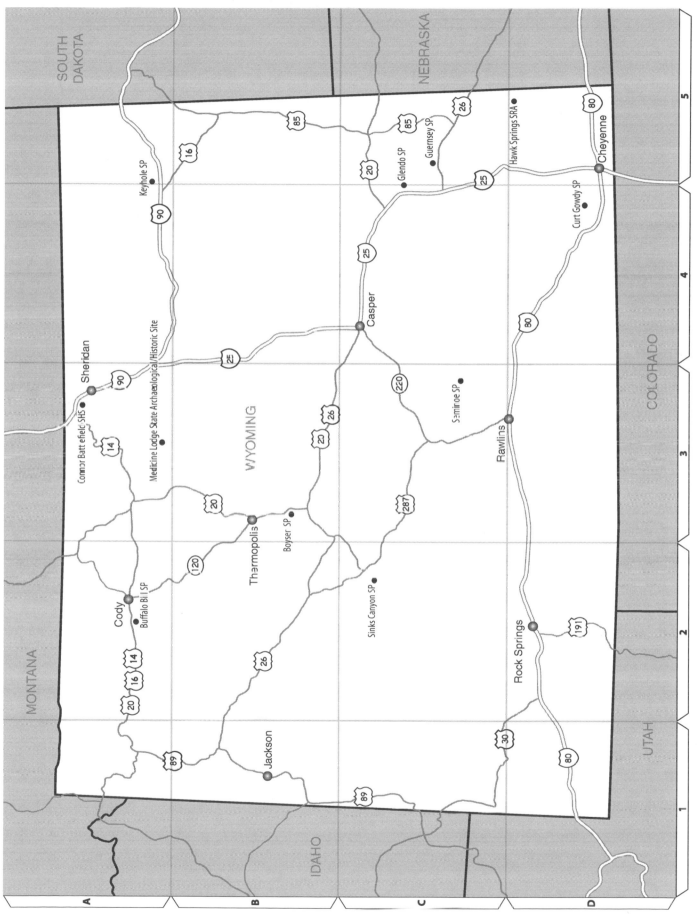

Wyoming

Eleven of Wyoming's state parks or recreation areas have RV parking spaces. Hawk Springs State Recreation Area has no designated sites so the RV spaces are "open" and available on a first-come basis; no reservations are accepted. While the other ten parks do have designated sites, there are no facilities at the sites; they are "dry camping" sites. These locations accept reservations. Some of the addresses are for mail; check park for location. All the parks offer drinking water and most have dump stations. There are no shower facilities in any park. Three parks have RV size limitations (see listings). Rate group: A

Wyoming State Parks & Historic Sites
2301 Central Ave.
Cheyenne, WY 82002

Information: (800) 225- 5996 or (307) 777-6303
Reservations: (877) 996-7275
Internet: www.wyoparks.state.wy.us
Reservations: www.wyo-park.com

Wyoming Park Locator

Wyoming Parks

Boysen State Park
120 Boysen Dr, Shoshoni, WY 82649. Phone: (307) 876-2796. Located 13 miles N of Shoshoni on Wyoming Reservoir on US 20; also accessible from US 26. 7 campgrounds, 277 sites; dump station. Swimming, fishing; boat ramp. 53 reservable sites. GPS: N 43-16.7 W 108-07.2

Buffalo Bill State Park
47 Lakeside Rd, Cody, WY 82414. Phone: (307) 587-9227. Located on Buffalo Bill Reservoir, 9 miles W of Cody on US 14.

Two campgrounds, 88 sites, 15 with electric, water; (some pull-through), 21 reservable sites; dump station. Fishing. Boat ramp. Reservable. GPS: N 44-30.3 W 109-15.0

Connor Battlefield State Historic Site
Ranchester, WY 82844. Phone: (307) 684-7629. Located on the Tongue River in Ranchester in northern Wyoming, just off US 14. 20 sites. Seasonal. Fishing. GPS: N 44-54.2 W 107-10.1

Curt Gowdy State Park
1264 Granite Springs Rd, Cheyenne, WY 82009. Phone: (307) 632-7946. Located between Cheyenne and Laramie on WY 210, just N of I-80. 139 sites, 15 with electric, water; 35 reservable sites; dump station. Three lakes in park. Fishing; boat ramp (15 h.p. limit). Horse corral. Reservable. GPS: N 41-11.5 W 105-15.3

Glendo State Park
397 Glendo Park Rd, Glendo, WY 82213. Phone: (307) 735-4433. Located on North Platte River, 6 miles SE of Glendo, off I-25 exit 104. Seven campgrounds, 419 sites, 87 reservable; dump station. Boat ramp. Marina. Swimming, fishing, boat ramp. GPS: N 42-28.5 W 104-59.9

Guernsey State Park/Museum
Guernsey, WY 82214. Phone: (307) 836-2334. Located on North Platte River off US 26, 2 miles NW of Guernsey. Seven campgrounds, 216 sites, 16 with electric, water, 120 reservable; dump station, showers. Swimming, fishing; boat ramp. Reservable. GPS: N 42-17.1 W 104-45.9

Hawk Springs State Recreation Area
c/o Guernsey State Park, Guernsey, WY 82214. Phone: (307) 836-2334. Located on Hawk Springs Reservoir in southeastern WY, off US 85, S of Torrington. 24 sites. Fishing; boat ramp. GPS: N 41-44.7 W 104-12.8

Keyhole State Park
22 Marina Rd, Moorcroft, WY 82721. Phone: (307) 756-3596. Located on Keyhole Reservoir between Moorcroft and Sundance, off I-90 exits 165 or 153/154; N to US 14 and WY 113. 256 sites, 31 electric, water, 49 reservable; dump station. Fishing; boat ramp. GPS: N 44-21.8 W 104-48.5

Medicine Lodge State Archaeological/Historical Site
Hyattville, WY 82428. Phone: (307) 469-2234. Located 6 miles NE of Hyattville, off WY 31 on W slope of Big Horn Mountains. 25 sites. Equestrian area, trails. Fishing. Reservable. GPS: N 44-18.5 W 107-36.0

Seminoe State Park
Seminoe Dam Rd, Sinclair, WY 82334. Phone: (307) 320-3013. Located on North Platte River, 40 miles NE of Rawlins off I-80 exits 219 or 221. Two campgrounds, 84 sites, 10 reservable. (Rough terrain.) Next to BLM land-ORV area. Swimming, fishing; boat ramp. GPS: N 42-08.9 W 106-54.3

Sinks Canyon State Park
3079 Sinks Canyon Rd, Lander, WY 82520. Phone: (307) 332-6333. Located on the Popo Agre River, 6 miles SW of Lander on WY 131. 29 sites, no reservations. 40-foot limit. Fishing. GPS: N 42-44.4 W 108-49.6